CHRIST
IS MY LIFE

A ONE YEAR DEVOTIONAL
ENCOURAGING SPIRITUAL GROWTH
TO BE AUTHENTIC, SPIRIT-LED,
AND CHRIST-CENTERED

PATRICIA MARAGH

WESTBOW
PRESS®
A DIVISION OF THOMAS NELSON
& ZONDERVAN

WestBow Press books may be ordered through booksellers or by contacting:

WestBow Press
A Division of Thomas Nelson & Zondervan
1663 Liberty Drive
Bloomington, IN 47403
www.westbowpress.com
844-714-3454

Unless otherwise noted, scripture taken from the King James Version of the Bible.

Scripture quotations marked TPT are from The Passion Translation®. Copyright © 2017, 2018, 2020 by Passion & Fire Ministries, Inc. Used by permission. All rights reserved. ThePassionTranslation.com.

Additional scripture quotations taken from the Amplified® Bible (AMP), Copyright © 2015 by The Lockman Foundation. Used by permission. www.lockman.org

ISBN: 978-1-6642-5764-1 (sc)
ISBN: 978-1-6642-5763-4 (e)

Library of Congress Control Number: 2022902875

Print information available on the last page.

WestBow Press rev. date: 12/20/2022

People come to Jesus at different times and for varied reasons. Some come to Him early in their childhood, some just simply as they heard the Word of God and believed, while others come in times of great difficulty and are rescued. Once the decision is made in the heart to follow Jesus, the path we choose to follow to obtain God's favor, joy, peace, healing, love, protection, prosperity, and deliverance is the determinant factor in how successful the Christian walk will be.

Will we receive and follow God by grace through faith in the relationship, receiving and pursuing His righteousness and holiness by His Word and Spirit, or will we follow by acting according to our interpretation or ideas of what we believe is right?

Instead of trying to live our life for God, we should depend on Him and live from His life and His power in the Holy Spirit in us. We should follow grace through faith by loving Jesus with all our hearts in loving dependence and trust, delighting in Him and His Word, abiding in Him, worshipping and praising Him, always progressing daily from faith to faith. When we fail or sin, because we are in loving dependence on God, we should keep our eyes on Jesus and the Cross and receive His grace and love in forgiveness. Always keep going forward, expecting His goodness. In this way, Christ becomes our life.

In stark opposition to God's grace, we can seek to pursue God by the Law in self-effort or self-righteousness, either learning or choosing to try to please God by what we do. Works and self-effort dominate our Christian life, and with it comes failure, struggle, despair, torment, and fear. When we sin, we look inward at our own and others' sins' shortcomings, bringing fear, strife, and dread. To grow spiritually, we must choose God's grace to keep us in faith—depending on His righteousness and grace, instead of the Law with rules to eliminate sin and make us good in His sight. No power or life exists in the efforts of self, others, or religion; only faith in God's love and Jesus Christ gives us new life.

Grace is our dependence on Christ alone, in His power and abilities working in and through us for our good. Because the Blood of Jesus was shed for us, He is the essence, activator, and substance of everything in our lives. See Galatians 2:20.

"And this is the record, that God hath given us eternal life, and this life is in His Son. He that hath the Son hath life; he that hath not the Son of God hath not life" (1 John 5:11-12).

This devotional will seek to ground the reader's faith in the foundations of the gospel and strengthen their belief and desire to grow in dependence on Christ in a relationship and into freedom. This will require hearing the Word and hearing it again until you genuinely believe. You may consider reading through in the morning and delving more profound in the evening as you read all the Scriptures for each day in total, opening your own Bible to build your faith. See Romans 10:17; Psalm 119:130. There is much to be grasped that you may read again next year. The key is to grow up more today in Christ than yesterday intentionally.

Secondly, this book is intended to be an asset to prepare and equip the believer to be fully able and confident to share the gospel and *"be ready always to answer every man that asketh you a reason of the hope that is in you with meekness and fear"* (1 Peter 3:15).

Third, each person must mature until Christ is formed in them and He is their life. Where do you need new life in your existence? Do you need salvation? Jesus says, *"I am the way, the truth, and the life"* (John 14:6). Do you need a provision? *"I am that bread of life"* (John 6:48). Do you need protection? *"I am the good shepherd"* (John 10:11). Do you need wisdom? He says in James 1:5, *"If any of you lack wisdom, let him ask of God, that giveth to all men liberally."* Do you need His grace in His sustenance? He says, *"I am the true vine"* (John 15:1).

He who knows the Father by His Words and by experiencing Him in a relationship and testifies of His Son in the power of the Holy Spirit will have eternal life within as Christ is formed within and He becomes your life.

Read, study, meditate, fellowship, and enjoy the journey as Christ becomes your life!

WHERE LIFE BEGINS

*"And the Lord God formed man...and breathed into his
nostrils the breath of life."* —Genesis 2:7

TRUTH: God is in a Father-child relationship with us, just as He was with Adam before he sinned. God is the source of our natural lives, as seen in Genesis 2:7. At salvation, He comes to live within our hearts by His Spirit. He quickens and changes the genuine, sinful hearts we are born with and recreates them to be alive unto God. See Psalm 51:5; Romans 6:11. In John 20:22, Jesus imparted new life into His disciples to be born again spiritually. Likewise, when we are born again, He is also the source of all spiritual life. See John 3:16; 2 Corinthians 5:17.

By faith, the life and love of God live in our hearts by His Spirit. See Romans 5:5; Romans 12:3; John 14:16-17. As believers, we possess the spiritual life of God in Christ in our natural being, our human spirit. In Him was life, and His life was the light of men. In Him, we live and move and have our being. See John 1:4; 8:12; Acts 17:28. So, let everything that hath breath praise the Lord and awake to the consciousness, the truth, and the reality that we are only alive unto God by Christ Jesus. If you are not born again, read, agree with, and speak Romans 10:9-10. Repent of sin, confess Jesus as Lord, and rejoice that you now have new life in God.

LIFE: Be grateful for your life. Give thanks that your very breath came from God. Each day breathe His breath of life in you by His Word and by prayer and fellowship with the Holy Spirit as you experience Christ as your life. Express your gratitude, praise, and thanksgiving, which will bring joy and, in turn, bring strength and trust in God. See Psalm 107:21-22; Nehemiah 8:10; Proverbs 3:5-6.

Prayer: Thank You, Father, that Jesus gives new life, and I choose Your breath of life in me today. This is the day the Lord has made; I will rejoice and be glad in it. As I read and meditate in Your Word, help me in every moment and situation I face to depend on Your goodness for abundant life, joy, and peace in the Holy Spirit, for indeed, I desire Christ as my life. Amen.

TRUTH AND LIFE IN GOD

"Jesus saith unto him, I am the way, the truth, and the life: no man cometh unto the Father but by me." —John 14:6

TRUTH: It is not a matter of what truth is, but who it is. God is truth. He is omnipotent, omniscient, omnipresent, and absolute. To know the truth is to know God in His Word and by His Spirit. He is true for all people and for all times. Truth is truth because God is faithful and gives His Word as truth. He has put His Words in a book called the Bible for all to see and use as the original standard of all truth. People and presidents swear that they speak the truth as they lay hands on it. Adam and Eve heard the truth from God's mouth but rejected it and consequently experienced death spiritually and later physically.

God is love. And when we choose His way by living in love, the truth comes into our hearts, making us accessible to His love and giving us new life. *"If ye continue in my word, then ye are my disciples indeed; And ye shall know the truth, and the truth shall make you free"* (John 8:31-32). God is truth. When we get to know God, we will see the truth, as His response to any prayer will be to speak only the truth. When our belief is aligned with God's character and His Word, we will know His truth. When the truth in God's promises is believed and spoken in faith, Jesus responds to bless us and give us liberty.

LIFE: We shy away from the truth because it is revealing and, at times, uncomfortable. Truth reveals our character, intent, and motives so, we often ignore, make excuses, or flat out deny the truth. But the truth is God Himself; we cannot hide from Him. We can have our ideas and opinions, but God and His ways are always true. He has set before us life and death; therefore, choose Jesus and choose life. See Deuteronomy 30:19. Hear and read the truth and gain Christ's eternal life, which will set you free from sin, destruction, and death. Jesus is the only way to heaven and your best life here on earth. Choose Jesus to be liberated and be renewed. See John 10:10; 13:34-35; 18:37. We will not know all truth all at once, but as we study the Word and remain in Christ Jesus, we will learn more and more truth as we learn of Him. Get to know Him more each day.

WHOSE TRUTH?

"A man's heart deviseth his way: but the Lord directeth his steps." —Proverbs 16:9

TRUTH: Today's society sees truth as relative to who is speaking. The majority seeks to rule by how many are loudly speaking and shouting or according to groups exerting power because of having the same intense personal desires. Also, when influential, charming, or charismatic people speak, many listen and are influenced to believe that what they say is automatically true.

Although God told Eve not to eat the fruit from the tree, she decided what was true for herself; she listened to Satan and sinned. She singlehandedly decided her truth. On the other hand, Adam listened to and believed his truth from his wife. Collective truth is not determined by the majority who speak in our tribe, circle, or group. They, too, are not always correct. See Genesis 11:4.

The Bible says God is truth, so we have truth when we listen to God and obey Him. *"I am the way, the truth, and the life: no man cometh unto the Father, but by me"* (John 14:6). Truth is God Himself, who is given to all people for them to live and abide by Him. We cannot respond like Eve and make up our truth or follow others like Adam. We must humble ourselves and agree with God that He alone is Truth. He alone is omniscient and has infinite knowledge, being aware of all the aspects of any situation to reveal the whole truth. God's truth is the standard and absolute truth for all. If you want to avoid making the same mistake Eve did, do not try to be god for yourself, deciding what you believe is right or wrong. Agree with God and His Word, for He alone is truth.

"The steps of a good man are ordered by the Lord: and he delighteth in his way" —Psalm 37:23.

"If so, be that ye have heard him, and have been taught by him, as the truth is in Jesus" —Ephesians 4:21.

LIFE: Choose God's Word as your way of life, and you will side with truth every time you seek God's wisdom, His heart, and direction. Only He can direct you with absolute accuracy and complete truth into a successful life. See John 17:17; 16:13.

OUR GOD

*"For who is God save the Lord? or who is a
rock save our God?"* —Psalm 18:31.

TRUTH: We are asked to look, seek to know, thank, and worship God. We know Him as Creator of heaven and earth, and most of all as Creator of ourselves and our loved ones who warm our hearts. We can get to know God and see His love for us as Father: He is God the Creator, as He made all things; nothing was made without Him. See John 1:3. Our God is love, and He is a loving Father worthy of worship and praise. See 1 John 4:16; Revelation 4:11; 5:12.

Our God is a Protector. See Isaiah 41:10; Psalm 91; Matthew 18:12-14. God is gracious and merciful; He does not deal with us as we deserve. See Psalm 145:8; Joel 2:13; Luke 6:36. God is our source, and we should always look to Him first. See Psalms 31:19; 107:8-9; Philippians 4:19.

Our God is El Shaddai, the All-Sufficient One who will take care of us; so, depend on Him. See Matthew 10:29-31; 18:12-14; 2 Corinthians 3:5. Our God is the giver of all good gifts. See Luke 11:13. When in faith, He gives His goodness in blessings and chastisement in judgment to correct, never judgment to hurt or condemn. See John 3:17; Hebrews 12:5-6; Romans 5:8-9.

LIFE: The deadly COVID 19 pandemic has been devastating yet invisible. God, our Father, is visible in His creation and can be experienced in our hearts and lives by His supernatural character and irrevocable, abundant promises and blessings. We heeded warnings about an unseen virus to stay six feet apart for natural protection; now heed God's call to you as a Father who loves you and calls you unto Himself to yield and draw closer to Him for a more excellent relationship or to obtain salvation. He is your great, good God, worthy of your surrendered heart to love and worship Him. See Hebrews 3:7-13.

SIN

"The wages of sin is death." —Romans 6:23

TRUTH: Sin is any thought, attitude, or action that falls short of God's Law and spiritual perfection of love. See John 13:34; Romans 13:8-10.

"Whosoever commit sin transgresseth also the law: for sin is the transgression of the law" (1 John 3:4).

"Owe no man anything, but to love one another: for he, that loveth another hath fulfilled the law..." (Romans 13: 8-10).

Sin is offensive to God because it is a rebellion against Him. See Deuteronomy 9:7-8. Jesus is God's answer for sin. Faith in Christ Jesus is the cure for sin. See John 3:16; 10:10; Romans 14:23.

As Christians, we have been delivered from sin; and we are the "just" who live by faith, not by focusing on sin or avoiding corruption. We are not to practice, cover up, or ignore sin either; it must be dealt with. See Romans 10:9-10; 1 John 1: 7-9.

Eve committed the first sin on earth when she exalted her way over God's way. Whatever we put above God, including self, is idolatry and a sin.

"Thou shalt worship the Lord thy God, and him only shalt thou serve" (Matthew 4: 10).

"To him, that knoweth to do good, and doeth it not; it is sin" (James 4:17).

LIFE: All people sin, including believers on occasion. See Romans 3:10-12; 23; 1 John 1:9-10. Because sin was destroyed in the sacrifice of Jesus, we should always look to Jesus and receive His forgiveness. If we sin and repent, sin loses its dominion, and no condemnation can come to us. Forgiveness, repentance, and continuing in righteousness are God's grace to us in Christ Jesus. He redeemed and freed us from the power of the Law, self, Satan, sin, and death. Believe this with every fiber of your being. Be righteousness conscious, believe God loves you and made a way of escape, take Him at His Word, and sin and its effects can have no power over you. See Romans 6:11-14; 5:17; 1 Corinthians 10:13.

DEAL WITH SIN

"For the wages of sin is death." —Romans 6:23

TRUTH: The church is now living under the New Covenant of grace with the commandment to love. See John 13:34; Romans 13:8-10. Under this New Covenant of grace, believers may have developed the tendency to be lax about sin, not examining our hearts before God in the moment or at the end of the day to deal with sin.

God hates sin and tells us not to practice immorality and to avoid the very appearance of evil. See 1 John 3:9; 1 Thessalonians 5:22; Proverbs 6:16-19. He also tells us to judge ourselves in 1 Corinthians 11:31. When we sin, and the Holy Spirit convicts us of righteousness, we should yield to Him. See John 16:7-9.

Some things like smoking may not be stated as sin in the Bible, but we must ask ourselves whether those things are good or healthy for us. Is it the best way to treat God's temple, or is it a good witness for God? Will it draw us closer to or farther from God? See 1 Corinthians 10:23-24. To determine which actions will bring life or death, we must ask whether the behavior will please, honor, or glorify God. Be always led by the Holy Spirit. See 1 Corinthians 6:19-20; 10:31-33; Romans 8:14.

We may also need to ask how our actions will affect others? If what we do causes them to stumble, we must submit to the Word. See 1 Corinthians 8. Let our conscience before God be our guide. See Colossians 3:17; Romans 14:23. What we do (sins of commission) and what we fail to do (sins of omission) must be addressed before God.

LIFE: Be habitual about seeking forgiveness of sins each night when you pray to close the door to Satan, his guilt, accusations, and any curse he may want to bring against you because of sin. See Micah 7:8-9; Galatians 3:13.

Repent for salvation. See Romans 10:9-10. And if you're already a believer, use 1 John 1:9 to be clean and accessible in the presence of your Father. Remember, sin's dominion was broken over our lives at the Cross. Therefore, always repent forward, looking to Jesus for cleansing and restoration. See Hebrews 4:16; James 4:17. Never backward-looking toward sin and condemnation. See 1 John 3:19-20. Then you'll continue to progress and enjoy Christ Jesus in sweet fellowship.

GRACE

"That I might finish my course with joy, and the ministry, which I have received of the Lord Jesus, to testify the gospel of the grace of God." —Acts 20: 24

TRUTH: Grace is God's power to live in and work with man, giving him the ability to do what he could not accomplish by or for himself. Humanity could not save himself from sin, so God sent His grace in the person of Jesus Christ to bring salvation. Secondly, man cannot always solve his problems without God's help in his daily life. We all need Jesus, by His Spirit, to help us. See Judges 6:17; John 1:17; 14:16. God is always a God of grace who loves man, His creation.

When Adam and Eve sinned, God gave them grace instead of immediate physical death and protected them. See Genesis 3:21-24. Noah found grace in the eyes of the Lord. See Genesis 6:8. The Lord was with Joseph, and he found grace in the eyes of Potiphar. See Genesis 39:2-4. Lot had God's grace in his deliverance from Sodom and Gomorrah. See Genesis 19. Even when God instituted the Law of Moses, it was His grace in substituting animals' blood to cover the sin of man temporarily until He could permanently remove evil in the body of Christ Jesus on the Cross. See Hebrews 9:11-15.

But because our God is perfect, He never leaves anything imperfect, temporary, or undone. He did not leave man in his sinful state, with an imperfect solution of animal blood to cover sin. Instead, He sent His grace in His Son Jesus to pay the total price for sin and our redemption. Jesus is God's grace in His fullness to us; embrace Him fully in a relationship, fellowship, and obedience.

LIFE: *"And the Word was made flesh and dwelt among us...full of grace and truth. John bare witness of him and cried, saying, This was he of whom I spake...for he was before me.... For the law was given by Moses, but grace and truth came by Jesus Christ"* (John 1: 14-17).

GRACE — DAY 2

*"And the ministry, I received of the Lord Jesus, and to testify
the gospel of the grace of God." —Acts 20:24*

TRUTH: The grace of God is the gospel given to us through Jesus Christ, His Son, and His shed Blood on the Cross and all He provided for us, in the power of the Holy Spirit to make us overcomers. See Ephesians 1:3; 19-20; 2 Peter 1:3. God has provided everything for our well-being, but it is all located in our spirit or the spirit realm. We access all that God has provided by believing in what Jesus did for our salvation. We must believe that the written Bible is true and received as truth. Believing in Jesus is our faith in action, placed in God's grace. See Ephesians 2:8.

When we accept all Jesus has done for us, our faith in God's grace will cause us to have joy in our salvation and our God. Grace will cause us to trust God in His joy, peace, abundance, rest, and triumph instead of living by the Law in trying, working, striving, and being frustrated in our efforts to live the Christian life. The latter will make your Christian life exceedingly difficult. Live as you were saved, grace through faith in Christ Jesus trusting His love. See Colossians 2:6.

Living by grace is having faith in and dependence on Jesus. God's way of grace is for us to receive and continue to walk out our salvation by faith, believing in what Jesus accomplished on the Cross. Jesus alone gives us salvation, freedom, and victory over Satan, sin, Law, and death. See Ephesians 2:8; Romans 6:14. And He alone, by His grace and His Holy Spirit, can sustain us. See Psalm 23.

LIFE: *"Therefore by the deeds of the law there shall no flesh be justified...Even the righteousness of God which is by faith of Jesus Christ unto all and upon all them that believe...Being justified freely by his grace through the redemption that is in Christ Jesus"* (Romans 3:20-24).

ONLY TRUE GOD

*"That they might know thee the only true God, and Jesus
Christ, whom thou hast sent."* —John 17:3

TRUTH: Some people have a hard time recognizing the heart and the love of God in the Old Testament. Under the Law of Moses, many have concluded that God is harsh, to be feared, wrathful, and vengeful. Jesus came to change our hearts and minds so that we might see the Father as He truly is, a God of love, kindness, goodness, peace, and justice. Before the Law, God said everything He created was good. After man sinned, God promised redemption and forgiveness in His kindness, grace, and mercy. See Genesis 3:15. God was not harsh or wrathful when He drove Adam from the garden; He did that as an act of His mercy to prevent them from eating the fruit from the tree of life and thus living forever in their sinful condition.

The killing of animals as a sacrifice under the Law of Moses was the mercy of God covering man's sin when they go to the priest once each year to atone and receive temporary forgiveness. To make forgiveness permanent and give humanity the ability to live free from sin, Jesus shed His Blood for the remission of sins. Despite the difference in the covenant God uses, Adam with innocence, Moses with the Law, and us as the church with grace, He is the same one true God of love, and grace, giving goodness and mercy. We must believe He is good all the time and that He loves us, or else we will begin to entertain the lies Satan tells us about Him. Satan will say that God does not care, He does not love us, that God will punish us for our sin and not respond to our cry for His help. All of this is false.

LIFE: You must have the correct image of God in your heart, as that will determine whether you have a close or a distant relationship with Him. Will you trust God or be afraid, doubting that He will not love, bless, deliver, heal, and provide for you? Believe He will and that He does! *"The righteous cry, and the Lord heareth, and delivereth them out of all their troubles"* (Psalm 34:17).

HEART OF OUR FATHER

"But when he was yet a great way off, his father saw him and had compassion and ran and fell on his neck and kissed him." —Luke 15:20

TRUTH: The story of the prodigal son in Luke 15 is well known as the restoration of the wayward son. Jesus came to earth to show us both the face of God and the heart of God, as a loving, good, and generous Father. Taking his inheritance, the son wanted to go as far away from his father as possible. Likewise, God also gave humanity free will; and He honors our choices even if they are to our detriment. The son's rejection did not stop his father from loving him. We are made in the image of God, and though some have rejected Him, He still loves us all and desires that all would be saved and turn to Him. As believers, when we sin, God still loves us and still sees us as His righteous children in need of forgiveness.

The wayward son was out of the father's house, but he was not out of his father's heart. See John 3:16; 2 Peter 3:9. The father was not angry, retaliatory, critical, or judgmental on his return. Instead, he ran to meet his son and warmly received him with love, a hug, and a kiss. See Luke 15:10. He was robed with the best robe, just as our Heavenly Father clothed us with His robe of righteousness, restoring us into a right love relationship with Him. See Isaiah 61:9-10. He was also given shoes for his feet and lifted from poverty and separation into his father's welcoming arms, overflowing with love, wealth, peace, blessings, and favor.

LIFE: The son, seeing his need for restoration, humbled himself, returned to his father, and received forgiveness. The father's love for him exceeded his rebellion and shame. You, too, must humble yourself before your Mighty God and loving Father, repent of your sins and shortcomings and receive His forgiveness, love, restoration, and peace. See John 1:12; 3:16. The heart of your Father has only love, goodness and mercy for you. Receive it. Meditate on Psalm 23.

HEART OF OUR FATHER — DAY 2

"Father, I have sinned against heaven, and before thee, and am no more worthy to be called thy son: make me as one of thy hired servants." —Luke 15:18-19

TRUTH: The truths in this story from the son's point of view are that the son wanted to live independently of the father, showing his pride and rebellion. People often wait until they have tried it all and failed before turning to God. However, despite any sin, He still will not turn anyone away. See John 6:37.

The son's repentance and restoration taught him the value of honoring and loving his father. This relationship demonstrates God's grace. However, although the older son stayed home and worked dutifully and never outrightly sinned against the father, he had little or no relationship because being jealous, he complained he was never given even a kid to throw a party with his friends. See Luke 15:29-30.

This older brother's response represents the Law or religion. He had a relationship of working, without much love or passion in the relationship with his father. Even in repentance, faith in God's grace honors God in a relationship more than our dutiful and self-sufficient behaviors, works, or actions for Him.

LIFE: We all may be prodigal in some area, but we are to run to God for His help and give our situations to Him. See Hebrews 4:16; 1 Peter 5:7; Psalm 34:15. Get in the Word, pray, and fellowship to develop a relationship with the Father through Jesus; talk to Him and hear from Him, as He is your way back or forward. Become a doer of the Word and do as your Father leads you. See Romans 8:14. Surround yourself with like-minded people of faith to maintain your desire for complete restoration. See Acts 4:23. Guard your mind as you stay close to your Father and follow His guidance. See Philippians 4:8. Remember to praise, worship, and give thanks for His love, forgiveness, wisdom, guidance, and unfailing love. Meditate on Luke 15:3-7.

JESUS

"For God so loved the world, that he gave his only begotten Son, that whosoever believeth in him should not perish, but have everlasting life." —John 3:16

TRUTH: Jesus of Nazareth is our Messiah, Savior, and Lord. He is the incarnate Son of God sent to earth to be crucified on the Cross for the salvation of humanity from their sins. He was wounded for our transgressions and marred beyond recognition as He took on our sins, sicknesses, disobedience, and death on the Cross. See Isaiah 53:4-5; Psalm 22. *"But now being made free from sin, and become servants to God, ye have your fruit unto holiness, and the end everlasting life"* (Romans 6:22).

Jesus Christ became sin and gave us redemption and forgiveness. See Ephesians 1:7. He took our curses and gave us His blessings, exchanged our sins for His righteousness, our self-efforts for the promised Helper in the Holy Spirit. He gave us power and authority over all creation and all evil. See Luke 10:19; 2 Corinthians 5:21; Galatians 3:13-14. Jesus walked this earth in dominion, might, power, grace, mercy, love, and compassion. He preached the Word, healed the sick, fed the hungry, and delivered people from demonic oppression and death. He showed us how to live a life pleasing to the Father and left His Holy Spirit to help and show us how to continue. See John 14; Romans 8:26. We are to have great joy in our salvation and rejoice that Jesus made us free from Satan, sin, sickness, death, and the Law, which held us captive to our self-efforts; He gave us His power in the Holy Spirit to overcome all things by faith. See 1 John 5:4.

LIFE: Believe Jesus. Pray, *"Jesus forgive me of my sins, cleanse my heart, be my Lord and Savior and make me your child. Give me a passion and great desire for Your Word and fellowship with You by Your Holy Spirit. Draw me close and help me to walk in Your ways. Help me depend on the Holy Spirit and talk to Him about helping me with everything. And for every situation I face, help me ask for Your wisdom and guidance to walk in holiness in Jesus' name. Amen."*

CHOOSE LIFE

"I call heaven and earth to record this day against you, that I have set before you, life, and death, blessing, and cursing: therefore, choose life." —Deuteronomy 30:19

TRUTH: During the COVID 19 pandemic, an attack of the spirit of fear came forcefully to me in a dream and said, "bow." Doing all I know to do by faith, I asked the Lord for help. The Word of the Lord came: *The longer you stay, the more you remain beneath."* Two words jumped out at me: *stay* and *beneath,* as they suggest I was at a place, below where I should be, battling this attack of fear of COVID 19. On awaking, I asked for wisdom, and the words *Arise, choose your position, and abide* came into my spirit. I refused to be sick! I rejected subtle symptoms because I am the head and not the tail, above and not beneath, the healed of the Lord. In God's Word, we are to abide, be seated, and hold up the stripes Jesus received as our banner for healing. We do not battle with fear of sickness or sickness itself and bow to the enemy. No! we rise and declare our healing and stand as the healed. See 1 Peter 2:24; Isaiah 53:4-5; Psalm 103:2-3.

Just as a man chooses a wife and remains faithful to her, so believers, having chosen Jesus, the kingdom, love, and light, must not be battling Satan to be free from fear or any other attack of the enemy, we instead must choose to be seated with Jesus in the heavenlies and stand firm. Therefore, every intruder of fear and any other darkness must be cast down as we choose life and rise above sickness and death every time. *"Who hath delivered us from the power of darkness, and hath translated us into the kingdom of his dear Son"* (Colossians 1:13).

LIFE: Jesus loves me, and I am on His side and under His wings. I am established in the kingdom, raised with Jesus, choosing His life to deliver, make and keep me free. I am in Christ, and the law of the Spirit of life in Christ Jesus frees me from the law of sin and death. No sickness can overcome me when I abide and rest in Christ. *"If ye abide in me, and my words abide in you, ye shall ask what ye will, and it shall be done unto you"* (John 15:7).

CHOOSE LIFE — DAY 2

*"...I have set before you life and death, blessing, and cursing,
therefore choose life."* —Deuteronomy 30:19

TRUTH: Confess life-giving words over yourself and others. In Christ Jesus was life and His life is my life, and the life of God in me is full of resurrection power. I am one spirit with the Father, and His life cancels all death and fear; in Him, I live, move, and have my being. There is no fear here, so spirit of fear, Go! in Jesus' name.

Jesus is my righteousness, and He loves me. I am seated with Him, and His unfailing love and care for me are boundless; I need not fear. This is my prayer: *Spirit of infirmity, accusation, and fear, Go! I choose life and shall not be moved! My mind stays on Jesus, and His love floods my soul. His perfect love casts out all fear; I reject you, spirit of fear. I choose Jesus as Lord over fear, and I am established in His love in Christ Jesus. You have no place here, for God has not given me a spirit of fear but of power, love, and a sound mind, in Jesus's name.*

No weapon formed against me can prosper, and I cancel every tongue risen against me. Christ was afflicted and oppressed, yet He bore it in silence; He opened not His mouth. See Isaiah 53:7. Therefore, I now open my mouth and command the accuser's voice speaking in my head to be silent: I reject your voice and your words of condemnation. I agree with God's Word that Christ in me is greater than your sickness or negative words against me. Go! I am healed and delivered in Jesus's name. I choose life and cancel your assignment against me as I send you back to the kingdom of darkness in Jesus's name. I rejoice in Him as my deliverer who made me more than a conqueror in Christ Jesus.

LIFE: Satan will come hard against you, but stand your ground, draw a line in the sand by choosing life in Christ, and resist him until he and his darkness bow. Now rejoice and say thanks be to God who gives me the victory in Christ Jesus and be free. See Romans 8; John 8:12; Colossians 1:13; John 1:4; Acts 17:28; 2 Corinthians 5:21; 1 John 4:18; Isaiah 54:17; 2 Timothy 1:7.

THE WISE FEAR THE LORD

"The fear of the Lord is the beginning of wisdom: and the knowledge of the holy is understanding." —Proverbs 9:10

TRUTH: We are wise when choosing God in His Word and are honoring and obedient to Him. By doing this, we give God Lordship over our lives, with Jesus sitting on the throne of our hearts reigning as King. You are not wise if you are in control, making all your life decisions. These verses say it well. *"In the fear of the Lord is strong confidence: and his children shall have a place of refuge. The fear of the Lord is a fountain of life, to depart from the snares of death"* (Proverbs 14:26-27).

Our purpose is to fear the Lord, walk in righteousness, and avoid living in devious ways. See Proverbs 14:2. *"Behold, the eye of the Lord is upon them that fear him, upon them that hope in his mercy"* (Psalm 33:18). See Proverbs 8:13; 17.

LIFE: In our daily lives, how can we show the fear of the Lord? We show the fear of the Lord when we make Him our priority and show Him respect, honor, love, thanksgiving, and worship for His great redemption. And with gratitude, we praise Him for His involvement in our daily lives, His goodness and mercy, blessings, and the people He places around to bless us. The eyes of our hearts are always turned to gazing toward the Lord, seeing His heart of love, greatness, holiness, and power towards us. In humility, we bow our heads and hearts to Him in surrender. See Revelation 1:17-18. We show fear as we receive Godly wisdom in our life by faith-righteousness, rejecting self-righteousness in any self-effort, and as we exhibit love for God by faith in His Son Jesus to be saved and continually depend on Him to live a successful life in a close relationship.

Meditate on Psalm 25:1-16.

FEAR OF THE LORD

"The fear of the Lord is the beginning of knowledge: but fools despise wisdom and instruction." —Proverbs 1:7

TRUTH: Genesis begins, "In the beginning, God created...." We are given no explanations of God's origin or His previous existence. For anyone to believe God and accept His Words in the Bible, they must do it by faith. He said it four times, *"The just shall live by faith."* See Habakkuk 2:4; Romans 1:17; Galatians 3:11; Hebrews 10:38. Jesus, God in the flesh who lived on earth, feared God His Father. "And *there shall come forth a rod from the stem of Jesse, and a Branch shall grow out of his roots. And the spirit of the Lord shall rest upon him, the spirit of wisdom, and understanding, the spirit of counsel and might, the spirit of knowledge and the fear of the Lord"* (Isaiah 11:1-2). We know Jesus feared His Father because He loved, honored, revered, trusted, submitted to, and obeyed His Father and do only what He saw His Father doing. See John 5:19.

We know God desires all men to fear Him because He says no one will have any excuse not to fear Him, as even a person seeing only His creation should pause to bow to Him as the Creator. See Romans 1:17-20. To fear God is to be in absolute and complete reverence, having holy gratitude toward and love for the Almighty God as the Creator, Sustainer, and Redeemer of all things. We are not only to recognize Him, but to believe Him, receive Him, and grow and increase in His love, faith, relationship, and obedience to Him.

LIFE: The opposite is true when we show a lack of Godly fear to the Almighty God, as the atheist and the sinner try to do by rejecting Him. Even believers can ignore Him by choosing to do our own will in the things we desire instead of according to God's Word. Personally, if you neglect God, you resist His love, care, truth, wisdom, and understanding for a prosperous life and therefore open yourself to failure. Fear the Lord and prosper. See 3 John 2-3.

FEAR OF THE LORD — DAY 2

"The fear of the Lord is the beginning of knowledge..." —Proverbs 1:7

TRUTH: Those who resist God and have no fear for Him will remain in a sin-conscious, fleshy, carnal, and sinful lifestyle instead of becoming Spirit-led and Christ-centered believers as Romans 8 requires.

When we fail to fear God, we will lack wisdom and become as fools. See Proverbs 9:10; Psalm 14:1-2. The Bible says about those who don't fear God.

- They are unthankful, vain in their imaginations, have foolish and darkened hearts, will have the wrong image and concept of God, and will be unclean and lustful in their hearts. See Romans 1:21- 32.
- They dishonor their bodies. Some look at the Word of God, which is truth, as a lie; they have a reprobate mind, thinking and doing ungodly things. They are filled with unrighteousness, showing no love for God or man. They yield to fornication, wickedness, arguments, and deceit; they are gossipers, backbiters, boasters, and inventors of evil things.
- Children become disobedient to parents, covenant-breakers, not loving and affectionate, implacable, without reason, and unmerciful. See 2 Timothy 3: 1-3.

If people choose not to surrender to God, for them, His death is in vain; and He will judge those who choose to continue living in sin as worthy of death. The end may come early in this life on earth, but they will also experience spiritual death in eternity. See Romans 1:21-32 and Revelation 21:8. For believers who are still in religion, self-will, self-effort, and carnality, Scripture says to judge ourselves. See 1 Corinthians 11:31-32. Instead, we are to change our ways and become dependent on God by His Spirit in a relationship and His Word to lead and guide us into forgiveness, repentance, and a more excellent relationship in fear of the Lord, for He is our greatest treasure.

LIFE: *"The fear of the Lord is to hate evil; pride, and arrogancy, and the evil way, and the forward mouth, do I hate"* (Proverbs 8:13). To fear the Lord is to love what He loves and hate what He hates. See Proverbs 6:16-22.

FEAR OF THE LORD — DAY 3

"Let all the earth fear the Lord: let all the inhabitants of the world stand in awe of him." —Psalm 33:8

TRUTH: *"Blessed is the man that feareth the Lord, that delighteth greatly in his commandments. His seed shall be mighty upon the earth: the generation of the upright shall be blessed"* (Psalm 112:1-2). We fear God because of His greatness and majesty; we are joyfully aware that He alone is worthy to be praised, and only in Him can we find salvation, righteousness, prosperity, and peace.

How do we fear God so that we can be blessed? Know that He loves us, provides for us, and desires us to have delight instead of dread when we come to Him as our Father. And as His church, we should expect to be blessed presently and for all our future generations.

We start by seeing God for who He is, great and powerful in His abilities to create and provide for humanity. In His character, He is Holy and hates sin enough to send His only Son to die to redeem humankind from sin, and awesome enough to love sinners as we are or were. For all His goodness, we should choose to look to Him as the source of all our lives. This is our first step in humility to acknowledge His supremacy, our inadequacy, and our desperate need for Him.

Because we see the greatness, wisdom, and awesomeness of God in His grace, this humility and fear of the Lord will eventually lead us to believe and accept Jesus as Savior and Lord of our lives, forgiving our sins and granting us His blessings. See John 3:16; Ephesians 2:8. We fear, praise, and worship Him for all His magnificence.

LIFE: *"Praise our God, all ye his servants, and ye that fear him, both small and great"* (Revelation 19:5).

FEAR OF THE LORD — DAY 4

"Who shall fear thee, O Lord, and glorify thy name?" —Revelation 15:4

TRUTH: We fear God when:

- We have a heart that reverences and honors Him for His greatness. See Psalm 89:7; Hebrews 12:28-29.
- We see Him as the one true God worthy of our love. See John 17:3.
- We agree that natural life by itself is vanity. See Ecclesiastes 1:14; 12:13.
- We become aware that God's love flows from His heart as a King's infinite love of grandeur, power, majesty, and holiness, requiring our positive response to Him. See Revelation 5:12-13.
- We see it as wisdom to surrender our hearts, willing to please Him as the God of our lives. See Hebrews 13:1-9.
- We honor God and do not fear man over Him. See Proverbs 29:25.
- We choose God's will over our desires. See Deuteronomy 30:19-20.
- Displeasing actions cause us to look to His grace. See Hebrews 4:16.
- We are careful to represent Him with Christlikeness in our behaviors. See 2 Timothy 2:19-26.
- We are careful to handle God's Word correctly. See 2 Timothy 3:7-17.
- After seeing that Jesus took sin in His body for us, we love what Jesus loves and hate sin. See Psalm 22; Proverbs 6:16-19.
- Choose to *"love the Lord thy God with all thy heart, and with all thy soul, and with all thy mind"* (Matthew 22:37).

LIFE: God loves us infinitely and with everlasting love, but we should never have the false hope that we can live as we wish, and God will always love us without judgment in correction. Some even ask how a good God could send anyone to hell. He doesn't send anyone to hell. The choice is ours to make. A holy fear of the Lord will cause believers to work out our salvation with fear and trembling and sinners to seek redemption. We are to run to our Father with temptations, weights, and sin for help and cleansing to maintain a relationship, blessings, and fellowship with our Holy Father.

FEAR THE LORD IN HIS GRACE

"Then had the churches rest throughout all Judea and Galilee and Samaria, and were edified; and walking in the fear of the Lord, and in the comfort of the Holy Ghost, were multiplied." —Acts 9:31

TRUTH: Saul of Damascus, possibly of Israelite parenthood, was living by a mistaken interpretation of the Law of Moses. God, knowing his error, had mercy on him and corrected him by stopping him from accomplishing his intent to continue murdering Christians. Saul had a powerful encounter with God on the road to Damascus, and he was blinded. God sent Ananias, His servant, to minister to Saul for him to receive his sight and the baptism of the Holy Spirit. Saul was converted and later preached the gospel of God's grace in power. See Acts 9.

Paul learned what it means to be in the presence of the Almighty God, who holds all people accountable according to our thoughts, motives, words, and actions, and he feared God. We also fear God and yield to His ways and His Word as our guide. See 2 Corinthians 7:1.

When Saul's knee hit the ground, he said, "Lord!" See Acts 9:5. To fear the Lord is to recognize Jesus' Lordship over our lives. God's grace was sufficient for Saul. For believers, God is to be the One sitting on the throne of our hearts to give us life, truth, and confidence; we are not to live for ourselves. See Romans 10:9-11, 1 Corinthians 6:19-20. To be led by God's grace, we must humble ourselves and see God as Saul did, Our Lord high and lifted, worthy to be praised and obeyed. See Psalm 86:11-12. Believers who fear God are led in God's grace by the Holy Spirit into goodness and mercy and are not self-directed as Saul was. See Romans 8:14.

LIFE: We fear God and keep His commandments not out of dread, but out of love, by dying to self and desiring to yield to Him. See John 14:21. The Lord says He will teach us how to fear Him. We do not have to be afraid that we do not know how. Ask Him to guide you, and He will. See Psalm 34:11-22.

BENEFITS OF FEARING THE LORD

"Behold the eye of the Lord is upon them that fear him...
To deliver their soul from death." —Psalm 33:18-19

TRUTH AND LIFE: *"O that there were such an heart in them, that they would fear me, and keep all my commandments always, that it might be well with them, and with their children forever"* (Deuteronomy 5:29).

"For as *the heaven is high above the earth, so great is his mercy towards them that fear him* (Psalm 103:11).

We will have favor in all areas of life. *"By humility and the fear of the Lord are riches, and honor, and life"* (Proverbs 22:4).

"O fear the lord, ye his saints; for there is no want to them that fear him. ...they that seek the Lord shall not want any good thing (Psalm 34:9-10).

"And *I will give them one heart, and one way, that they may fear me forever, for the good of them, and of their children after them... I will put my fear in their hearts, that they shall not depart from me"* (Jeremiah 32:39-40).

Passion and intimacy will increase with your Father. We will draw nigh. See James 4:8. *"But unto you that fear my name shall the Sun of righteousness arise with healing in his wings"* (Malachi 4:2).

"That his heart may not be lifted above his brethren, that he not turn aside from the commandment to the right hand, or to the left: to the end that he may prolong his days in his kingdom, he, and his children in the midst of Israel" (Deuteronomy 17:20).

"What man is he that feareth the Lord? him shall he teach in the way that he shall choose" (Psalm 25:12).

Philip feared God and left a revival to minister to one person. See Acts 8:26-28. Reverence to God will cause us to grow in obedience and power for Him to use us to minister, peace will increase, and we will have a clear conscience. See Acts 24:16. Strong faith and confidence will be our portion. See Proverbs 14:26-27. And we will receive our inheritance in His divine protection. He will give us the kingdom with all His blessings until we're satisfied. See Psalm 34:9-10; Proverbs 19:23; Luke 12:32.

JESUS DIED FOR RELATIONSHIP

"That ye might believe that Jesus is the Christ, the Son of God; and that believing ye might have life through his name." —John 20: 31

TRUTH: All true and authentic life begins with the only true God through Jesus Christ, His Son. Eternal life is the best quality of life here and now to eternity. It is a life established in union and fellowship with God, filled with power, love, and a sound mind. In God's abundant life, it is a life of righteousness, peace, and joy. We cannot know God through other means, such as religion and being good. See Isaiah 64:6; Matthew 5:20; 23:27; Titus 1:16. Living by religion is living by the devil's agenda. See John 8:42-44. Galatians was written to Christians who were saved by God's grace into a relationship, but we're turning back to religion, trying to live by self-effort through the Law of Moses.

A life of living by the human self-will, reasonings, feelings, strength, and independence opposes a relationship with God. Paul says in Philippians 3:7-10, *"But what things were gain to me, those I counted loss for Christ...that I may know him." To* know God in a greater relationship, we must believe in Jesus and experience Him in touching God's heart through believing and obeying His Word, always yielding to His Spirit's power by His love, wisdom, and peace.

LIFE: Know God through Jesus in a relationship, grace through faith, obeying Him by the Word and power of His Holy Spirit, both to be saved and live the Christian life each day. Never resort to self-will and your strength.

Prayer: *Father, help me rely on You, increase my resolve to depend on and trust You more in our relationship and in every situation I will face today. Help me look to God my Father first for all things and believe His promises. "That God hath given to us eternal life, and this life is in His Son. He that hath the Son hath life; and he that hath not the Son of God hath not life...That ye may know that ye have eternal life and that ye may believe on the name of the Son of God"* (1 John 5:11-13).

REPENTANCE

"Repent ye therefore, and be converted, that your sins may be blotted out, when the times of refreshing shall come from the presence of the Lord." —Acts 3:19

TRUTH: Repentance to be saved is one of the most significant decisions one will ever make. To repent is to be remorseful of our sin and wrongdoings enough to change our minds about the sin and turn to God from our hearts and to His way of living. In repentance, we acknowledge sin sincerely from the heart and turn our minds, thinking, and life towards God to bring a change in our lifestyle.

How repentance is sought is also essential as it must be grace through faith and not by our efforts or performance. Sin and repentance are not hot topics being taught regularly anymore, but when taught in the context of God's grace, they will assist greatly in keeping sinners and believers out of Satan's grasp. To repent is to reject sin and choose Christ Jesus as the person makes a 180-degree turnaround, running away from sin and religion to faith in God. See Matthew 3:8; Proverbs 28:13.

LIFE: If you are not born again, read John 3:16; Romans 10:9-10 and believe Jesus died for you and receive salvation. You must not try to clean up yourself or confess all your sins to feel worthy enough for God to accept you. Simply accept Jesus sincerely and with humility of heart. Then, as a believer, stop focusing on sin and focus on being in relationship with Jesus, raised and seated "in Christ" in heavenly places, abiding in Him. And when you do sin, repent and be cleansed to maintain unbroken fellowship and righteousness. You repent to keep Satan the accuser out of your life, not to get God to continue loving you. Repentance is critically important in these last days to remove sin, live life with God, and invite true refreshing times that come only from the presence of the Lord.

REPENTANCE DAY 2

"Repent ye therefore, and be converted, that your sins may be blotted out, when the times of refreshing shall come from the presence of the Lord." —Acts 3:19

TRUTH: When a believer sins, it should be thought of as one who accidentally drinks poison and must be rushed to the doctor immediately. Run to God for mercy and be freed from the sin by repenting and asking the Holy Spirit to help you pursue righteousness and show you how to avoid that sin from reoccurring. *"There hath no temptation taken you but such as is common to man: but God is faithful, who will not suffer you to be tempted above that ye are able; but will with the temptation also make a way to escape, that ye may be able to bear it"* (1 Corinthians 10:13).

God's greatest desire is for us to live so close to Him that at any time we sin, we know He is right there to respond to our repentance and, by His Blood and His Spirit, give forgiveness and lead us back into righteousness. This is the option and path we have in repentance, and when we take it, no condemnation can come to us because we walked after the Spirit of life in Christ Jesus. See Romans 8:1-2.

Therefore, name and admit the wrong or the sin, not justifying or making excuses. See Zechariah 1:3; 2 Chronicles 7:14; James 4:8.

Be remorseful that you broke fellowship. See Hebrews 4:16. Receive forgiveness and cleansing. See 1 John 1:9. Ask God through His Holy Spirt to keep you from that sin and make a commitment to yourself to resist future temptation. See 1 Peter 1:5. If another person was hurt, ask them to forgive you as well. See Matthew 3:8. Spend time in the Word and prayer to build yourself up to resist the devil so that he will flee. See Romans 10:17; James 4:7.

LIFE: Repent genuinely; don't just be sorrowful. Own up to the sin and give it to God. Get back into fellowship with Your Father and let His love and life flow in and through you as you seek to continue your Christian journey to make Christ your life. Read 2 Corinthians 7:8-13.

FORGIVENESS

"In whom we have redemption through his blood, even the forgiveness of sins." —Colossians 1:14

TRUTH: Psychologists define forgiveness as a conscious and deliberate decision to cancel and release sin, hurt, and the emerging feelings of resentment or judgment towards someone who has brought us harm. To be just and offer forgiveness, God had to pay the price for death in the crucified body and the shed Blood of Jesus. Forgiveness has a tremendous cost. It cost God the life of and separation from His only Son to offer us the grace of forgiveness. No one should receive forgiveness with repentance lightly, either at salvation or for daily sins, without accounting for the agony and suffering of Jesus at Calvary. Without the Cross, God could not forgive, *"and without shedding of blood is no remission* (or forgiveness)" (Hebrews 9:22). Jesus Christ died on the Cross and became the *"once and for all sacrifice"* for our sins. See 1 Peter 3:18; Hebrews 10:10-12. The death of His Son shows the degree to which God hates sin and His willingness to die to save sinners. See Romans 5:6-8. Forgiveness is an act of God's grace, and when faith is placed in Jesus and forgiveness is received, believers are eternally freed and cleansed from all sins. See 1 John 1:7-9; Colossians 2:13; Mark 3:28.

Therefore, the Blood of Jesus removes all guilt and the penalty of sin away from us, and God does not keep a record of them because He says He remembers them no more. See Psalm 32:1-2; 103:12; Isaiah 43:25. The ability for us to receive forgiveness from the Cross should be a deep source of joy and gratitude because, when God looks at us, He sees us in Jesus with our spirit as forgiven, cleansed, dead to sin, redeemed, and holy, children made in His image.

LIFE: See yourself in the same way God sees you: A new creation forgiven, redeemed, and restored in His love. See Psalms 107:1-2; Ephesians 1:7; 1 John 1:7; Romans 6:11-12; Colossians 1:22.

YOU ARE FORGIVEN

"Son be of good cheer; thy sins be forgiven thee." —Matthew 9:2

TRUTH: When we give and receive forgiveness, we are lifted from sin, sin-consciousness, and death to new life and freedom. How do we forgive? First, we realize only Jesus is perfect, and He forgave us our sins; therefore, we should look at the wrong done to us and pardon, by letting it go into Jesus' hands. Choose to see it as a thing of the past: *"But this one thing I do, forgetting those things which are behind, and reaching forth unto those things which are before"* (Philippians 3:13).

Secondly, we ask Jesus to remove the emotional and psychological pain and keep it from reaching our hearts to cause bitterness. See Romans 12:19.

Thirdly, we are to purpose in our hearts to release the person who sinned against us, cancel the offense, and forget it as we apply these Scriptures daily. See Romans 12:14; 2 Corinthians 10:4-5; Philippians 4:8; 1 Thessalonians 5:15.

Fourthly, refocus on Jesus and receive His healing with peace and reconciliation in our hearts. See Colossians 1:20.

We forgive because Jesus forgave us. Therefore, we are not allowed to hold others' sins against them. See Colossians 3:13. God said vengeance is His, and He only must repay. See Romans 12:17-19. We forgive because Jesus commands us to forgive. See Ephesians 4:30-32. Jesus showed us how to forgive, so just let it go! See Luke 23:34; Acts 7:60. We also forgive because God forgives us only as we forgive others. See Matthew 6:14-15.

An unforgiving spirit will hinder our prayers. See Psalm 66:18. Forgiveness brings freedom to the heart and the soul. See Hebrews 12:14-15; Proverbs 4:23-27. We also forgive as many times as necessary. See Luke 17:4-5.

LIFE: You are forgiven; believe it, receive it, and walk in total freedom by the power of Christ to obey, love, and remain joyful in your spirit even as you forgive others.

WALK IN FORGIVENESS

"Lord, how oft shall my brother sin against me, and I forgive him? till seven times?" —Matthew 18:21

TRUTH: Forgiveness is an essential part of our Christian life. It placed us into salvation, and it keeps us walking in the grace of our salvation. We are commanded to love, and forgiveness is one key that opens the door to experience God's love and keeps the door open for love in fellowship to continue. As believers, when Jesus forgave us, He delivered us from the judgment or wrath of God and gave us His discipline to judge ourselves, love, and forgive. See 1 Corinthians 11:31-32; Galatians 5:22. A believer may be judged with the consequences of his sin, but judgment with damnation is for the devil or the world, as God already spiritually judged and punished a believer's sin in Jesus.

Consequently, we do not walk with fear of punishment for sin from God but look to Jesus by receiving and giving forgiveness and cleansing. We receive forgiveness provided by Jesus' Blood to have a cleansed heart and a purged conscience, always seeking to walk in the newness of life. As offenses come, forgive and be forgiven and be freed from the grasp of Satan, the sin of unforgiveness, and its consequence of fear.

Forgive seventy times seven, meaning unlimited times; always live with a forgiving heart. Walking in forgiveness exercises the grace of God's love and avoids self-righteousness in fault finding, criticizing, bitterness, strife, and bringing condemnation on self and others. See Matthew 7:5. Walk in forgiveness one with another from the heart. See Matthew 5:43-45; 18:34-35. Receive forgiveness for yourself by faith and be free. See Romans 10:9-10; 1 John 1:7-9; Hebrews 8:12.

LIFE: Prayer: *Father, in Your name, I receive forgiveness for my sins and cleansing from any conscience of sin. As I am forgiven, I forgive others and pray for them. I thank You for cleansing and healing my wounded heart; please fill me with Your presence and peace in Jesus' name. Amen.*

CONFESSIONS ON FORGIVENESS

"Who forgiveth all thine iniquities: who health all thy diseases." —Psalm 103:3

TRUTH: Unless we acknowledge the need for forgiveness and receive it by faith and give forgiveness, we will not be free. As we forgive and do it quickly, we can rejoice in the freedom it brings as we rest in Jesus and have unlimited joy in our salvation. *"Be angry, and sin not: let not the sun go down upon your wrath"* (Ephesians 4:26).

Thank you, Father, for the sacrifice of your Son, Jesus, and His shed Blood to forgive all my sins. I receive your forgiveness and believe I am washed, cleansed, forgiven, and made right with God. See 1 Corinthians 1:30. I am forgiven, justified, made innocent, and freed from the guilt of sin; made righteous, acceptable, and restored into my Father's love. I am the righteousness of God in Christ by the Blood of Jesus alone. I look at nothing in and of myself in my actions or performance to gain God's love or His acceptance.

I am the just who lives by faith in God's grace, the Blood of Jesus, and the power of His Spirit. I reject the enemy's lie that I am justified, made right with God by my obedience and perfect performance, always doing what is right.

When I sin or am accused of sin by the devil, I look to Jesus, the Author, and Finisher of my faith. By His Spirit, I receive wisdom, direction, and repentance. I will not listen to Satan and his torment of how wrong I was and that I deserve punishment. The chastisement of my peace was upon Jesus; by His stripes, I am healed and free from torment. See Isaiah 53:5; Matthew 18:23-35.

LIFE: I am free from the stain of sin because I have Jesus' perfect righteousness. I am loved, forgiven, accepted, holy, blameless in God's sight. I lift Jesus' righteousness as my breastplate that protects God's love in my heart and keeps me free, joyful, and at peace. See 1 Thessalonians 5:8; 2 Corinthians 5:21.

OUR GREAT GOD

"For the Lord is a great God, and a great King above all gods." —Psalm 95:3

TRUTH: We sing songs about how great our God is and how great is His name. But if we truly fail to grasp the greatness of God, we will fail to choose the proper foundation on which to build our Christian life. We will select sand instead of solid rock. See Luke 6:46-49. Some reasons people do not see God in His greatness could be pride, selfishness, arrogance, ignorance, religion, lack of effort in meditating on His superiority, self-righteousness, a critical and judgmental spirit, doubting God, being afraid of God, and mocking God. It could also be other gods in the things we idolize more than we do God Himself—such as our family, money, job, sports and sports icons, clothes, food, career, pleasures, and possessions.

When we see God as our great God, the rock of our salvation, we are strengthened to trust Him, believe Him, and depend on Him. See Psalm 18:2. We see Old Testament saints who magnified their great God. Daniel defied the king's orders to bow and worship Him and testified how great his God was. See Daniel 3; 6:19-28. The Israelites worshipped and sang many praises unto God, their deliverer. See Exodus 15. We, too, must declare His greatness within our hearts and our lives to enlarge our expectation and faith to receive from Jesus.

LIFE: Will you do your self-examination by checking whether there is anything mentioned above that is hindering you from seeing the greatness of God in your life? Ask the Holy Spirit to change it. Meditate on these Scriptures to change your perspective and worship God's true greatness to you and in you.

See Isaiah 44:8; Psalms 29:1-2; 48:1-2; 66:1-5; 145:2-3; 147:4-5; Philippians 2:9-11; Titus 2:13.

SURRENDER TO GOD

"Come unto me, all ye that labor and are heavy laden,
and I will give you rest." —Matthew 11: 28

TRUTH: Jesus, as a good Father, is calling people to come to Him, and He promises rest and peace. He told us how to rest by taking His yoke upon us and to learn of Him. What is Jesus' yoke? It was not explained here, but I believe God's yoke is His love because we know God is love, and Jesus gave us a commandment of love to bind us to Himself and other believers. See John 13:34; Matthew 22:37; 1 John 4:11. He went as far as to say His yoke is easy and His burden light. Receiving God's love, delighting in it, and passing that love to others is easy and is not a burden. When we surrender to God, receive His love, and are willing to love others, we will have accomplished His will in obeying His New Covenant commandment for our lives to love. Jesus surrendered to His Father and fulfilled His purpose and destiny to bring salvation to humanity. When facing the Cross, Jesus prayed, *"O Father, if it be possible, let this cup pass from me: nevertheless, not as I will, but as thou wilt"* (Matthew 26:39). Jesus submitted to the Father, fully committed to living in agreement with God's will.

As believers, we know we have a great, good, faithful God to bless and do the impossible for us as His children. But what is our response to Him? Are we fully committed, half-hearted, unsure, or rebellious? The Rev. Elisha A. Hoffman wrote an old Hymn with the following chorus: *"Is your all on the altar of sacrifice laid? Your heart, does the Spirit control? You can only be blest and have peace and sweet rest, As you yield Him your body and soul."* Commit our all to our Father and watch His life in us bring real life to everything our hand touches.

LIFE: *Father, I give my entire life and all that I possess to You, that Your kingdom come to me and Thy will in heaven be done in my life here on earth. Father, let my every desire be first and foremost for You through Jesus Christ, Your Son. I choose to die to myself, surrender to and live for You. Holy Spirit, I ask for You to lead me into total commitment. In Jesus' name, I pray, Amen.*

GOD IS LOVE

"He that loveth not knoweth not God: for God is love." —1 John 4:8

TRUTH: God is love, and all believers have Him in the fullness of His nature in their hearts. We have been commanded to love and live a life of love, first towards God. As we receive Him for ourselves, we then share Him with others. We get to know God's love and develop His supernatural life within as we accept Him by faith, maintain a union relationship, and abide in the Word and fellowship. See John 15; Ephesians 3:17-18. 1 Corinthians 13 tells us precisely what God's unconditional love is like—a love that gives without conditions and continues to give even when rejected.

The greatest battle of our Christian journey is to stop Satan from keeping God's love from growing in our hearts to fulfill God's purpose and destiny for our lives. But we must draw sustenance from the Vine; we must draw on His love, His Word, and His Spirit, the most incredible power on earth to destroy all evil. His supernatural life in us by the power of the Holy Spirit connects God's love to our spirits and helps us daily to crucify the flesh. By allowing God's love to grow in and flow from us, we can bless others. Fear in our soul is expelled as we acknowledge and practice God's love. As Christ is being formed within our hearts, God's love increases faith and authority to cast out all fear. See Galatians 4:19; 5:6.

"There is no fear in love; but perfect love casteth out all fear...he that feareth is not made perfect in love" (1 John 4:18).

LIFE: I will always depend on God's love and power, not on my self-effort or works, which breed fear and insecurity. I am established in righteousness, in my Father's love. I walk by faith in His love and care, which makes me secure, healed, delivered, triumphant, and victorious over all fear and all evil. See Isaiah 54:14.

LOVE IS OF GOD

"He that loveth not knoweth not God; for God is love" —1 John 4:8

TRUTH: Everything the Word says about love in 1 Corinthians 13 is true of God. "God is love" means more than just the acts of love He does. He is the very essence, nature, and character of love. Everything He is and does is out of love. When we understand this, we will not take things He does personally, especially those we do not understand. For example, we won't take all trials to mean God does not love us. From His character, we see God is all-encompassing; He loves the whole world...the good, the bad, and the undeserving, and He loves us.

God's greatest act of love was seen in extending His love to us in Jesus for salvation, the forgiveness of sin, and His acceptance in Jesus' righteousness. See John 3:16; Ephesians 1:6-7. He is still with us in our daily lives with provision instead of poverty, deliverance instead of bondage, comfort for grief, healing for sickness, and love instead of fear. No darkness, insecurity, infirmity, torment, bondage, or fear can harm us because, by His Spirit, we possess the power to rest in His love, strength, and grace, and by faith to command fear and all evil to bow in the name of Jesus.

"But let him that glorieth glory in this, that he understandeth and knoweth me, that I am the Lord which exercise lovingkindness, judgment, and righteousness, in the earth: for in these things I delight, saith the Lord" (Jeremiah 9:24).

LIFE: Love is who God is, and love is what He demonstrates. Knowing God's love and His unfailing goodness and loving-kindness gives assurance and confidence that He saved us and He is for us, and nothing can stand against us and succeed to harm us. His perfect love eliminates all fear. See 1 John 4:18.

"And we have known and believed the love that God hath to us. God is love: and he that dwelleth in love dwelleth in God, and God in him" (1 John 4: 16-18).

GOD IS LIGHT

"God is light, and in him is no darkness at all." —1 John 1:5

TRUTH: At creation, God spoke natural light into being by creating the sun, moon, and stars. Humanity enjoyed God's splendid creation with spiritual and natural light until Adam's sin brought spiritual darkness. The corruption and the darkness it brought reigned until Jesus came to earth and brought the remedy in Himself as spiritual light.

Ephesians 5:8 says, *"For ye were sometimes darkness, but now are ye the light in the Lord: walk as children of the light."*

God is light and born again believers have the Spirit of God dwelling inside their hearts filled with life and light. *"In him was life: and the life was the light of men"* (John 1:4). Satan's domain is darkness, and with any step away from God in the opposite direction of love and light, darkness begins.

"He that saith he is in the light, and hateth his brother, is in darkness even until now. He that loveth his brother abideth in the light, and there is none occasion of stumbling in him" (1 John 2:9-10).

God is light and represents love, joy, peace, patience, faithfulness, goodness, meekness, temperance, obedience, worship, power, love, a sound mind, righteousness, and peace. Satan controls darkness, sin, fear, hate, and disobedience. We must dethrone him with Christ's life, light, and love within and with the knowledge of His Word. "The entrance of thy words giveth light; it giveth understanding unto the simple" (Psalm 119:130).

His Word believed, spoken in faith and authority, and acted on as truth will always set us free and keep us in God's light. See John 8:32,36.

LIFE: Walk in the light of God's Word and guard your mind by practicing its truth. Stay always in the truth of God's Word, in fellowship, worship, and the exaltation of Jesus, and He will cause you to triumph and fill you with light.

Meditate on John 1:4, 9; 8:12; Revelation 22:1-5.

GOD'S HIGHER LOVE

"And now abideth faith, hope, charity, these three; but the greatest of these is charity (love)." —1 Corinthians 13:13

TRUTH: God's love is divine, an everlasting forever love, always available and freely given, never withheld until conditions are met. We get to enter when we love Jesus. He will never disappoint and will never fail. God is love, and His nature of love will manifest in actions of love. God's love motivated Him to send His Son Jesus to die on the Cross to grant humanity forgiveness of sins and, in exchange, receive His righteousness or right standing before the Father. The ability to love God from the heart, which Adam lost, was restored. *The love of God is shed abroad in our hearts by the Holy Ghost, which is given unto us"* (Romans 5:5). We are to live in the Kingdom of God from this place of love in our hearts to fulfill His commandment for us to love. See John 13:34-35.

How do we do this? We receive His gift of righteousness, and we worship God for who He is, LOVE. We worship Him as our healer. We worship Him as our provider. We worship Him as our deliverer, but we must also worship Him as our Great Love, our righteousness, and as we do, His love will be formed in our hearts to love and trust Him. His perfect love, once formed, builds faith which drives out all fear. God's love in our hearts as trust is greater than any fear of Satan coming against us in this world. Thank You, Heavenly Father, for multiplying Your love in my heart as I worship You. Thank you, Father, that you are a God full of compassion, gracious, long-suffering, and plenteous in mercy and truth. See Psalm 86:15. Because of Your great love and grace, I can see past the sin and mistakes of myself and others and see the need to forgive, pray, and extend love as Stephen did when he forgave those who stoned him to death. See Acts 7:59-60.

LIFE: Read and meditate on these Scriptures on trusting God's love and become established in His righteousness, which will drive out fear and oppression. Isaiah 54:14; Jeremiah 31:3; Zephaniah 3:17; John 3:16; 1 Corinthians 13; Ephesians 2:4-10; 1 John 4:17-21; Romans 8:37-39.

THY WORD IS LIFE

"Man shall not live by bread alone, but by every word that proceedeth out of the mouth of God." —Matthew 4:4

TRUTH: Bread here is the natural sustenance for the body, but Jesus is saying to us that we need more than physical food for our bodies. We are also made up of a spirit within to be fed by the Word of God and a soul where the intellect and study feed the mind. God desires that our human spirit, where He dwells, become the engine that drives our soul and body unto holiness. God is love, and He deposited Himself in our human spirit. See Romans 5:5; Galatians 5:22. Living by love through the Word of truth from our spirit-man is walking in the Spirit. We live the New Covenant of grace when we obey God's new commandment to love. *"A new commandment I give unto you, That ye love one another: as I have loved you, that ye also love one another"* (John 13:34). Jesus and His Word are one, and His Word is the truth, our spiritual food, and sustenance for life. See John 1:1, 14-17.

If we are concerned chiefly about our natural existence, we will not become spiritually mature in the things of God. We will not develop an increasing and passionate relationship with God the Father. Instead, we will live carnal lives full of worry and struggle. Faith works by love. When we love God, we will connect with Him in a relationship, believe Him by His Word and His Spirit and walk by faith. Living by the soul in a carnal existence is not living by faith, and whatever is not of faith is sin. See Romans 14:23. Wherever faith is lacking, evil lurks, and Satan has an open door to access your life.

"Holding forth the word of life; that I may rejoice in the day of Christ, that I have not run in vain" (Philippians 2:16).

LIFE: Living by the Word of God is a necessity for you as a believer to succeed, just as Jesus speaks the Word, "It is written," enabled Him to succeed against Satan. Practice saying the Word daily in your life situations, and you will prosper. See Isaiah 55:11-12; 3 John 2.

THY WORD IS LIFE -DAY 2

*"Man shall not live by bread alone, but by every word that
proceedeth out of the mouth of God"* —Matthew 4:4

TRUTH: The Word of God is the bread of life. God's Word caused Jesus to overcome Satan. God's people are destroyed for lack of knowledge and application of His Word. If we do not know the truth, we will be held in bondage. It is the truth that we know, believe in our hearts, and speak in power and authority that will set us free. See Hosea 4:6; John 8:31-32.

The Word of God is our solid foundation to keep us strong, in His light and His life. See Matthew 7:24-27. *"Thy Word have I hid in mine heart, that I might not sin against thee"* (Psalm 119: 11). God's Word is unfailing because He is love, and love never fails. See Numbers 23:19; Romans 4:18-21; 1 Corinthians 13:8. The Word of God is the power to heal, deliver, and give life. See Isaiah 55:11; Psalm 107:20. The Word of God gives wisdom and direction. See Psalm 32:8, 37:23.

Hearing and believing God's Word brings faith to our hearts and the possibilities for all blessings. See Romans 10:17; Acts 14:9-10. God's Word brings comfort to the grieving and peace to troubled hearts. See Isaiah 41:13; Psalm 85:8-13. God's Word as life protects us defensively to destroy evil and, when used offensively, grants us blessings and peace. See Psalm 91; Hebrews 4:12.

LIFE: Jesus is the bread of life; feed on Him by His Words, fellowship with His Spirit, and be led by Him in His ways and character. Let His Words lead you into deeper fellowship and relationship. As you hear from His heart and obey, you will be kept and sustained with His power and His life into everything good.

OUR SECURITY

"Blessed is the man that trusteth in the Lord, and whose hope the Lord is. For he shall be as a tree planted by the waters..." —Jeremiah 17:7-8

TRUTH: Wherever there is insecurity, anxiety, and fear in our lives, some dependence on the flesh exists. The flesh here can refer to anything we trust or prioritize above God. In verse 5, God mentioned those who trusted in man. But we can also trust in ourselves, our intellectual abilities, status, money, and so on.

In today's digital media age, many people are living in discontentment and discouragement because of the high level of misinformation, comparison, and false exhibition being displayed. Everyone tends to show only their side or the good side, while reality may be vastly different behind the scenes, and they are struggling. There are often comparisons of houses, properties, clothes, beauty, bodily features, and wealth. Verse 6 tells us the negative results of insecurity; they will be parched; eyes will be dimmed with anguish, and they will not even see any good in their situation. They will lack fresh drinking water to quench their thirst and suffer. We will have these negative results, as nothing else in the world can satisfy the deep longings of our hearts for connection and relationship with God.

To build security in our hearts, we need Jesus to uphold, support, and keep our feet from falling. When we place ourselves in His care, He will watch over, deliver and keep us safe. As we meditate on His Word and fellowship, He will help us, delight in us, provide and comfort us. In turn, we will have a higher level of trust, greater self-esteem, joy, genuine love, and peace.

LIFE: We can be secure because we are sealed unto God and cannot be plucked from His hand. Therefore, trust Him. See Ephesians 1:13-14; John 10:28-30; Proverbs 3:5-7. *"Now unto him, that is able to keep you from falling and to present you faultless before the presence of his glory with exceeding joy"* (Jude 24-25).

OUR SECURITY — DAY 2

"...He shall be like a tree planted by the rivers of water, that bringeth forth his fruit in his season; his leaf also shall not wither, and whatsoever he doeth shall prosper." —Psalm 1:3

TRUTH: Placing our need for security in transient and temporary things will cause us to be fearful because they are subject to change, and it will be as if we are always moving with shifting winds. We can lose our beauty, our friends can turn their backs on us, and we can lose our money along with our hope.

But when we make God our assurance and our source, then no matter what happens, we look to Him and still have hope. Where is your hope? Hope thou in God. See Psalm 42:5-6. As Psalm 23:4 tells us, yea, though we walk through the valley of the shadow of death, we will fear no evil: for God is with us. And because God is with us, He says we are blessed, and we shall be like a tree planted by the waters that spread out her roots.

Can we hear Psalm 1 from our hearts echoing the Scripture in Jeremiah 17:5-8? When we commit ourselves to God and put our complete trust in Him, looking to His ways, His Word, and His Spirit to lead, guide, and provide, He will never fail us. We become secure as our faith rests in Him to meet our needs and care for us. Reject insecurity and fear, receive your Father's love and obey Proverbs 3:5-10 and be blessed and secure in God through Jesus Christ His Son.

"Commit thy way unto the Lord; trust also in him; he shall bring it to pass" (Psalm 37:5).

LIFE: The righteous are blessed. He is like a tree, flourishing and fruitful, bearing fruit. If you translate this to your life, what would it look like? Are your roots deep in God? Are you drawing your sustenance from Him to bear fruit? Are you prospering in your soul, mind, will, emotions, family, and finances? Be secure in God alone and receive His love, joy, wisdom, direction, and peace in His loving care to prosper in every area of your life. Begin today on your path to being secure in God and yourself and as in His love you learn to trust others.

SURETY OF SALVATION

*"He that hath the Son hath life: and he that hath not
the Son of God hath not life."* —1 John 5:12

TRUTH: It is tough for many people to accept that salvation could come so easy, while others believe all that is required is to say the sinner's prayer and then continue their life as usual. Neither path is God's way as the person is not looking to God in faith; instead, he is in the sin of self-righteousness, having no assurance of God's grace in His salvation. See Romans 14:23; Acts 16:31; Isaiah 32:17-18. In addition to the lack of assurance before God, they will be completely exposed to the ravages of Satan in their soul, living by their senses in thoughts, feelings, and self-choices in their human will as the devil bombards them with lies and accusations. The lies may be about you not being saved, or being unworthy, or about God not being good. This will result in a lack of confidence in their salvation, low self-esteem, instability, and fear.

After one receives salvation and chooses to live as one pleases or in self-righteousness, this opens the door to sin, sin-consciousness, sickness, lack, poverty, and lack of protection. That person might then wonder why God is not taking care of them. It is unscriptural to use our feelings to measure our salvation, as we are not acting in faith. Satan then has access to the soul, and he can torment us with temptations of sin, sin-consciousness, guilt, doubt, accusation, condemnation, and fear until our mind is no longer sound. We must live by faith in a relationship from our spirit that is sealed and secure in God. Our soul (mind, will, and emotions) must be renewed with the Word for us to stand firm in the faith. Faith in God's Word, His love, and grace is our shield against the enemy of our souls with insecurity. We will become secure in God and life as we walk with renewed minds in the Word and the Spirit (love, grace, faith), not the flesh (our thinking, feeling, natural actions). See Romans 12:1-2.

LIFE: Increase your security of salvation as you meditate on John 5:24; Acts 2:22-28; 4:12; 16:30-31; Romans 10:9-11,13; 8:15-16; Ephesians 1:13.

ACCESS

"By whom also we have access by faith into this grace wherein we stand and rejoice in hope of the glory of God." —Romans 5:2

TRUTH: Adam's sin plunged the entire human race into separation from God. We should all have been put to death for our sins. But God, in His grace and mercy, caused Jesus to die for us on the Cross. When we are born again, we gain access to God's grace, blessings, and compassion in salvation. We gain entrance into God's kingdom and His family in a relationship, where we can rejoice in hope and the glory of God. See Romans 5:17-19. All believers can now access the highest place of privilege in the presence of God in the heavenlies, seated "in Christ" at the right hand of the Father. See Ephesians 2:6. We must believe we're in a perfect relationship, delivered from sin, and can rejoice in Jesus, our great hope and Savior. See Psalm 42:11. We have a hope that because the veil was torn, believers have access granted to all Jesus has provided in salvation by His resurrection power. See Mark 15:38-39. The Lord broke down the veil that separated us and drew us near the Blood of Jesus to give us access. See Ephesians 2:13-14.

As new creation spirit-beings, we have been given power in relationship to relate to the Father in love, in righteousness, in His Word, and His blessings. Access also gives us power and authority in Christ to enforce Satan's defeat. See Luke 10:19. What has access into the kingdom brought to you? The keys to the kingdom are to access indescribable joy and blessings in all of God's goodness. See Matthew 16:19; Ephesians 1:3. If you think there must be more, there is always more... more joy, peace, blessings, and victory in Christ Jesus!

LIFE: Access is granted! If you need more, put your hope in Jesus alone and His Word to guide you in all your endeavors, to end struggle and weariness. Choose Jesus and depend on His Holy Spirit to gain even greater access to more incredible blessings and greater peace.

THE KINGDOM

"Who hath delivered us from the power of darkness, and hath translated us into the kingdom of his dear Son." —Colossians 1:13.

TRUTH: *"Then Pilate ... said unto him, Art thou the king of the Jews? And Jesus answered him, Sayest thou the thing thyself, My kingdom is not of this world."* See John 18:33-36. A king is a supreme ruler of a kingdom. Jesus is King of heaven, the universe, earth, hell, and its inhabitants. See Philippians 2:9-11; Revelation 19:16. Every king is a lord and has a kingdom with subjects, resources, and decrees or laws. See Matthew 6:13. The king is absolute, and none is superior to Him. But as King, Jesus the Son of man puts on flesh and became a man to deliver humanity from their sin by offering redemption and forgiveness. The Blood of Jesus purchased humanity as children, kings, and priests in the kingdom of God to reign with King Jesus. See Romans 5:17; Revelation 17:14. He is the Lord of lords and King of kings.

As children of the King, we are heirs and joint-heirs, not servants but sons, a chosen generation, kings of the King, friends, and partakers of the kingdom filled with power, love, and a sound mind. Jesus' kingdom is love, righteousness, light, peace, and joy. See Romans 8:17; John 15:15; 2 Peter 3:10-18; Romans 14:17. Our King is infinitely powerful, and no one can defeat Him. He is wealthy, good, kind, faithful, and true. He loves and cares for those of us in His kingdom. We have nothing to fear. We can trust our King Jesus by faith to provide, deliver, heal, and always protect.

"And heal the sick that are therein, and say unto them, The kingdom of God is come nigh unto you" (Luke 10:9).

LIFE: I belong to King Jesus and possess the kingdom of God filled with love, light, life, righteousness, peace, and joy in the Holy Ghost because the kingdom is within me. See Luke 17:21. I have a covenant of love with my King, and by faith, every blessing in the kingdom given as a promise is mine as I depend on Jesus by faith. I am loved, secure, and free because my trust is in my King Jesus, who reigns supreme and brings success to every area of my life.

TO DIE IS TO LIVE

"For in that he died, he died unto sin once: but in that he liveth, he liveth unto God." —Romans 6:10

TRUTH: Jesus' death on the Cross accomplished the remission of Adam's original sin, which we inherited as well as the forgiveness of the personal sins we commit. Jesus accomplished this by absorbing all sin and its consequences of sicknesses and all the diseases of the earth into His body, which marred Him almost beyond recognition. See Psalm 22; Isaiah 52:14; John 1:29; 1 John 3:5.

This act of God's grace separated sin and its consequences from us and freed us. When we sin, we can repent without suffering any immediate spiritual consequences from God. The immediate pain of sin and any suffering we experience is from the natural consequences of our sin or Satan. See Romans 6:16.

When we sin, we repent to close the door to Satan; even when we may have caused the pain of sin on ourselves, we can still look to Jesus and claim our deliverance. See 2 Corinthians 5:21; 1 John 1:9; Colossians 1:13-14; Hebrews 4:16. Romans 6 tells us that at the point of being born again, we must believe we are dead to sin because we were on the Cross with Jesus and baptized into His death. We must believe that *"he that is dead is freed from sin."*

We are to reckon ourselves to be dead indeed to sin and know that sin has no more dominion over us because we are living by God's grace in the power of His Holy Spirit in repentance, forgiveness, and self-control. We are not living by the Law of self in our efforts, which leads to sin.

LIFE: To begin our Christian life aright, we must acknowledge Jesus took our sins, and we are freed from sin and are no longer the same person, doing the same things we used to do. Reckoning ourselves dead with genuine repentance and becoming alive in Jesus' righteousness will free us from the bondage of Satan. Death to self and sin and becoming empowered by God's grace in the power of the Holy Spirit will give us new life in God. We die to live. Read Romans 6:4, 11-14.

TO DIE IS TO LIVE - DAY 2

"In Christ Jesus our Lord, I die daily." —1 Corinthians 15:31

TRUTH: As believers, we cannot continue to live a self-directed life using the reasonings of our minds, emotion-based feelings, having bad attitudes and the same unsaved friends, and going to the same places we visited before we were saved. No! We are dead to that old person we used to be because of Christ. He now lives in our hearts and wants us to recognize Him, love Him, honor Him, thank Him, and worship Him for so great a salvation He procured for us.

To overcome Satan, we must die to the flesh, selfishness, rebellion, and defiance and choose to live by the power of the Holy Spirit. This will be so when we die to sin and the old man and accept that Jesus gave us salvation by His power and grace, and of nothing, we did ourselves. We receive of Him in our daily lives the same way we got saved. See Colossians 2:6; 1 John 2:6. That is by grace through faith, living not with an earthly perspective but from an eternal one of love. See Romans 5:8-9; 10: 9-10; Ephesians 2:8; 2 Corinthians 4:18.

God recreated us with a new heart by His grace, and He now desires to direct our lives by His Holy Spirit in our hearts, also by His grace. Grace means we accept that Jesus did it all by His power on the Cross to position us into His kingdom. We are empowered by His grace within to bless us by His many promises. God gave us truths and promises we are to believe and receive. Our belief in God's grace exalts Jesus to the throne of our hearts, and by the Holy Spirit, we are dead not only to sin but also to Satan, self, others, the Law, and death. We have responded to God's choice of us and have yielded to Him, and we are now saved.

"Know ye not, that to whom ye yield yourselves servant to obey...whether of sin unto death; or of obedience unto righteousness" (Romans 6:16).

LIFE: You are dead to sin, so turn away from dependence on self, others, the world, religion, and anyone or anything that will hinder your growing relationship with Jesus, and yield to Him. Meditate on Romans 8:13-14; Ephesians 4:22-24; Colossians 1:20-23; 3:5;1 Peter 4:1-2.

ALIVE UNTO GOD

"Likewise reckon ye also yourselves to be dead indeed unto sin, but alive unto God through Jesus Christ our Lord." —Romans 6: 11

TRUTH: The resurrection of Jesus from the dead defeated Satan, death, hell, and the Law. Jesus rose, and we also arose with Him when we believed in Him. We become alive unto God when Jesus, by His Spirit, indwelled our hearts. Jesus' resurrection justified us when His Blood made us innocent, just as if we had never sinned. We are innocent and no longer guilty of sin and its death penalty. We have been cleansed from sin, washed, sanctified, and made righteous. We were made the righteousness of God when He removed the old sinful heart within and gave us His love by His Spirit. See Romans 7:23-25; 5:17; 1 Corinthians 1:30.

God gave us Jesus' righteousness, His right standing of a love relationship with the Father. God's love in our hearts needed the breastplate of righteousness to protect our hearts and our faith in His love. See Ephesians 6:14;1 Thessalonians 5:8-9. When we believe God's love for us by faith, we are the righteous, made alive unto God by His Spirit, and by faith, we can obey Him. God now sees us through the lens of Jesus' Blood by His crucifixion to His ascension as new creation beings forgiven, cleansed, innocent, loved, dead to sin, and alive unto God.

Alive unto God, we are to see ourselves "in Christ," a chosen generation, a royal priesthood, a holy nation, a peculiar people, that ye should shew forth the praises of Him who hath called us out of darkness into His marvelous light. See 1 Peter 2:9. The power of the Holy Spirit in our hearts raised us alive unto God, not only to lead by His Spirit but also to sustain us in God our Father.

LIFE: You are not born again to continue old business as usual. Alive unto God in Christ, you are now to depend on God, by His Word, and by His Spirit, for the proper stance before God in righteousness, the right thoughts to think, words to speak, decisions to make, and actions to take. Surrender in dependence on God, His Word, and the leading of His Spirit who will keep you alive unto God, abiding in Him and blessed.

AS CHILDREN

*"The Spirit itself beareth witness with our spirit, that
we are the children of God." —Romans 8:16*

TRUTH: God is the creator of all men, but He gives each person a choice for Him to be their Father or not. Adam's sin separated God's love from man's heart, but Jesus came and ended that separation in Himself.

When we believe in Jesus, the Spirit of God enters our hearts and deposits Himself within. Because God is love, with salvation, love enters our hearts. And by living in our hearts, God has given us His life and restored His relationship of love with us through Jesus. To be a Christian does not mean we belong to a particular church, denomination, religion, or faith. It does not mean we are good or perfect persons who never miss church one Sunday or that we are very dedicated workers, in the nursery, in the choir, or at the door as a greeter. We are not Christians because we fulfill our obligations to tithe, read our Bible, fast, and pray daily.

The way for each of us to know we are a Christian is to know that *"The Spirit beareth witness with our spirit, that we are children of God..."* (Romans 8:15-17). It is about a relationship.

You are a child of God when you receive Jesus, the forgiveness of sin, and the gift of righteousness and yield to God in having a loving, dynamic relationship with Your Heavenly Father. You are a Christian when you know for sure God loves you with an everlasting love, you live by faith from His grace, and therefore you know you will never be abandoned or have the need to fear. See Acts 16:30-31; Hebrews 13:5; Romans 8:33-39; 1 John 4:18

LIFE: We love God because He first loved us to give us His best, and therefore we love Him in return. We can now seek His leading and His help to give our best and then do the necessary spiritual disciplines like attending church, praying and reading the Bible, and tithe, without any guilt or condemnation. See Romans 12:1-2; James 2; 17-24. Because as His children, we live by faith, which pleases God, and receives His forgiveness and guidance continually when needed, we can be sure of our place with our Father in His heart and in heaven. See John 16:13.

AS CHILDREN — DAY 2

"That we are children of God." —Romans 8: 16

TRUTH: As children, the very start of our Christian life must be about believing God's great love for us and returning His love in a dynamic relationship. It should never be about being good, doing works of religion, serving God, or of obligation.

We cannot please God without faith. See Hebrews 11:6. And faith works by God's love in us. See Galatians 5:6. It is receiving the love of God which allows us to be His children in a love relationship with the Father, living by faith. Our faith rests in God's love as we look to Jesus, read His Word, and hear Him speak and encouraging us to build trust. See Romans 10:17.

Our hearts become assured as we listen to the Holy Spirit speak to our inner man, and we joy in our divine connection and relationship with Him. We respond to our Father by doing what He says to us, and we are blessed because He is love. His love will never fail but takes us from faith to faith and from glory to glory.

A child looks to their parents for acceptance, love, nurture, provision, protection, and forgiveness. We should expect the same from our Heavenly Father and even more because He is absolutely good. Believe that your salvation gave you a new life in a relationship with God with His love flowing from your heart. You are a bonafide child of God filled with the fullness of God and His love. See John 3:16-17; Romans 10:9-10; John 1:12; Titus 3:5; John 4:13-15; Hebrews 11:11.

LIFE: I am a Christian in a relationship with my Heavenly Father. I walk with Him, talk with Him, and listen to Him as I connect in the Word, prayer, and fellowship. I will not substitute religion or works for my relationship. As His child, I fully expect to be divinely blessed in every area of my life. Even in the difficult times, I will look for His blessings because He is always there, always good, and will never leave me nor forsake me. My Father is faithful and true to me, as His child.

IN CHRIST

"For ye are all the children of God by faith in Christ Jesus." —Galatians 3:26

TRUTH: We are children of God not because He created us all as His creation but because, by faith, we believe in His Son, Jesus. Just as we don't go to heaven because we are good and perfect but because we are forgiven in Christ. Those whose sin is forgiven when Jesus becomes their Savior are saved and placed "in Christ." You believe you are forgiven, justified, made innocent, righteous, accepted, and reconciled unto God into a relationship, knowing that He loves you and promises to care for you. You have a faith relationship abiding and resting in Christ.

In this new or renewed relationship with God your Father through Jesus, you have been made an entirely new creation being on the inside of your human spirit where the Spirit of Christ came to live. God Himself in the person of the Holy Spirit now takes up residence in your spirit or heart, giving you on the inside the complete fullness and holy nature of God. See Ephesians 1:4; Colossians 1:22-23. The love among the Father, Son, and Holy Spirit is now shared with us. See 1 Corinthians 6:17; John 17:21-23.

Without Jesus, we are sinners and dead in sin, carnal in nature, and dominated by selfishness. But when born again by believing in Jesus by faith, we are now in Christ – in a new kingdom, a new family, possessing a new heart with a new nature of love given in our spirit, with new desires, for the eternal things of God above, to walk by faith in His love, and to walk in the Spirit to inherit the kingdom of God and all His blessings.

LIFE: See yourself and others as made new and loved by your Father and hidden in the cleft of the rock, blessed with all His righteousness becomes our righteousness. His power is our power. His authority becomes our authority and His life our life.

"For we are his workmanship, created in Christ Jesus unto good works which God hath before ordained that we should walk in them" (Ephesians 2:10).

Meditate on Ephesians 2: 6,10,13; Romans 8:1-2; Philippians 4:13.

IN CHRIST — DAY 2

"For ye are all children of God..." —Galatians 3:26

TRUTH: In Christ, we are made new creation beings by the Blood of Jesus. See 2 Corinthians 5:17. Conformed into God's image. See Romans 8:29. As partakers of His divine nature. See 2 Peter 1:1-4. No longer our own, we belong to God. See 1 Corinthians 6:19. Made alive in the newness of life. See Romans 6:4. Made part of the body of Christ with other believers. See Romans 12:5. We are blessed to obtain an inheritance. See Ephesians 1:11. And made unto wisdom, righteousness, sanctification, and redemption. See 1 Corinthians 1:30. And the list could continue.

Become a true believer by believing in Jesus and live with the full assurance that you have a privileged place in your Father's heart because He made you loved, forgiven, justified, innocent, chosen, redeemed, free, righteous, accepted, and victorious in Christ Jesus.

You are in Him, and He is in you, one spirit; therefore, live every moment of your life with the knowledge that you are new within. Living from this place of union abiding in Christ, you have been reconciled in love, hope, faith, power, and victory. See Colossians 1:12-21.

Believe also that nothing can separate you from the love of your Father. Your position or relationship "in Christ" does not change with your carnal behavior or sin, but your fellowship and intimacy do. Sin affects your ability to interact with and be led by the Holy Spirit. When we sin, we should repent quickly and draw near. Our Father will forgive, forget, restore, and help us.

LIFE: "Father, in the name of Jesus, I thank You that I am one spirit with You because I belong to You. You chose me as Your own because You love me, and I thank and praise You. Father, I thank You that I am crucified with You on the Cross. I am dead, and my life is hidden with Christ in God. As I continue to behold the beauty of Jesus, help me to see His beauty in myself as I increasingly grow to become more of the new person You made me in Christ — one with Him in His glory, with the ability to love others and conquer Satan. Thank you, Jesus. See Colossians 3:3-4; 1 John 4:8-21; Luke 10:19.

POOR IN SPIRIT

"Blessed are the poor in spirit; for theirs is the kingdom of heaven." —Matthew 5:3

TRUTH: Here in Matthew 5, Jesus is beginning to tell others what the kingdom of God really looks like. The values of grace He was putting forward were the very opposite of what the Pharisees and Sadducees upheld by the Law. Jesus was ushering in His new kingdom, expounding a backward kingdom—to be rich, one must become poor in spirit. When is it ever good to be poor? It depends on what we are to be poor in.

God is not calling us to become poor in possessions, so we can love and serve Him better. He says we are blessed if our spirit or heart is poor of worldly lusts but is richly turned towards God in meekness, humility, and dependence on Jesus, having faith in God and trusting Him as our source.

God's call to be poor in spirit is for us not to be like the olden Jews, who sought only external conformity in obeying rules, rituals, and hand washings while their hearts were far from Him, being puffed up with pride, social standing, and the need for power. *"Woe unto you, scribes and Pharisees, hypocrites! For ye pay tithes of mint and anise and cumin, and have omitted the weightier matters of the law, judgment, mercy, and faith: these ought ye to have done, and not to leave the other undone."* See Matthew 23:23.

They sought external things to prop themselves up to be significant, just as many today seek the same things such as status, money, intellectual pursuits, megachurches, fitness in physical appearance, possessions, careers, and pleasures.

LIFE: We are poor in spirit when we humble ourselves, believe in Jesus, and receive a new heart, making God and His ways our priority. We need a broken and contrite heart, willing to depend on God by faith, trust Him daily, to lead us by His Spirit into a lifestyle of love.

Meditate on Psalm 51:17; Matthew 5:1-12.

POOR IN SPIRIT — DAY 2

"Blessed are the poor in spirit." —Matthew 5:1

TRUTH: The verse in Matthew 6:33 feeds right into this thought.

"But seek ye first the kingdom of God, and his righteousness and all these things shall be added unto you."

Solomon could be considered poor in spirit at the beginning of his reign. When the Lord appeared to him in a dream and asked him how He could bless him, Solomon asked for an understanding heart to discern between good and evil. His answer pleased God because he did not ask for personal riches or long life. God, therefore, said He would also give him the things he did not ask for, such as wealth, riches, and honor. See 1 Kings 3.

Like Solomon, at the beginning of his reign, we are pleasing God by not being haughty, prideful, self-directed, independent, and self-absorbed in our attitude, but by acknowledging we are helpless and in need of Him. See Romans 7:12-25.

God hates these seven things: a proud look, a lying tongue, hands that shed innocent blood, a heart that devises wicked imaginations, feet that are swift in running to mischief, a false witness that speaks lies, sowing discord among the brethren. See Proverbs 6:16-19.

Be poor in spirit and humble ourselves before the Father as we ask Him to keep us from these sins and instead keep us risen with Christ, seeking things above, where Christ sits on the right hand of the Father. See Colossians 3: 1-3.

LIFE: Christianity is not just about going to church, being a faithful and dutiful member, trying to live a respectful life, but more about humbly yielding to God your Father and daily living dependently on Jesus and the power of the Holy Spirit with childlike faith abiding in Him. You should always be looking to your Father to meet all your needs and help you grow up in Christ Jesus in His image and likeness. See Psalm 34:6; Philippians 2:13.

GOODNESS OF GOD

"I had fainted, unless I had believed to see, the goodness of the Lord in the land of the living." —Psalm 27:13

TRUTH: *"O give thanks unto the Lord, for he is good"* (Psalm 107:1). Every person must make a conclusion about Jesus; either we see Him as a good God worthy to be thanked and worshipped, or we see Him as just a Deity people fuss about unnecessarily. You cannot see and ignore Him. But as we look at Jesus, we see God's goodness because Jesus has shown that He is good.

 "They shall abundantly utter the memory of thy great goodness and shall sing of thy righteousness. The Lord is gracious, and full of compassion: slow to anger, and of great mercy. The Lord is good to all: and his tender mercies are over all his works" (Psalm 145:7-9).

 As we embrace God's goodness, we can relax in His presence and believe and trust Him more by faith. God's character is beyond reproach because we saw Jesus' natural way of living and walking among man, and yet He never sinned. See Hebrews 4:15. He has His Father's integrity as He does not lie. See Titus 1:2. He is authentic as the God of love. See 1 John 4:8. God's goodness seen in His character, His approach, His will in His Word, and His performances towards us is completely good, as seen in Jesus. *"Surely goodness and mercy shall follow me all the days of my life* (Psalm 23:6).

LIFE: God is always ready to do good. See Luke 4:18. He has good things for you to receive, so receive them by faith. See 2 Peter 1:3; 1 Corinthians 2:9-12. Do you have a lack? In need of healing? Need deliverance? Believe God is good, ready, and willing; so, take Him at His Word, stand in faith, and trust His goodness as He is willing. See Jeremiah 29:11-14; Luke 5:12-13; Mark 1:4–41. And He is also able. See Jude 24; 3 John 2; Psalm 31:19.

TRUTH FREES US

"And ye shall know the truth, and the truth shall make you free." —John 8:32

TRUTH: Jesus, the Living Word, tells us He is Truth. See John 14:6. When we believe in Jesus, the truth of God's Word brings salvation. We are saved or born again. The gospel of Jesus Christ gives us redemption or freedom from Satan's slavery of sin in our human spirit. See John 3:16; Romans 10:9-10; Galatians 5:1.

We are free within our spirit, but God's Word will continue to make us free from all bondage in our soul and body as we apply it. See 2 Corinthians 3:17. Jesus told His disciples, *"If ye continue in my word, then are ye my disciples indeed; And ye shall know the truth, and the truth shall make you free"* (John 8:31-32) as we continue in a growing relationship with Jesus and His Word and make Him our priority, truth increases, and faith will grow in the heart to set us free. See John 17:3; Romans 10:17. Faith in God while abiding, trusting, believing, speaking, and acting on God's Word causes Jesus to go to work on our behalf and bring blessings and freedom. See John 8:36; Revelation 12:11.

We are one spirit with Jesus, just as He was one with His Father and walked in power, dominion, and complete freedom from Satan and sin. To know the truth is to know Jesus and believe His Word as truth rigidly fixed in our hearts so that we will not waver but stand passionately in Christ's victory, believing and speaking the Word until the promise of deliverance comes to pass and brings us freedom. See Psalm 112:7; 2 Corinthians 4:13.

LIFE: Believe Jesus and settle His Word in your heart as truth. The truth of the gospel believed, spoken in authority and confidence, and acted upon in faith will set you free. Let the truth of God in the life of Christ set you free to walk in the liberty Jesus purchased for you. It will not happen all at once, but as you continually abide in Christ Jesus, His Spirit will bring freedom. *"Now the Lord is that Spirit: and where the Spirit of the Lord is, there is liberty"* (2 Corinthians 3:17).

ACCEPTED AND LOVED

"To the praise of the glory of his grace, wherein he hath made us accepted in the beloved." —Ephesians 1:6

TRUTH: When we genuinely love, we give our acceptance of the total package or being of the other person—the good and the bad, the achievements and failures, the glad and the sad. From the father's point of view, the story of the prodigal son best demonstrates God's love and acceptance for us despite our rebelliousness and failures. See Luke 15:11-24.

The youngest son rebelled against the authority of his father by asking for his inheritance early so that he could find his way in life. He joined himself as a citizen of another country and wasted all his money, becoming destitute and eating pigs' food. He looked at his life and remembered that his father's servants were living a better life than himself, so he returned home.

His father, anxiously awaiting his return, ran to greet him in compassion, welcomed him inside the house, and kissed him. The son repented and was willing to be accepted at a status less than being a son. But the father would not have it. He welcomed, embraced, and gave him a robe and a ring to show his love, acceptance, and sonship. Jesus is our righteousness, our robe of love and acceptance.

LIFE: Sons are never mere servants or workers but are closer and more intimate with the Heavenly Father. You are a branch on the Vine, so experience life in Christ as a son and daughter and see yourself loved and accepted by God your Beloved. Despite your failures, always run to your Father as a son or a daughter and be clothed in His robe of righteousness, His love, and receive the ring of acceptance as His child restored in love and fellowship and enjoy the party in the family of God!

Meditate on Jeremiah 31:3; John 15:1-17.

SONS

"But as many as received him, to them gave he power to become the sons of God, even to them that believe on his name." —John 1:12

TRUTH: Every boy, girl, man, or woman is born to natural parents. It is undisputed that we are the product of a man and a woman, and we are called sons or daughters. When Satan was kicked out of heaven, he landed on earth and later entered the garden of Eden, where Adam and Eve lived. He tricked and deceived them into giving up their sonship in a relationship for slavery to himself. See Genesis 1:28; 3:1-9; Ezekiel 28:13-15. Instead of a man in union relationship with God, man became slaves to Satan. Those living under the Law of the Old Testament whose hearts were inclined to God became kings, priests, prophets, and servants, but God wanted sons and daughters in a love relationship.

We lost our sonship to Satan, but God sent Jesus to restore it and sustain this relationship by His Holy Spirit. Through Jesus, we relate to God as our Father and us as His sons. We should, by the Holy Spirit's help, be looking like His image, behaving like Him, and receiving from His inheritance as well as ruling and reigning with Him. *"They which receive abundance of grace and the gift of righteousness shall reign in life by one, Jesus Christ"* (Romans 5:17). When we believe in Jesus, we are sons and daughters of our Father God, heirs to the kingdom of God, and citizens of heaven. Always see yourself as a child of the Most -High God, both by position in the family and by receiving your inheritance as blessings to be enjoyed. See John 3:1-3; Romans 8:16-17.

LIFE: A relationship comes with responsibilities, but always relationship first. First, God desires sons and daughters in a loving faith relationship of dependence on Him, not just workers. See James 2:14-20. Take your rightful place as sons and claim your kinship to God first in His love, authority, power, Word, and Spirit, and rule over all things on earth except man. *"For ye are all the children of God by faith in Christ Jesus"* (Galatians 3:26).

GRACE NOT EFFORT

"For by grace are ye saved through faith; and that not of yourselves; it is the gift of God. Not of works, lest any man should boast." —Ephesians 2:8-9

TRUTH: God saved us by His grace through our faith when we believed in Jesus. On the Cross, Jesus ended the power of all sin and separation from God and, in exchange, gave us Jesus' righteousness, His restored love relationship with the Father, and new life.

Grace is God's gift, favor, and power to do good and provide for people who did nothing to deserve His gift. But God saw us as deserving of His love and gave it. For our salvation, Jesus' death on the Cross was God's grace to us. It was His power in His goodness and His mercy doing for us what we could not do to save ourselves from sin.

Therefore, Grace is the basis of our salvation, and grace requires that one acknowledge their sinfulness and hopelessness to save themselves and choose to humble themselves and accept God through Jesus and the work of the Cross. God desires that we receive everything from Him by grace looking unto Jesus. See Colossians 2:6; 1 John 2:6; Matthew 11:28-29; Romans 5:17, 21; 6:14-18.

Faith: Faith is our believing. It is the only means by which salvation can be procured; when faith lays hold of God's grace, we will be saved. Jesus did it all on the Cross; we are to believe and receive the truth of the Cross in our hearts and be saved from our sins, self-effort by the Law, sicknesses, and the dominion of Satan.

LIFE: Jesus did it all; we did nothing to be saved. Jesus, by His grace, took our sins and gave us His righteousness or His right love relationship with the Father. When we believe His love and receive Him into our hearts, we are saved; and as we continue to live by faith in God's grace, we are continually being saved from evil in this world and are being kept by His grace. See John 3:3; Philippians 2:12-13; Psalm 91; 1 Peter 1:5.

GRACE NOT EFFORT — DAY 2

"And of his fullness have all we received, and grace for grace." —John 1:16

TRUTH: Grace is what God did through Jesus. Faith is how we respond once we have heard. We have faith when we believe. God's gift of salvation did not require our obedience, goodness, any acts of service, works, or our performance, only our belief and response. See Romans 4:16; Ephesians 2:8-9.

When we humble ourselves and accept our great need for Jesus by faith, we are acknowledging His grace that we did nothing, that we expended no effort for our salvation. No amount of religion, good works, self-effort, church activity, or attendance, membership to the right church, no trying hard enough to do more, not to sin, or to obey the rules is acceptable to God. This is what religion is about, our efforts towards God for salvation and sanctification without the power of the Cross and the Holy Spirit.

Religion dishonors God because it rejects or minimizes His grace in Jesus and His work in us. The posture of dependence for salvation grace through faith honors God for all He did for us through Jesus, and we gladly accept Him and worship Him. Grace cannot be earned, only received.

Humble yourself and receive God's grace because you did nothing to gain your salvation, and you cannot by yourself keep it. It is the life of Christ Jesus by His Spirit that will save and sustain you.

"I am the vine, and ye are the branches; He that abideth in me, and I in him, the same bringeth forth much fruit: for without me you can do nothing" (John 15: 5). However, with faith in God's grace, we can do all things as our connection to Christ Jesus releases His grace, His power, and His life to us.

LIFE: Meditate on these Scriptures on God's grace as you learn to depend on Him and make Christ your life. See John 1:17; Acts 20:24; Romans 4:16; 5:20; 11:6; 2 Corinthians 4:15; 8:7; 12:9; Ephesians 1:7; 2:8; 4:7; Colossians 1:6; 4:6; James 4:6-7; 2 Timothy 1:9; 1 Peter 4:10.

JESUS IS LORD

*"That if thou shalt confess with thy mouth the Lord Jesus,
and shalt believe in thine heart that God hath raise him from
the dead, thou shalt be saved..."* —Romans 10:9-10

TRUTH: Some people believe the wrong thing. They are told, *"Just say this prayer after me, and you will be saved."* So, they say the prayer in John 3:16 or Romans 10:9-10 without any real commitment from a sincere heart. That is not salvation. But someone who prays this prayer from a sincere heart, willing to surrender to Jesus as Lord, will receive salvation.

Jesus is Savior in forgiving sins, and He is Lord as we surrender to and acknowledge His rulership over our whole life, just as the thief on the Cross and Saul yielded their destinies to Him as Lord in the Scriptures. See Luke 23:37-43; Acts 26. As Lord, He is our supreme Leader, and we belong to and are governed by Him. See 1 Corinthians 6:19-20.

We ought to give Jesus full authority over our lives. The Lordship of Jesus requires dying to sin, self, the Law, and the world in a continuing process of daily surrendering all the different areas of our lives to God through Jesus, His Son. This process of daily yielding for purification is called sanctification. Sanctification is the process of dying to ourselves by saying no to the old negative thoughts, desires, and actions of our old life and instead turning them over to God. And as we ask Him by His Spirit to change them, continuing to make us new, with His life, we will reign in our hearts. *"Sanctify them through thy truth: thy word is truth* (John 17:17). *"Much more they which receive abundance of grace and the gift of righteousness shall reign in life by one, Jesus Christ"* (Romans 5:17).

LIFE: Allow the Holy Spirit to dominate every area and everything negative of the old life, which may still challenge your new life in Christ. See Romans 8. Let God's Word be your final authority to keep Jesus as Lord of your life, and He will reward you with the power of His Spirit working in and through you to empower and lift you to reign over all evil. See Philippians 2: 9-11,13.

JESUS HOLDS MY HEART

"I will never leave thee nor forsake thee." —Hebrews 13:5

TRUTH: Jesus as Savior and Lord guarantee that the Holy Spirit lives and abides in our hearts as a seal, a down payment, that we are God's possession, the children of God. See John 15; 2 Corinthians 5:5; Ephesians 1:13, 14; 4:30; 2 Timothy 2:19; 1 John 4:15-18.

The Holy Spirit within is God's guarantee that we belong to Him and that He will never leave us. See John 14:16; Hebrews 13:5. In the heart, the Holy Spirit is God's GPS or Global positioning system to keep us going forward and connected to Him in a relationship. When we get lost, He will redirect us to the correct path. We are in a relationship where we can hear Him speak to our hearts, and by faith, we can respond to our Heavenly Father. With God's promise to us, we can be content in our hearts that our God is in us, for us, and with us. Therefore, we do not need to doubt His presence, character, Word, power, or response when we call on Him.

"And behold, I am with thee, and I will keep thee in all places whither thou goest and will bring thee again into this land; for I will not leave thee until I have done that which I have spoken to thee of" (Genesis 28:15).

LIFE: *"God is not a man, that he should lie; neither the son of man, that he should repent: hath he said, and shall he not do it? or hath he spoken, and shall he not make good"* (Numbers 23:19). Will you let Him hold your heart? Then confess this prayer and surrender your life fully to Him.

Father God, Your Word says if I confess with my mouth that Jesus is Lord and believe in my heart that God raised Him from the dead, I am saved. I believe, and I receive You as my Savior, Father, and Lord. I accept all my sins forgiven. Thank You for Your love and salvation. Lord help me to daily surrender to you In Jesus' name. Amen. Jesus is now Your Lord and Savior, and you are His precious child. If you are already born again, share with someone to be born again too.

JESUS HOLDS MY HEART — DAY 2

"I will never leave thee nor forsake thee." —Hebrews 13:5

TRUTH: Has God got your heart? Are you close enough to Him to hear His heart and His words of commitment to you? Are you willingly sharing Jesus with others? Are you afraid to share and afraid when trouble strikes? Jesus wants to hold your heart so that with Him on your side, every beat, every pulse, and rhythm will generate hope and faith, causing you to look to Him to keep, provide, deliver and sustain.

Our faith in God's grace, depending on His Holy Spirit within, is our guarantee that God will never leave us. Maintain your divine connection with God through Jesus, receive all He provided at the Cross and have faith to believe and receive. The Blood of Jesus by His Spirit has divinely connected us to God's heart of love, power, and blessings, and nothing can separate us from His love.

"Who shall separate us from the love of Christ? Shall tribulation or distress... or famine... nor principalities, nor powers...nor any other creature, shall be able to separate us from the love of God, which is in Christ Jesus our Lord" (Romans 8:35-39).

Live in the Spirit, live by God's Word of truth, believe, yield, and obey Him, and He will forever be near you because He has a covenant of love with you by His Holy Spirit. And His love will never fail. His Spirit in us will always tell us what is true, and when we listen and yield to Him, we touch His heart, and His truth will lead us to into good as we make Christ our life.

LIFE: Jesus' said, *"Lo, I am with you alway, even unto the end of the world"* (Matthew 28:20). Jesus can and will keep His promise because He can't lie. See Hebrews 6:18. *"But he that is joined unto the Lord is one spirit"* (1 Corinthians 6:17). We are one spirit in union relationship with God the Father through the Spirit of His Son, which is sealed within our hearts. He is Your Lord. Be confident of His love, His promises, His nearness, and His pledge to forever be with you and to care for and deliver you as He holds your heart.

TRIUMPH IN JESUS

"Now thanks be unto God, which always causeth us to triumph in Christ." —2 Corinthians 2:14

TRUTH: Jesus triumphed over Satan, sin, death, and the Law. We know Satan is defeated because Jesus robbed him of his power and gave it to us as believers. God stripped him of all his power. See Luke 10:19; Romans 6:6; Colossians 2:14-15; 1 Corinthians 15:54-57. We triumph with believing and receiving the Word of God and with prayer. All believers must live by faith, and faith comes by hearing and hearing the Word again until faith arises in our hearts. All this can only happen when we love God and is passionate about His Word. His love in us will build faith because we know faith works by love. And as we love God and believe His Word and speak it from our hearts, our faith moves God on our behalf to bring us our desired blessing. See Galatians 5:6. *"For whatsoever is born of God overcometh the world: and this is the victory that overcometh the world, even our faith"* (1 John 5:4).

"It is written, Man shall not live by bread alone, but by every word that proceedeth out of the mouth of God" (Matthew 4:4).

"And hath raised us up together, and made us to sit in heavenly places in Christ Jesus (Ephesians 2:6).

We have victory in the power of the Holy Spirit. See Acts 1:8. The Holy Spirit will help us in all things. He will lead us out of error and into truth, teach and bring all things to our remembrance, and show us things to come. See John 14. He will help us to pray. See Romans 8:26. He goes before us and leads us. See Romans 8:14. He helps us to please the Father. See Hebrews 13:21.

LIFE: Let us stand in faith, always rejoicing before we see the blessing, as our good and faithful Father who cares enough to defeat Satan will cause us to triumph every time!

IDENTIFICATION STRENGTHENS THE INNER MAN

"For ye are dead, and your life is hid with Christ in God." —Colossians 3:3

TRUTH: Believing in Jesus and being born again places God's Spirit within with a new nature in Christ, dead to sin, the old man and self. We are alive unto God as our human spirit is now hidden in God's Spirit within us. In Jesus' resurrection and exaltation, we were raised with Him, and His victory was given to us. See Ephesians 1:19-23. To live a victorious Christian life, God's Spirit within must be fed by the truth of the Word of God, nurtured by prayer and fellowship to help us grow spiritually. Our strengthened spirit-man, identifying more and more with Christ's character, can dominate both soul and body to make us victorious. The breastplate of righteousness protects the love of Jesus deposited in our hearts and keeps us seated in Christ. See 1 Thessalonians 5:8; 1 Peter 1:5. Failure to be identified with Christ will leave a vacuum for Satan to attack our hearts with insecurities and unworthiness about whom we are in Christ, trying to displace our newfound position in Christ, His peace and love within. Be identified knowing you are in Christ. See Ephesians 1 -3.

The joy and excitement sensed when first born again would dwindle and open the door for Satan to tell us the lie that we're not saved and begin to distort our identity. The more we believe his lies, the more we lose our identity and the joy of our salvation. The Christian life will become burdensome with struggling, trying, and failures. If this is your case, you have slipped from the Gospel and Christianity in relationship with Jesus into religion, legalism, self-effort, or works. Turn back to the identity given you in God's Word and let the Holy Spirit as your Helper confirms whom God says you are in Christ. He will strengthen you with Jesus' righteousness and love. God's identity in you wins the battle against Satan for your soul. Do not be identified as the one whom Satan can devour, be recognized as an overcomer and more than a conqueror.

LIFE: Identification silences Satan's lies against your position of right relationship in Christ or Christ's righteousness in you. Do not let him steal your identity and your faith in God's grace. It is not what you do, but believing in Jesus, by His Blood, made you right. Meditate on 1 Peter 5:8; Colossians 3:1-4.

PROPERLY IDENTIFIED

*"But let it be the hidden man of the heart, in that
which is not corruptible."* —1 Peter 3:4

TRUTH: If we are to succeed in the Christian life, we must first win the battle of our identification in Christ on the inside. Whom is the new creature in Christ God has re-made you to be? And what is the significance of being correctly identified? John 8:32 and 36 says, *"And ye shall know the truth, and the truth shall make you free. If the Son, therefore, shall make you free, ye are free indeed."*

When we receive the truth of our new identity in Christ Jesus, we are completely set free from Satan's lies and the inner battles that bring the shame, guilt, fear, insecurities, accusations, and condemnation that rob us of relationship and peace with the Father. Pull out your Christ I. D. card in Satan's face and tell him you are Christ's.

LIFE: Properly identified, I am the redeemed of the Lord, saved from the hand of the enemy. See Psalm 107:2. In my Lord's exaltation, His victory was given to me. I am seated victoriously in heavenly realms. See Ephesians 1:3. I am forgiven, cleansed, purged of, and dead to sin; He cast all my sins into the depths of the sea. See Micah 7: 19. I am justified by the Blood of Jesus, made innocent, blameless, loved, and acceptable to Him.

I reject Satan's lie that I am justified and loved by my Father only when I obey God or do everything right. See Romans 5:1-2. I am free from the stain of sin because the Blood gave me Jesus' perfect righteousness; I am led by my Father's love and the presence of His Holy Spirit into obedience, never by my self-effort and performance, which invites Satan's fear and torment. See Romans 6; Romans 8:14; Philippians 2:13; 1 John 4:18. I am the righteousness of God in Christ by Jesus' obedience to the Cross and His shed Blood alone, and nothing of myself. See 2 Corinthians 5:21; Ephesians 2:8-9. I overcome by the Blood of Jesus, and no weapon formed against me can prosper because I'm Christs'. See Revelation 12:11; Isaiah 54:17.

ESTABLISHED IN IDENTITY

"For it is a good thing that the heart be established with grace; not with meats." —Hebrews 13:9

TRUTH: The sentiment of instability and insecurity previously echoed in this verse in Hebrews was also stated in James 1:6— *"But let him ask in faith, nothing wavering. For he that wavereth is like a wave of the sea driven with the wind and tossed."* Whether in our doctrine, which gives us righteousness in standing before God, or in our daily walk of faith, we are to be established and secure in our identity and relationship with our Heavenly Father. We are not to be carried or tossed about by Satan or anyone or anything else. Instead, we are to be fully assured in our hearts that we are covenant children of God, secure by our faith in the Father's love, peace, and blessings. See Isaiah 32:17-18; 54:14

Firstly, be established by faith in your standing before God in His covenant love of grace. Believe your righteousness is by God's grace in Jesus and His shed Blood. The Blood reconciled you into a love relationship and an everlasting covenant with God, which cannot end and cannot be broken. See Hebrews 13:20-21. With faith, nothing, not even sin, can separate us from our Father's love because He made a way of escape with forgiveness. See 2 Corinthians 5:17-20; Romans 8:38-39; 1 Corinthians 10:13. Believe God loves us infinitely because of the Blood of Jesus in an unbreakable marriage covenant, never again for us to be destabilized by insecurity or a lack of peace in our relationship with our Father.

LIFE: Never think that if you sin, God is mad, and therefore Satan has a right to torment you. No! Do not let Satan cause you to look at yourself; always look to Jesus and your identity in Him. Claim your victory seated at the right hand of the Father, and you are in Him. Now repent, and stand delivered and victorious to go on. Read Ephesians 1 to 3 to find thirty identification Scriptures telling you who you are in Christ Jesus. Start with Ephesians 1:2. I am filled with grace and peace. Verse 3, I am blessed with all spiritual blessings in heavenly places in Christ.

SURETY OF SALVATION GOD'S WAY

*"The Spirit itself beareth witness with our spirit, that
we are the children of God."* —Romans 8: 16

TRUTH: We are saved by God's Word (grace) in the Gospel. And with humble and surrendered hearts, we believe (faith) and receive Jesus. Faith is of the heart. See 1 Corinthians 15:3-4. We can know and be sure we are saved when we can accept the Word on God's salvation as incorruptible truth that not even sin can change. *"Being born again, not of corruptible seed, but of incorruptible, by the word of God, which liveth and abideth forever"* (1 Peter 1:23).

- We have the assurance of our place in God by believing Jesus died to forgive all our sins and establish us in His righteousness. God loves us as much as He loves Jesus. See John 3:16; Mark 3:38.
- We are sure of our salvation because Jesus accepted our prayer of repentance and delivered us. See Ephesians 1:6-7; Colossians 1:1-14; John 6:37.
- We have an assurance of our salvation in the Word. See 1 John 5:11-13; Ezekiel 36:26, 28; Jeremiah 31:33; 2 Corinthians 5:17; Ephesians 1:13.
- Resist Satan and all His lies telling you that you are not saved. See John 8:44. We do not live by our conscience of whether we are right or wrong or feelings of deserving punishment. Instead, believe by faith that you are saved by God's Word of truth and the witness of the Holy Spirit within you. See Hebrews 10:2; Romans 10:4; 9-10, 13, 16-17; Romans 8:14-16; Acts 16:31. Believe that you do not lose your salvation because you sinned, but only if you deliberately renounce and reject Jesus. See Hebrews 6:4-6; 10:29. If faith is placed in Jesus and you continue in faith, your salvation is sure, as He will always lead you to please Him even with repentance. See Philippians 1:6; 2:13; Colossians 1:23.

LIFE: God loves you in Jesus, forgiving and restoring you into a relationship that nothing can break. Believe God by faith, not your feelings. See Romans 8:32-37; Hebrews 13:5, 8-9. You have been raised and seated in Christ Jesus at the right hand of the Father, so reject any insecurity about your salvation.

GOD'S MIND IN YOU

"Let this mind be in you, which was also in Christ Jesus." —Philippians 2:5

TRUTH: The Word tells us we have the mind of Christ. See 1 Corinthians 2:16. Once we are born again, we are given the mind of Christ in our spirit through the Holy Spirit. With His mind within, we can commune with the Father, be led by His Spirit into obedience, endure trials, pray, be God-centered, Word-centered, and hear clearly from the Father to do the same works He did through Jesus. Though given in its fulness, the mind of Christ is in a mustard seed form which must be nurtured, watered, and cultivated with the Word of God and praying in the Spirit. This will help us grow and become mature Christians, no longer feeding on milk but meat, the weightier principles of the gospel necessary for spiritual growth. See 1 Corinthians 3:1-3.

LIFE: We grow our understanding of the mind of Christ in the Word as we hear, read, meditate, speak, and act on the Word. See Romans 10:17. We grow in the mind of Christ as we diligently meditate on the Word until our hearts believe and receive from the heart of God. See 1 John 5:13.

We grow in the mind of Christ as we not only believe but act on the Word of God that we believe to be true and become doers of the Word. See James 1:22; 2:17.

We grow in the mind of Christ in His character by developing the fruit of the Spirit and walking in His love. See Galatians 5:22; 1 John 3:14-15.

We grow in the mind of Christ being led by His Holy Spirit in His Word and His presence and as we respond to Him by faith. See 1 Corinthians 2:10-12.

We grow in the mind of Christ when every thought that does not fit the image of God in us is cast down. See 2 Corinthians 10:4-5; Matthew 16:23.

We grow the mind of Christ as we walk by faith, humility, obedience, and love desiring to glorify God. See 1 Corinthians 10:31.

GOD'S MIND IN YOU — DAY 2

"Let this mind be in you...." —Philippians 2:5

TRUTH AND LIFE: We grow in the mind of Christ as we know God by the eternal, above the temporal; also, as our hearts pulses with His heart for the lost or the unsaved. See 2 Corinthians 4:18; Luke 19:10.

We grow in the mind of Christ, praying all kinds of prayers, listening and hearing His heart, and is led by His Spirit. See Ephesians 6:18; Romans 8:14.

We grow in the mind of Christ as we take negative thoughts captive and hold them to obedience to Christ as we rejoice. See Philippians 4:8; 1 Peter 5:7.

We grow in the mind of Christ fighting the good fight of faith, with spiritual weapons to defeat Satan. 1 Timothy 6:12; Ephesians 6:10-18.

We grow in the mind of Christ as we obey His commandment to love. See John 13:34-35; Mark 12:33.

We grow in the mind of Christ as we use the keys of the kingdom to access His inheritances and His revelations to us. See Matthew 16:19.

We will grow in the mind of Christ as we choose to fellowship with Christ-minded Christians. See Psalm 1; Proverbs 14:9.

We grow in the mind of Christ as we listen to His prophets and prosper. See 2 Chronicles 20:20.

We grow in the mind of Christ as we trust. See Proverbs 3: 5-7; Psalms 31:14-15; 37:3-5.

God's Word is truth. Truth dispels Satan's lies and accusations against us, seeking as a roaring lion whom to destroy. The enemy tries to force us to walk out of our position of righteousness in Christ and His love and into fear. As we make God's Word written or spoken by His Holy Spirit our final authority, we will stand immovable in Christ's victory. And as His mind is formed in us by God's love, grace, and faith in His Word, darkness, and fear will flee as God's light, love, power, and peace in Jesus. The mind of Christ will dominate and change us progressively into Christlikeness for us to be like Jesus.

MADE NEW PARTAKERS

"...Given unto us exceeding great and precious promises: that by these ye might be partakers of the divine nature..." —2 Peter 1:4

TRUTH: A born again believer has the very nature of God Himself within his heart. However, there are some aspects of His character that God has reserved for Himself in His omniscience, omnipotence, omnipresence, and His immutability. Some other aspects of His nature have been imparted to us, such as His wisdom, righteousness, holiness, the fruit of His Spirit, His gifts, and His peace. See 1 Corinthians 1:30; Galatians 5:22; 1 Corinthians 12, 14. Although all believers receive God's divine nature, not all do partake, grow, and live like true followers with the image of Christ. Many live lesser lives because they may not know or believe what Jesus did for them to make them new creations and overcomers in Christ. They may not believe they are recreated or made new into God's image within their human spirit sealed with the nature of God by the Holy Spirit. Or they may not have believed and used their authority over the evil one. See Ephesians 1:13-14; Luke 10:19.

Therefore, they neglect to feed their new spirit with the true gospel in the Word of God to be renewed in their mind and thus have failed to take hold of God's promises. They were unable to believe and receive God's promises as true. Had they allowed the Word of God by the power of the Holy Spirit to impact their souls and bodies, it would transform them by God's grace into God's image into becoming more like Jesus. Partaking of Christ in the Word and fellowship will draw us closer in His love, in a relationship, and into the Father's blessings.

LIFE: We have been made new to partake of every blessing God has given us in Christ Jesus. Accept His gift of salvation and His gift of righteousness in God's love. Yield to Jesus as Lord, hear and be a doer of His Word. Be led by His Holy Spirit to be a partaker of His eternal and abundant nature and prosper as your soul prospers. See 2 Corinthians 5:17-21; James 4:8; Romans 12:1-2; Psalm 23; Philippians 2:10-12; 1 Peter 1:15-16; 3 John 2.

PARTAKERS OF HIS DIVINE NATURE — DAY 2

"...Ye all are partakers of grace." —Philippians 1:7

TRUTH: If you are a believer, you must by faith receive God's grace given by the shed Blood of Jesus and His finished work of the Cross confirming the gospel and all its blessings and provisions given to you, *"According as his divine power hath given unto us all things that pertain unto life and godliness, through the knowledge of him that hath called us to glory and virtue... are given unto us exceeding great and precious promises: that by these ye might be partakers of the divine nature"* (2 Peter 1:3-4).

We are children of the living God who made us new to live and abide in Him as we trust His grace in His love, power, and ability. Without the power of God working on our behalf, we will struggle and strive, reverting to self-effort in religion and self-righteousness depending on ourselves or others. We can see the good things or blessings in this life, but we will not access them in our strength. However, in Christ Jesus, acknowledging that we are righteous, loved, accepted, worthy, and qualified to be one with Jesus in spirit, made wise, holy, and redeemed, by faith in God's grace, we can by the Holy Spirit confidently access God's graces, to sit, and partake. See 1 Corinthians 1:30; Philippians 1:7; 1 John 5:14-15. We can partake as we see God's goodness with a heart of love giving us good things, and as we see ourselves as righteous or worthy to take hold by faith in the power of His Spirit to access all blessings promised by our Father.

LIFE: No longer do we have to try to be sufficiently good or to feel holy enough to come boldly to our Father and receive of Him because we are made righteous and accepted to run to Him. See Hebrews 4:16. Instead, we discern the body and the Blood of Jesus in His sacrifice as His provision and blessings to us. We must believe we are qualified because the wall of partition between us and our blessings is torn in two in Christ Jesus, who made all things accessible for us to receive. See Matthew 27:51-53; Ephesians 2:15-22. Be led by the Holy Spirit to sit, sup, and partake with Jesus, to enjoy Him and all His blessings forever.

JUSTIFIED

"Therefore, being justified by faith, we have peace with God through our Lord Jesus Christ." —Romans 5:1

TRUTH: Fallen man was condemned with sin in his heart to death. Death ranges from sadness, defeat, anxiety, fear, sickness, disease, accident, and destruction to physical death. Jesus was crucified on the Cross to provide forgiveness of our sins and our complete redemption. His resurrection justified us as "the Just," to live by faith and to believe we have been made innocent and no longer guilty. As the just, we have been freed, made dead to all sin, declared righteous, and made right with God in a love relationship. When we believe in Jesus, we must believe that His perfect righteousness, in His love and right standing with the Father, was given to us. The same love God has for Jesus, He gives us the moment we believe and are born again. See Romans 5:5; 1 John 4:8-9.

The truth that God made us justified and righteous means He made us innocent, not guilty, freed from the bondage of sin and death; instead, we are made loved, worthy, and acceptable to God as His children. As His children, living by faith, we have peace because we are wrapped in His arms of love and care. We have peace with God because He did all the work at the Cross and restored our standing on the solid rock, Jesus by His Blood. If we begin to look at ourselves to feel and be right with God by our obedience, action, or performance, we have jumped into the quicksand of the flesh. We will lose our peace, and fear will come into our hearts. We are seeking to be justified by our performance which is not faith. As the Just, we must come by faith having a sense of innocence and freedom to go into our Father's presence at any time as loved, accepted, and worthy of being received by Him. See Ephesians 1; Hebrews 4:16.

LIFE: I am justified, made loved, righteous, acceptable, and pleasing to my Father by the Blood of Jesus alone. I reject the lie that I am justified by my obedience and performance; therefore, I deserve torment when I sin. The Blood of Jesus gives me access and peace in Christ Jesus, my Jehovah Shalom. See Isaiah 32:17-18; Romans 5:1; 1 Corinthians 1:30.

DESERVING PUNISHMENT

"Know therefore that God exacteth of thee less than thine iniquity deserveth." —Job 11:6

TRUTH: The life of Job is charged with much need for our greater understanding of God and His ways with man. God said Job was perfect and upright, and on many occasions, Job stood up for his innocence, yet he suffered. He lost it all, his health, livestock, servants, and children. His three friends tried to counsel him to repent of sin before God to be free from His calamity. One even suggested in Job 11:6 that he deserved more punishment than God was giving him for his self-righteousness. Job replied to him in Job 9:12-35.

God said Job was blameless and righteous, yet Satan attacked him. See Job 1:8; 2:3. Scriptures tell us that God forgets not even the sparrows, and we are of more value than them. See Luke 12:6-7. God was with Job and supervised his entry into his test and the processing during his trial, to the end. God's purposes may have been: (1) To prove Job was righteous and faithful as He said to Satan. (2) To sanctify and increase Job's faith from self-effort to greater dependence on God. See Job 1:5. (3) That God is sovereign and has a greater purpose in His dealings with our lives (4) To help us to see ourselves as righteous and blameless as He says in His Word and to reject Satan's voice speaking to us to condemn, as Job's friends did. See Ephesians 1:4; Colossians 1:22. Believers must reject the idea that every trial or suffering must be because of sin or of them deserving punishment or that lack of immediate relief means God is absent. No! We do experience trials for God's purpose of sanctification. See James 1:2-6; 1 Peter 1:7-9.

LIFE: God is always present in our trials or any sanctification process we are going through. He is there to help, give understanding, wisdom, guidance, and comfort, but the sanctification ends not when we confess sin to get relief, but when God is done increasing us. So, yield, lean into God your Father and learn of Him quickly so that your time of sanctification will be shorter. Amen.

MADE UNTO WISDOM

"But of him are ye in Christ Jesus, who of God is made unto us wisdom, and righteousness, and sanctification, and redemption." —1 Corinthians 1:30

TRUTH: Jesus was made the Son of man. See John 1:14. And we have been made sons of God. See Galatians 3:26; 4:6; Romans 8:14. Our verse tells us God made us new. With His wisdom, He increased our capacity to be supernaturally wise; His righteousness gave us love, value, and acceptance. God in Christ made us sanctified when He made us holy in character in our spirit-man. Redemption deals with our status in that God made us free to be His. God remade us in Christ, wise, accepted, holy, and free. When God looks at us through Jesus' Blood, He sees us remade in His image; and this is how He wants us to see ourselves.

God's wisdom is the expression of divine knowledge and truth. See 1 Corinthians 1:24; Colossians 2:2-3; James 3:17. God's wisdom is infinite as He can see the big picture, the end before the beginning. He also has complete knowledge of "how" to achieve the desired goal. Lastly, God's wisdom can bring all the parts, people, places, and resources together to achieve His goal. Although we see in part, God's view is complete. Jeremiah 29:11 says God has good thoughts of peace to give us an expected end of blessings. Jesus had great wisdom to discern His Father's heart and accomplish salvation, to do good, as well as to answer His accusers wisely. Likewise, in Christ, we have the wisdom of God in our spirit -man to navigate our earthly life successfully because we have His eternal life in us.

Life: Receive Jesus as Savior and Lord. Fear God hear and study His Word. Receive Jesus the Baptizer and the baptism of the Holy Spirit. Fellowship with the Holy Spirit and start praying out mysteries that will give you the wisdom of God concerning any situation you face that needs a direct answer from your Father's heart. See Romans 10:9-19; John 1:33; 1 Corinthians 14:2-4; James 1:5-8.

MADE UNTO RIGHTEOUSNESS

"But of him are ye in Christ Jesus, who of God is made unto...righteousness." —1 Corinthians 1:30

TRUTH: We are made righteous the moment we are born again. God deposited His gift of righteousness within us in His love by the Holy Spirit. See Romans 5:5; Galatians 5:22; 1 John 4: 7-8. Righteousness causes us to have right standing before God, the God of love, to be loved by Him. We are being made right with God. His righteousness results in our humbly doing right by God and others because we belong to a righteous God of love who helps us to love. We live passionately to show our love for God in our obedience and lifestyle. See Romans 13:8-10. Righteousness orients us to live by faith with God-centered, Jesus-focused, and Holy Spirit-led lives. We will be led to live in humility, having our human will submitted to God and His eternal life. *"In the way of righteousness is life; and in the pathway thereof there is no death"* (Proverbs 12:28).

As we walk in our Christian journey, we accept the work of the Cross and the shed Blood in Christ Jesus as our righteousness. Jesus is our path to love God and to give love to others. He alone made us right before God. He alone tells us that we are loved, acceptable, and worthy to our Father. Now we should always see ourselves in our character as forgiven, redeemed, adopted by God, loved, Holy Spirit-directed, dependent on God, and making every choice a sacrifice of self to exalt Jesus. We die to ourselves, sin, and the Law, always desiring only to love, worship, obey God, and prosper in Him. When we fail and sin, as the righteous, we run to God the Father and cry out by faith, trusting God for His forgiveness and grace to help and restore us into righteousness and fellowship in His love.

LIFE: You are righteous when you receive Jesus as the One who makes you right with God. And are focused on God by Jesus Christ His Son, grace through faith for your salvation, and His love and power in the Holy Spirit to help you love in daily life. You are accepted as His beloved. Always look to Jesus, your righteousness, to make all things right, never self-righteousness. You'll then be able to relax and enjoy His presence. See 2 Peter 2:10; Isaiah 54:14

MADE UNTO SANCTIFICATION

"Through sanctification of the Spirit, unto obedience and sprinkling of the blood of Jesus Christ." —1 Peter 1:2

TRUTH: Every born again person is sanctified, made holy in their spirit by the grace of God, called out of the world of sin, possessing the presence of God, and set apart for His sacred use. See Exodus 33:16; Ephesians 1:4; Colossians 1:22; 2 Timothy 1:9. As we acknowledge that we are made holy and cling to God to lead and help us by His Word and Holy Spirit, we are working out the holiness within our spirit to grow and manifest purity into our souls and bodies, showing forth the holiness of God from within to the outside in our behavior. How we live matters to God, and He expects us to live in holiness, which can happen only as we depend on the Holy Spirit in relationship to illuminate the Word of God to us and then give us the power to yield to God our Father and obey Him. *"Sanctify them through thy truth, thy word is truth"* (John 17:17).

A believer is sanctified and made holy by the Blood of Jesus Christ. See Hebrews 10:10, 14. We are to believe this is our position in Christ by faith. In our daily life, we must believe we are being sanctified as we read and meditate in the Word of God, reverently seeking the help of the Holy Spirit to give revelation truths. He will help us be doers of the Word, putting off the old man in our sinful habits and putting on the new man created in Christ Jesus after holiness and righteousness. See 2 Corinthians 5:21; Ephesians 4:21-32; 1 Thessalonians 4:4, 7; 5:23-24; 1 Peter 3:15; Romans 5:17; 12:1-2.

LIFE: *"Be ye Holy for I am Holy"* (1 Peter 1:16). Sanctification is not refraining from sinning, as this is of the flesh, but it is drawing near to the Father so the Holy Spirit can lead you into truth, righteousness, and holiness. Maturing in God must be by the Holy Spirit; otherwise, the enemy will accuse you of failure and condemn you. See Romans 8:14; John 3:17-18; Romans 8:1-2.

MADE UNTO REDEMPTION

*"But of him are ye in Christ Jesus who of God made
unto us ...redemption."* —1 Corinthians 1:30

TRUTH: Redemption speaks of freedom. Jesus cleared our sin debt by His shed Blood on the Cross redeemed and made us free from bondage. See Galatians 3:13 -14; Ephesians 5:1. Jesus delivered humanity from alienation and separation from God. See Romans 5:6-11. He reversed the effects of the fall when He made us free in the Spirit realm from sin, Satan, death, sickness, and the Law. Jesus made us free unto God to love and worship Him and for us to walk in freedom in our daily lives. See Exodus 3:18; Romans 8:4. There may be many Christians who are not walking in the freedom God intended and are still sin-conscious and afraid of Satan or at least may not have complete dominion over him. Some are dying too quickly from sickness and accidents as if we do not have a healer and a protector. We may still be attached to the Law and the flesh in our self-directed and independent lifestyles, not fully surrendered and taking our position in Christ as the redeemed of the Lord made free.

"Who redeemeth thy life from destruction; who crowneth thee with lovingkindness and tender mercies" (Psalm 103:4).

Walk as the redeemed, believe all your sins are forgiven, and that sin is not imputed to you (held against you). See Romans 4: 8,15; 5:13; 2 Corinthians 5:19. Your heart is to be free and lifted in Jesus' righteousness to the Father. He is our passkey to resist and defeat Satan and draw from the spiritual realm, by faith, every blessing we will ever need here on earth to be made free, made whole, and enjoy our redemption.

LIFE: *"If ye continue in my word, then ye are my disciples indeed. And ye shall know the truth, and the truth shall make you free. If the Son therefore shall make you free, ye shall be free indeed"* (John 8:31-32, 36). We can change our adverse circumstances by genuine faith in God's grace, Christ Jesus, our redeemer, and be free. See Mark 11:22-24.

GIFT OF RIGHTEOUSNESS

"For if by one man's offence death reigned by one; much more they which receive abundance of grace and of the gift of righteousness shall reign in life by one, Jesus Christ." —Romans 5:17

TRUTH: Righteousness is right standing or right relationship with God. Humanity was in sin and separated from God the Father. To restore man unto God, He sent His Son Jesus, whose shed Blood provided redemption and forgiveness for sin. Through Jesus, the man was forgiven, cleansed, and delivered from sin, guilt, shame, and condemnation. See John 3:16-17. Jesus paid the debt for sin, removed its power of the curse, and gave us His righteousness or right love relationship with His Father as a gift. Jesus' righteousness which is the love of the Father in us, justified and declared us innocent, freed from all sin, made righteous, approved, and acceptable to God our Heavenly Father. When people believe in Jesus, they have faith in God's love, are born again, and are made righteous. Jesus loves you, and Jesus loved God, so God loves you and by His Spirit deposited the fruit of love in your heart. See Galatians 5:22.

Jesus is now your righteousness, your reason for God loving you. And He loves you with an everlasting love. Rest in His love and never fear. See Isaiah 41:10; 54:14. Believe by faith that God gave you the gift of love in Christ Jesus, who loves you and made you righteous and acceptable to your Father. Your righteousness, or your acceptance by God through Jesus' love, now gives you peace with Him. You can rest and delight in His great love for you and never feel you must earn His love. For this, His gift of love, our hearts are open to praise, thank, and worship God for this great gift of righteousness, His love in a restored relationship builds faith and now releases His grace. Grace flows from righteousness.

LIFE: God loves me. His perfect love deposited in my heart gives me peace with Him and frees my heart from fear. See Romans 5:1; Colossians 1:20;1 John 4:18.

RIGHTEOUSNESS AND PEACE

"For by one man's offence death reigned by one: much more they which receive abundance of grace and the gift of righteousness shall reign in life by one Jesus Christ." —Romans 5:17

TRUTH: When we acknowledge that we are righteous and God loves us, we will rest in His love and have peace in our hearts with God. And as the righteous, when we learn to trust and rest in Him, we will depend on Him and obey Him. Obedience brings peace. We will do right according to the Word of God, which then conveys the peace of God to our hearts. *"Mercy and truth are met together: righteousness and peace have kissed each other"* (Psalm 85:10).

The Holy Spirit dwelling in our hearts will lead us into obeying God's commandment to love. And as we love God and one another, others will know we are believers, peacemakers, and disciples of Christ. See John 13:34-35; Matthew 5:9. The opposite of righteousness is unrighteousness or sin. *"All unrighteousness is sin"* (1 John 5:17). Righteousness or faith in God's love will result in increased faith in His Word. Faith releases God's power to keep us from sin, provide, and deliver. Because God's love delivers, fear is canceled, and we reign in peace and succeed in life. See 1 Corinthians 13:8; Romans 5:17; 1 John 4:18.

LIFE: Jesus' righteousness is most important as God imparts His love and acceptance of us by the Blood of Jesus, giving assurance and peace. Not receiving the gift of righteousness leads one to other means of working out our salvation with religion or works. As we seek God's love in self-effort, striving, struggle and torment come to the soul. Receiving Jesus' righteousness and peace gives rest in your soul and freedom from fear as you trust His love for you. Confess God's love often over yourself. Say, *Jesus loves me, and You Lord is my righteousness and peace. I trust You, Lord, and will not be afraid. I rest in Your peace. When You provide, I have financial peace, and when You heal my body, I have physical peace and look forward to enjoying my relationship with my Father.* Meditate on Isaiah 32: 17-18.

RIGHTEOUSNESS AT WORK

"They which receive the abundance of grace and the gift of righteousness shall reign in life by one, Jesus Christ." —Romans 5:17

TRUTH: Everyone likes to receive gifts. They peak the imagination and bring excitement, joy, and love to one's life. God also loves to bestow blessings to His children. First, He gave the gift of His Son to provide us with eternal life and the gift of righteousness in His love. God gave us a right relationship with Him when we believe in Jesus with His righteousness. Open your gifts; read about them in the Word of God. Have joy that you are no longer separated from God and that you have no need to work to earn His love and acceptance.

In our natural life, God gives us gifts in people: parents, spouses, other relatives, teachers, employers, and friends. We received Jesus' righteousness, His right standing with the Father, and with the gift of righteousness, God made us right with Himself. Through the sacrifice of Jesus' Blood, God restored us into a love relationship with Him.

When we are at variance with others in our lives, especially our loved ones or employers, we may sometimes feel them more of a weight than a gift to our life. But when we look to Jesus our righteousness, He will help us walk in His grace, love, and peace with ourselves, with others, and even our enemies.

LIFE: God gave us His gift of righteousness when He allowed Jesus by His Blood to take us to Himself, into His presence, as loved, acceptable, worthy, chosen, valuable, free from sin, guilt, shame, and condemnation. As believers, Jesus' righteousness will equip us to receive love; and we are now able to give God's love and allow His love to build faith. See Galatians 5:6. We see righteousness at work when we sin or fall into unrighteousness. The Holy Spirit convicts us of righteousness (not sin). See John 16:10. Once we receive His conviction, we turn to God in repentance, receive forgiveness and restoration into righteousness or right love relationship with God our Father, self, and even others for us to continue with God going forward in peace. Peace sets the atmosphere for enjoying our relationships.

RIGHTEOUSNESS AT WORK — DAY 2

"...The gift of righteousness shall reign in life by one Jesus Christ." —Romans 5:17

TRUTH: *"Lord, how oft shall my brother sin against me, and I forgive him? till seven times. Jesus saith unto him, I say not unto thee, Until seventy times seven"* (Matthew 18:21-22). Satan's lie to us is that we can be selfish, self-focused, and self-directed and still be happy in life.

Grace is God, with His power through Jesus, all by Himself doing for us that we cannot do for ourselves. God did it all in Jesus and gave us His love as a gift. Receive it by faith. We are righteous by the Blood of Jesus alone. We are righteous the moment we receive Jesus. When we say Jesus is our righteousness, it means Jesus, by what He has done on the Cross, makes us right, restored into a love relationship with God the Father. Jesus has our hearts; though we may be weak, flawed, broken, and carnal, He still holds us. We can depend on and trust the Father by the Holy Spirit to change and mold us into becoming more like Jesus every day. When we are offended by others, because we are looking to God and His Word, we can release them, trusting God's grace in His righteousness to go to work to flow towards them to turn the situation around. In the end, both parties will escape Satan's bondage of strife and reign in righteousness and peace.

LIFE: The gift of righteousness lets you know you are loved with everlasting love and accepted by God. And with His love, you become established in righteousness, trusting your Father, who gives you peace and cancels fear. See Isaiah 32:17; 54:14. When the Holy Spirit is acknowledged as God's perfect love in you...greater than Satan and all other forces...you can say in your heart about others that you bless and curse not. I will not fear, neither will I render evil for good. I trust God and expect Him to work that which is right and good, perfecting what concerns me. Righteousness releases love, which gives faith, trust, rest and peace. Jesus is our righteousness, and we are the righteousness of God in Christ. He is our love. See Isaiah 32:17-18; Romans 5:17, 8:28; Psalm 138:7-8.

STAND IN RIGHTEOUSNESS

"And the work of righteousness shall be peace, and the effect of righteousness quietness and assurance forever." —Isaiah 32:17

TRUTH: Receiving the gift of righteousness is receiving by faith God's love in His grace, Jesus Christ. The opposite is to receive Him by works:

- We are trying to work to please or to earn God's love. This is performance, self-effort, and self-righteousness. See Galatians 3; 2 Peter 2:10.
- We live by a law mentality of right and wrong thinking, not giving compassion from the heart by the leading of the Spirit. Mark 2: 24-28.
- We are critical, judgmental, and quick to punish. See Matthew 7:1-5.
- Fear and insecurities come when we're exposed to Satan's attack and lack faith in God's love and care. See Isaiah 54:14.
- Relationship with God not being close and loving, but distanced and frustrating. See Luke 15:11.
- One's heart is not fully surrendered to the Father in rest but is still trying and striving to accomplish in self-effort. See Hebrews 4:11.

LIFE: When you stand in righteousness, your relationship with God is of faith or in faith-righteousness. You trust His love and care for you. You have received Jesus, God's grace, and all He did on the Cross to give you His love and blessings. You know God loves and accepts you, and you depend on Him and trust Him enough to listen, hear, and be led to obey Him by faith. See Philippians 2:13. God said to Abram, *"Look now toward heaven, and tell the stars, if thou be able to number them: and he said unto him, So, shall thy seed be"* (Genesis 15:5). Abram believed the Lord; and it was counted unto him for righteousness. The opposite of not receiving God's love and depending on Jesus is self-righteousness. Stand as the righteous and believe God loves you, cares for you and will direct and fight for your good every time. Enjoy His goodness and His love.

STAND IN RIGHTEOUSNESS — DAY 2

"And the work of righteousness shall be peace..." —Isaiah 32:17

TRUTH: Let us stand in our righteousness in Jesus and believe only the Blood makes us righteous, not our right actions or performance. When we believe that Jesus alone is our righteousness, we know our hearts are knitted to our Father's heart as one spirit, and in gratitude, we abide, worship, and yield to Him as the Author of our salvation. We continually depend on the Holy Spirit to lead, change, and mold us into the image of God's Son. Because we rely on Jesus and not our performance, the devil can never accuse us of being unworthy or unacceptable to God and therefore worthy of his condemnation or punishment. We stand in righteousness and believe that by God's grace in Jesus and His Spirit, we gain God's love and acceptance in a relationship with Him. God's perfect love deposited in our hearts closes the door to Satan and the spirit of fear. Stand in righteousness, as loved by the Father, a new creation being, living in the newness of life by the power of the Holy Spirit. Righteousness leads to holiness, which brings peace.

Stand in righteousness and receive God's peace. See James 3:18. Jesus reconciled us to our Father in love, and nothing can separate us from His love. See Romans 8:32-39. Stand in righteousness and see our Heavenly Father rightly—a Father who loves us and is not angry with us and does not desire to punish us. Accepting we are righteous will cause us to depend on God by the Holy Spirit, who will lead us into rest, quietness, and assurance of our Father's love and care for us. See Isaiah 32:17-18; James 5:16.

LIFE: When I stand in righteousness, my relationship with my Heavenly Father is by faith, believing He loves me infinitely; and I yield to Him. Through the Blood of Jesus, I see myself rightly and God rightly; I also know the devil rightly as defeated, and I relate accordingly to each by the Word, resulting in a life of peace. In righteousness, I daily learn to trust God more each day, increasing my desire for His continued blessings in every area of my life.

FAITH LIVES OUT OF RELATIONSHIP

"I am the vine, ye are the branches: He that abideth in me, and I in him, the same bringeth more much fruit." —John 15:5

TRUTH: Scripture tells us we are made in God's image, and we enter His family to love, worship, and serve Him intimately. In return, we expect His love, faithfulness, and care of us. Our relationship with God is a Father-child relationship, one with Him as the branch is to the vine. It is a relationship of connectedness and oneness through Jesus' Blood, who saved and reconciled us. And it is with humility we acknowledge that the God who saved us is greater because of our inability to save and care for ourselves. We are needy to Jesus as a child needs their parents at birth, and our dependence and neediness are upon God's grace through Christ Jesus and all He accomplished on the Cross for us. We have redemption from Satan, sin, sickness, death, and self in the law because of god's grace. Jesus, our Good Shepherd, provided everything we need for life and godliness in salvation. See 1 Kings 8:56; Psalm 84:11; John 3:16; Ephesians 1:3; 2 Peter 1:2-4. We know who God our Father is, that He is great, mighty, loving, kind, all-powerful, and all-knowing. But we must be as His children living by faith in a Father-child relationship with Him.

LIFE: We are born again through Jesus Christ in a relationship with God our Father. We are new creation beings in Him, who by His Spirit gave us a new heart or a new nature, forgiven of sin, made righteous, restored into a right relationship or right standing, being justified just as if we never sinned. We have peace with God our Father. We are divinely connected to Him by God, the Holy Spirit who indwells and gives us the capability to be taught and led by God. We can go to Him at any time for His grace in times of need or mercy in times of sin and failure. See Hebrews 4:16. Run to Him, talk to Him, find His heart in His Word, defer to Him, have fellowship as you listen, act or rest in Him as led by His Spirit. Let Christ be your life by faith in a relationship. Believe Him and live out of your relationship by always trusting Him. Trust builds intimacy.

FAITH LIVES OUT OF RELATIONSHIP — DAY 2

"I believe and therefore have I spoken: we also believe,
and therefore speak." —2 Corinthians 4:13

TRUTH: The character of God was given to us in our spirit to help us grow and transform into the very image of Christ—an image of love which provides us with peace, boldness, confidence, and power to be gracious and to bless people just as Jesus did on earth, bringing glory to God our Father. We can now live by faith in all our relationships with His character of love within. See Galatians 5:6. We have the Father's character in us as we are in a union relationship with Him. See Galatians 5:22; John 14:16-17. He deposited faith in us to believe Him. See Romans 12:3. Now we can connect to God in His presence and grow in our faith as we accept His Words, both written and spoken by His Spirit.

The measure of faith we develop is directly proportional to our relationship with God through His Word and our communion with the Holy Spirit. A little relationship with Jesus by the Word and the Holy Spirit means little faith. See Romans 10:17. The little relationship results from being distanced from God and being more self-directed and self-reliant in what we do to please or receive from God. One may also live a carnal lifestyle. As believers living under the New Covenant of God's grace, we believe all Jesus accomplished on the Cross for us to be saved and live by grace through faith, resting in a relationship. We do only what He reveals to our hearts as we hear from the Father. We believe and speak the Words of the Father, and through faith and patience in a relationship, receive all the blessings in His promises.

LIFE: The opposite of living your faith in a relationship with the Father through Jesus and the Holy Spirit is to live by the Law, trying to obey doctrine and principles to be acceptable and pleasing to God by what we do or do not do in our strength. God wants us to commune and fellowship with His Word and His Spirit and live by faith in a relationship with Him to make Christ our life so that, even with mustard-size faith, we can do mighty things through Him and exalt the name of Jesus. See Luke 17:5-6.

FAITH LIVES OUT OF RELATIONSHIP — DAY 3

"For I know that this shall turn to my salvation through your prayer, and the supply of the Spirit of Jesus Christ." —Philippians 1:19

TRUTH: The Old Testament saints connected to God externally by the cloud by day and fire by night; they heard from God amid thunder, lightning, smoke, and through kings, priests, and prophets. They obeyed an external Law by their self-action and were judged for sin by death when they failed. In today's church, God's relationship with His children connects internally by His Spirit. He is in us, with us, and for us, teaching and guiding us from the heart by His Word and His Spirit into faith, truth, and obedience. See John 16:13; Philippians 2:13. God will hear as we speak His Word, believe by faith, listen, and trust Him to answer in a relationship. Because we love Him, we hear His answer, agree with Him, act on His Word, and obey. See 1 John 5:2-4. God speaks to us in many ways, some of which are:

- By an inner witness by His Holy Spirit (Romans 8: 14, 16; 9:1).
- By His Word (1 Timothy 3:16).
- Through His prophets/ pastors/teachers/Angels (1 Corinthians 12:28).
- Through nature (Romans 1:20).
- By an audible voice (Mark 1:11).
- As a burden to pray or help (Galatians 6:2).
- Through providence – God's care in open or closed doors.

Only in a relationship, in fellowshipping to listen, believe, and act on God's Word, will we be complete in Him. See Colossians 1:10; 1 John 5:14-15.

LIFE: We live by faith out of our relationship with the Father because Jesus' Blood gave us His Spirit with God's nature to live a supernatural life. One in spirit with the Godhead. This is our secret place, our union in God. See Psalm 91:1; 1 Corinthians 6:17. As we feed our spirit with the Word of God, faith comes to establish us in God's grace, His love, and His faithfulness. We rest in the victory Christ won for us. We live from our spirit where the love, faith, and power of God flows from within to bring Jesus to us with all His blessings to prosper us.

EYES OF FAITH

"Lift up now thine eyes... for all the land which thou seeth, to thee will I give it, and to thy seed." —Genesis 13:14-15

TRUTH: God gave His church a command to live by faith. See Galatians 3:11. God can meet our needs sovereignly by a miracle and through exercising our faith. However, believers are required to live by faith. Faith hears God's Word, believes it is true, confidently holds fast to His character, and acts on what is believed until our desire comes to pass. Before the eyes of faith can see the blessing, they should first see their Blesser, God, through Jesus Christ His Son. Accept His grace and love in all He did on the Cross and hear what He has to say to us, just as when He spoke to Abram. God told Abram to lift his eyes, the eyes of faith, to the stars and see the promised blessings He had for him. As a childless man, the promise to make his seed as the dust of the earth must have been overwhelming for Abram to understand. God always gives us promised blessings beyond the grasp of our understanding. That is because the enormity of the promise means it must be claimed by faith. First to be received in the heart, envisioned in the soul, and acted upon before seeing it with the eyes. The eye of faith is of the heart. The desired blessing must be believed in faith, conceived in the heart, and acted upon.

The eye of faith sees into the Spirit realm and lays hold of the blessing. Abram lived under the covenant of promise, so he depended on his ability to hear and follow God to receive His promise. He made many mistakes along the way. But as the church, we live under the New Covenant of Grace by faith and are led by God's Word and His Holy Spirit. That is why grace is a better covenant, as we can trust God's Word and His Spirit to sharpen our eyes of faith for us to "only believe" and receive our blessing. See Hebrews 8:6.

LIFE: *"And all things whatsoever ye shall ask in prayer, believing, ye shall receive"* (Matthew 21:22). If you're sick, believe by faith you're healed and act on what you believe; get out of bed, even sit up in a chair and be healed. Meditate on Mark 11:22-24.

EYES OF FAITH — DAY 2

"Lift up now thine eyes..." —Genesis 13: 14-15

TRUTH: Always look with eyes of faith at the promises given if they have a spiritual law attached. This law must be obeyed to demonstrate our love and trust in the Father for Him to act and fulfill the promise we desire.

Let your eyes of faith see the spiritual law to yield and obey, as only then will we see all God has for us and to receive all His blessings. For example, Romans 8:1 – *"There is therefore now no condemnation to them which are in Christ Jesus..."* [then the spiritual law is:] *"who walk not after the flesh, but after the Spirit."*

A second example is found in Deuteronomy 28:2: *"And all these blessings shall come on thee, and overtake thee..."* [then the spiritual law is:] *"if thou shalt hearken unto the voice of the Lord thy God."* Hearken diligently and do all His commands.

We see the third example in Malachi 3:10. The spiritual law is given first: *"Bring ye all the tithes into the storehouse, that there may be meat in mine house."* Then we see the promise of faith: *"Prove me now...if I will not open you the window of heaven, and pour you out a blessing, that there shall not be room enough to receive it."* The eyes of faith must turn not only to hear and believe what God says but also to be a doer by acting on the whole counsel of the Word as we rejoice in His goodness and let our eyes of faith see Jesus as the One to manifest our blessing as we yield to and obey the spiritual law given.

LIFE: Let us see the desired promises and the connected spiritual law as if one is present, it must be obeyed. Just as Abram looked north, south, east, and west to physically see his promise, we must look to Jesus and the finished work of the Cross, obey any spiritual law given by God and believe Him completely. Take Him at His Word and watch Him respond to your faith to bless everything you put your hands to in Jesus' name. See Genesis 12 and 13; Joshua 1:3.

FAITH

"But without faith it is impossible to please him: for he that cometh to God must believe that he is, and that he is a rewarder of them that diligently seek him." —Hebrews 11:6.

TRUTH: The Bible begins in Genesis 1, *"In the beginning God created the heaven and the earth."* The Bible does not attempt to explain the existence of God either then or before creation. But before creation, there was an eternity. God existed in eternity past, and He is free from the succession of time as He is an infinite Spirit without beginning and end. Colossians 1:17 says, *"And he is before all things, and by him all things consist (are held together)."* God is to be believed and responded to as His very existence can be received only by faith.

After Jesus came to earth and died on the Cross, a New Covenant of Grace was instituted, and the Law of Love governs it. The New Covenant is lived by faith in God's love. Love is relational, and it pleases God that we relate to Him and other people in love. That is why faith works by love. Love for God first and then for others cancels Satan's attacks. See Matthew 22:37-40; John 13:34.

Faith believes that God is precisely who He says He is and that He will do exactly what He says He will do in His Word. God is a Spirit living in heaven, and we are here on earth. But as we live by faith, we relate and connect to Him by His Holy Spirit. By believing, we put action to our faith and trust that God will accomplish our desires. Hebrews 11:1 says, *"Now faith is the substance of things hoped for, the evidence of things not seen."* Faith requires us to believe God by His Word, then act on what we believe because He is true, and His Word is truth. If you're believing God for finances and prayed and have the unction to give to another, do it according to the Word, which says, *"Give and it shall be given unto you..."* (Luke 6:38). God never lies. See John 14:6; Numbers 23:19.

LIFE: All people should accept God and His Word by faith and be saved, both for heaven and a prosperous life here on earth because He is the beginning and the end of all things good. See Hebrews 12:2; Revelation 1:8; 22:20.

FAITH — DAY 2

"But without faith it is impossible to please Him." —Hebrews 11:6

TRUTH: Jesus Christ has called us to live by faith, and He is the same yesterday, today, and forever. See Hebrews 13:8. We can live by faith in Jesus every day because His love is constant, and faith works by how much we love and believe Him. When we hear, read, or listen to testimony about Jesus, agree with God's Word and believe His power is available to do what we are expecting, we have faith. Faith is an unwavering belief and agreement with God and His Word, and with patience, we can wait and see our desired manifestation.

It pleases God when His children believe and take Him at His Word. God calls it faith, and faith pleases Him. See Hebrews 11:6. The story in John 20:24-29 tells us Thomas doubted and was without faith. He did not connect to God's heart, and he did not please Jesus by his unbelief.

It pleases God when we humble ourselves and, by faith, believe Him. When He speaks, we are to hear and respond as we connect to Him in a relationship through our belief in Jesus His Son. We demonstrate faith in Jesus as we read His Word, pray, fellowship, and listen to Him to hear what He says to us; and as we do these things, the more faith will come to our hearts, and the greater will be our capacity to respond and to receive God's blessings. See Romans 10:17.

LIFE: Christ is your life as you humble yourself and believe Him. Take Him at His Word and draw strength and power to stand in the face of any challenge, any opposition, and have the confident expectation that God is your reality of goodness, favor, love, provision, and peace. He is faithful to His character and His Word to bless as you stand in faith and patience and wait until your desire becomes a reality for you in the natural. Christ is your reality, and He is your real life. Meditate on Mark 11:24.

FAITH VS MENTAL ASSENT

"So, then faith cometh by hearing and hearing by the word of God." —Romans 10:17

TRUTH: Faith takes our hope to a higher level by having belief, confidence, and assurance in God's Words. Faith is not taking a bunch of Scriptures and saying them repeatedly, knowing the Word is true while still waiting anxiously for the result, or even complaining while waiting. When the result is not seen in a reasonable time, the person backs off, thinking God has forgotten about them. This is mental assent because the Word of God is only in the head, not the heart. Faith is of the heart. When God's Word is believed, anchored in God's love on the finished work of the Cross, faith comes. See Romans 10:9-10. *"Faith is the substance of things hoped for, the evidence of things not seen"* (Hebrews 11:1).

Because faith comes by hearing the Word of God, we can increase confidence in our hearts as we read the Word and listen to preaching. Notice our text used the word *hearing* twice; this means we must rest in relationship with Jesus and keep hearing, thinking about, and meditating on the Word and what He did on the Cross to meet our needs. We do this until we believe in our hearts that God's Word is true and that it will cause His blessing to manifest in our lives. If you have a problem that you need God to fix, first take your stand in oneness in Christ, who is seated at the right hand of the Father, then claim your blessing as already received from this place of victory. Then find promises for your deliverance in Scripture and write out those verses. Feed your spirit with the Word; hear, meditate, and memorize the Scriptures that minister to you the most. Speak the Word forth, knowing you believe you've already received the promise. *Then,* you pray and ask God to meet your need. Agree with God and receive your blessing; say, "It's mine; praise God, I believe, and I receive. If the Lord gives you an instruction, do it. Worship and thank God your Father in advance until your desire manifests. See Mark 11:22-24.

LIFE: Faith comes alive; after hearing, speaking, and mediating, we believe, pray and stand victorious to receive with joy as we continue to worship until our blessing comes in God's timing.

OVER FAMILIARITY

"A prophet is not without honor, but in his own country, and among his own kin, and his own house." —Mark 6: 4

TRUTH: Many Jews knew Jesus in the natural and heard Him teach the Word with great authority, yet they questioned His legitimacy because of over-familiarity. Verse 5 says He could not do any mighty work except lay hands on a few sick folks and heal them. It was just in the chapter before that the woman with the issue of blood was healed, and the ruler of the synagogue's daughter was miraculously raised from the dead. See Mark 5:25-30.

Presently in the church, we must be careful not to find ourselves in the same position with over-familiarity by glossing over the written Word and neglecting our relationship with Jesus through the Holy Spirit. We may be going to church daily, but our lives are not changing to align with the Word of God because we dismiss it by thinking, "we know that already." Or where the Word demands a change of us, we skip over it and move on to some other part of the Word we find more palatable. Just as the Jews would not receive Jesus, we may be doing the same by becoming religious, glossing over His Word, and letting neglect and over-familiarity cause lack of revelation, close relationship, personal intimacy, and affection. We can also wrongly assume we know God's way and use our energy to resist God's dealings by thinking it is the devil; we start binding and rebuking Satan instead of yielding to God's work in our lives, especially in times of trials and times of sanctification with refining fires. In tests, we must go to God first and ask for revelation. Then we act only on what He says, as we should never assume.

LIFE: Repent of any over-familiarity. If we see it, ask Jesus to give us a fresh revelation of Himself in a personal relationship and fellowship to receive fresh manna and blessings each day, not only for ourselves but to be able to minister to others. Because our life is hidden in Christ, and He has become our life, we can be a channel for God to be formed in our hearts in a more significant way so we can minister powerfully to bless others. See Colossians 3.

O YE OF LITTLE FAITH

"Wherefore, if God so clothe the grass of the field...shall he not much more clothe you, O ye of little faith?"—Matthew 6:30

TRUTH: Shall I find faith on the earth when I come? If Jesus asked you this question, what would your answer be? Shall He find faith in you? In me? See Luke 18:8. Faith is living out of our relationship with Jesus. Faith is us embracing Jesus and His Word as truth and as our final authority until our blessing manifests. Faith comes when, in relationship and fellowship, one hears and keeps on hearing the Word of God, continually drawing near to Jesus. Let His Word get deep in the heart until we believe it is true, and faith arises to dispel any doubt that our blessing will manifest.

Abraham believed in God, and it was counted to him as righteousness. See Romans 4:3. Just like Abraham, you are to know how much God loves you and will take care of you so you can rest and trust in Him by faith to provide.

The Bible tells us about those who will not have faith when Jesus comes.

- Those who worry about their daily provisions (Matthew 6:30).
- Those who are fearful (Matthew 8:26; Luke 8:25).
- Those who doubt (Matthew 14:31, 17:20).
- Those following false doctrine with much reasoning and questioning (Matthew 16:8).

To all of these, Jesus says, *"O ye of little faith."*

LIFE: When Jesus comes, let Him find faith in you. Believe Him. Think on Him, meditate on Him, speak God's Word until faith comes. And when worrying thoughts come while you wait on your need to be met, take your seat, abide, and rest in Christ Jesus being one in spirit with Him. Declare Him Lord over your situation and command Satan to bow. Be thankful in all things, praise Him, worship Him, and give Him thanks in advance. Let your joy give strength until your manifestation comes. See: 2 Timothy 1:7, 14; 1 John 4:18; 1 Thessalonians 2:13, 18.

DAVID'S CONFIDENCE

"David said to Saul, Let no man's heart fail because of him; thy servant will go and fight." —1 Samuel 17:32 (24-53)

TRUTH: All people in life, including believers, can face insurmountable obstacles yet overcome. We may begin to tremble and may even become paralyzed with fear, but this lesson from David shows us that the battle is the Lord's, and He will give victory if we trust in Him to fight for us.

First, there was a promise to the man who could kill Goliath, and David enquired about the reward. Have you inquired and found the promises, fully expecting your reward in the blessing of the Word God gave concerning the situation you are facing?

Second, David saw the enemy just as God saw him, an uncircumcised Philistine. David knew he was circumcised and was guaranteed God's protection because of His covenant.

Third, David refused to listen to the nay-sayers. He turned away from them twice until his request reached the king's ears, which honored David's desire. *"Be careful about nothing; but in everything by prayer and supplication with thanksgiving let your requests be made known to God"* (Philippians 4:6).

Fourth, David spoke in faith, not in fear, to the king about how he planned to face and fight the enemy. David remembered times before when he had defeated attacks of lions and bears (Vv. 32-36). Always remember the victories the Lord has given you in the past. He is the same yesterday, today, and forever.

Fifth, David could not fight with Saul's armor and weapon; he chose his own. The words on the page of the Bible will not deliver you. It is hearing God's Word and placing it deep into your heart, believing, speaking, then acting in faith on what the Word says in boldness and authority; The truth will bring your victory.

It is the truth we know, believe, and speak in authority that will set you free.

LIFE: Let us put our faith and trust in God and face the giant with God's Word in a relationship and confidence, knowing the power of our God will deliver. See Exodus 14:5-31; 2 Samuel 22:2-4; Psalm 18:1-3.

CONFESSIONS ON RIGHTEOUSNESS

"In thy name shall they rejoice all the day: and in thy righteousness shall they be exalted." —Psalm 89:16

TRUTH AND LIFE: In the resurrected Christ...I am forgiven of all sins, cleansed, and made free. See Mark 3:28; Acts 13:38-39.

- I am freed from all guilt, innocent, chosen, approved, and favored because of the Blood of Jesus. See Hebrews 10:22; Ephesians 1:4.
- I am the righteousness of God in Christ Jesus. God loves me because Jesus is my righteousness. See 2 Corinthians 5:21; 1 John 4:19.
- Jesus loves me perfectly, and I'm acceptable to Him. See Ephesians 1:6.
- I am God's beloved; He loves me as He loves Jesus. See John 17:21-23.
- I have a right relationship with God my Father through Jesus' shed Blood. See Philippians 3:9-10; 1 John 1:7, 9.
- The law of the Spirit of life in Christ Jesus hath made me free from the law of sin and death. See Romans 8:2.
- I reject the lie that my rightness with God comes from my being good with perfect performance; no, my righteousness is from the Blood of Jesus. He gave me God's love in my heart to love Him and others. See Romans 5:5, 19.
- I receive God's grace through faith and His righteousness (love) which gives me the eternal life of God. See Romans 4: 17, 21.
- Jesus loves me. I assure my heart to trust the Father's help never to doubt His love. See John 3:16; Psalm 27:3-5; Romans 8:31-39.
- God's love deposited in my heart, full of power in the anointing the Greater One drives out all fear. See Romans 5:5; 1 John 2:27; 2 Timothy 1:7.
- I am righteous, loved by God, one spirit with Him raised and seated in Christ in the heavenlies far above all evil. See Ephesians 1:3, 16-23.
- His Spirit, the Anointing in me, is greater than any force of darkness on the outside — greater than Satan the accuser, greater than fear, greater than sickness, greater than lack, greater than all the hosts of hell. My God is greater than all. See 1 John 4:4; Psalm 34:15, 17.

GOD'S RIGHTEOUS STANDARD

"But after that faith is come, we are no longer under a schoolmaster." —Galatians 3:25

TRUTH: Some people try to love God or be Christians by religiosity, seeking to obey the Ten Commandments as a list of do's and don'ts without regard for what the Blood of Jesus accomplished. Some believe only the New Testament of grace is acceptable because the Law has become obsolete. Neither of these two positions is correct for the church. The Law is good and holy, but grace through faith is the standard of righteousness God accepts. It is willing obedience to His love that God requires for the church and believers to yield to the leading of His Spirit of love. See Ephesians 2:8; Romans 3 and 4; Romans 13:8-10; John 13:34-35; Philippians 2:13.

While on earth, Jesus began to introduce the New Covenant by preaching the sermon on the Mount in Matthew 5. He showed a new way to follow God that required a new heart and living a completely new life in Christ. Under the New Covenant of grace, God needed and commanded a love relationship through Jesus Christ—not religious rules, not a list of do's and don'ts in works, and not permissiveness. See Romans 6:1-3. To the person who chooses any of these as their standard of righteousness, as their way of loving God, He will say, *"I never knew you; depart from me, ye workers of iniquity"* (Matthew 7:23). It is our faith in God's grace, our trust in His Word, and being led by the Holy Spirit willingly into obedience to God that will keep us out of religiosity. When we look to Jesus and the Cross, we must realize how much we need Him, be grateful, humble ourselves, turn to God in faith, believe in Jesus, receive Him, surrender and worship Him.

LIFE: Belief in Jesus, God's grace who makes us forgiven, cleansed, righteous and acceptable to Himself. God's standard of righteousness is our love in relationship with Himself and others. See John 13:34-35. On encountering Jesus, we are persuaded to follow and obey Him. Christ is indeed our life as His Spirit leads us. Meditate on Colossians 3:1-4.

GOD'S RIGHTEOUS STANDARD — DAY 2

"...We are no longer under a schoolmaster." —Galatians 3:25

TRUTH: God gave the Law to Moses, which remained in effect until Jesus came. God gave the Ten Commandments for His people to obey both as worship to Him and as a means of maintaining holiness among them. The Israelites couldn't obey the Law because of their sinful hearts and unwillingness to yield fully. See Psalm 51:5; Acts 7:53. Jesus came and fulfilled all the Law by obeying it and ended the Law as a standard of our righteousness. He did not make the Law obsolete, only unnecessary for us to follow as rules. See Galatians 3:11-26; Matthew 5:17-18; Romans 10:4.

Moses, living under and obeying the Law, achieved holiness enough to experience God in such a glorious way that his face shone with God's glory. As the church who are born again with God's Spirit and His righteousness living within our hearts, how much more can we receive more grace upon grace. And as we continually depend on God by the Holy Spirit, He will cause us to experience His glory, peace, deliverance, provision, protection, and power to minister to ourselves and others. See 2 Corinthians 3:6-18. In Acts 21:26, Paul knew he did not have to obey the Law, but he did because it helped minister to others spiritually weaker than himself. See Matthew 7:12; Acts 21.

LIFE: Instead of the Law being obsolete, God said the Law is holy, good, and acceptable anytime it is used legitimately. See 1 Timothy 1:8; 1 Corinthians 9:20-23; Galatians 3:24. The Law can still be used to lead a sinner to Christ when using God's love shown in John 3:16 doesn't persuade a person or help a weaker believer remain in Christ, but it cannot be the church's standard of righteousness. It must be set aside to reveal God's grace, in His goodness, mercy, and love given in Jesus Christ His Son by His Holy Spirit in His covenant of love. God's covenant of grace fills us with His love equipping us to enjoy loving relationships with God Himself and others.

POWER OF THE CROSS

"For the preaching of the cross is to them that perish foolishness; but unto us which are saved it is the power of God." —1 Corinthians 1:18

TRUTH AND LIFE: At this time of the year, we celebrate the crucifixion and resurrection of our Lord and Savior Jesus Christ, and we celebrate the power of the Cross to save and deliver humanity. The Cross destroyed the power of Satan and sin and provided for our salvation in forgiveness and righteousness. We were also given faith to access the Kingdom of God and the Kingdom of heaven. See Romans 14:17; Revelation 21:27. The Cross gave us power in the Gospel, the Word of God, the name of Jesus, and the Blood of Jesus. See Romans 1:16-17; 1 Corinthians 1:18; 2 Timothy 3:16; Philippians 2:9-10; Revelation 12:11. The Cross has the power to change, to bless and prosper us. We have been given all spiritual blessings in heavenly places in Christ Jesus to meet our every earthly need. See Ephesians 1:3; 1 Peter 1:2-4.

The power of the Cross made us a brand-new species of spiritual beings, one spirit with God through Jesus in a relationship for mutual benefit to believe, receive, and spread the gospel and the love of God. See Ephesians 2:10; Mark 16:15-18. We have been given a New Covenant of God's love with forgiveness in His grace; we do not live by strict obedience to the Law with threats of punishment with failure. See Hebrews 8:6. The Cross defeated Satan and gave us power over him, sin, death, and the Law. See Luke 10:18-19; Romans 6:14.

The resurrection of Jesus Christ gave us eternal life and raised us to be seated at the right hand of the Father, where we were made alive with Him, imputed His victory, and made unmovable in faith. See 1 Corinthians 15:57-58; Ephesians 1:3. We rest in Christ Jesus as Lord, and every evil must bow to His presence in us. See Philippians 2:9-11. The resurrected Jesus was the first to preach the gospel. See Luke 24:13-32. The resurrection is central to the Gospel as the only religion with a living, divine leader. See Romans 1:4. Jesus' faith in the Cross gave us power in our faith and authority over Satan and death, ensuring our place in eternity. Let us always first look to the Cross and its power for eternal life, walk out our salvation, and prosper in our everyday lives. See Philippians 2:12; 3 John 2. Embrace the Cross; receive Jesus, for He is the only way, the truth, and true life of victory.

CHRIST IS MY LIFE

"He restoreth my soul." —Psalm 23:3

TRUTH: God through Jesus is in the restoration and reconciliation business. He can take what is dead, broken, stagnant, lifeless, and impossible in your life and bring restoration. In Ezekiel 37, the Lord was with the prophet and took him to the valley of dry bones, where he saw only death and degradation surrounding him. The Lord caused him to walk around in the valley to see the hopelessness and lifelessness, what seems like only death and the end of all things. But God did not allow him to despair.

God spoke and told him to prophesy and speak life to those dry bones. Ezekiel obeyed, and *"there was a noise, and behold a shaking, and the bones came together, bone to his bone...the sinews and flesh came upon them, and the skin covered them above... and the breath came upon them, and they lived and stood upon their feet"* See Ezekiel 37:4-10.

Let us spend time with Jesus in a relationship, fellowship, and worship; look to Him and hear His Word to us. Listen and obey. Jesus is our perfection; as we believe His Word by faith, prophesy, and speak the Word given to us, He will perfect that seemingly hopeless situation concerning us and let the Word of life in Christ Jesus bring restoration and new life.

God came to earth in the flesh as Jesus to walk among us, to show us how to live in His eternal life of power. Jesus lived in perfect obedience to God the Father, and He brought life to the world. In this demonstration with Ezekiel, God shows us how to yoke with Him through Jesus in love and obedience, hear, speak His Word in faith, and let Him by His Spirit bring life to us just as He did the dry bones.

LIFE: Christ's life in you will change death to life, sickness to health, darkness to light, torment to peace, fear to faith in His love and care, a spirit of heaviness to joy and defeat to victory. Christ is the actual reality of your life. Choose Him, relax and let Him work on your behalf.

Meditate on Ezekiel 36:26-28; John 1:4; 5:24, 26; Acts 17:28; 1 John 5:11-12.

NEW CREATION DIRECTION

"O Lord, I know that the way of man is not in himself: it is not in man that walketh to direct his steps." —Jeremiah 10:23

TRUTH: In the garden, man chose to be self-directed when he decided to disobey God. Humanity ever since has tended toward walking this path of self-righteousness, self-reasoning, and self-dependence, usually relying on self-help techniques to fix themselves. See Ecclesiastes 1:14. Paul had to correct the Galatians who began in God's grace but returned to the Law with religion and self-effort instead of maintaining the relationship and real life in Christ Jesus. See Galatians 3, 4; Ephesians 3:6; Colossians 1:12; Psalms 5:12; 37:23.

Man tries hard, even working several jobs at once, speaking proudly of this attempt to direct their own lives, achieve, remain in control, and make sure they can sustain themselves. In the eyes of the world, this is very noble. Some people look to the world and its opinion or the government for their direction. The world says more is better—more money, more pleasure, more education, more promotion, more power will supposedly satisfy. However, these are temporary fixes that can and will still leave man dissatisfied.

Because the Word of God says, *"The Lord looked down from heaven upon the children of men, to see if there were any that did understand, and seek God"* (Psalm 14: 2).

LIFE: I am a partaker of God's divine nature, on a new path, directed to receive His love and promises, which by faith guarantees a new inheritance in Christ Jesus filled with His grace and favor. Turn away from self-effort to dependence on God and faith in Jesus. Turn from depending on your power to relying on His power by the Holy Spirit working on your behalf in all things and all situations. God will make you feel loved and cared for, joyful, provided for, and protected by the power of Christ in you. He is the hope of your glory to ensure that you stand in authority and gain His victory. Meditate on Philippians 1:19.

NEW CREATION BEING

"Therefore, if any man be in Christ, he is a new creature: old things are passed away: behold all things are become new." —2 Corinthians 5:17

TRUTH: As a new creation we are the children of God, embodied with the Spirit of God within, full of eternal life, innocent, righteous, and qualified to enter our Father's presence by faith whenever we choose. We now possess the keys to the Kingdom of God which, gives us access to relationships and blessings from the Father through Jesus Christ His Son, *"In whom are hid all the treasures of wisdom and knowledge"* (Colossians 2:3).

LIFE: New creation Scriptures – "Who am I in Christ." Confess these over yourself often until you see yourself as God recreated you to be in your born again spirit. See your identity in Him as the real you. - Ephesians 1-3.

- Made new – Jeremiah 31:3; 1 Corinthians 1:30.
- Adopted – Galatians 4:5-6; Ephesians 2:19.
- Chosen, loved and accepted – Ephesians 1:4; 2:15, 16-18; 3:6; 1 Peter 2:9.
- I am filled with power, love, and a sound mind – 2 Timothy 1:7; Romans 8:11.
- The righteousness of God – 2 Corinthians 5:17,21; Ephesians 4:24.
- Justified and innocent – Romans 3:24; 5:1.
- Dead to sin, alive unto God – Romans 6:2.
- We are delivered from vain imaginations – 2 Corinthians 10:4-5; Philippians 4:8.
- A new creation and partaker of God's promises – Ephesians 3:6; Colossians 1:12.
- Raised and seated in heavenly places – Ephesians 1:3; 2:6.
- Have new access to God the Father in relationship grace through faith into all spiritual blessings and His resurrection power – Hebrews 10:20; Ephesians 1:3, 19-20.
- More than a conqueror – Romans 8:37.
- Who can do all things through Christ- Philippians 4:13.
- An overcomer by the Blood of Jesus — 1 John 5:4-5; Revelation 12:11.

PUT OFF THE OLD MAN

"That ye put off concerning the former conversation the old man, which is corrupt according to the deceitful lusts." —Ephesians 4:22

TRUTH: Ephesians 4, starting with verses 1-3, tells us that we should walk worthy in our calling as Christians, empowered by the fruit of the Spirit with the results of unity and peace. We are one spirit living as one body in Christ because we have the same Heavenly Father.

We must put off the old man because we are forgiven of all sins. First, acknowledge that our old self died with Christ on the Cross, and we are dead to sin. Sin no longer has dominion over us, and we do not have to sin. See Romans 6; Ephesians 1:7. Because we are born again, the Word of God said we are not to walk as those left in the world of sin, having a carnal mindset, with no understanding of the life of God in us requiring holiness. Those in the world have not yet put off uncleanness, greed, lying, anger, stealing, foul speaking, bitterness, wrath, unforgiveness, and malice.

The power of Christ in us, if we let Him, will keep the old man dead. And if carnal behaviors are found among believers, they must be put off. We do that by first recognizing the truth Jesus spoke about the old man, that he is dead and that he remains dead as we continually live a surrendered life, daily putting the flesh to death and choosing to live by the power of the Holy Spirit with forgiveness, repentance, and self-control. See Ephesians 4:20-24; John 14; 1 Corinthians 9:27; 1 John 1:9.

LIFE: Repent by believing the truth of the Word and be sorrowful for your sin. Romans 10:9-10; 1 John 1:8-10. Be joyful and rejoice in God's grace and mercy in that Jesus died to provide your ability to receive forgiveness and new life. Remember, the Old Testament saints were stoned to death for some of the sins we commit today. So, by the power of God's Word, renew your mind and live from your new heart where Christ lives. As you yield, repent, forgive, exercise self-control, and speak the Word in authority, God will make Christ your life by the power of His Spirit. Meditate on Galatians 2:20.

PUT OFF THE OLD MAN — DAY 2

*"That ye put off concerning the former conversation, the
old man which is corrupt..."* —Ephesians 4:22

TRUTH: As it concerns our weaknesses of the old man, recognize them and give them to God as care. See 1 Peter 5:7. Take your place seated in Christ, claiming His victory to help you overcome. See Ephesians 1:16-23; Acts 17:28.

Meditate on the Word. For unforgiveness/forgiveness, greed/giving, anger/meekness, and peace. Let these Scriptures cause you to believe in your heart and be willing to submit your human will to Christ's Word while casting down the voice of the enemy. Trust God to work on your behalf to cause you to become strong.

Find Scriptures teaching the opposite virtue to your problem. Ask the Holy Spirit to alert you and help you first recognize and then resist any attack from the devil to live like the old man of the past. Pray and ask your Father to remove those weaknesses or sins from your life by His grace. Look to your Father, through Jesus His Son, by the power of the Holy Spirit, fully expecting Him to work the death of Christ in you, to keep you and to help you, as you yield and seek to follow Him. See 1 Corinthians 9:27; Philippians 1:6; 2:13; 1 Peter 1:5.

When temptations come to fall back into the old pattern of living, obey Hebrews 4:16 and run to your Father and say, *"Father give me the grace to overcome this temptation in Jesus's name."* If you have sinned, still run to your Father, repent, and ask for His mercy in forgiveness and for His help to keep going forward and to keep you from falling again. See Philippians 1:6; Jude 24.

LIFE: *"And that, knowing the time, that now it is high time to awake out of sleep: for now is our salvation nearer than when we believed. The night is far spent, the day is at hand: let us therefore cast off the works of darkness and let us put on the armor of light"* (Romans 13:11-12).

PUT ON THE NEW MAN

"And that ye put on the new man, which after God is created in righteousness and true holiness." —Ephesians 4:24

TRUTH: Although we have looked separately at putting off the old man and putting on the new man, they are to be done simultaneously. Put off by being dead to sin, self, Satan, and the Law and put on by being alive or freed unto God by growing in His Word, Spirit, and His love. When we believe in Jesus, we are clothed with His resurrection power in our hearts, the same power which raised Him from the grave with the eternal life of God. We have Jesus' righteousness, the newness of life in His love when His Spirit enters our hearts. See John 13:34-35; Romans 6:11; 5:5; Galatians 5:22-23.

"And if Christ be in you, the body is dead because of sin: but the Spirit is life because of righteousness" (Romans 8:10).

Jesus, by exchange took our sin and gave us His righteousness, His right standing of a love relationship with the Father, making us loved and accepted. Ephesians 4 admonishes us to remember that we have been given grace in the power of the Holy Spirit to help us to put on Christ. That is to renew our minds and to think God's thoughts, cast down the enemy's thoughts, speak God's Words, and walk by faith in His commandment to love as Jesus loves. Further, God gave us apostles, prophets, evangelists, pastors, and teachers to help us mature in Christ, and away from unrighteousness or sin and unto righteousness, holiness, and power of Christ's life in us. See Ephesians 4:7-8, 11- 32.

LIFE: *"And have put on the new man, which is renewed in knowledge after the image of him that created him. Where there is neither Greek nor Jew, circumcision nor uncircumcision, Barbarian, Scythian, bond nor free but Christ is all, and in all"* Put on therefore as the elect of God, holy and beloved, bowels of mercies, kindness, humbleness of mind, meekness, longsuffering forbearing one another ... (Colossians 3:10-13).

PUT ON THE NEW MAN — DAY 2

*"And that ye put on the new man, which after God is
created in righteousness..."* —Ephesians 4:24

TRUTH: God desires we put on the Word and the fruit of the Spirit of love, joy, peace, patience, gentleness, goodness, faith, meekness, and self-control (Galatians 5:22); righteousness, peace, and joy in the Holy Ghost (Romans 14:17); power, love and a sound mind (2 Timothy 1:7). As we depend on Jesus by the power of the Holy Spirit, the Word of God, and the ministry from fellow brothers and sisters led by the Spirit, we will hear from and be led by God. His life will lead us into the newness of His eternal life, walking in the Spirit and not in the flesh. We must also be aware that we have an enemy, Satan, who will do his best to prevent us. But we have the authority to cast him down and overcome him. See Luke 10:19; 2 Corinthians 10:4-5; Philippians 2:9-11.

The new man living in the newness of life knows they are righteous, loved, accepted, approved, and qualified to enter and fellowship in our Father's presence at any time because of the shed Blood of Jesus. We see ourselves as His workmanship, the recreated new creation being in Christ, heirs to all God's blessings, raised and seated with Christ, anointed and qualified to love as He loves and to do the works of Jesus. You have a brand-new start with a brand-new life, placed in a brand-new family, headed by a brand-new Father with a brand-New Covenant of love led by the Spirit of Love, the Spirit of Jesus Christ Himself; so, follow Him. See John 13:34; Galatians 5:22; Romans 8:14.

"And no man putteth new wine into old bottles; else the new wine will burst the bottles, and be spilled, and the bottles shall perish. But new wine must be put into new bottles; and both are preserved" (Luke 5:37-38).

LIFE: Meditate on these Scriptures: Colossians 3:10-14; Romans 13:13-14; Ephesians 6:11; 1 Peter 2:2; John 17:17; Titus 2:14; Hebrews 12:14.

HIS WORKMANSHIP

"For we are His workmanship, created in Christ Jesus unto good works, which God hath before ordained that we should walk in them." —Ephesians 2:10

TRUTH: Many times, we perceive ourselves by the negative thoughts we have of ourselves, other people and those the devil projects into our minds. At times, much of what we believe are the enemy's lies, reducing us to live a struggling, defeated life, leading to condemnation.

Those who live by the dictates of self, Satan, the flesh, and the world live by their senses, and the impulses of their situation or environment and live below God's creative workmanship in them.

But that is not God's best for us. He says we are His workmanship. Here, the Greek word for workmanship is poiema, meaning masterful creativity or masterpiece. Each believer is created perfect in God, purposefully and intentionally, with a destiny that only God Himself can accomplish in you. See Jeremiah 29:11.

You are not flawed, weak, sin-stained, incapable of getting it right, or incapable of being all God says you are in the Scriptures. And as the body of Christ, we should not allow Satan or others to cause us to focus so much on sin, the avoidance of sin, or on self so that we forget we are God's workmanship created anew and are new creatures in Christ Jesus and kept by His grace. See 1 Peter 1:5.

LIFE: You and I are made new when we were made one in God in our human spirit. We were fashioned by His Word and the work of the Cross. We must accept that the life of Christ, the Greater One in us, raised us as His workmanship, His new creation seated with Christ in victory. Whatever we face in life always begin to see the situation seated from this place of victory. We are His victorious masterpieces. Jesus is the only answer for true success. Let's put Jesus on display by our love for Him and one another. And as we share the Gospel and God's blessings in Christ Jesus we show forth as His workmanship and masterpieces a people living our best life. Meditate on John 17: 11-12.

HIS WORKMANSHIP — DAY 2

"For we are his workmanship created in Christ Jesus..." —Ephesians 2:10

TRUTH: We are created new, His workmanship with new life in Christ.

- God's grace saves me through faith in Jesus, as I believe (Ephesians 2:8).
- I am God's workmanship, made new and loved (Jeremiah 31:3; 1 Corinthians 1:30).
- I am loved, accepted, holy, and without blame before God (1 John 4:19; Colossians 1:22).
- The triumph and exaltation of Christ ensure my victory, and I shall not be moved into sin, sickness, or destruction (Psalms 16:8; 112:7).
- I am a chosen child, to a forever Father (Ephesians 1:4; 1 Peter 2:9).
- I have the mind of Christ, and I will not live a discouraged life. I will lift Jesus high and exalt His name forever (1 Corinthians 2:16).
- I am delivered from the powers of darkness into Christ's light. I will let His light continually guide me into truth and life (John 8:12; Colossians 1:13-14).
- God loves me as His child. I will trust with childlike faith (1 John 3:1-2).
- I am an overcomer by the Blood and have victory in Christ (Revelation 12:11).

LIFE: Each person must see yourself as God sees you and let faith in His opinion of you lift you into heavenly places, thinking on things above, the eternal things in Christ Jesus. Focus on Jesus, not evil; the goodness of God, not His wrath; the presence of God in all things and situations, not His absence; the benefits of trials, not the trouble; the love of God to keep and care for you, not the fear that He won't. Focus on crossing over into light and life, not lingering in the darkness. Lift your head high; you are a masterpiece created to live by faith in God's love and doing good works because Christ is your life. Let us begin to act like it.

NAAMAN

"Would God my Lord were with the prophet ...for he would recover him of his leprosy." —2 Kings 5:3

TRUTH: Naaman was a Gentile commander of the army of the king of Syria, a great leader and highly respected, but he suffered from leprosy. He mistakenly heard that Israel's king could help. When he went to the king, he could not help; and the king tore his robe, declaring he was not God. Elisha, the man of God, heard and sent for Naaman because indeed there was a prophet in Israel to help. May the time return soon in the body of Christ when people in need once again seeks out the church and the people of God, who can bring Christ into any situation needing healing or deliverance. See Mark 16:17.

Naaman went to Elisha, but he was met by a messenger to go wash in the river Jordan seven times. Pride got the better of him, and he was angry because possibly he was not offered healing fitting to the status he felt he deserved. However, his servants reasoned with him until he submitted to do as Elisha instructed, and he was healed.

When he saw the greatness and the glory of God in his healing, he went back to Elisha. He confessed, "Behold n*ow I know that there is no God in all the earth, but in Israel... henceforth offer neither burnt offerings nor sacrifices unto other gods, but unto the Lord"* (2 Kings 5: 15-17).

LIFE: Jesus told us we must be like little children to enter the kingdom of heaven. See Matthew 18:3. Likewise, we must humble ourselves as Naaman did, both to receive salvation and to successfully prosper in good health and to be blessed in our daily Christian life. See 3 John 2. We must forsake pride, our way, religion, or legalism's way of works and choose God's way of grace through faith depending on His power. His way given us in His love, for healing, or deliverance.

Teach me Your way of humility, Jesus and help me to follow. Amen.

"Teach me to do thy will; for thou art my God: thy Spirit is good; lead me into the land of uprightness" Psalm 143:10.

NEW CREATION BENEFITS

*"The Lord had said to Abram...And in thee shall all families
of the earth be blessed."* —Genesis 12:1-3

TRUTH: Every promise God gave to Abram, as a believer, we can also inherit because in Christ we are Abraham's seed. See Galatians 3:29. Believers are blessed in our spirit with all spiritual blessings. See Ephesians 1:3; 1 Peter 1:3. Every blessing we will ever need is in Christ Jesus and can be obtained by faith.

Benefits and Privileges:

- To have a Father who loves us with unfailing love (1 Corinthians 13).
- Sins forgiven, guilt and condemnation removed (John 3:16-17).
- Given gifts (Romans 10:9-10; 1 Corinthians 12: 1-12; Galatians 5:22).
- Spiritual blessings: healing and protection (Ephesians 1:3; Psalm 91).
- We are the "just" and made to live by faith (Galatians 3:11).
- We are helped to obey God's commands (John 3:34; Philippians 2:13).
- We are to be cheerful givers (Luke 6:38).
- Holy Spirit dominated - we are led by Him (Romans 8: 14).
- There is no condemnation as we walk in the Spirit (Romans 8:1-2).
- New relationship walking in the Spirit not the flesh (Galatians 5:16).
- Heirs and joint-heirs as new creation beings (Romans 8:17).
- A new heart of righteousness with eternal life (John 17:17).
- We can be transformed into our Father's image by the Word (Romans 12:1-2).
- We bless and curse not (Romans 13:14).
- Made righteous to reign in life through Jesus (Romans 5:17).

LIFE: Each believer must seek to know Your God, who made you a new creation being. Your salvation is just the beginning. Become familiar with the new person you are in Christ. Know your status, position, or standing in Christ, your privileges and benefits, and by faith and grow and transform into the image of your Father seen in the love and Word of His Son, Jesus. You can then, by faith, consciously receive and release God's power to those with whom you come into contact and those who need Christ and His life of blessing flowing through you.

CHRIST IN YOU

"To whom God would make known what is the riches of the glory of this mystery among the Gentiles; which is Christ in you, the hope of glory."—Colossians 1:27

TRUTH: A born again believer must acknowledge that Christ lives within his heart by God's spirit and is made a new creation. Christ is in you by His Spirit, and He is the controlling factor in your life. For believers, God's Spirit should now wholly dominate our lives. We are full of the fullness of the Godhead bodily, complete in Christ Jesus to live new lives of faith and power. See Colossians 2:9-10.

The first sign that God is in you is knowing that you are His child as the Spirit gives witness. See Romans 8:15-16. The Spirit of God indwells us with the love of God. See John 14:6-17; Romans 5:5. The love of God deposited in the anointing produces sanctification and transformation of our character from selfishness unto love, the very nature of Christ within. See John 17:17; Philippians 1:6. Secondly, He provides power to do the work of God. See Acts 1:8.

"Beloved, *now are we the sons of God... but we know that, when he shall appear, we shall be like him: for we shall see him as he is"* (1 John 3:2).

Acknowledge you're new on the inside because of Christ. There is nothing you cannot be or do, nothing you cannot overcome, and no one you need to fear because the Greater One lives in you. See 1 John 4:4.

LIFE: You are in Christ, one spirit with the Father, Jesus, and the Holy Spirit. You are aligned with God, delivered from the kingdom of darkness into the kingdom of light, Colossians 1:13; 1 Corinthians 6: 17-20. You are dead to sin and alive unto God in righteousness seated at the right hand of God in Christ. See Romans 6; Ephesians 1:3. The Holy Spirit will work both Jesus' death and His life in you. Christ in you is not only love but holiness and power in the anointing to overcome all because Jesus by His Spirit in you is Lord and is greater than all. See Isaiah 10:27; 1 John 2:27; Philippians 2:9-11.

CHRIST IN YOU — DAY 2

"...Christ in you the hope of glory." —Colossians 1:27

TRUTH AND LIFE: Let us make this personal. We are sons and daughters of the Most High. We have His DNA. Christ in you guarantees that you belong to God and that you have an inheritance and a destiny in Him. See Ephesians 1:13; John 14:2-3.

Christ in you is God's love deposited which gives, covers, lifts, heals, provides, and leads us in a relationship by His Spirit. Christ in you is the wisdom, the very mind, and ways of God to lead you into all truth. See Romans 8:14. Christ in you is the Comforter who will never leave you. See John 14:16-18; Hebrews 13:5. Your life is hidden in Christ, and He becomes your righteousness, your right standing before the Father, making you loved and accepted. He is your all in all. Christ in you is the; Anointing to take authority over the devil, to lead you into all truth and deliver you from your enemies. See Isaiah 10:27; Psalm 91; Romans 5:17.

As the body of Christ, Jesus dwells in us; and He rules and reigns by His Spirit. We have been bought with the price of the Precious Blood of Jesus. We are no longer our own. We are to surrender our human will to God to be led by His Word and His Spirit and are not to continue living by our self-directed efforts. When He speaks, we yield and obey because we trust in Him and His goodness and delight to do His will.

Christ in us causes us to reverence our body as His temple and purify our hearts. See Romans 12:1-2; 1 Corinthians 6:19-20; 9:27; 10:31-33. Christ in us made us alive unto God, giving Him our hearts to keep loving us from now until all eternity. Christ in us makes us a light set upon a hill, walking in love as peacemakers, giving grace, and showing the life and love of Christ to all. Christ in you is the hope of glory who establishes us in Christ for healing, deliverance, protection, provision, peace, and glorification into eternity. We have a great hope of rest and joy awaiting us.

HOPE OF GLORY

"To whom God would make known what is the riches of the glory of this mystery among the Gentiles; which is Christ in you, the hope of glory." —Colossians 1:27

TRUTH: The mystery spoken of was the once hidden truth of Christ living in our human spirit when one is born again. This truth was revealed in the gospel, which included the Gentiles alongside the Jews into the kingdom of God. See Ephesians 3:4-7. This mystery was anticipated as the Psalms were read and God praised. See Psalms 96, 97, 98.

Moses had a close relationship with God his Father, and he asked God to show him His glory. God replied that He would show him His goodness. Since we have come to know that God's glory is manifested in His Word and His Holy Spirit, He had to reveal to Moses what could be displayed at that time, a limited aspect of Himself, the Living Word, as His goodness. See John 1: 1-14.

God's glory today manifests, also by His Spirit in Jesus, His grace, who in His goodness and mercy. See Psalm 23:6. We see His Glory when His Spirit manifests God's love in His goodness in revelation knowledge, righteousness, healing, deliverance, authority over death, and in His teaching and preaching. His glory in His mercy in repentance and forgiveness will give restoration. See Matthew 9:35; Romans 8:19-22.

LIFE: The riches of the glory is Christ indwelling us by His Spirit. God's glory by His Spirit lives in you and me. It was God's love that sent Jesus to the Cross. When we believe in Jesus, God transfers His love by His Holy Spirit into our hearts or our human spirits. He is a well of water springing up into everlasting life, for us to walk in the newness of life with the same glory which raised Jesus from the dead. Christ is our life and the hope of our glory from now until eternity. See John 4:14; Romans 5:5; 6:4.

THE HOPE OF GLORY — DAY 2

"Christ in you the hope of glory." —Colossians 1:27

TRUTH: Romans 8:11 says, *"But if the Spirit of him that raised up Jesus from the dead dwell in you, he that raised up Christ from the dead shall also quicken your mortal bodies by his Spirit that dwelleth in you."*

God's Spirit, which raised Jesus from the dead, is in us and with us. He raised us and seated and exalted us with Jesus. It took God's power to raise Jesus from the dead. When we believe in Jesus, God deposits Himself in us by His Spirit full of love and power. See Romans 8:11; Acts 1:8; 2:4. The Holy Spirit, full of power, dwells in and upon us. He will bring life not only for our self-deliverance but also for the deliverance, healing, revelation knowledge, and wisdom to those around us who are in need.

We are one spirit with God the Father. See John 14:20; 1 Corinthians 6:17. The same Spirit of God in Jesus is in us, and with Him, we can do His works and greater works. See John 14:12. Because of Christ in us, we have the hope of glory to receive all our needs as met in Jesus because, *"Greater is he that is in you, than he that is in the world"* (1 John 4:4).

LIFE: God's glory and Spirit of love and power are in you. Embrace this truth meditate on Scriptures about your oneness with God until the knowledge of the Spirit within grows. He will take His rightful place to rule and direct your soul and body in God's love and power for His glory. Take a seat within your spirit, yield your human will to Him and embrace your oneness: "I am one spirit with Jesus. He is my righteousness. My life is hidden in Him. I abide in Him, and He is my resting place. See Hebrews 4. He makes me right, and, by His stripes, power flows to me to give me healing." Do the same for lack, deliverance, and other needs, for Christ indeed is the hope of our glory.

FORSAKE SELF-RELIANCE

"Woe unto them that are wise in their own eyes, and prudent in their own sight." —Isaiah 5:21

TRUTH: The fear of the Lord is the beginning of wisdom. We do not have all the answers for ourselves, and we do not entirely understand God's ways of thinking all the time. But as believers, we are chosen and called by God to be transformed to be like Him, follow His ways, and do His will. See Proverbs 3:7-8. He has given us His Word, His pastors, and prophets, and His presence in the Holy Spirit to be led by Him. Yet, we often read the Word or hear Him speak by His Spirit to us, and we skip over it, do as we please, neglect to pay attention, and ignore. We may outright reject by saying we do not understand or feel we cannot do what is required. When we do this, we are not living by faith, but self-reliance and are exposed to Satan, sin, and fear. See Romans 14:23; Isaiah 54:14.

When we neglect Jesus and His Spirit, we have chosen to exhibit self-will, self-righteousness or self-reliance, pride in our hearts, living in our strength, which is the independence we inherited from Adam. See Proverbs 1:31-33. Following one's mind, instinct, interpretation of the Bible, emotions, and physical needs is a recipe for failure. We must surrender and yield to follow God by the leading of His Spirit. He is the One who leads us into all truth. See John 16:13. We are being deceived when we do otherwise, just as Eve was deceived in the garden. Eve did not believe God's Word to her and left a gap for Satan to come in with lies, half-truths, and deception for her to fulfill her selfish desires in her strength. Forsake self-reliance and trust God. We do this as we allow God by His Spirit to work His death in us for us to die to self, and to make us alive unto Him, filled with His love to walk by faith and not by sight.

LIFE: *"For the eyes of the Lord run to and fro throughout the whole earth, to shew himself strong in behalf of them whose heart is perfect toward him..."* (2 Chronicles 16:9). Yield to God Your Father and let Him bless you.

FORSAKE SELF-RELIANCE — DAY 2

"Woe unto them that are wise in their own eyes..." —Isaiah 5:21

TRUTH: The result of Adam and Eve's sin and being deceived brought self-reliance into man's heart. Had they foreseen the negative consequences, they would have paused and not listened to Satan. See Proverbs 16:6-7.

As believers, we must learn from their mistakes that self-reliance is pride and that independence from God will lead to disobedience and a strain on our relationship with the Father. Choose instead humility, listening, and yielding to God, depending on His Holy Spirit to save, transform, establish, lead, help and deliver. See Romans 12:16; 8:13-14.

Only by faith, not self-will, can we be sure that His righteousness by grace will work for us to bring forth the fruit of the Spirit of love, God's power, favor, and blessings. When we read or hear God's voice in the Word or our spirit, we must take the time to write it down, or we will forget and neglect to meditate and pray for God's will to be done. Therefore, we will fail to saturate our hearts with truth, the place where faith begins and will cause God's Word to come to naught. See Joshua 1:8; Matthew 13.

Repent of self-will, self-reliance, and self-interest as these lead only to death. Change self-focus to God-focus and have the life of God living in and growing through you. In righteousness and holiness, let Christ be your life and, in all things, depend on Him. Dependence on Jesus will always bring victory, just as the walls of Jericho came down when His instructions were carefully followed. See Joshua 6.

LIFE: Repent of self-will and self-righteousness and receive God's righteousness in His Word, love, and care for you. Depend on Jesus for everything. Begin to thank, praise, and worship Him. Self can be subdued, as the human will is surrendered, and Christ is exalted. Surrender your selfishness to Him and become lost in His love, mercy, beauty, and goodness. See Psalm 23.

OUR WORDS

"For by thy words thou shalt be justified, and by thy words thou shalt be condemned." —Matthew 12:37

TRUTH: God's Word tells us we are either given life and peace by our words or are destroyed by them. Words are powerful, either building up or tearing down, positive or negative. We must make a deliberate choice for them not to be negative because, as believers, this ought not to be: *"Doth a fountain send forth at the same place sweet water and bitter?"* (James 3:11). As believers, many of us struggle to keep our minds, thinking, and words aligned with God, as we know, we should. We vacillate in the blink of an eye between speaking the truth or speaking negatively. Peter had that same trouble when he declared Jesus as the Son of God with one breath and denied Him with the next. See Mark 8:29-33.

Life and death are in the tongue. See Proverbs 18:21. When we speak death, we are being destroyed. When we talk about sickness and death instead of life, when we accuse and condemn instead of praise, when we curse instead of blessing others, when we speak doubt instead of faith, if we talk fear instead of the knowledge of God's love and His promises, we attract negative results. We hinder our faith when we align with the spirit of the law of sin and death. Death comes when we give judgment, encourage gossip, display anger, allow jealousy, act in bitterness, as well as many other sins mentioned in Romans 1:29-31; 1 Corinthians 6:5-17; 2 Timothy 2:16-26; James 3:9-18. As believers, we are of God and must seek after His life in Christ Jesus. See John 6:68-69.

LIFE: Fill your thoughts and words with life, not death; quench not the Spirit. Give Him room to work the life of Christ in your life. Meditate on Proverbs 12:18; 15:4; Psalm 141:3; Matthew 5:9; Ephesians 4:30-32; 1 Corinthians 13:1-8.

OUR WORDS — DAY 2

"Let no corrupt communication proceed out of your mouth... but that which is good to the use of edifying." —Ephesians 4:29

TRUTH: Whatever thoughts and words fill our hearts will fill our mouths. See Luke 6:45. Instead of being gracious, a self-righteous heart will be critical and judgmental and stir up strife, but a peaceful heart will seek to bring peace, reconciliation, and unity. Let our thoughts, words, and actions bring life and not death. What are you reading, watching, and meditating on? Choose wisely because that is what will fill your heart, and from your heart, your mouth will speak. See Matthew 15:18-20.

When we wake up in the morning, we should declare each new day as the day which the Lord hath made we should determine to rejoice, be glad to be filled with the Holy Spirit and be ready to start anew. See Psalm 118:24. How will we rejoice? By speaking God's Word and finding joy in all His grace accomplished on the Cross for us. See Colossians 1:13-20. Be expectant; His grace is sufficient to see us through each day.

We should never let our souls, especially our minds, become bullied, entrapped, or captured by Satan into negative thinking and speaking. Be quick to assign each thought to its owner. Negative thoughts come from Satan, and life-filled Words are from God. Once you have identified the spirit behind the voice speaking, choose God's side immediately, and cast down those negative thoughts. Replace them with God's Word concerning that area, be it your health, finances, children, others...whatever. Be slow to speak and quick to listen. Deuteronomy 30:19-20; 2 Corinthians 10:4-5; Philippians 4:8-9; James 1:19.

LIFE: When negative words come out of your mouth, capture them; say, "I reverse that in Jesus' name, and I cast it down to the obedience of Christ." See 2 Corinthians 10:4-5. Then replace it with what is true in God's Word to your situation. See Philippians 4:8. Always sow blessing, offer encouragement, be kindhearted, and give grace and peace to those who hear you. The Lord will bless you as a peacemaker. Meditate Colossians 4:5-6; Matthew 5:9.

HAVE WISDOM

*"If any of you lack wisdom, let him ask of God, that
giveth to all men liberally."* —James 1:5

TRUTH: Our God is of infinite wisdom. He is omniscient, knows all things, and holds all power and truth in Himself. Nothing escapes His knowledge. He knows about each sparrow's wellbeing, the number of hairs on our heads, and what we need before asking. See Matthew 6:8.

God told us in His Word that He is faithful and true. He says that His eyes are going to and fro seeking those to bless and that when the righteous cry unto Him, He hears and delivers.

So why do we, as God's children, live and behave as if we are orphans trying to scratch out a living or fathom life on our own as if we are without a Father? See Proverbs 16:9. Jesus gave us access to the Father of wisdom in all things eternal and good. *"According as his divine power hath given unto us all things that pertain unto life and godliness, through the knowledge of him that hath called us to glory and virtue"* (2 Peter 1:3).

"He layeth up sound wisdom for the righteous: he is a buckler to them that walk uprightly" (Proverbs 2:7).

"Hear, O my son, and receive my sayings; and the years of thy life shall be many. I have taught thee in the way of wisdom; I have led thee in right paths" (Proverbs 4:10-11).

As a believer, consider yourself wise because God made you wise when you were made one with His Holy Spirit of wisdom. Christ will be our life as His Word, and His Spirit helps us to grow by faith into His wisdom, knowledge, and understanding to gain His mind and His goodness in every area of life. Embrace Him by embracing the Holy Spirit and make Him your path into His eternal life and gain wisdom. Wisdom is our path to a successful life. See 1 Corinthians 1:30; Luke 2:52.

LIFE: Meditate on Ephesians 1:16-23.

HAVE WISDOM — DAY 2

"If any man lack wisdom let him ask of God..." —James 1:5

TRUTH: We have the mind of Christ, and we can engage God's Holy Spirit living within us to gain wisdom about any situation we are facing.

As we study His Word, He can speak to us through Scripture; as we pray in the Holy Ghost, we can tap into our Father's mind, thoughts, and heart to pray out mysteries and gain His wisdom and understanding as to the way forward or the way out. See 1 Corinthians 14.

As we draw closer to the Father in the Word, prayer, fellowship, and communion, we will hear from Him to gain the wisdom of His heart and get what we need to make informed and successful decisions.

We must ask God for His mind, heart, and wisdom in every situation that concerns us. We must resist the temptation to try to figure out things on our own as we can look only at the pro and cons, while God, in His wisdom, sees the whole picture from beginning to a successful end.

The Father wants us to seek Him and maintain the relationship by staying connected in faith, fellowship, hearing, asking, speaking, believing, and receiving.

Seek relationship and the wisdom of your Father in the Word. Pray in the Holy Spirit and listen for His revealed knowledge to you as a Rhema Word. Hear, listen, follow Him and obey, and you will never fail.

"For the Lord giveth wisdom: out of his mouth cometh knowledge and understanding. He layeth up sound wisdom for the righteous: he is a buckler to them that walk uprightly" (Proverbs 2:6-7).

LIFE: Meditate on Daniel 2:16-22; Proverbs 2:1-8; James 1:5-6.

MIND OF CHRIST

"But we have the mind of Christ." —1 Corinthians 2:16

TRUTH: The Bible tells us that God in Christ Jesus made us wise. See 1 Corinthians 1:30. We have the wisdom of God in our human spirit or the inner man by the Holy Ghost. God's mind is autonomous. The Scripture says, *"Who hath directed the Spirit of the Lord. or being his counsellor hath taught him? With whom took he counsel, and who instructed him, and who taught him in the path of judgment, and taught him knowledge, and shewed to him the way of understanding?"* (Isaiah 40:13-14).

We receive from God what Jesus has given us of Him, not to direct God or give Him instructions, but for us to communicate in prayer. Abraham communicated with God and got His mind on the Sodom situation. See Genesis 18:22-23.

LIFE: Christ's mind in us...

- Is by the Holy Spirit's indwelling. See Acts 2:38.
- Is opposite to the wisdom in the mind of man having finite and limited possibilities. See 1 Corinthians 2:4-6.
- Has revelations to impart. See 1 Corinthians 2:7-12.
- Knows the supernatural things of God by the Holy Spirit and will impart them if we ask. See 1 Corinthians 2:10-12; 1 John 5:14-15.
- Compares spiritual things with spiritual because He interfaces with and understands God. See 1 Corinthians 2:13.
- Is alive when we activate our union or oneness of spirit in relationship. See 1 John 4:13.
- Is love. See John 13:34; Mathew 22:37, 39.
- Is of faith. See Hebrews 11:6; Galatians 3:11; Romans 4:17.
- Is of faith righteousness. See Romans 4:3-5; 2 Corinthians 5:21.
- Is ever present NOW. See Hebrews 11:1; Exodus 3:12-14; 16:21-27.
- Is eternal. See 2 Corinthians 4:18; Colossians 3:2-3.
- Honors the Word of God. See 1 Thessalonians 2:13; Psalm 119:10-12.

THE MIND OF CHRIST — DAY 2

"But we have the mind of Christ." —1 Corinthians 2:16

TRUTH: We can spiritually discern the mind of Christ. By God's Spirit, we have spiritual discernment of eternal things. See 1 Corinthians 2:4-15.

- The mind of Christ can be given to our mind by the ministry gift of tongues and interpretation and prophecy. See 1 Corinthians 14.
- The mind of Christ is filled with the power of God. See Romans 8:11.

When we are born again, every believer has the mind of Christ in the Holy Spirit sealed and abiding within our human spirit. See Ephesians 1:13. However, we still have the remnants of the old mindset and old ways of thinking in our natural mind in the soul realm. Our natural mind does not know everything because it is finite and tainted with remnants and memories of our old life and open access to our enemy. Therefore, to make decisions, our finite minds engage in self-reasoning, the listing of pros and cons, and the processes of elimination by answering "what if."

However, the mind of God, which knows all things and is full of wisdom, is available to us as we tap into the supernatural by faith through the Spirit of God by prayer, praying in the Holy Ghost, fasting, meditating on God, and His Word. If we listen, we will hear the mind of God. See John 1:12; Romans 5:2; 1 Corinthians 14.

"Eye hath not seen, nor ear heard, neither have entered into the heart of man, the things which God hath prepared for them that love him. But God hath revealed them unto us by his Spirit; for the Spirit searcheth all things, yea, the deep things of God. For what man knoweth the things of a man, save the spirit of man which is in him? even so the things of God knoweth no man, but the Spirit of God" (1 Corinthians 2:9-11).

LIFE: By faith, we possess the mind of Christ in our spirit. He will bless us when we believe God's Word is true and begin to depend on it for the life of Christ within to instruct and lead us into our best life. Life at its highest is only available in God, through Jesus Christ His Son and the Holy Spirit giving us His heart and mind. See Romans 8:14; Galatians 5:16.

THE MIND OF CHRIST — DAY 3

"Let this mind be in you...." —Philippians 2:5-11

TRUTH: The mind of Christ has God as a priority. See Matthew 6:33; 1 Kings 3:11-13; Psalm 84:11-12.

- The mind of Christ exalts God the Father. See 1 Corinthians 8:6; John 17:20-26; John 5:30.
- The mind of Christ is thankful. See Philippians 4:6-7; Colossians 3:15; Psalm 106:1-2.
- The mind of Christ accepts by faith trials in sanctification as a necessity for spiritual growth. See James 1:2-5; 1 John 3:2-3; Proverbs 3:12.

Although the mind of Christ is in us, we have a responsibility to cultivate and nurture and guard it with the Word of God, prayer, fellowship, and casting down imaginations, for it to grow from our spirit to influence our soul and body unto righteousness in our actions. We do that as we take the Word of God as truth and as we pray, worship, speak, believe, abide, rejoice and receive.

The Word of God is living and may come as a blessing, comfort, discipline, or the fire of sanctification. But they are all His Words from His mind, for us to take into our hearts and with the help of the Holy Spirit, let them disperse to our soul and bodies to transform us more and more into the image and likeness of Christ. So that we may show forth the beauty of our beautiful Lord and Savior. See Romans 12:1-2.

God is love, and John 13:34-35 says, *"A new commandment I give unto you, That ye love one another; as I have loved you, that ye also love one another. By this shall all men know that ye are my disciples, if ye love one another."*

LIFE: Love God and love one another, walk by faith in God's grace, always seeking to develop the character, attitudes, and actions in the mind of Christ. As believers, we must see each person through Jesus' eyes of faith and love. By God's grace and with His love, we will fulfill God's command to love from the heart, even our enemies.

HOLY SPIRIT IN PRAISE

"But thou art holy, O thou that inhabitest the praises of Israel." —Psalm 22:3

TRUTH: Praise is boasting about God our Father, exuding joy and adoration for His salvation, grace, mercy, and goodness because He gave us eternal life and all things in life to enjoy. We praise God because He is our source for all things good, and He is worthy of our worship. We sing songs of praise, boasting of His love in giving us Jesus, His greatness, His faithfulness, His infinite power and grace, the glory of His Spirit, His leading and guidance, and His wisdom. There is no end to the good things for which we can praise Him. God inhabits the praises of His people. He comes and dwells with us by His Spirit when we praise Him. So, let us praise Him! Make it personal!

LIFE: *"I will praise thee, O Lord, with my whole heart; I will shew forth all thy marvelous works. I will be glad and rejoice in thee; I will sing praise to thy name, O thou my most High"* (Psalm 9:1-2).

"I will love thee, O Lord, my strength. The Lord is my rock, and my fortress, and my deliverer; my God, my strength, in whom I will trust; my buckler, and the horn of my salvation, and my high tower. I will call upon the Lord, who is worthy to be praised" (Psalm 18:1-3).

"The Lord is my strength and my shield; my heart trusted in him, and I am helped: therefore, my heart greatly rejoiceth; and with my song will I praise him" (Psalm 28:7).

"Praise ye the Lord. O give thanks unto the Lord; for he is good: for his mercy endureth for ever" (Psalm 106:1).

HOLY SPIRIT IN PRAISE — DAY 2

"But thou are holy, O thou that inhabitest the praises of Israel." —Psalm 22:3

TRUTH AND LIFE: *"Rejoice in the Lord, O ye righteous: for praise is comely for the upright. Blessed be the Lord God the God of Israel, who only doth wondrous things. And blessed be his glorious name forever: and let the whole earth be filled with his glory; Amen"* (Psalm 33:1; 72:18-19).

"Bless the Lord, O my soul: and all that is within me, bless his holy name. Bless the Lord, O my soul, and forget not his benefits: who forgiveth all thine iniquities; who healeth all thy diseases; Who redeemeth thy life from destruction; who crowneth thee with lovingkindness and tender mercies" (Psalm 103:1-4).

"O give thanks unto the Lord, for he is good: for his mercy endureth forever. Let the redeemed of the Lord say so, whom he hath redeemed from the hand of the enemy" (Psalm 107:1-2).

"Thine, O Lord, is the greatness, and the power, and the glory, and the victory, and the majesty: for all that is in heaven and the earth is thine; thine is the kingdom, O Lord, and thou art exalted as head above all" (1 Chronicles 29:11).

"Thou art worthy, O Lord, to receive glory and honor and power: for thou hast created all things, and for thy pleasure they are and were created. Saying with a loud voice, Worthy is the Lamb that was slain to receive power, and riches, and riches, and wisdom, and strength, and honor, and glory, and blessing (Revelation 4:11; 5:12).

CAST DOWN

"Casting down imaginations, and every high thing that exalteth ...against the knowledge of God." —2 Corinthians 10:5

TRUTH: We are to cast down every thought and lie of the enemy and forget as Paul did. We are to see our past and sins forgiven as God sees and cast their memory into the depths of the sea. See Micah 7:19; Psalm 103:12. We are to give past hurts and wounds from family, friends, and spouses to the Lord and forgive as we cast down and forget. This is hard because we battle pride which the enemy fuels to keep us in turmoil, pain, bitterness, and strife. But Jesus' death on the Cross and the power of His Blood will purge our conscience from sin's effects, dead works, and cares to release the power and truth which sets us free.

To stop the enemy's negative thoughts from harming us, we recognize him early as the source. Realize how potentially destructive they are and cast them down to the obedience of Christ. This means the Word of God is the standard of our obedience, and anything which deviates us from God's Word must be cast down.

We are not to entertain the enemy by listening to what he says. Cast down and replace. See 2 Corinthians 10:4-5; Philippians 4:8. We have God's power and authority in the anointing to cast those thoughts down, forgive, and be healed from our wounds. Just as a stranger has no business disciplining our children, Satan has no place trying to correct us as God's children. Telling us, we deserve whipping for sin. We have the Word and the Holy Spirit to convict us of righteousness and lead us into truth. Reject His voice trying to convict us of sin, as it'll bring fear and condemnation. Yield only to the voice of the Holy Spirit and Jesus' righteousness as you embrace God's Word.

LIFE: When Satan tries to tell you that you are in sin and deserve punishment or torment, take authority over him and command him to leave. Declare Jesus is your righteousness. Turn to God as you seek to hear the Holy Spirit's voice and His leading into righteousness to make you free. His instruction may be for repentance, forgiveness, standing in righteousness, avoiding evil, yielding to God, or simply an apology. Just do it!

CAST DOWN — DAY 2

"Casting down imaginations, and every high thing that exalteth itself against the knowledge of God, and bringing into captivity every thought to the obedience of Christ." —2 Corinthians 10:5

TRUTH: If we do not know that all our sins are forgiven, Satan can continue to accuse us and bring on sin-consciousness and condemnation. Let us cast down every vain imagination from the enemy, speak the Word, and believe in our hearts that all our sins are cleansed. See Acts 13:38-39; Colossians 2:13; 1 John 1:7.

Secondly, know the true character of God and whom He has made us in Christ. This will protect our standing and keep us hidden in the exalted Christ. See 2 Corinthians 1:3; Ephesians 1:16-23; Hebrews 1:3. Never focus on ourselves, our feelings, or the enemy; instead, focus on Jesus and what His Blood has done for us and hold fast to our confession of His promises. This will protect us from condemnation. See Romans 8:1-2; 1 John 3:18-21; 10:10; 1 Peter 2:9.

For each person, after you repent of sin, if Satan is still nagging you with feelings of unworthiness and condemnation, call out that spirit and cast it out. Then tell him to stop his talking and go! You are dead to him, dead to sin and that evil spirit's power because of the truth in Isaiah 53:7; 54:14, 17; Revelation 12:11; and 1 John 4:4. Command every lying tongue to leave in Jesus' name. Replace every lie with the truth of God's Word. If the enemy says, you will die, cast down his lies (2 Corinthians 10:4-5), and replace them with God's Word. If sick, say, *"I shall not die, but live and declare the works of the Lord"* (Psalm 118:17).

LIFE: Stand in faith and believe God to defend and deliver you. Do not yield to Satan's negative thoughts and feelings. Cast them down and replace them with God's Word. See 1 Corinthians 15:57; Romans 8:37. As you arise and stand in God's resurrection power, victory, and strength in Christ Jesus your Lord, you will overcome. You win!

FORGET WHAT IS BEHIND

"Brethren, I count not myself to have apprehended: but this one thing I do forgetting those things which are behind..." —Philippians 3:13

TRUTH: Life is made up of the thoughts, words, decisions, choices, and actions that we make daily. Some of these are good, and some are just bad. Often, we wish we hadn't made the bad ones in the first place. Most times, we would have preferred to forget some of them instantly. But there is a devil whose job is to steal, kill, and destroy. He makes every effort to remind us of our sins, faults, and weaknesses. He harasses us with guilt, doubt, torment, anxiety, and fear, always working hard to keep us remembering the bad stuff and keeping us in bondage to him.

Remembering and harboring negative thoughts, suggestions, emotions, and feelings from the enemy will bog us down with guilt, fear, and torment. But God has commanded us to forget those things which are behind. God knows that having a mind cluttered with negative thoughts will hinder believers from prospering and growing spiritually in their faith.

LIFE: Once you are born again, you are to repent and forget past sins and cast down thoughts of past failures, forgive offenses both past and present because Christ took sin in His own body and removed its power to harm us. Every sin starts with a thought, a suggestion, or an idea from self, others, or the devil. Cast those negatives down to the obedience of Christ. Choose God, His goodness, His mercy, His way to protect us from the evil one, Satan.

"Remember ye not the former things, neither consider the things of old. Behold I will do a new thing; now it shall spring forth" (Isaiah 43:19).

We forget as we cast our cares to Jesus, cast down imaginations, worship God and keep our minds stayed on Jesus by speaking His Word, rejoicing, and giving thanks in the situation. Also, as we pray about the situation and others, the enemy will be kept under our feet as we keep pressing forward-thinking and speaking of our great redemption in Christ. Meditate on 1 Peter 5:7; Isaiah 26:3; 1 Thessalonians 5:16-18.

FORGET WHAT IS BEHIND — DAY 2

"And reaching forth unto those things which are before." —Philippians 3:13b

TRUTH: As we forget the things of the past, we reach forth into the newness of life when we run to God with our temptations for His grace and mercy in those times of need. See Hebrews 4:16. Here God has given us a way to get His help to forget sin. (1) In obedience, we run to the Father for help to keep us from sin in times of temptation. (2) When we do sin, He has provided a way of escape for us to run to Him for mercy in repentance and forgiveness. When we receive grace to help and forgiveness and cleansing of sin, its effects can have no dominion over us. When others offend us, speak evil against us, cheat, lie, and stab us in the back, we can look to Jesus. We can forgive and forget to close the door to Satan, maintain our peace and move on in our walk with God. Jesus will, by His Spirit, help us to forget if we ask Him and receive by faith. Also, as we trust Him, He will avenge us. See Colossians 3:13-17; Hebrews 10:30.

Saul, who had letters to kill the Jews and personally supervised Stephen's death, was confronted by God to change his life's direction and heart. When God was finished dealing with him, not only was his heart changed but also his mind, his name, his direction, and his purpose. Saul became Apostle Paul.

The change in his life caused him to see himself just as God said about him being a new creature; he forgot his past and said, *"Receive us; we have wronged no man, we have corrupted no man, we have defrauded no man"* (2 Corinthians 7:2). Paul chooses to forgive, forget and restore, beginning with himself. He overcame his past and was then able to tell us that it must be done.

LIFE: Paul was a doer of the Word. He obeyed God and forgot His past by leaving old things behind and went on to be a significant minister of the gospel of God's grace, sharing His goodness, love, and power to all. Secondly, he obeyed 1 Thessalonians 5:18 that in all things, which is in every situation he found himself, he gave thanks and worshipped God. Let us follow Paul as he followed Christ. See Acts 16:16-31.

THE KINGDOM MINDSET

"And exhorting them to continue in the faith, and that we must through much tribulation enter the kingdom of God." —Acts 14:22

TRUTH AND LIFE: The kingdom of God is righteousness, peace, and joy in the Holy Ghost. The kingdom is within as the Spirit of God in us confirms we are children of God. As children of God, when we humble ourselves to the Father and receive His righteousness in His love, we can then be thankful for all the great things Jesus did to justify us by faith. His love gives us peace. Having His peace in our hearts and minds and peace with others will fill us with joy. We can then rejoice in Christ Jesus, the captain of our salvation, and live a righteous lifestyle in the kingdom by the power of His Spirit.

As we live by the Word, our right thinking and right words demonstrate our love for God, leading to the right actions. Love always does the right thing. The kingdom of God is righteousness, God's love, which leads to peace and joy in the Holy Spirit because He helps us do the right thing even in trials. See Romans 14:17; 13:8-10. Romans 5:3 says, *"...knowing that tribulation worketh patience: and patience, experience, and experience, hope."*

Humility is a primary virtue in the kingdom. In Numbers 12, Miriam and Aaron opposed Moses as the leader, and God struck Miriam with leprosy. Moses pleaded with the Lord, and He gave her a time-out for seven days. She was prideful instead of humble, and the Lord allowed her to go through the fire to humble her heart.

Another kingdom mindset is esteeming others better than ourselves. Philippians 2:3 says we must humble ourselves, putting others' needs before our own. This is the kingdom mindset of God's grace in Jesus, giving His life for us and empowering us as His people to live in faith, love, humility, patience, and forgiveness. God's virtues empower us to be conquerors in the kingdom of God. See Galatians 5:22; Mark 11:22-25; James 1:3-4.

THE KINGDOM MINDSET — DAY 2

*"And that we must through much tribulation enter
into the Kingdom of God."* —Acts 14:22b

TRUTH AND LIFE: In the kingdom, it takes much dying to self and suffering in the flesh to give up on pride in the heart, which must be done for a believer to master and enjoy their Christian journey. As we give up pride, we become modest instead of self-promoting; we give the benefit of the doubt to others rather than being judgmental. See Romans 12:3. The kingdom mindset values the well-being of others as and or above our own.

We love our enemies: It is painful on the flesh to love those who have hurt or even harmed us. Having the mind of Christ is choosing to die to our ways and choose Christ's. This walk is challenging but not impossible, as we saw Stephen ask God to forgive those who were stoning him to death. He prayed for their ability to receive forgiveness. See Acts 7:59-60; Acts 8. Saul, who consented to this stoning, went through the fire of tribulation himself to be converted. We are to love our enemies, as God at times uses them to agitate our fleshly nature so that we run to Him for deliverance. The processing of our character with this agitation increases our praying and sharpens our faith and trust in God.

We learn obedience: Christ Himself went through the fire at Gethsemane, sweating drops of Blood to yield His will to the Father's will of going to the Cross. For the joy set before Him, He went to the Cross. He esteemed us above Himself to accomplish God's will to establish the kingdom. Likewise, we will often suffer in the flesh to obey God. It may be to forgive, to give up the comforts of home for the jungle, to withhold judgment, to feed our enemy, or to bless those who curse us.

"Humble yourselves in the sight of the Lord, and he shall lift you up" (James 4:10). When we humble ourselves to live a kingdom life focused on Jesus, we appear to live in reverse. We die to self to live in Christ, give to receive, and increase in stature is to decrease into humility to bring forth God's glory. And as we pray for God's kingdom in heaven to come on earth, we will become more and more established in kingdom living and God's heart.

LIVING AS ONE PLEASES

*"And he turned aside to see the carcase of the lion: and
he took...went on eating." —Judges 14:8-9*

TRUTH: Samson was chosen from birth to deliver the children of Israel from the Philistines. He was blessed with enormous strength to get the job done. He was given instructions not to cut his hair, drink wine or strong drink, or eat any unclean thing. See Judges 13:4-5. But Samson was rebellious, as seen in our text; he disobeyed God and ate from a dead carcass, womanized, took revenge, vandalized other's possessions, became angry, and killed many men. When we are under assault from the enemy, we must be careful to fast and pray as he will use food to distract us or cause us to sin—as he also did with both Esau and Judas, whom he entered after he ate at the Passover. See Genesis 25:27-34; John 13:2.

Instead of living within the boundaries God gave him, Samson pushed the envelope and lived as he pleased. He allowed his passions for women, food, and drink to cause him to make bad decisions one after another. Finally, when he went to Delilah and toyed with her, playing her games, he played into her hands. He was overtaken by his enemies, bound, and his eyes were plucked out. The boundaries set by God for a believer are not to quell our passions and pleasures but to protect us from our enemy Satan, sin, and destruction. God has commanded us in John 13:34 to love, and if Samson had loved, he would not have intimately defrauded God's child and his sister, Delilah, who is made in God's image. See 1 Thessalonians 4:4-7. Samson disregarded the instructions of God and reaped the consequences as he was finally humiliated. Realizing his life was not his to live as he pleased, he turned to God in faith, and God once again, in His mercy, caused him to accomplish his destiny, but with great anguish.

LIFE: Let us learn from Samson and yield early to God's Word, the spiritual boundaries, and the conviction of His Holy Spirit. He will protect us from destruction and give us a fruitful life with no added sorrows. We will reap what we sow, so sow seeds of humility, yieldedness, obedience, and reap God's blessings. See Proverbs 10:22; Galatians 6:7.

DRINKING ALCOHOL

"It is not for kings to drink wine; nor for princes strong drink. Lest they drink, and forget the law, and prevent the judgment of any of the afflicted" —Proverbs 31:4-5

TRUTH: Drinking alcohol has become a severe problem in our society, especially among young people falling prey to strong drinks. Even Christians are being seduced into social drinking.

When drunk people are arrested, they are charged with DUI driving under the influence. So, the question first and foremost is, whose influence should a Christian be under? Gods' or of alcohol? Deuteronomy 30:19-20 tells us that God has set before us life and death, blessing and cursing, and for us to choose life, that our children and we may live. What does alcohol give to a believer, life or death? *"For to be carnally minded is death: but to be spiritually minded is life and peace"* (Romans 8: 6). The question to be answered is, does drinking alcohol for pleasure satisfy a carnal or spiritual need? 1 Timothy 3:3; 5:23.

There are only two forces in this world—God for love, life, and godliness or Satan for sin, death, and lawlessness. Christianity is about allegiance, and as Christians, our allegiance must be for God; it cannot be a mixture of the spiritual and the carnal together. This is spiritual adultery. See Genesis 21:9-21. We can even say there is no rule in the New Testament that forbids drinking strong drinks, but God did not call us as the New Testament church to live by rules; instead, we are to live by His grace through faith depending on His Spirit. Did you ask Him what is right for you? Let the Holy Spirit lead you into His truth for you. See John 2:1-12; Galatians 5:1-16; 1 Corinthians 6:11-20.

LIFE: We can choose the "fruit of the Spirit" (Galatians 5:22), or can we select "wine and spirits" (Isaiah 28:7). Our life must be a clear choice for God, one that leads to a life of peace and victory, or you can ignore God and choose the world, a path that can lead to fear, frustration, and death. Choose you this day whom you will serve. Choose Jesus and choose life. Stay in God's Word and His presence until He removes every desire not of Him. Meditate on Deuteronomy 30:19-20.

PRAYING MOTHERS

*"Lo, children are an heritage of the Lord, and the fruit
of the womb is his reward."* —Psalm 127:3

TRUTH: Mothers are a great blessing from the Lord to take care of the family. A Mother's great responsibility is to nurture, care, protect, train, teach morals and integrity, and to be examples for our children growing up with the image of God in their hearts. Above all, mothers are prayer warriors for our children. See Deuteronomy 6:6-8; Jeremiah 31:17. Pray for them in these areas:

- General—Psalm 115:14; Proverbs 11:21; 20:7; Isaiah 54:13-14; 61:9.
- Protection—Psalms 18:1-2; 32:7; 46:10-11; 107:20; Psalm 91; Zechariah 2:5.
- School/grades/confidence—1 Kings 4:29; Daniel 1:4, 7; Daniel 2:21-23; Proverbs 10:7; John 14:13, 17-18, 26; John 16:13; Romans 8:37; Ephesians 1:16-20; Philippians 1:6; 4:13; James 1:5-6; 1 John 5:14-15.
- Sexual purity—1 Corinthians 6:9, 19-20; 7:1-2; 1 Thessalonians 4:3-6; Ephesians 4:22; Romans 12:1-2.
- Favor—Psalms 5:12; 37:23; 89:17; 102:13; Proverbs 3:4; 16:15; 22:1.
- Friendships—Deuteronomy 13:6-8; Proverbs 18:24; 29:35; Micah 7:4-5; John 5:44; Acts 4:23-24; 1 Corinthians 2:5; James 4:4; Psalm 147:3.
- Obedience—Joshua 24:15; Isaiah 1:19; Jeremiah 7:23; Ephesians 6:1-2; Philippians 2:13; James 4:7.
- Mate- Isaiah 34:16; 62:5; Jeremiah 1:12; Proverbs 18:24, 29:35.

LIFE: Trust your children to God's grace. Father, I thank you for my child. I ask for wisdom and Your best solution in this situation (name it) to help my child. Help me hear Your answer and do as You say to guide, correct, and help them. For adult children: Father, in the name of Jesus, I cast the care of (name) to You and trust Your righteousness and abundant grace to make things right for them, because all my children shall be taught by You, Lord, and I trust in You. Cause them to hunger and thirst after your righteousness until they are filled. Amen. See Romans 5:17; Isaiah 54:13; Matthew 5:6.

DRINKING IN GOD'S WORD

"Whether therefore ye eat, or drink, or whatever ye do, do all to the glory of God." —1 Corinthians 10:31

TRUTH: Every choice we make as believers should be based on the Word of God and should glorify God. In the same way, God ended death in our hearts and gave us life. He ended the Law of self-effort and gave us grace in the power of the Holy Spirit to depend on Him. We are to end walking in the flesh and begin walking in the Spirit. See Galatians 5:16. Many times, we have excuses. King Solomon, called by God, started well in a humble way before God. See 1 Kings 1-10. Later, Solomon disobeyed God in Deuteronomy 7:3-4 and 17:17; he began to live a mixed lifestyle, seen in 1 Kings 11:6. Solomon lived as the other kings, probably having excuses as we sometimes do, such as, other kings were doing it, or there's nothing wrong with it, or the Bible doesn't say it is a sin.

Solomon's disobedience and appetite for women and pleasure led to his downfall. We too, can be enticed and deceived by all the drinking and partying we see advertised in commercials, showing people immorally frolicking, having fun and a good time, and slowly increasing our desire for the same. But no one sees the pain on the other side of their immorality, with addictions, sickness, mangled bodies or death from accident or abuse, and the separation caused in families. Jesus must become the priority in our lives, loving Him and allowing His love to flow to others, as all are lifted into God's presence. *"All things are lawful for me, but all things are not expedient: all things are lawful for me, but all things edify not* (1 Corinthians 10:23).

"But take heed lest by any means this liberty of yours become a stumbling block to them that are weak" (1 Corinthians 8:8-12).

LIFE: Alcohol dulls our discernment, giving a false sense of happiness and well-being. See Genesis 9:20-2; 19:30-38. But we can drink in God's Word and be made joyous and whole as God's Word is eternal and indestructible; therefore, we can trust His Word and His life in us to give us peace, prosperity, and real joy in the relationship.

DRINKING IN GOD'S WORD — DAY 2

"Wine is a mocker, strong drink is raging: and whosoever
is deceived thereby is not wise." —Proverbs 20:1

TRUTH: Alcohol makes the heart weak, and many Old Testament Scriptures discourage its use. See Isaiah 5:11-22; Hosea 4:11; Proverbs 23:29-33. One wonders if the strong wine the Scriptures speak of as mixed wine when red in the cup was different from the wine Jesus made, which was not intoxicating. See Numbers 6:3; John 2:1-12. Verse 12 tells us people believed in Jesus because of this miracle, not that people became merry, drunk, and turned away.

Wine mocks causes anger and deceives. When people are filled with the Holy Spirit, He will teach and give revelation knowledge and lead them into rest. See Proverbs 20:1; Isaiah 28:7-12. When Paul told Timothy to drink wine in 1 Timothy 5:23, it was possible for the health benefit of Resveratrol found in the skin of grapes before fermentation into wine, which has many health benefits, as an antioxidant. Don't get all religious about this; by saying you won't take medicine with alcohol, ask the waitress if food is cooked with wine, use the whole counsel of God remember God blessed wine but condemned excess, abuse, and encourages abstinence. See Deuteronomy 7:13; 14: 26; Psalm 104: 14-15; Ephesians 5:18; Proverbs 31:4-5 Be led by the Holy Spirit. Worship in His presence until He fills you with the fullness of His joy. He knows what is suitable for your life.

- Drinking alcohol just for pleasure or relaxation will open the door to Satan and keep us from consecration and complete separation of our life unto God and be captured and used by Him. See Numbers 6:1-3; Luke 1:15; 1 Timothy 3:8.
- The Word says before we were drunkards and revilers, but we have been washed, sanctified, justified in the name of the Lord Jesus Christ, and we should seek to honor Him with our bodies. See 1 Corinthians 6:10-11.
- We are not to avail ourselves of everything available to us; alcohol for pleasure delights the flesh, not the spirit. See 1 Corinthians 6:9-20; Romans 8.

LIFE: Put off the old lifestyle and put on the new man. Let God guide you to enjoy the best wine, the Spirit of Jesus. *"And be not drunk with wine, wherein is excess; but be filled with the Spirit"* (Ephesians 5:18). Meditate on Acts 2:15-17.

DRINKING IN GOD'S WORD — DAY 3

"And be not drunk with wine, wherein is excess; but be filled with the Spirit." —Ephesians 5:18

TRUTH: Allegiance to God is our priority; nothing else but His Spirit should control us. Anything that can control, harm, or cause death should be avoided in excess, including food. See Ephesians 5:18. We also should not by our liberty partake of things not mentioned as sin, but which cause someone else to stumble or turn from God. See 1 Corinthians 8:6-11. Secondly, all things are lawful, but not all are expedient or edifies. See 1 Corinthians 10:23. Rules saying do not; are not the issue. Allegiance to God is. Let Him control and lead our hearts. God is to be glorified in all we do. See 1 Corinthians 9:19-25, 31-33.

The Word tells us which Spirit we should choose to exalt. *"And I will pour out my spirit upon all flesh; and your sons and daughters shall prophesy.* See Joel 2:28. These are the latter days, and we must choose God's Spirit, desiring to be sanctified, set apart as holy ready to display His goodness in our lives and to be prepared to be used of God to minister His righteousness in the earth.

LIFE: Prayer: Father, in the name of Jesus, I desire to put off the old man drinking alcohol as a formed habit and choose to live in Your newness of life. (Or pray this for someone else or the body of Christ). You told me in Your Word to run to You for grace, mercy, and help in times of need. So, Father, I come as I no longer want to progress until the habit of drinking becomes bondage, and I am its slave. Lead me by Your Word and Your Spirit into truth and deliverance. I plead the Blood of Jesus over my soul and put on the whole armor as I lift Your Word as the shield of faith. Give me the wisdom to cast the enemy's thoughts and feelings down and for strength in self-discipline and restraint to reject his temptations. I receive my deliverance by faith and declare God in me is greater than Satan without, and no weapon formed against me shall prosper. I yield to the power of the Holy Spirit's help in Jesus' name. Amen. Meditate on Psalm 103:1-5; Hebrews 4:16.

WORSHIP

*"Give unto the Lord, O ye mighty, give unto the Lord glory and strength...
worship the Lord in the beauty of holiness." —Psalm 29:1-2*

TRUTH: First Chronicles 16 is a mainstay as an example to help us to worship. We see that God's people were assembled and had the presence of God in their midst. They offered up sacrifices, thanks, and praise in the Psalms. They sang songs, played instruments, and rejoiced. They laid aside their troubles, anxieties, fears, and cares and purposed in their hearts to worship God. They decided He was worthy of all their praise, and they worshipped and crowned Him with honor.

They called to remembrance all God's wondrous works and were mindful of His covenant. As they worshipped, they encouraged each other to declare His glory, give an offering and declare His strength. They worshipped, in 1 Chronicles 16:34 saying, *"O give thanks unto the Lord; for he is good; for his mercy endureth forever."* They ended their worship in verse 36 by saying, *"Blessed be the Lord God of Israel forever and ever. And all the people said, Amen, and praised the Lord."* When we are trapped in weakness or habitual sin, a heart humbled in worship is an effective force against Satan, as praising and exalting God as our deliverer brings His presence and power on the scene with deliverance, healing, and provision.

LIFE: As we saw in this example, worship took them beyond themselves as they engaged their spirit, soul, and body, immersing themselves in the greater presence of God. They were in awe of God, expectant and jubilant, worshipping as if they could not be kept silent. They worshipped God for His character as deliverer and for His acts of goodness which blessed them and brought deliverance. God came to their rescue, and He will come to you, making every crooked way in your life straight and causing streams to flow in your dry places to refresh uplift, and rescue as you worship God your Father.

Meditate on 1 Chronicles 16 and worship the Lord to build intimacy!

BELIEVERS ARE JUST

"But that no man is justified by the law in the sight of God, it is evident: for The just shall live by faith." —Galatians 3:11

TRUTH: For a person to be saved, they must believe by faith that God exists, and they must believe that He sent Jesus to die for their sin and offer salvation by grace through faith in Christ alone. See Hebrews 11:6; John 3:16; Ephesians 2:8; Romans 10:9-10. A person who believes in God through Jesus Christ and His shed Blood on the Cross is said to be "just." The word *just* is derived from *justification,* which means *to acquit, found not guilty, declared innocent, righteous, freed from sin, and is saved.*

Our text says no man can be found innocent or not guilty in the sight of God, by the Law of works or the Ten Commandments. This means no one can be saved by anything they attempt to satisfy God or be in right standing before Him outside of Jesus. Any effort of self to be saved or to be sanctified, purified, or to become holy during the Christian walk is self-righteousness, and God will reject it. See Isaiah 64:6; 53:10; 57:12-13; Job 25:4; Romans 3:21-24.

God requires not self-righteousness but faith-righteousness, believing in the love of God which Jesus displayed on the Cross. To be born again, you must receive Jesus and the forgiveness He offered from the Cross. We can only say God loves us if we believe and receive by faith Jesus' righteousness as our own. When by faith you accept Jesus and His love, He will cause you to be in the right standing with God or restored into the right relationship with Him. You will have your love for the Father when you receive Jesus. You will be declared just or innocent, just as if you never sinned. The Word says the just shall live by faith, knowing and believing you are innocent, free from sin, loved and reconciled to the Father will give you peace and make you bold as a lion. See Romans 5:1; Proverbs 28:1.

LIFE: *"But now the righteousness of God without the law is manifested... Even the righteousness of God which is by faith of Jesus Christ unto all and upon all them that believe"* (Romans 3:21-22).

BELIEVERS ARE JUST — DAY 2

"The just shall live by faith..." —Galatians 3:11

TRUTH: The person who is 'just' believes Jesus died on the Cross for their sins rose again and lifted them with Himself into a new life in Christ. Christ gave us eternal life, life changed from sinner to saved, from guilty to innocent, from being unacceptable to loved and accepted by God in the beloved.

The just have exchanged their sin for Jesus' righteousness... righteousness which can be received only by faith. You are just because you exchanged your sin for Jesus' righteousness in His love by faith.

Only Jesus' righteousness can give you salvation with a new heart, new nature, and new life. By Jesus' righteousness, God's Holy Spirit in us can live the life of Christ in and through us by grace through faith and into peace.

"But to him that worketh not, but believeth on him, that justifieth the ungodly, his faith is counted for righteousness" (Romans 4:5).

I am just because I am born again as I accept that Jesus took my sins in His body on the Cross and in exchange gave me His righteousness, His standing of love before the Father. I am justified, loved, made innocent, chosen, approved, wise, accepted, holy, redeemed, and reconciled by the Blood of Jesus, and I live by His Faith because Christ is my life. See Colossians 3:1-4. When the enemy accuses that you are unworthy, unloved, sin-stained, and flawed tell him that is why Jesus died for you and that His Blood cleansed and justified you. Tell him you are not right by your correct actions, but you are made right by the Blood of Jesus.

LIFE: I am saved by grace through faith, and I am just. I must continue to live by grace through faith, trusting God's Word daily. I live a life dependent on my Father for everything. Being just makes me innocent and free, loved, and bold to live by faith in Christ and receive His blessings. I am blessed! See Mark 11:22-24; Romans 5:1; Ephesians 1:4; 1 Corinthians 1:30; Galatians 2:20.

LEGALISM

*"Now go and smite Amalek, and utterly destroy all...And he took
Agag the King of the Amalekites alive..."* —1 Samuel 15: 3, 8

TRUTH: God gave Saul instructions to kill all the Amalekites, including all they possessed, their ox, sheep, camel, and asses. Saul disobeyed and chose to do things his way. He spared the king and the best of the animals. When Samuel the prophet confronted him, he responded that the people wanted the animals to sacrifice. It was not his job nor his place to offer a sacrifice, not being a priest. Legalism is religion or works towards God without the Holy Spirit. It is man choosing to serve God in his way, hoping God will be pleased, just as Saul did. God requires man not only to believe in Jesus by grace through faith to be saved, but also to give Him our whole heart, mind, and soul and live our daily lives in total submission to Him. See Ephesians 2:8; Colossians 2:6.

For many, God is their hope for salvation, but then in daily life, they try their ways living by their own rules or interpretation to achieve a right relationship with God. Some with special water baptisms, holy days, and ways to dress to be holy and pleasing to God. They try hard not to sin, harder to be good Christians, and even harder to walk in love so their faith will work because they know, *"Faith works by love"* See Galatians 5:6. There is much self-sacrifice in trying to do their best working for Jesus in the church, but at times they end up expending so much energy in competition, struggle, self-promotion, pride, or jockeying for position that they become frustrated, burnt out, and tired. All of this is legalism or works.

LIFE: Give it up! Die to yourself, give up your control and surrender to the life of Christ in you and live by the love and power of the Holy Spirit in and with you to have real-life in Christ Jesus. Focus on Christ Jesus in a relationship through His Word, worship, and praise to reach His heart, not through the things you do. Love Him with all your heart and give Him everything, and His love and life will flow from His Spirit to yours to give you, His life.

Meditate on Deuteronomy 30:20; Romans 3:19-28; Galatians 2:20.

LEGALISM — DAY 2

*"Are ye so foolish? Having begun in the Spirit, are ye now
made perfect by the flesh?"* —Galatians 3:3

TRUTH: These believers were trying to live their Christian life in their strength, trying to be good in their way and trying even harder not to sin so God would be pleased with them. This is legalism or religion of works. Man in self-effort seeking to find or please God is not pleasing to Him, just as He was not pleased with Saul. Religion minimizes what Jesus has done on the Cross. And shortchanges the believer in God's blessings. God was pleased with Jesus obeying Him to go to the Cross, and God is pleased with us when we believe in and accept Jesus as our righteousness or our right love relationship with Him. Legalism is self-righteousness, which is not faith and is therefore sin. See Romans 14:23. God called us into a relationship for us to hold up Jesus to Him as our righteousness, the One who makes us right in His presence and to receive His every blessing.

The results of legalism and self-righteousness are pride, self-dependence, self-sufficiency, control, being judgmental, frustrated, burnt out, and having an overly critical spirit. When there is a failure, there is suffering, feelings of unworthiness, insecurity, fear, condemnation, and strife in relationships. Satan also has his sway, creating anxiety and torment because we are never sufficient unto ourselves or for others. Believers who practice legalism have received Jesus by humbling themselves, but they went back from putting their full faith on Jesus and began to live in their own strength. See Galatians 3.

LIFE: You are to continue your Christian life with God's grace through faith in complete dependence on Jesus. Jesus is your center, so be God-centered, always depending on His Word and Spirit through all Jesus did for you at the Cross as your first step to meeting any need, including relationships. Always rest in Jesus and the power of the Cross, His Word, and shed Blood, never self or otherwise, and you'll have peace. Read Romans 3 and 4.

GOD'S GRACE

"For the grace of God that bringeth salvation hath appeared to all men." —Titus 2:11

TRUTH: Grace is God's gift of the power of His Son's Spirit living in us to transform us into our Father's image. Jesus gave us the Gospel with salvation in the New Covenant of Grace established by His Blood. See Luke 22:20; Titus 2:11-14. Grace is God giving His favor and power within man by His Spirit. God also exercises His favor and power, doing for man what man could not do for himself. For example, man was born in sin and could not achieve salvation to save himself, so God purchased our salvation with the Blood of His Son Jesus by His grace. Likewise, after being saved, the Christian cannot purify himself of his old bad habits or earn God's blessings to achieve holiness or success. Only grace in God's power of His Holy Spirit can cleanse, help, deliver, transform, and bless us.

LIFE: God's grace in salvation: Adams's sin infected every human being with a sinful heart. To reverse this, Jesus died on the Cross, took all our sins upon Himself to the grave, wrestled with death for three days, and rose triumphantly, defeating Satan, sin, death, and the Law. His resurrection justified us, declared us forgiven and innocent, free from sin and all its consequences such as guilt, shame, fear, and condemnation, and made us righteous and loved. God's grace in Jesus exchanged our sin. It gave us Jesus' righteousness, love, and holy standing with the Father, therefore reconciling us to God in a love relationship empowered by His Spirit to grow in Christ's image. We are raised and seated in victory with Christ Jesus at the right hand of the Father. We have overcome by the Blood of Jesus. With Jesus' righteousness, we can enter God's presence at any time without rebuke, even with sin, desiring repentance. In the presence of God, His grace made us wise, accepted, holy, and free to live by faith and become victorious in every area of our lives. Even when we fall, His grace will lift us and restore us. What a joy to be loved by Jesus. See Proverbs 24:16; Hebrews 4:16; 1 Corinthians 1:30; 15:57.

GOD'S GRACE — DAY 2

"For the grace of God that bringeth salvation hath appeared to all men." —Titus 2:11

TRUTH: The opposite of grace is the Law, religion, or works where one tries to work for or earn salvation or sanctification by their efforts. When we humble ourselves, knowing that we did nothing and can do nothing to be saved but simply believe in Jesus, we depend on what He did on the Cross and are saved by God's grace. We live by grace as we rely on Jesus by His Spirit to guide us in our daily lives.

God's grace for daily living: After being saved, our Christian life must be lived just as we got saved, by grace through faith. See Colossians 2:6. We are to take our position of victory, which Jesus gave when He seated us with Him at the right hand of the Father. From this place of victory, believe His Word is true, stand in authority, and refuse to be afraid of anything. Humble ourselves to stand in faith and, by the power of the Holy Spirit, receive God's favor, power, direction, ability, and help to achieve whatever we need to succeed.

We are to continue to depend on His grace from the Cross and all His finished work to the ascension to provide for us. The life and work of Jesus on the Cross provided God's Word in the New Testament with truths, promises, blessings, and power in the Holy Spirit for us to live by. God's grace provided ability in the power of the Holy Spirit to lead us into all truth. This broke all Satan's powers against us to live by rules of the Law, as we can now walk by faith and not by sight and walk in love so that our faith works. See Colossians 1:13-14; 2 Corinthians 1:9, 12; 2 Corinthians 5:7; Galatians 5:6.

LIFE: Grace sees what Jesus has already done for us at the Cross and believes it as true. We believe in God's grace for healing when we think on the Cross that He bore stripes on His back for our healing and His power rises within to heal. We therefore must refuse to accept sickness because grace provided healing. To live God's grace is to daily live Psalm 23 and Galatians 2:20 as qualified by faith to receive all His blessings as we depend on and trust His Word and His Spirit for all things.

HE BEGAN A GOOD WORK

"Being confident of this very thing, that he which hath begun a good work in you will perform it until the day of Jesus Christ." —Philippians 1:6

TRUTH: In Genesis, at creation, God created the world and said it was good. He recreated our hearts and told us that He began a good work in us. God made us new in our spirit man when He gave us a new heart filled with Himself by His Holy Spirit. See Galatians 5:22. He took our sin in His own body and redeemed us from all sins, casting them as far as the east is from the west. See Psalm 103: 12. He justified us by the Blood of Jesus and made us righteous, reconciled unto God into our Father's love. We have His peace and character in us by His Spirit. We have been given faith to receive Him as Savior and Lord and be raised in heavenly places, seated in Christ, able to receive all His spiritual blessings. See Romans 12:3; Ephesians 1:3. We have been given the Holy Spirit to be our Helper, to lead us into the things of God and Christlikeness. See John 14:16-17.

According to His divine power, God has given us all things that pertain to life and Godliness. We have everything we will ever need to live an abundant life here on earth, and God says we have His abundant life as we live by faith in His grace, depending on His Son Jesus Christ and His Holy Spirit. God has begun a good work, and as we receive Him by faith, we will continue to grow in Him from grace to grace, from faith to faith, and from glory to glory.

LIFE: As you yield to the Father by His Holy Spirit and let Him lead you through all three processes of your salvation—regeneration or new birth, See John 3:16. Sanctification or transformation. See Romans 12:1-2. And glorification. See Romans 8:17-18. He will prepare you to live here and for heaven. He will continue the work He began to help you in everything which concerns your life. *"Make you perfect in every good work to do his will, working in you that which is well-pleasing in His sight through Jesus Christ"* (Hebrews 13:21).

Christ Jesus is our path to abundant living.

LOVE IS RIGHTEOUSNESS

"For if by one man's offence death reigned by one; much more they which receive abundance of grace and of the gift of righteousness shall reign in life by one, Jesus Christ." —Romans 5:17

TRUTH: To reign in life, we must abide and live by the commandment God has given us. *"Thou shalt love the Lord thy God with all thy heart, and with all thy soul, and with all thy mind...Thou shalt love thy neighbor as thyself"* (Matthew 22:37-39). This commandment is designed to perpetuate the union relationship of a righteous God who loves us, makes us righteous by the Blood of Jesus, and qualifies us to love other people.

"Owe no man anything, but to love one another: for he that loveth another hath fulfilled the law...Love worketh no ill to his neighbor: therefore, love is the fulfilling of the law" (Romans 13:8-10).

"But let us, who are of the day, be sober, putting on the breastplate of faith and love" (1 Thessalonians 5:8).

Loving God, grace through faith, is seeing Jesus and believing that all He did on the Cross was done for our salvation. Then in our hearts, we humble ourselves by faith to receive Jesus by His Spirit. Being incredibly grateful, we receive His love in humility enough to bow before Him and worship Him. When by faith, we receive God's love, worship, and trust Him to lead us, we are in right standing, or a right love relationship, and we are righteous. Loving God by faith righteousness pleases God. See Hebrews 11:6.

LIFE: Just as Job was considered righteous (see Job 1:1), your faith in your Heavenly Father's love will always lead you to surrender your human will to trust Him in all things, in the good times and in the bad times. You too will say, *"Though he slay me, yet will I trust in him: but I will maintain mine own ways before him"* (Job 13:15).

LOVE IS RIGHTEOUSNESS — DAY 2

"...Gift of righteousness shall reign in life by one Jesus Christ." —Romans 5:17

TRUTH: At times when we sin or fall into unrighteousness, let the unfailing love of God shed abroad in our hearts minister to us that we are still His righteous children who sinned and need repentance. Obey God and repent, that God's love given in Jesus' Blood will cleanse us to keep going forward in His grace. God's gift of righteousness, the grace of His love in receiving forgiveness by faith, will save us from despair and condemnation about that sin.

We express love in righteousness when we run to our Father with all our needs by faith. God loves it when we depend on Him in all things. When we need grace in times of temptation or need help for protection, God's love will deliver us. Or even after we have missed it and sinned, His righteousness in His mercy will restore us. See Hebrews 4:16; 8:12.

We love in righteousness when we depend on God to keep us by His grace, power, and ability and not by our thinking, efforts, or ways. See 1 Peter 1:5. We love in righteousness when we depend on God's power in the Holy Spirit to lead, guide, and help us to grow in fruitfulness and Christlikeness. As we yield to God, His deposit of the fruit of the Spirit will work in us to bring the needed change. See Galatians 4:19; 2:20; 5:22; Philippians 2:13.

LIFE: God loves me just as much as He loves Jesus. Jesus' Blood opened the way for the Holy Spirit to come into my spirit or my heart, depositing His love. Romans 5:5. His love removed sin and gave me new life in Christ Jesus. I can now love God, and His love causes me to yield, abide, and obey Him. I am the righteousness of God in Christ Jesus because I am loved, and in return, I depend on His love. He molds me and leads me by His Spirit to do right by God and man. I live by love in Jesus' righteousness and receive help from the Holy Spirit to obey God's command to love all, even my enemies, and receive His blessings by faith. See Matthew 5:44; Philippians 2:13; Mark 11:24.

REST IN RIGHTEOUSNESS

"And my people shall dwell in a peaceable habitation, and in sure dwellings, and in quiet resting places." —Isaiah 32:18

TRUTH: Righteousness determines what kind of relationship we will have with our Heavenly Father, with others, and with the devil. God has commanded us to love, but without acknowledging His gift of love occupying our hearts, we cannot experience His love fully and love others well or be assured of God's love enough to resist the enemy and be free from fear. Isaiah 54:14. God's love must be acknowledged, believed, and received by faith. We are righteous when we think our Father's unfailing love is shed abroad in our hearts along with His faithfulness. See Romans 5:5; 12:3. It is not about our being sinless or perfect, but about us having faith in the perfect One, Jesus, whose love will lead us to yield to Him, receive forgiveness and blessings and love others. Our faith in God's love and His Word produces authentic obedience, as it did for our Father of faith, Abraham. See Romans 4:3-4; 1 John 4:7-8; 1 Thessalonians 5:8-10.

LIFE: Some of the net results of righteousness are:

1. Your standing with the Father is one of faith-righteousness, loving Him enough to give up control of yourself in surrender and believe God by faith. It is the opposite of self-righteousness, where you choose to remain in control and try to work for or work out your salvation and blessings in self-effort. It would be best if you chose to determine that your posture in salvation and your Christian walk: is one of faith in a close relationship of abiding and rest, not one of self-effort and struggle.

2. Self-righteousness keeps your self-will activated, working to be spiritual enough to be saved and loved. There is little rest instead; there is striving and struggling to reach a state where you feel good enough for God to love and accept you. Instead of rest, you have frustration, fear, and torment. Jesus gave up His self-will in Gethsemane when He said, *"nevertheless not as I will, but as thou wilt"* (Matthew 26:39. That is why He could say, *"the prince of this world cometh and has nothing in me."* (John 14:30).

REST IN RIGHTEOUSNESS — DAY 2

And my people shall dwell... in quiet resting places. –Isaiah 32:18

LIFE: Continued -

3. Faith-righteousness receives God's grace, in Jesus Christ His Son, through faith, trusting only the Blood of Jesus for salvation and sanctification. You have submitted your will to God and have gained His peace in Jesus. You have a closer love relationship in obedience to your Heavenly Father, led by the Holy Spirit into rest for your soul. See Romans 3: 21-22; 5:1.

4. We are made righteous in our spirit so that our spirit, filled with God's love, will influence our soul and body to think, feel, and choose to live by God's love. After having received God's love, we are to stand in the correct posture or love relationship in faith, trusting in God's grace, Jesus, and the accomplishments of the Cross. We can now walk in righteousness and by His love to do right by others. See Romans 13: 8: -10. *"As ye have therefore received Christ Jesus the Lord, so walk in him"* (Colossians 2:6).

5. Walking in self-righteousness is walking in the law of self-effort, trying to fix everything oneself, which is sin, as whatever is not of faith is sin. See Romans 14:23. Selfishness results in strife, fights, and strained relationships. There is no peace or rest because we are incapable of always finding all the correct solutions ourselves.

6. Walking in righteousness by faith with other people will mean we love and obey God's commandment instead of living in selfishness. We also will trust God's grace and power working in us to love or do right by others. Our trust in God brings rest and peace. See Hebrews 4:9-11.

Jesus is our righteousness. His love leads us into rest as we trust. Trust causes Him to go to work to make all things right and for things to work for our good because Christ is our life. See Romans 8:28; Philippians 1:6; Exodus 14:14.

NEW CREATION IN RIGHTEOUSNESS

*"And that ye put on the new man, which after God is created
in righteousness and true holiness." —Ephesians 4:24*

TRUTH: Righteousness gives a believer a restored love relationship with God their Heavenly Father. They will feel loved, accepted, forgiven, worthy, and accepted. The believer now has a sense of belonging. They know they belong to the family of God. Their righteousness is of faith, always depending on God, and this pleases their Father, who in response acts on their faith to bless them.

Righteousness results in acceptance and belonging, which gives blessings and peace. If a believer does not understand the need to receive the gift of righteousness, they will struggle, strive, and try to be acceptable to God by works, in what they do for Christ or their lifestyle choices. Self-effort is religion and works, which lacks righteousness or a right relationship with the Father because it lacks faith.

New creation beings live by faith in God's grace and have a new Father who gave them a heart for delighting in Him; they have new desires, living in a new Kingdom and having joy in their salvation. Those who do not see themselves as new creation beings are religious and live by legalistic rules, duty, and self-effort. The religious person is in self-righteousness, which is as filthy rags to God. See Isaiah 64:6. The success of our Christian journey rests on a believer living in the newness of life by faith in God's grace by His Spirit, knowing and believing they are righteous. Remember, the prayer of a righteous man gets results. See James 5:16.

LIFE: God loves me in Jesus, and I receive His love in His righteousness by faith. Every day I rest and trust His love to care for me. I will always depend on Jesus and trust Him, never on myself, to fix all my situations or meet my own needs. I am a new creation having Jesus' righteousness His great love and care for me will never fail, and I am eternally blessed as I depend on Him and therefore have no fear or worry. I will trust Jesus and have joy and peace in believing. See Romans 15:13.

WORK OF RIGHTEOUSNESS

"And the work of righteousness shall be peace; and the effect of righteousness, quietness, and assurance forever." —Isaiah 32:17

TRUTH: Righteousness is the rightness of thoughts, words, and actions of love conforming to God's will. We can apply righteousness in two areas:

First, in our standing before God: When we go before God, the only approach He will accept is one of humility, faith, and obedience. First, we must hear the Gospel preached to us to be saved, even if it is only by nature. See John 3:16; Romans 1:20-21. Our response is to humble our hearts, believe in God, and receive Jesus. See Romans 10:9-10. This is faith (our believing) in God's grace (the Gospel). See Ephesians 2:8. Faith in God's grace is the righteousness that pleases God. We have conformed to His will, to love God by faith, and believe in Jesus.

Jesus' righteousness in us then works peace in our hearts in the presence of God our Father when we accept that His Blood made us righteous, holy, innocent, blameless, united in spirit as one, and seated in heavenly places. See Romans 5:1-2; 1 Corinthians 6:17; Isaiah 9:6-7; Colossians 1:20-22.

Jesus' righteousness by faith in our hearts gives us right standing or acceptance with God, giving us a peaceful heart full of assurance of His love, Fatherhood, and care. In our standing before God, His love and care eliminate struggling, striving, and trying in our way to find God's favor, acceptance, worth, and blessings. An example of righteousness before God is the story of Abel being righteous and Cain being unrighteous. See Genesis 4:4, 13-16.

LIFE: When you believe with all your heart that God loves you and will never fail you, by faith, you are righteous. In Jesus, you are acceptable to God in the right relationship, and therefore you will have peace with God. Peace with God gives you a heart filled with quietness and assurance in connection to God, love, fellowship, belief, trust, and receive from Him. Meditate on Isaiah 32:17.

WORK OF RIGHTEOUSNESS — DAY 2

"And the work of righteousness shall be peace; and the effect of righteousness quietness and assurance forever." —Isaiah 32:17

TRUTH: Righteousness can be applied in your standing before God and:

Second, in our lifestyle or standing before man: In our Christian walk, the goal is that our lifestyle represents the character and life of Christ, that we have the rightness of thoughts, words, and actions conforming to God's will, His Word, and His Law to love others. We now live in the church age of grace, and its law is for us to love. See John 13:34.

Love fulfills the law of righteousness by faith. See Romans 13:8-10. God calls us to love, and the spirit of love flowing from our hearts always brings peace. We are called to love one another, forgive one another, give and share with others, love our enemies, and submit to one another.

Because we love, we should not be quick to take offense or retaliate, and we should refrain from judging others negatively and condemning others; instead, we bless and curse not. See Romans 12:14, 21. We are righteous when we walk in faith and love towards God and others. This will bring peace to our hearts, homes, communities, and the world around us. With love and peace in our hearts, Christ is seen in our character and lives. John 13:35 says that people will know that we are God's disciples by this.

LIFE: When you love, you bless with your thoughts, words, and actions and have peace with others. As you fellowship and God shows you the qualities He needs to change, you and I are to give them to Him and ask Him to change our hearts in that area. Read and meditate opposite Scriptures. For example, for stealing, meditate on honesty. Ask the Holy Spirit to help you while expectantly listening to His leading. Yield to the work of righteousness and be led by the Spirit to prosper as your soul prospers to live in peace with all men if possible. See Philippians 2:13; 3 John 2; Romans 12:18.

RIGHTEOUSNESS AND FEAR

"In righteousness shalt thou be established: thou shalt be far from oppression; for thou shalt not fear..." —Isaiah 54:14

TRUTH: God's righteousness is faith in His grace, His love sent in Jesus Christ. We live by His faith to love God, love others, receive blessings and resist Satan. Fear comes because love for God is lacking, and therefore faith is lacking because faith works by love. We lack faith because we did not receive the gift of righteousness in God's love. See Galatians 5:6.

Whatever is not of faith is sin, and sin brings fear. Romans 14:23. A believer gets saved by wholly depending and believing in the love of Jesus, demonstrated on the Cross. We exchange our sin and receive Jesus' righteousness by faith, holding it as our own. Our faith in receiving God's love in Christ Jesus pleases God, and we are then established in righteousness. God's love builds faith and trust, causes us to stand in power and authority, and drive out Satan's fear. See 1 John 4:18.

Any self-effort to be saved, pleasing to God, or resisting Satan that is not of faith is religion or legalism. The person is not established in righteousness, and fear will come. However, when our response is established in righteousness, by grace through faith, believing in Jesus and His Word, the believer's heart becomes assured and has peace with God. He is not afraid of God but will love Him and want to be near Him, delighting in Him and being willing to stand in faith, obey, worship, and trust Him. He is God-loved, assured, blessed, and can also stand God-directed by faith in Jesus' strength and gain victory over Satan. See Romans 8:14.

LIFE: Believe Jesus is your righteousness, your GREAT LOVE. Believe you are anchored in Him for everything. Any suggestion by Satan or others to gain your focus or get your needs met outside of your anchor, Christ Jesus, will bring fear. Oppression is far from you because you depend on God's love in Jesus and your faith releases His power to save, bless, provide and care for you as you trust in Him and do not fear. Meditate on Isaiah 41:10.

RIGHTEOUSNESS AND FEAR — DAY 2

*"In righteousness shalt thou be established...thou shalt be far
from oppression; for thou shalt not fear..."* —Isaiah 54:14

TRUTH: As an example, when we are established in the righteousness of faith in healing according to Isaiah 53:4-5 and believe God is the healer, not the doctor, we will be established in righteousness for recovery, and no fear in sickness can take hold, because the expectation is that we were healed from above along with the doctor's help. See 1 Peter 2:24. The oppression of sickness will be far removed from you because you are in the faith.

When you are established in the righteousness of prosperity. See Malachi 3:10; Philippians 4:18, 19; 3 John 2; 2 Corinthians 9:8, the oppression of poverty and lack will be far removed because you are in faith that God is your supply instead of your job. And He will never see the righteous forsaken.

When you are established by faith in the righteousness of God's deep, abiding, and everlasting love, torment and fear will be far from you because God's love deposited in your heart by His anointing is greater than fear, and perfect love full of God's power casts out all fear. See 1 John 4:18. Oppression with fear and torment will be far from you because your love and trust in God's care, not yourself and not others, frees you from being uncertain, doubtful, and fearful.

When you are established in God as your protector, you will not live in fear of gun violence or the coronavirus because you know God is your protection. See Psalm 91. Have rightness in your thinking, speaking, and actions, grace through faith depending on God for every promise as you grow to trust Him more, and fear will be eliminated for Christ is your life.

LIFE: Faith works by love. When you love God in a relationship and believe His Words, faith comes. Faith then causes you to *"Not be afraid of evil tidings; his heart is fixed, trusting in the Lord"* (Psalm 112:7).

"But I trusted in thee, O Lord: I said, Thou art my God...My times are in thy hand (Psalm 31:14-15).

PURSUE RIGHTEOUSNESS

"Blessed are they which do hunger and thirst after righteousness for they shall be filled." —Matthew 5:6

TRUTH: This Scripture verse is one of my favorites in praying for others. God will move on their hearts and draw them unto Himself as we pray this. Righteousness is trusting a God of love with the situations of our lives and the lives of others. But for yourself, what is your greatest hunger? What are you striving for? Is it that you primarily hunger for yourself in self-indulgence—your stomach with food and drink, personal pleasures, intellect, status, or appearance—more than you are hungering after God? All selfish attitudes toward self, neglecting God, is self-righteousness. God desires that we yearn after Him, believing what He says is right. As we read God's Word or hear it preached and by faith believe, Jesus will come to us and fill our hearts with Himself who is love and power, and we are considered as righteous. See 1 John 3:16, 4:8; Romans 4:3-5.

We are blessed when we hunger after God—after His love, His character, His ways, His desires, and eternity. God now calls us righteous. God no longer looks at us for sin because "in Christ" we are dead to sin and seen as honest to God. Now see yourself the same way God sees you, as righteous and in a right love relationship with Him, forgiven, chosen, and loved. You are free from sin and accepted by God your Father. Faith in His love in your heart will lead you to love God and yield to Him as you delight in Him and love others. The result:

LIFE:
"The effectual fervent prayer of a righteous man availeth much" (James 5:16).

"The righteous cry and the Lord heareth, and delivereth them out of all their troubles. Many are the afflictions of the righteous, but the Lord delivereth him out of them all" (Psalm 34:17).

"For the kingdom of God is not meat and drink; but righteousness, and peace, and joy in the Holy Ghost (Romans 14:17).

BENEFITS OF RIGHTEOUSNESS

"And work of righteousness shall be peace; and the effect of righteousness quietness and assurance forever." —Isaiah 32:17

TRUTH: Righteousness establishes in us our Father's love. Faith in His love and the finished work of the Cross brings blessings and power in His promises and in our faith against the devil to eliminate fear. Faith and trust in God's love and goodness bring the heart and mind peace and quietness. You will have the assurance of being deeply loved in a relationship, knowing you are deeply cared for by your Father.

LIFE: God's grace, in what Jesus did on the Cross, can be accessed only by God's righteousness that is His love grace through faith. See Romans 4; Galatians 3:11. Righteousness builds faith which releases grace.

Other benefits include:

1. Gives the correct perception of a good God and not one of a wrathful God. (Romans 5:8, 9; 1 Thessalonians 5:9).
2. It gives a correct view of oneself as a new creation worthy of being loved (2 Corinthians 5:17,21).
3. Increases intimacy and trust (Deuteronomy 6:5; John 15:4-6).
4. Gives assurance and acceptance (Romans 15:6-7; Ephesians 1:6).
5. Eliminates sin-consciousness and condemnation (Hebrews 10:2; Romans 8:1-2).
6. Increases faith to receive from God (Mark 11:22-24).
7. It helps us walk in the Spirit and not in the flesh (Romans 8:2).
8. It helps us reign in life as we depend on God's abundant grace and His gift of righteousness (Romans 5:17, 21).
9. Gives boldness (Proverbs 28:1; Ephesians 3:12).
10. Provides power and authority over Satan (Luke 10:18-19; Philippians 2:9-11).
11. It gives an eternal perspective, not earthly or temporal (2 Corinthians 4:18).

THE WORD

*"But the Word of the Lord endureth forever. And this is the word
which by the gospel is preached unto you."* —1 Peter 1:25

TRUTH: Our God is a forever God because He has no beginning and no end. He is the Word, and He is eternal. He spoke creation into being, and its result is still here and will remain until God says otherwise. *"While the earth remaineth, seedtime and harvest, and cold and heat, and summer and winter, and day and night shall not cease"* (Genesis 8:22). We are told in John 1:1 that Jesus is the Living Word, which was made flesh and dwelt among us.

God's Word is truth. See John 17:17. The Word further says heaven and earth shall pass away, but God's Words shall not pass away. See Mark 13:31. In God's Word, we have truths to believe (John 20:31), commands to keep (John 13:34), and promises to receive (John 3:16). As we read the Word, we are not just to seek information or lists of things to do to become more spiritual or to be better Christians; instead, we are to ask the Holy Spirit to teach us and draw us into a closer relationship, to hear God's revealed truth, and for Him to help us apply the truth to change our lives.

The Word of God brings faith to our hearts. The more often we hear the Word, the greater the relationship and the quicker faith will come to our hearts. See Romans 10:17. Keep hearing the Word of God in as many ways as you can. In our still and quiet time, hear from the Holy Spirit, listen in a Bible study, hear the Word preached electronically, and in testimonies; faith will be formed in the heart when the Word is believed.

"Thy word have I hid in mine heart, that I might not sin against thee" (Psalm 119:11).

LIFE: Just as food nurtures the body and study cultivate the mind, the Word of God feeds and grows your spirit to activate the Holy Spirit within to communicate better, teach and lead us into all of God's truth, guiding the soul and body into righteousness, and holiness to give us blessings, and victory. See John 14:26, 16:13.

THE WORD — DAY 2

"But the word of the Lord endureth forever." —1 Peter 1:25

TRUTH: The Word of God is a seed to be seen, heard, read, studied, meditated upon, spoken, and planted in our hearts. As we nurture and water the seed of God's Word with fellowship and prayer, faith begins to grow so we can believe and receive. See Mark 4:14-20. The seed of the Word sown into our hearts will transform the mind and fortify the soul so that we can gain God's promises and withstand the attacks of the enemy. When the enemy comes as a stealer of the Word, we must stand against him, rebuke and cast him down, and exalt God's power in His Lordship to cause us to overcome. See Isaiah 59:19;1 Timothy 6:12.

There is power in speaking God's Word. When we speak the Word, God's power is released to defeat the enemy of our soul, just as Jesus used the Word to defeat Satan in Luke 4. As our soul prospers with the Word of God, we will have good health and prosperity. See 3 John 2. We should never reduce the Word of God to rote learning, an obligation, or just daily confessions without connecting with Jesus the Living Word, God's love in the finished work on the Cross, and the Holy Spirit. Victory comes in knowing what Jesus, the Living Word as truth, accomplished for us that when we believe, faith arises for us to receive. The truth we know, think, believe, speak, and act on will set us free to receive our blessing. See John 8:32, 36.

"It is written, man shall not live by bread alone but by every word that proceedeth out of the mouth of God" (Matthew 4:4).

"Your word is a lamp unto my feet, and a light unto my path" (Psalm 119:105).

LIFE: The Word is truth. Truth closes the door to the enemy's lies and his torment. Humble yourself, believe the Word and get greater light, revelation, correction, and peace. Let God's Spirit in you wield the Word of God, which is quick and powerful and sharper than any two-edged sword, to give you, on the one hand, blessings from God your Father and on the other a weapon against all evil. See Hebrews 4:12; Ephesians 6:16-17.

DOERS OF THE WORD — DAY 1

"But be ye doers of the word, and not hearers only deceiving your own selves..." —James 1:22-25

TRUTH: The Word of God is a lamp unto our feet and a light to our path; it will shine onto the right way for God to guide and to bless us. It is not enough to only hear the Word, and it remains superficial as the enemy will jump right in and steal the Word. How many times after hearing a good message does someone offends us, and we get upset? That is the stealer of the Word at work, and if we entertain the offense, we allow him to succeed and rob us of the Word sown into our hearts earlier. Matthew 13:4, 19.

How many times do we read the Word and just skip over it and move on? How many believers read the Word just to complete a Bible yearly plan? Do we read the Bible just because it is the right thing to do as a Christian? Some may not even bother to read it unless they need God in a trying situation. James says that hearing without doing the Word is like looking at our faces in the mirror, seeing a spot or a flaw, and walking away without cleaning the area. What we are doing with the Word of God is hearing it and doing nothing about it. The Bible says we are deceiving ourselves. When we do not delve deeper into God's Word, allowing the Holy Spirit to speak revelation to us, we will miss what God wants us to see or hear, first to believe, to bless, as well as to bring change to the heart, character, and situation as the Holy Spirit seek to make us into Jesus' image.

LIFE: With the neglect of the Word, we are deceiving ourselves as when temptations come, we will be unable to resist the devil. We'll try all we know to do but to no avail because we desperately need more Word deposited in our hearts for the Holy Spirit to use and build faith to resist. With more Word in us, the Holy Spirit will give us more revelation knowledge to help us to understand better how to use our faith to stand and overcome life's challenges. See Ephesians 1:17-18. Hear, but yield to the Holy Spirit, and become a doer not only of God's Word in the Bible but also of His revealed Word by the Holy Spirit to overcome.

DOERS OF THE WORD — DAY 2

"But be ye doers of the word..." —James 1:22

TRUTH: As doers of the Word, we are to read, hear, meditate on the Word, and hear again in our hearts what the Holy Spirit is saying to us concerning the Word. We are to see ourselves and our standing with God reflected in and by the Word. Are we in right standing with God our Heavenly Father? Or are we in a strained relationship because of carrying weights or sins? After spending time in the Word, God will show us our reflection. We should then ask the Holy Spirit to help us apply the truth revealed to us in the Word to renew our minds and soul so they both will begin to align with God's ways. See Romans 12:1-2.

Don't let us walk away and forget what God said, but let the Word connect us in relationship to Jesus the Living Word, by His Holy Spirit, to bring power within to be a doer of God's Word. *"Jesus saith unto him, I am the way, the truth, and the life: no man cometh unto the Father but by me"* (John 14:6).

We must seek understanding from God's Word and then, by faith, apply the truth of God's Word that we understand and believe for God to change our situation. God's Word has the power within it to cause us to be steadfast, to prevail, and to overcome. James 1: 25 tells us to examine the perfect law of liberty, the Law of God's grace in His Word, and to continue in it to build our faith and act on it so that we can become a doer of the Word. In any situation we encounter, we must first look to the Word as seen in the gospel from the Cross and thank God for what Jesus did for us concerning that situation. His stripes are for our healing. Then use the Word on healing, which contains God's power, to stand and overcome all sickness and receive His blessing and recover.

LIFE: In Revelation 1:3, God said He would bless those who read the book. We can be sure we will be doubly blessed if we read and become doers of the Word. In this evil world, our lives may be the only Bible people see, so let our lives become living epistles to be lights and testimonies of Christ Jesus so that we can become a blessing to others. See 2 Corinthians 3:2-3; Genesis 12:2.

SPEAK THE WORD

"This book of the law shall not depart out of thy mouth; but thou shalt meditate herein day and night... for then thou shalt make thy way prosperous, and then thou shalt have good success." —Joshua 1:8

TRUTH: The Word tells us in this verse how to have good success—not just win, but success. How? *"The blessing of the Lord, maketh rich, and he addeth no sorrow with it"* (Proverbs 10:22). However, some of us as Christians may not have the outstanding level of success we desire. Why? We may not fully believe our text in Joshua 1:8.

Speaking and believing God's Word will make us successful. That is a fact and a truth. You will not be successful just by speaking the Word from your mouth, or as we say, "confessing the Word." No! We are to confess the Word based on what the shed Blood of Jesus accomplished on the Cross with the goal of it going deep in our hearts until we believe what Jesus accomplished is true in the promise He gives.

As we meditate on and speak the Word we believe, it will, without a shadow of a doubt, bring faith and God on the scene to change our situation for the better. God's Word has the power to do the impossible when by faith, we believe it from our hearts and speak it from our mouths. We cannot face one situation in life that the Word cannot change.

Mark 11:23-24 says, *"That whosoever shall say unto this mountain, Be thou removed, and be thou cast into the sea: and shall not doubt in his heart, but shall believe that those things which he saith shall come to pass, he shall have whatsoever he saith."*

LIFE: Unbelief is sin. Sin keeps the enemy at work to bring torment. Jesus is my righteousness. I believe and trust His Word of truth, which shuts down the enemy, delivers me from his grasp, and sets me free. The Word I think, believe, speak, and execute by the power of the Holy Spirit activates faith to bring my needed change as God makes things right for me. See 2 Corinthians 4:13.

SPEAK THE WORD — DAY 2

"This book of the law shall not depart out of thy mouth." —Joshua 1:8

TRUTH: If we are sick, the first thing is to take our seat in the place of victory by believing that the Cross and Christ's resurrection power imputed our success to us and therefore, we can stand as the healed. Next, speak God's Words because they are life and health, believe and receive. See Proverbs 4:20-23. If we are broke, He is our provision. See Philippians 4:18-19. If we need protection, we trust His Word in Psalm 91. When we speak the Word of God, faith comes into our hearts by the power of the Holy Spirit for us to believe and receive. As we already have the victory. Then in the process of building our faith for success, remain steadfast and patient in praise and thanksgiving to receive as we wait on the manifestation.

Speaking contrary to the Word of God gives Satan access to cause our negative situation to remain or potentially worsen. Satan can keep us down only if we join him in thinking, speaking, and acting on His suggestions and lies. He will project one lie after another to keep our focus on him. See Ephesians 4:26-28. Speak God's Word, which is truth. John 8:32 says, *"And ye shall know the truth, and the truth shall make you free."* The Word, which God Himself speaks about our situation, that we believe to be true in our hearts and then speak from our mouths and act upon, will set us free.

Our natural situations will change as we are faithful to the Word of God to speak, believe, receive, and act on it. Let our thinking line up with God's Word as our eyes remain on Jesus. Stick with Him by staying unmovable, for Christ already gave us the victory; speak it and meditate on it until we get the revelation we need. It is the revealed truth of God's Word upon which we stand; believe and speak that which shall set us free to have good success.

LIFE: Believe Jesus. *"So shall my word be that goeth forth out of my mouth: it shall not return unto me void, but it shall accomplish that which I please, and it shall prosper in the thing whereto I sent it"* (Isaiah 55:11).

JOY, THE FORCE OF FAITH

"For the joy of the Lord is your strength." —Nehemiah 8:10

TRUTH: The fruit of the Spirit is the life and character of God deposited in our human spirit when we become born again. Jesus' character demonstrated in our daily life is the greatest proof that the fruit of the Spirit is operating in us to produce holiness. Every believer must allow the Holy Spirit to cultivate the fruit in their hearts and apply it to their lives. Joy is one fruit of the Spirit, and we all have joy. See Galatians 5:22; 1 Peter 1:8-9. We all try to obtain things in life to increase our natural joy. Parents may take their children to Disneyland, and it is the dream of most to vacation in Hawaii for pleasure. People have parties where they eat, drink, and are merry. Many find joy in their work. The writer of Ecclesiastes says he experienced all these things, and they are vanity of vanities. He says all is vanity. The truth is that real joy is not attained from the outside because joy is of the Lord, and it is from within our spirit.

Joy springs in our reborn hearts where the Holy Spirit dwells. As we meditate on the Word and worship the Father, the Holy Spirit will respond with joy, and we will sense His joyful excitement.

"Thou wilt shew me the path of life: in thy presence is fulness of joy; at thy right hand there are pleasures forevermore" (Psalm 16:11).

LIFE: Spiritual joy is from the Spirit of God. We experience the joy of our salvation when we unload the burden of sin. See Acts 16:28-34. Our hope in God stimulates joy, which strengthens our faith. We can have joy when we see others saved and receive blessings from God. See Acts 15:3-4. Express joy during your trials and while waiting on your blessings. Joy is the force of faith to help us endure to the end or until victory comes. See Habakkuk 3:17; Isaiah 35:10. Paul and Silas's praise and rejoicing in faith brought their freedom. See Acts 16:16-40. Do not let problems, people, or pride squash your joy, rejoice and build inner strength for Christ in you full of joy sustains you to give you life.

JOY, THE FORCE OF FAITH — DAY 2

"These things have I spoken unto you, that my joy might remain in you, and that your joy might be full." —John 15:11

TRUTH: God deposited joy within, and we can access His joy as we become grateful for His great love and grace and for so great a salvation, in which we can rejoice because of all Jesus did for us. The fruit of joy planted in our hearts, when nurtured and watered, will grow. When we study, we encourage our spirit, meditate on the Word, worship, give thanks, and rejoice to stir up the joy within. The Holy Spirit will take over and bring true joy to our hearts as we rest in and depend on God. God Himself will cause the life of Christ in us to arise and live through us to bring prosperity in every area so that our joy may be complete. See John 15:1-11. Abiding in Jesus and fellowshipping with the Holy Spirit will cause joy to bubble from our spirit into our soul to lift and sustain us during difficult times.

Philippians 4:4 says, *"Rejoice in the Lord always: and again I say, rejoice."* Why rejoice always? Christ is our life, so rejoice in the God of our salvation and all He did for us on the Cross. And again, we rejoice in the faithfulness of His character as we stand in faith, believing Him to bring forth the blessing we desire to enrich our daily lives. Next, we should also rejoice when the answered prayer manifests. Joy always causes us to bless the Lord and to have His praise continually in our mouths. With joy we can be sustained as we patiently wait to receive our inheritance from the Lord and to go forth to spread the joy and blessing to others.

LIFE: Meditate on rejoicing Scriptures and let the joy of the Lord strengthen you. See Psalms 5:11; 34:1-2; 86:10-12; 95:1-11; Proverbs 17:22; Isaiah 61:3; Jeremiah 15:16; Matthew 5:11-12; Romans 14:17; Ephesians 5:18-19; James 1:12; Revelation 19:7.

JOY, THE BUCKET FOR FAITH

"Thou wilt shew me the path of life: in thy presence is fulness of joy; at thy right hand there are pleasures for evermore." —Psalm 16:11

TRUTH: Attacks and trials from the enemy can plunge us into dark places if we do not know that Jesus is Lord over darkness. He is light, and darkness is dispelled when light shines. Christians who know God has called them to live by faith and are battling with anxiety, fear, worry, despair, or depression may have just not yet been applying all that they know about receiving God's love to build their faith, and therefore, may not be receiving from God; or they may have missed this essential aspect of their faith, which is their joy. Joy is the carrier and sustainer of faith.

Isaiah 12:2-4 says, *"Behold, God is my salvation; I will trust, and not be afraid: for the Lord, JEHOVAH is my strength and my song; he also is become my salvation. Therefore, with joy shall ye draw water out of the wells of salvation. And in that day shall ye say, Praise the Lord, call upon his name, declare his doings among the people, make mention that his name is exalted."*

From these verses and our main text in Psalm 16:11, we learn that our salvation or deliverance from troubles is in God through Christ Jesus. If we trust in Him, we will not be afraid. But we need His strength to move us from trial and trouble through the process of faith and trust into deliverance and victory. Joy is the bucket that brings us strength, taking us from trial to triumph. To receive our salvation, deliverance, or victory, we need to get into our Father's presence to receive of Him by faith rejoicing so His joy will sustain us until our blessing comes.

LIFE: The path into God's presence is joy, praise, rejoicing, and worship. Joy will keep you steadfast in your faith even in difficult situations as you draw from the well of salvation the blessing you need to prosper. So, always rejoice!

JOY, THE BUCKET FOR FAITH — DAY 2

"Therefore, with joy shall ye draw water out of the wells of salvation. And in that day shall ye say, Praise the Lord, call upon his name... —Isaiah 12:3-4

TRUTH: What is in the well of salvation? It is whatever we need from Jesus: He is our well for healing, deliverance, salvation for loved ones, finances, assurance for the future, career, children, family, job. God in Christ Jesus has done it all on the Cross to meet our every need.

Do not focus on the negative circumstances or feelings the devil is giving to distract you. Hear God's Word concerning your situation, and let faith arise in you. See Romans 10:17. Find Scriptures to support God's promise for your need. In your heart, tie those Scriptures of God's Word to Jesus' accomplishment on the Cross, providing those promises. Always incorporate the Blood of Jesus. For example, your healing and the stripes He received. Hear the Word, speak them, use your imagination to see Jesus taking away in His body your sickness, and believe in your heart that it is true that you are free from it. After knowing that you believe in your heart, pray and ask God for the promised blessing and receive. Believe then, pray. See Mark 11:24; 1 Peter 2:24.

Start rejoicing that you have it already, even though you do not yet see it. See Hebrews 11:1; Philippians 3:3. Joy is the bridge between our believing and receiving. Rejoice in God's truth to us in Jesus, His promises, His help in the Holy Spirit, and His blessings. Let our joy take us across the bridge from believing to receiving and be made whole and full of joy.

LIFE: Receive what you have prayed for as yours by an act of faith. If depressed and locked inside, get joy from reading and meditating in the Word, speaking and rejoicing, then go outside and enjoy the sunshine, flowers, and butterflies. The Word believed and spoken and acted on with joy will reap great blessings. Be joyful and enjoy your life in Christ.

LAZINESS

"For we hear that there are some which walk among you disorderly, working not at all, but are busybodies." —2 Thessalonians 3:11

TRUTH: We know people who do not want to work in this natural world. They may do some work, but only the very minimum, as if they are saving themselves. If they are not sick, these people are often those who have an entitlement personality. They feel others owe them something and are sometimes angry when they do not get what they think should be available. Some people always have Monday morning blues when it is time to work. Work is simply a necessity to pay the bills. They have no passion or desire to be creative or improve themselves at their workplace. They live for Friday and the coming weekend for happy hour and personal pleasures.

God has His ideas about work. He set the stage with Adam when He told Adam and Eve to be fruitful and multiply and replenish the earth. Adam was given work and responsibilities in the garden, and we have them too. Sometimes Christians can feel guilty or be made to feel guilty for not supporting those who do not want to work, for example, some non-disabled panhandlers on the street. God does not encourage laziness.

One good reason to pray before supporting such needs is that you may unwittingly join forces with the spirit that keeps these people bound. It may be a spirit of oppression, Poverty, or laziness. See 2 John 10-11 Always be led by the Holy Spirit and do as He says, but do not feel guilty. Some ways to help are preaching the gospel, praying for them, and supporting organizations and churches responsible for caring for and supporting them into rehabilitation. We can also encourage them to register in these helpful organizations and churches or to receive salvation and deliverance.

LIFE: *"This we commanded you, that if any would not work, neither should he eat"* (2 Thessalonians 3:10).

"He becometh poor that dealeth with a slack hand: but the hand of he diligent maketh rich" (Proverbs 10:4).

LAZINESS — DAY 2

*"In all labor there is profit: but the talk of lips tendeth
only to penury (poverty)." —Proverbs 14:23*

TRUTH: It is God's will for people to work. If He gave Adam work and the church the great commission, work must be a good thing, a necessity, a responsibility, and a privilege. See Mark 16:15- 17. One old saying goes, "The devil finds work for idle hands." Whether we are working at the marketplace or in the kingdom, God desires that we do so with purpose and passion and do it well. God has no room for laziness, either natural or spiritual.

"And whatsoever ye do, do it heartily, as to the Lord, and not unto men" (Colossians 3:23).

"Whatsoever thy hand findeth to do, do it with thy might; for there is no work, nor device, nor knowledge, nor wisdom, in the grave, whither thou goest" (Ecclesiastes 9:10).

"So, then faith cometh by hearing and hearing by the word of God" (Romans 10:17).

Expend effort working to hear and hear again the Word of God to build faith. Build faith believe God's Word is true in every area of your life, at work, in relationships, children, and in times of failure and success. Growing our love for the Father and increasing our faith to trust God is the labor we expend to enter God's rest. See Galatians 5:6; Romans 10:17; Hebrews 4.

LIFE: Paul worked a job to set an example that a believer should not be lazy. See Acts 20:33-35. Neither should you be spiritually lazy, but instead seek to build your faith with the Word of God, to renew your soul (mind, will, and emotions), and to be strong in the Lord. Do not be lazy about prayer and meeting to fellowship with other believers. See Hebrews 10:23-25. If overcome by laziness, you will have a tough time exercising your faith, believing, and receiving God's promises of prosperity, peace, and the deliverance which He promised you. Let the weak say he is strong and receive God's help to change. See Psalm 34:9-10.

SPIRITUAL VACATION

"But David tarried still in Jerusalem... and from the
roof he saw a woman..." —2 Samuel 11:1-27

TRUTH: Believers live by faith and continue by faith daily, hourly, and moment by moment. See Galatians 3:11; Colossians 1:22-23. It was a time when kings went to war, but David decided to take a natural and spiritual vacation. He sent his men to war while he stayed home relaxing on his balcony, where he saw Bathsheba, Uriah's wife, and was tempted with lust. His spiritual vacation led him down a path of sin, selfishness, lust, coveting, adultery, murder, and un-repented sin. After taking another man's wife, he tried to cover up his sin. Remember that God is omniscient; we cannot hide anything from Him. David suffered in anguish greatly from his sin. See 2 Samuel 12:9-13, 18-20.

Christians should grasp from David's life that when opportunities to sin present themselves for momentary pleasure or gain, we should first honor God's presence in us and call on His grace for help to resist that temptation. See Hebrews 4:16. Then choose to believe God's Word, cast the thoughts down, and be sober and vigilant against our adversary, the devil, who is seeking to devour us. See 1 Peter 5:8.

Can anyone remember a time when you basked in a momentary pleasure that led to great pain? Was the pleasure worth the price? Every answer in hindsight should be a "significant no"! So, be encouraged to run away from temptation and run to God. Ask for His grace to resist the temptation. And if like David, we do sin, it is better to own up, ask for mercy and repent; we shouldn't wait for God to call us out. See 1 Samuel 15:13-24. God hates sin because sin diminishes not only His character and witness in us but also our reputation and our physical bodies.

LIFE: Believers spend much time with Jesus; we have no time for a spiritual vacation. Daily live your faith in a close and intimate relationship with the Lord and His Word; as you commit wholeheartedly to Him, He will help you to walk in righteousness, always doing right as you walk by faith and not by sight.

GUARD OUR HEARTS

"Keep thy heart with all diligence; for out of it are the issues of life." —Proverbs 4:23

TRUTH: Before we were saved, we would allow any and many thoughts to flow through our minds freely, and Satan was okay with that. But after salvation, he will more aggressively seek to attack our thoughts to steer us away from the gospel and from obeying the Scriptures. God, therefore, encourages us to abide and continue. See John 15:7-9; Acts 13:43; Acts 14:22; Colossians 1:22-23. The enemy will also seek to prevent us from continuing to the end to receive all our blessings. See Matthew 24:13; Hebrews 3:14; 6:11-14. We must first guard our minds to protect our hearts as we continue and endure.

Satan deceived Eve because she did not watch over her mind; she listened and did the opposite of what God commanded. Satan will attack and destroy any person's life with an unguarded mind. He will infiltrate to overload with worry, distract, confuse, tempt, lie, guilt, accuse, intimidate, and condemn. We have a responsibility first to recognize the source and then to compare our thoughts against the Word of God, our main guide. Afterward, we are to reject Satan and depend on the power of the Holy Spirit to teach, guide, and sustain us.

"And be not conformed to this world: but be ye transformed by the renewing of your mind" (Romans 12:2).

"Wherewithal shall a young man cleanse his way? By taking heed thereto according to thy word" (Psalm 119:9).

Life: Guard your heart in what you hear, think, and see. Hide the Word in your heart, lift it as your sword of faith to defend yourself from the onslaught of the enemy. Secondly, filter all your thoughts, words, attitudes, and actions to align with God's Word. Cast down and reject evil thoughts and embrace the good. See 2 Corinthians 10:4-5; Philippians 4:8. A guarded heart will create a disciplined mind to believe in God. Keep trusting Him, and He will keep you prosperous and in peace to the end.

TILL CHRIST BE FORMED IN YOU

"My little children, of whom I travail in birth again until Christ be formed in you." —Galatians 4: 19

TRUTH: God's whole aim is for His Word and Spirit to remake us into the image of His Son, Jesus. This will happen as we receive Jesus as King and daily seek to become like the King in Christlikeness. As we see the Kingship of Jesus, we accept that He exercises authority, dominion, or rulership and control over all believers as children of the Kingdom of God. As King, He rules over our hearts by His Word in the Bible and by the voice of His Spirit. What God says is what He means, and we are to depend on His Spirit to bring us into obedience. See Philippians 2:13. We obey as we walk by faith, hearing, believing, acting on the Word, and responding according to our beliefs. Christ is formed in us when we are born again, changed in the heart to possess the Spirit of Jesus, then willingly live by faith until His Word dominates our spirit, enabling us to be led by the Holy Spirit to obey His voice. As believers, Christ is being formed in our hearts when we are willing to be transformed by renewing the mind, exchanging fear for love, unbelief for faith, Law for grace, a weakness for strength, pride for humility, torment for peace, darkness for light, bondage for deliverance, and being led by the Holy Spirit instead of being driven by Satan and fear. See Romans 8:1-2.

LIFE: Acknowledge Jesus as Savior, King, Ruler, Lord, and Owner of your life. Acknowledge that you live in the Kingdom of God here on earth, full of faith, life, light, and love while always looking forward to the eternal Kingdom of heaven where Jesus dwells. Acknowledge and believe that because of Jesus, Satan is defeated and must flee at your command because Christ is formed in you, and you abide in and depend on Him in the relationship for everything. Embrace God's love; it will increase your connection, faith, trust, God's presence, and His divine blessings in your life. Let God the Holy Spirit become prominent on the inside. Believe Him and live like He's the Greater One in you! Causing you to reign in life. Meditate on Romans 8:37; 1 John 4:4.

TILL CHRIST BE FORMED IN YOU — DAY 2

"I travail in birth again until Christ be formed in you." Galatians 4:19

TRUTH: As we spend time in the Word, we are daily maturing to love God with all the heart, mind, and soul to build faith to believe, receive, and love others as God loves us. See Mark 11:24; Matthew 22:37.

As we become doers of the Word, we acknowledge that the Holy Spirit living in us is continually sanctifying us from sin and idolatry, from pride to righteousness, from lies to truth, and from self-centeredness to Christ-centeredness. God desires His Spirit to dominate our lives and change our character to be like Jesus, as Christ is daily being formed within.

When we are faithful to God, His Word, and His Spirit enduring even through trials and difficulties, Christ in us will cause us to be strong. As we learn to see tests allowed by God as a necessary purification step, we will draw closer to our Father and endure until the flesh is subdued and Christ is formed in our hearts. We trust our Father's heart, even if in the circumstances we do not understand, but His love assures our hearts that He will provide. We can stand unmovable with our spirit aligned with God's Spirit, agreeing with His Word, saying the same thing until our enemy is defeated, and Christ is exalted to bring our blessing to pass.

LIFE: I am the child of the King, King Jesus. I live in His Kingdom of life and light. Death and darkness have no power over me. See John 8:12; Colossians 1:13. Christ lives in my heart, being formed full of power and boldness; He is my life. The hope of my glory is in Him. He is my reality, my great love, and my truth. His Word says by His stripes I am healed; therefore, I am healed. I agree with His Word; I shall not be moved, for Christ's Word of healing is formed in me. His love, which purchased my healing, frees me from fear, sickness, and destruction because I believe He flows by His Spirit with the power to heal and deliver. I believe, and I receive. Amen.

GROW UP SPIRITUALLY

"But grow in grace, and in the knowledge of our Lord and Savior Jesus Christ. To him be glory both now and forever. Amen." —2 Peter 3:18

TRUTH: *"As newborn babes, desire the sincere milk of the word, that ye may grow thereby. For everyone that useth milk is unskillful in the word of righteousness: for he is a babe. But strong meat belongeth to them that are of full age, even those who by reason of use have their senses exercised to discern both good and evil"* (1 Peter 2:2; Hebrews 5:13-14).

LIFE: I receive God's grace in His goodness and mercy at the Cross. And daily, I seek to grow up in the things of God. I am 'just,' and I live by faith. My faith pleases God because I depend on His grace given me in Jesus, His Spirit, and His written Word. I listen to the Word; I meditate the Word until faith in Christ is formed in my heart to believe and receive the promise I need, which was given to me in the Word.

I read the promised Word, meditate on it, speak it in faith, and believe with my heart. I now rest in Jesus and trust Him to bring my need into manifestation. I desire to grow in the things of God and to be transformed by the renewing of my mind with the Word until Christ is formed in my heart, and I continually think, speak, and live by faith, trusting Jesus like He trusted His Father. *"And the glory which thou gavest me I have given them; that they may be one, even as we are one"* (John 17:22).

I study the Word to show myself approved that though my outward man perishes, my inward man is being renewed day by day. I walk by faith and not by sight and look not at the things which are seen but at the things which are not seen, for the things which are seen are temporary, but the things which are not seen are eternal and bring the life of Christ to me. See 2 Timothy 2:15; 2 Corinthians 4:16-18. I fully believe God will bring my desires to pass because I believe His Word, His power, and authority in me rise to cancel Satan's attacks. I seek to grow up in Christ Jesus daily and walk continually in His victory.

GROW UP SPIRITUALLY — DAY 2

*"But grow in grace, and in the knowledge of our Lord
and Savior Jesus Christ."* —2 Peter 3:18

TRUTH AND LIFE: As I grow up spiritually, I am God-centered and God- inside minded. I seek first the kingdom of God and His righteousness, and all things are added unto me. See Matthew 6:33. I refuse to be cluttered in my soul with negative thoughts and worry. I choose instead to surrender my human will to God and cast down imaginations and every high thing that exalteth itself against the knowledge of God in my life. I cast every care and worry to God to the obedience of Jesus, and I know He will work everything out for my good. See 2 Corinthians 10:4-5; 1 Peter 5:7; Romans 8: 28.

I guard my heart and mind against Satan's negative influences and negative people and keep my eyes on Jesus, the Author and Finisher of my faith. By this, I am kept in God's grace until I have the victory. See Proverbs 4:23-26; Hebrews 12:2; 1 Peter 1:5.

I am established in my faith, trusting the Lord with all my heart, and I lean not to my understanding, but in all my ways, I acknowledge Jesus, and He directs my path. See Proverbs 3:5-6. I am not afraid of evil tidings because my heart is fixed, trusting in the Lord, and I choose to trust my Father's Word and His promises as I await the fulfillment of my desire.

When the enemy comes against me, the Spirit of God raises a standard against him like a flood and causes me to overcome. Thanks be to God, which causes me to triumph in Christ Jesus. See Isaiah 59:19; 54:17; Revelation 12:11; 2 Corinthians 2:14. I embrace by faith the trials sent by God to purify my heart, and to refine and mature my character to be more like His. See 1 Peter 1:6-7. I can do all things through Christ because I am more than a conqueror in Him. His love keeps me in Christ, and nothing can separate me from the love of my God as I grow daily in His love and into His image. See Philippians 4:13; Romans 8:37-39.

WHOSE REPORT?

"And these all, having obtained a good report through faith, received not the promise." —Hebrews 11:39

TRUTH: A Christian movie titled "I Still Believe" tells a true story about actor Jeremy Kemp, a twenty-year-old young man starting his college experience in music. Jeremy had a platform as a musician, which he used to showcase the entire journey of his undying love for Melissa, who had cancer. The movie showed:

1. Just as Jeremy was faithful to the end, God's love will never leave us nor forsake us. See Hebrews 13:5.
2. Despite all the challenges in our lives, we must still believe. Stephen, who, even at the point of being stoned to death, kept his eyes on his eternal destiny, said, *"Father, forgive them for they know not what they do"* (Luke 23:24).
3. As our text shows, God's promises to us are sure; and we will receive of Him. However, God did not say when or how to receive the promise.

In this movie, as she was dying, this young lady demonstrated complete faith and confidence in her Heavenly Father, whom she knew was in complete control of her life, just like the men and women in Hebrews 11. Many of whom never lived to see the promise but were mentioned in the Kingdom for their faithfulness, courage, and faith. Sometimes believers in the faith camp have given up on their faith because their desire did not manifest or didn't manifest as expected. When we direct our faith towards God, we must release the how, why, and when to Him, as He alone decides how our lives will benefit us and the kingdom. We are His, and He can write the story of our lives as He sees fit. He did the same for His twelve disciples.

LIFE: Some people stand in faith and still die. But it is not our place to form conclusions. Firstly, in their faith, they may have had hindrances or doubts we are unaware of. Secondly, God is sovereign, and He can use any situation, even our lives, for the greater good of the gospel. Whose report will you believe? We must trust God completely, for He is always absolutely good.

FATHERHOOD

"And thou shalt teach them diligently unto thy children, and shalt talk of them when thou...sittest...walketh... liest down, and when thou riseth up" —Deuteronomy 6:7

TRUTH: Fathers are of utmost importance in the home and family. In many children, negative behavior patterns have been traced to absentee fathers. In the latest ongoing discussions during the recent riots on U.S. streets in 2020 during the COVID 19, pandemic it was stated that fatherlessness was the main factor why many young African Americans are in prison. The nuclear family is God's answer for a stable home and society. Fathers who love God and love their families are often great role models in diligently teaching their children good values, good decision-making skills, how to take responsibility for their thought life, their actions, and their future. Children look up to their fathers as good examples in relationship interactions and for provision, protection, and wisdom. They should learn about accountability, responsibility, punctuality, facing difficulties, and enduring until success comes. I know these all sound like high ideals, and while, as fathers, you are not perfect and will not execute fatherhood flawlessly, with God, all things are possible. Spend time in the Word and ask for God's grace in His wisdom and the help of the Holy Spirit to guide you with each child.

LIFE: Fathers, spend time with your children and let them know you love God and love them too. Let them know they are accepted and loved in your father-child relationship. Love plus time and faith equal a relationship. Seek to communicate with your children by God's grace in humility and not always in an authoritarian way, causing them to rebel. Teach your children God's Christian values to love God, pray, walk in faith, be honest, keep their word, have a good work ethic, and esteem others to show God's love. Fathers, it is not about perfection but your sincerity to seek to walk in the Spirit of truth and humility, always asking the Holy Spirit to aid you in helping your children grow in fear of the Lord. God will honor your efforts and assist you in pointing your children to Him as you take them to church with you.

TRUE PATH OF LIFE

"Neither is there salvation in any other: for there is none other name... whereby we must be saved." —Acts 4:12

TRUTH: Increasingly, people are clamoring to live their way with many sayings. "Do what you want, you do you, float your boat, live your best life." People want to have the right to make any choice, thinking they can create their truth and their path. But that is not God's way. We are created by God and for Him. The Bible says, *"For of him, and through him, and to him, are all things: to whom be glory forever"* (Romans 11:36). Every person born needs to be saved. Every person needs Jesus. As we live our daily lives, we can heed that there is a way which seems right unto man, but the end thereof are the ways of death. See Proverbs 14:12. Jesus died on the Cross to give us eternal life and entry into the kingdom of God. A path of life we should all desire and take.

The Spirit of God has given us salvation within our human spirit. He will keep us continually being saved in our soul and body and lead us in the ways of God and away from evil. Living God's way is yielding to the Word and receiving it as truth, which releases power to set us free. See John 8:32,36. As we abide in Jesus the Vine, our Sustenance, the Great I Am, as our Source, we will have everything we need. He becomes the path to our best life. If we allow God through Jesus His Son to lead us by His Spirit and His life, we will walk in the ways of God, His truth, and gain a life full of His wisdom, blessings, and abundant peace. *"Thou wilt shew me the path of life: in thy presence is fullness of joy; at thy right hand there are pleasures for evermore"* (Psalm 16:11).

LIFE: There is no other path to God but Jesus, and there is no other way to meaningful success in every area of your life in the family, health, vocation, good choices, or your finances without God. Jesus is the fullness and completeness of your life. *"In him was life, and the life was the light of men."* See John 1:4.

Meditate on John 1.

WALK AS JESUS WALKED

"As ye have therefore received Christ Jesus the Lord,
so walk ye in him." —Colossians 2:6

TRUTH: God loves us and made for us to love Him in return. Faith in God's love led us to believe and have faith in Jesus to receive salvation. God is now commanding us to maintain faith and to walk in the same posture of grace through faith in the power of the Holy Spirit.

Grace: Our Christian walk is to be grace through faith in freedom with sincerity and thanksgiving unto God for all Jesus did for us on the Cross, and not in the Law or works at any stage of our walk. God's grace did it all through Jesus: *"Therefore it is of faith, that it might be by grace; to the end the promise might be sure to all the seed; not to that only... also which is of the faith of Abraham; who is the father of us all"* (Romans 4:16). See 2 Corinthians 9:8.

"Be it known unto you therefore, men and brethren, that through this man is preached unto you the forgiveness of sins. And by him all that believe are justified from all things" (Acts 13:38-39).

"Christ hath redeemed us from the curse of the law, being made a curse for us: for it is written, Cursed is everyone that hangeth on a tree: That the blessing of Abraham might come on the gentiles ..." (Galatians 3:13-14).

Believe: *"He that believeth on the Son hath everlasting life: and he that believeth not on the Son shall not see life; but the wrath of God abideth on him."* (John 3:36). See John 20:31; 2 Corinthians 4:13-14.

Walk in Faith: *"Now the God of hope fill you with all joy and peace in believing, that ye may abound in hope, through the power of the Holy Ghost."* (Romans 15:13) See Mark 11:22-24.

LIFE: Let us always keep our eyes on Jesus just as He kept His eyes on God His Father. Whatever we face, go to Jesus first; hear from Him, believe, and receive. Walk by faith in God's grace and not by sight, just as Jesus walked by faith in perfect union relationship with His Father. Meditate on John 5:19.

WALK AS JESUS WALKED — DAY 2

*"He that saith he abideth in him ought himself also so
to walk, even as he walked."* —1 John 2:6.

TRUTH: Salvation is much more than saying a salvation prayer and waiting until we die to go to heaven. It is not an experience like buying fire insurance where we pay the premiums and then wait until there is a fire to collect the settlement. First John was written to help believers know whether they are true believers with genuine faith.

If we say we are Christians, God says that we must surrender to Him and be imitators of Him to talk, walk, and act like Jesus. We are to have a Christ-like lifestyle just as Jesus had a union relationship with the Father. See John 17: 21-23; 1 Corinthians 11:1.

How did Jesus Himself walk? He had fellowship with His Father in heaven and walked in His Word. See 1 John 1:7-9. Jesus often prayed, followed His Father's instructions, and was without sin. He imitated His Father and said and did only as He saw Him do. See Ephesians 5:2; John 5:19. He walked in love. See 1 John 4:8-12.

He walked in faith, power, authority, purity, and holiness. See Matthew 15:34-39; 1 Peter 1:15-16. He was obedient and kept the Law perfectly to free us from it. See Romans 8:2-4; 10:4. He was zealous after the eternal things of God. He pleased the Father and lived a miraculous life producing good fruit wherever He went.

LIFE: We show forth Christ not by our attire, chains with crosses, or our bumper stickers but as a people submitted to their Lord by dying to sin and self and in dependence on the Holy Spirit to transform our soul by Christ's life, love, and light. We must acknowledge we have been bought with a price by the grace of our King. We are children of a King who exerts His will and rule by His love. He asks us to be willing to be led by the Holy Spirit into His love and Christlikeness by faith. Be willing! And walk as Jesus walked and let the world see your love, light, and the good following. Meditate Matthew 5:14-15.

COMMITMENT

"But Daniel purposed in his heart that he would not defile himself with the portion of the king's meat, nor with the wine which he drank." —Daniel 1:8

TRUTH: God had given His people the Law in the Ten Commandments and many other religious, social, and dietary rules to set them apart as followers of God from the rest of society. Daniel and his friends were captured by the Babylonians and were chosen to serve in the king's palace. The king instructed them to be fed with the king's meat and drink, which would violate their covenant with God. Some of us in the church today would possibly jump at the chance and say, "Yes! this *is the favor of the Lord,*" but Daniel and his friends thought about it and decided not to eat the defiling foods and disobey God. They committed themselves to do what was right in the eyes of the Lord.

What has been offered to you and me that seems like favor but could defile our bodies or our witness for the Lord? Is it overeating, drinking, music that doesn't honor God, or friends who aren't the best for us? What has Satan enticed us with to distract us? Notice Daniel was with friends of like beliefs; they agreed on the choice of foods. We are under a New Covenant of grace not strictly bound by the Ten Commandments, but if we are to love God with all our hearts, soul, and body, we too must be committed to loving God and putting the things which honor God first. With the help of the Holy Spirit, let us commit and decide in our hearts what is helpful to our Christian life and stick with it.

LIFE: Like Daniel, purpose in your heart what is the good and acceptable and perfect will of God and be committed to Him and the life of Christ in you. See Romans 12:1-2. What change is needed for a greater commitment? Is it spending more time in the Word, prayer, or fellowship? Is it your spending habits that mostly exclude God? Is it a need to guard your mind? Ask the Holy Spirit; He will help you commit to the things most honoring to God.

"But seek ye first the kingdom of God, and his righteousness; and all these things shall be added unto you" (Matthew 6:33).

OUR COMMITMENT

"Let your heart therefore be perfect with the Lord our God, to walk in his statutes, and to keep his commandments, as at this day" —1 Kings 8:61

TRUTH: The essence of a genuine relationship is commitment. Jesus died for us and drew us out of the world and sin as the *Ecclesia*. These are believers, the called-out ones in relationship with Him. God was committed to us with a covenant of love. See John 3:16; 13:34. We are commanded to love and to commit to God to love Him with all our hearts, and all our soul, and with all our minds. See Matthew 22:37-39. When we commit to receiving and cultivating God's love in our hearts, we are being empowered with the most significant force on earth, God Himself, because He is Love. See 1 John 4:8; 18-19. Love in relationship with God and others is the only thing we can take to heaven and into eternity. Paul tells us that what pleases God is faith, which will work when we love God and others; the Word says, *"But faith works by love"* (Galatians 5:6).

Our commitment to God can only be genuine, restful, peaceful, and rewarding when we receive His love by faith in His grace. Only then can we see ourselves as we are, new creation children of God, loved and accepted by the Father, cared for and protected, blessed with all the blessings we need, having no sin held to our account, forgiven, led by the Holy Spirit, and given gifts to share the relationship and commitment we have with the Father with others. Without grace, we live self-centered lives, which keep us trying, striving, and struggling to establish our commitment with ourselves and then with God. Still, with grace and the Holy Spirit, we can settle our hearts into a loving dependence on God, having the assurance of His love, and faithfully yield to committing to Him.

LIFE: Have a perfect, wholly committed heart, giving God priority and having a desire for Him above all else. With your commitment, He will make His life flow in and through you to give you, His best. See Psalm 37:5; John 14: 17-18; Colossians 2:2-3; 3:2-4.

PRIDE

"God resisteth the proud, but giveth grace unto the humble." —James 4:6

TRUTH: One definition of *pride* is *an assumed superiority or loftiness or a sense of unwarranted self-importance.* This contrasts with Colossians 1:16, which tells us that God created all things for Himself. All people are to be submitted to God.

When we take what God has given us and corrupt it with selfishness, self-sufficiency, and self-glorification, we have become prideful, and God resists the proud. See James 4:6.

Pride got Satan kicked out of heaven because God hates pride. See Isaiah 14:13-14; Proverbs 8:13; James 4:13-16. We should avoid actions of selfish ambition or vain conceit. Instead, in humility, value God and others above ourselves. See Psalm 34:3; Philippians 2:3. When pride comes, strife, disgrace, destruction, and ultimately a fall.

"Pride goeth before destruction, and an haughty spirit before a fall (Proverbs 16:18).

God desires the opposite of pride for us; He wants us to be pure and humble in heart, submitted, trusting, and obedient. A humble heart can receive Jesus as Savior, Lord, Baptizer, obey His commandment to love, depend on God, and yield to Jesus to be led by His Holy Spirit. See Matthew 5:8; John 1:33; Romans 8:14.

LIFE: Pride must be recognized, rejected, and repented of. As it will cause God to fight against you. He will put you in fiery trials until you run to Him to help you to repent and reject pride and self. Until you accept, it is impossible to live the Christian life in your strength and way; and instead to yield to Him and worship Him as Lord and Master. The remedy for pride is love, humility, faith, and trust in God's grace to be led by Him in the power of His Holy Spirit. God's love will lead you unto Himself, truth, humility, and peace, in relationship with your Heavenly Father.

HUMILITY AND PRIDE

"The sacrifices of God are a broken spirit: a broken and a contrite heart. O God, thou wilt not despise." —Psalm 51:17

TRUTH: We must be aware of how our character aligns with the nature of Christ and ask God to help us to be transformed by the renewing of our minds and hearts to His character and His will. See Romans 12:1-2.

LIFE: The prideful and the humble: The prideful are self-righteous; they are often judgmental, critical and look for weakness in others. The humble are loving, compassionate, and forgiving. The prideful are self-reliant instead of dependent on God and love strife, but the humble seek peace. The proud are selfish and demanding like Miriam, but the humble are meek like Moses. Pride leads to quarrels and strife for self-preservation, but the humble deny self and give others the benefit of the doubt for the sake of peace, like David's response to Saul.

Pride demands to be seen and catered to, but humility looks like Jesus washing His disciples' feet. Pride puts others down to uplift self, but Scripture tells us to esteem others like ourselves in humility. The prideful have a haughty spirit, but the humble know they are nothing without God. See John 15:5.

The proud love God from a distance because they are too self-conscious to draw close, but the humble, knowing their worth is in God, are willing to draw near. The proud are quick to blame, but the humble follow the Word and judge themselves first.

At times, the prideful believer usually hides needs by asking for prayer as an "unspoken request." The humble are willing to expose the devil and be opened to getting God's help. The prideful have great difficulty admitting they are wrong and often are not forgiving. The humble are quick to repent and quick to forgive. Choose Christ and humility over pride in self.

"Better it is to be of an humble spirit with the lowly, than to divide the spoil with the proud" (Proverbs 16:19).

INSUBORDINATION

"And Miriam and Aaron spoke against Moses because of the Ethiopian woman whom he married..." —Numbers 12:1-3

TRUTH: *"Let every soul be subject unto the higher powers. For there is no power but of God: the powers that be are ordained of God... and they that resist shall receive to themselves damnation"* (Romans 13:1-2).

It may be quite a common behavior in our nation and churches where, when we don't like some of the choices our leaders make, we become rebellious in our thinking and drawback, step down, form cliques, or even walk away. The Old Testament stories are relevant to us today as examples to guide us into truth and away from error. See 1 Corinthians 10:11; 2 Peter 2:6; 1 Thessalonians 1:7-10.

Miriam and Aaron did not like Moses' choice of his wife and began to resent his leadership. They went so far as to question if Moses was the only one God could speak to because they contended God could speak to them also. They used his wife as an excuse to be discontented and to rebel against God's chosen leader.

We can be like Miriam and Aaron, pointing out the flaws of our leaders, becoming critical, opinionated, backseat leaders, developing a sullen and rebellious attitude. God dealt severely, judging Miriam, and she became leprous.

Whatever our thoughts about the person or the decisions of those placed in authority over us, we are to be respectful, honoring, and supportive of God in them by our prayers. By our prayers, let God correct them. See Hebrews 12:6. We can only rebel when we are asked to do wrong and to honor man over God. See Daniel 3:10-12; Acts 4:18-20; 5:29. We are to speak the truth in love and trust God to work out the situation.

LIFE: Respect your leaders and trust God's grace in everyone, for building the body and for the unity of peace. See 1 Timothy 2:1-5. Pray Matthew 5:6; Ephesians 1:16-23; Colossians 1:9-14.

GRACE VS. LAW

"Therefore it is of faith, that it might be by grace: to the end the promise might be sure to all the seed; not to that only which is of the law, but to that also which is of the faith of Abraham: who is the father of us all." —Romans 4:16

TRUTH: Grace is God's power and ability in us and working on our behalf to accomplish what we are unable to do for ourselves. Our redemption starts on the correct footing when, by faith, we depend entirely on Jesus for our salvation and not on any of our efforts. If we know that we have received Jesus into our hearts as our Savior and are still not getting all the good things the Bible says we possess or should possess, it means we still have not fully understood God's grace and all He did for us. Instead, we may be living by religion, rules, self-restraints, and self-corrections. This lack of understanding of God's grace has left many living less than God intended, still trying, striving, and struggling to achieve God's blessings or to attain what God says we already have. Be it salvation to make us free, the ability to live above sin, seeking holiness to feel close to God, gaining blessings to prosper, or fighting to gain authority to overcome the evil one. Any efforts initiated by us are the works of our hands or of the flesh, which Jesus rejects just as God rejected the works of Adam and Eve, Cain, and Saul, in Genesis 3 and 4 and 1 Samuel 15.

LIFE: Grace, on the other hand, requires faith which believes God in Jesus, just as His Word says. Grace in our dependence on Jesus and His work on the Cross and receiving the gift of righteousness to make us righteous and accepted by the Father, qualified for His blessings and His help. Grace through faith brings hope, expectancy, faith, and anticipation of God's response to His goodness into our life—just as we saw God brought in the lives of Abraham and Peter the Apostle.

GRACE VS. LAW — DAY 2

"Therefore, it is of faith that it might be by grace..." —Romans 4:16

TRUTH: *"Abraham believed God, and it was counted unto him for righteousness"* (Romans 4:3). Abraham had faith in God's Words to Him, and he acted and obeyed, showing that he loved and honored God by having faith in His grace and spoken Word.

God requires us to live by His grace, looking unto Jesus and showing we love Him by believing His every Word, then acting on it by faith. Grace takes us away from living by rules, looking at ourselves and our efforts, trying to prove that we love God, and afterward expressing despair with feelings of condemnation when we fail.

The Law of Moses, which demands obedience and living by rules, was replaced with the commandment to love God with sincerity of heart by the power of His Spirit.

"A new commandment I give unto you. That you love one another; as I have loved you, that ye also love one another" (John 13:34).

"Owe no man anything, but to love one another: for he that loveth another has fulfilled the law. For this, Thou shalt not commit adultery, Thou shalt not kill, Thou shalt not steal...and if there be any other commandment, it is briefly comprehended in this saying, namely, Thou shalt love thy neighbour as thyself. Love worketh no ill to his neighbour: therefore love is the fulfilling of the law" (Romans 13:8-10).

LIFE: Believers live in God's grace by faith in His love. The opposite is living by religion or legalism with rules and regulations, trying hard to please God; this will keep you in bondage. God removed the wrath, dread, and fear of the Law of works of the flesh which worked against us and gave us His power of love through the Holy Spirit, which frees us to live in peace and love with God, ourselves, and others. See Romans 5:1-2; Colossians 2:14-17.

CHRIST ENDED THE LAW

"For Christ is the end of the law for righteousness to everyone that believeth." —Romans 10:4

TRUTH: The Law refers to Moses' Law or the Ten Commandments and all the accompanying rituals and ordinances in the Old Testament. God is perfect and demands perfect performance and obedience under the Law. See Deuteronomy 27:26; James 2:10. The Law pointed out people's sins and their inability to perform perfectly before God. See Acts 7:53; 15:10; Romans 3:20-23; 7:5-6; Hebrews 7:18-19; 10:1. In this church age, we still live by the Law when:

- We live by external rules, neglecting the sacrifice of the Blood of Jesus.
- We choose to study the Word for information, principles, and standards to follow instead of seeking a relationship with God our Father through Jesus.
- When we live in our strength and do not rely on the Holy Spirit, Satan will keep us in bondage to the flesh, which lacks faith and is sin. See Romans 14:23.

A lack of faith creates doubt, looking at self, others, obstacles, trials, or listening to Satan's lies. A lack of trust makes the human will come alive with a Law or works mentality of self-sufficiency, self-effort, control, self-righteousness, striving, and struggling in our Christian walk. The results are pride, lack of faith, worship, ingratitude, and un-thankfulness. There is strife, division, and an absence of following God's will. The law increases the enemy's activity in our lives and expresses itself in behaviors such as self-effort, unworthiness, failure, increased judgment, harshness, and condemnation of self and others.

LIFE: *"But the scripture (Law) hath concluded (shut up) all under sin, that the promise by faith of Jesus Christ might be given to them that believe...But before faith came, we were kept under the law... But after that faith is come, we are no longer under a schoolmaster"* (Galatians 3:22-25). In Jesus, God ended the Law and gave us His grace, His goodness, and mercy for us to depend on Him and not ourselves in self-effort. Complete knowledge of God's love in Christ Jesus and your dependence on the Holy Spirit will end the Law and its effects in your life.

CHRIST ENDED THE LAW — DAY 2

"For Christ is the end of the law for righteousness." —Romans 10:4

TRUTH: Man could not save himself from sin, so God sent His grace in the person of Jesus Christ to bring salvation. The strictness of the Law caused the man to have the wrong image of God as being hard and angry when He dealt with sin. Jesus, God's Grace, was sent in love; when we receive Jesus as our salvation by faith, we receive grace in God's ability, power, and strength for our Christian walk. See Romans 10:9-10; Hebrews 13:20-21. We live by grace when:

- By faith, we believe in the finished work of the Cross and receive Jesus.
- We live depending on Jesus by His Spirit to meet all our daily needs.
- We are dead to sin, self, the Law and are alive unto God and His love.
- We have a love union relationship of oneness with our Father, daily drawing nearer declaring Him as Lord over all things.
- We worship, honor God and His Word, fellowship and respond by faith as we abide in Him.
- Instead of demanding perfection, resulting in struggling and self-effort, we rest by faith, abide and believe God's Word as true and receive of Him with love and sincerity of heart and overcome.
- We surrender control of our human will to God and are willing to be led by Him into obedience by the Holy Spirit. See Philippians 2:13.
- Jesus is Lord and you reign through His life in you conquering in every situation you face. See Romans 5:17; 8:37.

The results of grace—instead of pride, struggle, fear, and negative behaviors—we display faith, humility, the fruit of the Spirit, rest, trust, peace, and blessings.

LIFE: Christ has ended the Law as the way for us to live in righteousness and attain holiness. Scripture says we will not see God without holiness. He gave us a New Covenant, His grace in Christ Jesus, for us to receive Him and to live by His life of love and by His power. We are to live by faith in the relationship, allowing God to work His death and life in us and love God and others. Grace is our total dependence on Jesus and His life of love in and through us. See Romans 4, 5, 8; Galatians 2:20, and Galatians 3.

GRACE IN AND FOR YOU

*"But unto every one of us is given grace according to the
measure of the gift of Christ."* —Ephesians 4:7

TRUTH: Grace is given to everyone in Christ Jesus. He comes into our hearts by the love deposited in our human spirit when we become born again. See Galatians 5:22; John 1:14-16. A believer must receive God's grace by faith both for salvation and sanctification or purification of the soul in their daily Christian walk. Any other way to God would cause belief in the lie that doing works of the flesh will satisfy God the Father. Religion engages in self-righteousness, self-effort, labor, fearfulness, and critical and judgmental thinking, all ending in fear and despair. God desires that we die to self and allow the Holy Spirit in us to lead, teach, and help us in all things. The Holy Spirit in union relationship through Jesus Christ God's Son has deposited all the power of God's grace within to empower us.

Read and meditate on the Word of God to build faith in God's grace in our hearts, so we are no longer the one in control trying to create our reality or success. Instead, we surrender to the Lordship of Jesus as our Love, our Righteousness, our Stronghold, and our Anchor. His power in His grace does the work to heal, deliver, protect, and provide. When we are in faith, His grace works for us to make all the wrong things right. When in faith, God will release His grace, which is His power and ability, on our behalf, every time. See Romans 8:11. When our righteousness or standing before God is of faith, His power is released to work on our behalf all things for our good. See John 15:5; 14:10; Romans 8:28.

LIFE: Grace is the power of God's Spirit at work in, with, and through you to empower, as you rely on Jesus to help you to receive His blessings. He will effect the change or transformation necessary within to put off the old man and put on righteousness, so grace, God's power, can flow to bring deliverance and blessings *"Much more they which receive abundance of grace and the gift of righteousness shall reign in life by one, Jesus Christ* (Romans 5:17).

GOD'S GRACE BRINGS FREEDOM

"But the Father that dwelleth in me, he doeth the works." —John 14:10b

TRUTH: Jesus very often declared He and the Father were one. See John 17:11-23. He said that, through Him, we too are one with God. Jesus gave us the same relationship He had with the Father, fully equipped with all His love, righteousness, grace, and power. Without grace, a believer will depend on their human ability and will struggle to overcome sin and evil habits and change into Christlikeness. Grace through faith establishes one in righteousness in God's love and ways, which builds faith, trust, peace, confidence, rest, and victory. We believe and trust what Jesus did on the Cross, and in a union, relationship put His Word in our mouths to speak faith and learn to trust Him to bring our desires to pass and make us free. See Mark 11:22-24; John 8:32, 36.

Grace is God's goodness and mercy offered in our Father's love, gifts, power, and blessings. Grace is released to us in Jesus' righteousness in His love and care. He will respond to our call upon Him for help. See Psalm 34:17. Faith in God's grace will release His power on our behalf to bring healing, joy in our hearts, deliverance, prosperity, a sound mind of peace, restoration in our broken relationships, favor, strength, the elimination of fear and freedom. See Luke 7:1-19. God's grace will free us from sin and bondages and help us to accept God's truth as to who we are "in Christ." Every promise God made to Abraham is ours as we depend on Jesus. See Galatians 3:13-14. This is what it means when we say Jesus is our righteousness. We believe He loves us enough to make all things right when we trust Him to make us free to fulfill our potential and bring glory to God.

LIFE: I tap into God's grace by faith, and I am dependent on Jesus, trusting His Holy Spirit and putting no confidence in myself. Jesus is my righteousness, and I have freedom as I depend on Him. In a relationship when I am weak, He gives me strength and new life in His grace to daily keep on going and to walk in freedom. Jesus, God's grace, is the answer to my every need.

WALK IN GRACE

"I am crucified with Christ: nevertheless I live; yet not I, but Christ liveth in me: and the life which I now live in the flesh I live by the faith of the Son of God, who loved me..." —Galatians 2:20

TRUTH AND LIFE: The walk of grace is to live the true gospel empowered by faith as we acknowledge God in Jesus as our Savior, Lord, Master, Baptizer, Author, and Finisher of our faith. In all areas and stages, our Christian life is initiated and sustained by God through Jesus His Son and the Holy Spirit (grace) and as we believe and depend on Him (faith). See Ephesians 2:8. The gospel of grace made us new creatures in Christ, dead to our old self and restored into a relationship with our loving Father by His Holy Spirit living in us. We are to fellowship with Him, abide in Him, honor, worship, and yield to Him in loving surrender to repent, obey, believe, and receive all His blessings given to us. By His Word and Spirit, we let Him live in and through us to provide us with new life. See Galatians 2:20; Philippians 2:13; Romans 6:11.

A believer walking in grace starts their Christian walk being born again by believing in Jesus and joining his heart to the Spirit of God. See Romans 10:9-10; 1 Corinthians 12:13. Now everything Jesus is and has in the kingdom of God is ours by faith because we are "in Christ." We must be united with Christ in His victory to receive His blessings. Begin at the Cross by being crucified with Christ dead to sin, the old man, the old life, and be given over to God in the loving surrender of His new life in us. Ask Him to work His death and His life to remove the old stuff and daily make us new and help us abide in Him. Jesus is not a Home Depot God who came to do a self-improvement project. He died to eradicate the old in us and make us new by His grace, Jesus. Let us examine our text.

I am crucified with Christ: I am dead to the old me with the sinful heart inherited from Adam plus my sins and bad habits committed against God. Like the thief on the Cross, I humble myself and choose Jesus. All my sins were crucified and died on the Cross with Jesus. I am dead to sin and self. See Romans 6; Galatians 6:14.

WALK IN GRACE — DAY 2

"I live by the faith of the Son of God." —Galatians 2:20

TRUTH AND LIFE: I am crucified with Christ: Likewise, like the thief at Jesus' side, we are spiritually dead to sin, self/Law, and Satan in Christ Jesus. Receive our old self and sins, not some but all, removed and canceled; and in its place, we have a new heart which is forgiven, cleansed, and free from sin and purged of sin-consciousness. At the born again experience, we have a divine exchange of our sinful self to God; in exchange, we get God's love in Jesus' righteousness, His right relationship with the Father.

Nevertheless, I live: That thief who believed in Jesus did not die forever; Jesus said he would be in Paradise with Him. We live because we now have the life of Christ in the Holy Spirit living in us, full of God's love, power, and eternal life. We are freed to love God, live for Him, follow Him as our leader, and live by His righteousness because He is our Lord of righteousness. Our Lord of right living. See Jeremiah 33:16; Romans 8: 10-11.

Yet not I: This is the crux of living the Christian life by the true gospel of grace. This is where the rubber meets the road. How are we going to live our Christian life? In the flesh? In our strength? Or dead to the old man and alive by faith in newness, living by the power of the Holy Spirit in God's love? John 14:16-17; 2 Corinthians 4:15; Colossians 3: 3-4. We abide in Christ and live by His love and power.

But Christ liveth in me: Christ lives in us by His Spirit. We trusted Him to be saved, and we must continue to trust Him to help us live our daily Christian life. If we do otherwise and begin to trust ourselves, others, the world system, or the church, we will start to struggle, become fearful, fail, sin, and wonder why our salvation isn't working the way our Bible tells us it should. Living in God's grace by Christ's power in the Holy Spirit empowers us to live our daily lives in the sincerity of God's love and His strength. Jesus living in and through us is our only way to faith, victory, and peace. See Romans 8:11; 1 John 4:8-9; Isaiah 26:3.

WALK IN GRACE — DAY 3

"I live by the faith of the Son of God." —Galatians 2:20

TRUTH AND LIFE: Christ lives in us by His Word and His Spirit, who teaches us all things and leads us to Jesus, who is Truth. We are to believe God's Word, agree with Him, speak the same things He says, and His life will flow from within our spirit with faith to our soul and body for us to have His abundant life. And the life which we now live in the flesh, we will live by the faith of the Son of God.

Live by the faith of the Son of God: We are flesh and blood living in this world, but we are also spiritual beings with an inheritance of blessings in Christ Jesus located in the spiritual realm. It was Jesus' faith on the Cross which accomplished for us. When we connect with Jesus, we can receive His faith. See Romans 12:3; Galatians 5:22. We, therefore, must set our affections and love on Jesus and therefore on things above connecting by faith with the spiritual realm. When we believe in Jesus, we stand with His faith, claiming His victory given to us to meet our needs and to overcome, just as He overcame it all. See John 16:33. Our focus is always to be on Jesus. Our faith must always rest in Jesus' love expressed in His shed Blood, giving His life for our salvation and sustenance. The Blood of Jesus and what He did for us on the Cross must be the only source of our faith for redemption, sanctification, and glorification living on earth and as we prepare for heaven.

LIFE: The means of walking in God's grace is to depend on God through Jesus and His shed Blood on the Cross as our source. Depend on the Spirit of grace, God's Holy Spirit who will lead us to walk by grace into the deeper things of God, Christlikeness, all spiritual blessings, and spiritual maturity.

"And be found in him, not having mine own righteousness, which is of the law, but that which is through the faith of Christ, the righteousness which is of God by faith" (Philippians 3:9).

Galatians 2:20 is the path of God's grace for us as New Covenant believers, to walk grace through faith with Christ as our life and our daily victory!

FRUSTRATING GRACE

"I do not frustrate the grace of God: for if righteousness come by the law, then Christ is dead in vain." —Galatians 2:21

TRUTH: This verse tells us how not to approach the Christian life. We are not to allow our faith to be shifted from God's grace in Jesus over into works or legalism. To frustrate means "to be cut off from." If we shift our focus from Jesus to anything or anyone else, we are cutting off God's grace, His love in His power, and His ability to work on our behalf to do what we need done but cannot do for ourselves. We cannot be saved if we depend on anything besides Jesus and His shed Blood for salvation. In our daily living, if we add self-effort ahead of the work of the Holy Spirit, we will get into spiritual adultery (combining Law and grace) to frustrate God's grace and become frustrated ourselves.

If we place our faith in ourselves by what we do, depending on Christian disciplines such as our confessions, lengthy prayers, fasting, church membership and attendance, tithing, we will be cut off from God's grace and the Holy Spirit's power. This is because we are doing them in our own strength, expecting results in what we do and for God to respond to us based on our performance. These disciplines are good and should be done out of faith in our love for the Father, not to earn love and favor from Him. Dependence on Christian disciplines has shifted faith from Jesus to us, someone, or something else. See Romans 4:4-5; 11:6; Galatians 3:3-7.

To be sure we receive from God and receive His grace and His power to help us, we must always turn to Him. Always look to Him, keep our eyes on Jesus, and trust that the power in His grace is greater. We must trust His provision for us and have faith in Him in all things; He will hear our prayers and come through for us.

LIFE: Keep your eyes securely on Jesus, the work of the Cross, and His Word alone while trusting His Spirit to work on our behalf. Never Jesus plus something else. Your faith will arise for you to believe and receive His life abundantly.

GRACE AND CONDEMNATION

"For it is good that the heart be established with grace." —Hebrews 13:9

TRUTH: If you have done good, enjoy your blessings in peace and righteousness and rejoice. If you are wrong or have sinned, let Jesus, by the convicting power by His Holy Spirit lead you into repentance and righteousness and rejoice for His goodness to you in forgiveness. We are now in a better and more secure covenant of love and peace, and therefore God's grace brings us rest. See Hebrews 8:6; 4:11. Not being established in God's covenant of grace, having faith in His love, will cause the devil to toss us to and fro with the lie that we are justified, made innocent and right with God only when we obey God perfectly and when our actions are right.

When we are wrong, the devil accuses our conscience and torments us that we do not measure up to God and that He does not love us and is not pleased with us; or that we failed God again and therefore deserves condemnation! When we are unsure of our Father's love, accusations bring fear. See Hebrews 10:2; Revelation 12:10. But remember we are justified by the Blood of Jesus alone. See Romans 3:24; Galatians 2:16. It is only the deep-rooted knowledge and understanding of God's covenant love of mercy and care that can drive out fear and settle us in God's peace. See Psalm 23:1; Romans 5:1. We must be secure that God loves us because of the Blood of Jesus, and not because of our performance. See Romans 3:21-31. The power in the Blood of Jesus secured our forgiveness, cleansing, peace and God's blessings, upholds us in Jesus' righteousness, and keeps us from condemnation.

LIFE: As a covenant child of God, receive His mercy and plead the Blood of Jesus upon your mind and situation. Believe you receive Jesus and His love and acceptance by faith, call those things which be not as though they are, rejoice and receive. If you lack, declare you are God's covenant child of love and the Lord is your Shepherd, so you shall not want; or if you are wrong or sinned, walk in His forgiveness, declare you are justified, made innocent by the Blood, and not by your actions, right or wrong. Then repent and be free from condemnation. See Psalm 23; Romans 8:1-2. Rejoice in your God for so great a salvation to make us free in His righteousness and from condemnation.

LOVE IN JESUS

"...And a voice came out of the cloud, saying, This is my beloved Son; hear him." —Mark 9:7

TRUTH: Jesus established the New Covenant of grace, enabling us to receive the love of the Father in forgiveness and redemption without working for it or receiving punishment from Him when we sin. Because of Jesus, we no longer need to relate to God by the system of the Law and self-effort to obey or be punished. In His great love, Jesus obeyed for us on the Cross and destroyed sin and death, and canceled Satan's power and dominion over us. When Jesus took our sin, He removed its power and gave us His righteousness in His love and blessings. In redemption and justification, His love made us flawless, innocent, and without blame in our spirit before the Father when He gave us His power in the Holy Spirit within. See Colossians 1:22. We can now relate to our Father by faith, trusting His love and the power of His Spirit to care, bless, provide, guide, and protect us. Jesus' righteousness gives us access to our Father's love.

Because of Jesus, we must sincerely believe God loves us with everlasting love. Believe Jesus' righteousness releases God's grace to us in His power, rest, and peace; no more trying and struggling to receive from God. We can now, by faith, believe we are justified and made right with God by the Blood of Jesus to abide, not the Law requiring us to be qualified by our performance to be in His presence and to receive His blessings. We are not justified by the Law, demanding obedience or punishment when we fail. When you sin, never look at yourself and feel condemned. Look to Jesus and the Cross, always repent forward, seeing Jesus as your hope to move forward in God. Never backward-looking at sin and feeling condemnation. Believe and receive the Blood of Jesus as your justification, the keeper of your feet from falling, and your peace. See Romans 3:19-25; 5:1; Jude 24.

LIFE: We are to resist any push of Satan to depend on ourselves, our obedience, on our works or performance to please God. God is pleased with Jesus, and when we believe in Jesus and by faith make Him the priority in every part of our life, He is pleased with our willingness and faith. Because our faith in Jesus pleases God, He will work all things for our good. See Hebrews 11:6; 13:21; Romans 8:28.

LOVE, THE KEY IN RELATIONSHIP

"That he who loveth God love his brother also." —1 John 4:21

TRUTH: God has called us into a relationship with Him and commands that we love because He is love. The fruit of love is the person and character of God in the Holy Spirit. Love as God can be thought of like the whole fruit, including the skin. See Colossians 1:17. Jesus is flesh part of the fruit. See John 6:54-58; Galatians 5:22. The other eight segments of the fruit mentioned, from joy to temperance can be thought of as seeds in the fruit of the Spirit. When we take hold of God as whole fruit, eat the flesh and plant the seeds into our lives, they bring virtue into our relationships and Christlike qualities to further increase and propagate the fruit of love. We get more fruit. We are children of God living in the kingdom of God by the Law of love. It is by God's love that the world will know that we are Christ's disciples. See John 13:34-35; Matthew 22:37-40; Ephesians 3:17-19.

Every intimate relationship starts with the hope of love and is sustained by the seeds of God's love mentioned above and practiced with forgiveness when wrong. See Romans 5:8; Colossians 3:1-15; 1 John 1: 7-9. We are drawn to Jesus because of His great love. When we receive God's love deep into our hearts, only then can we overcome selfishness and fear and can genuinely love. *"We love him because he first loved us"* (1 John 4:19). By faith, we are to receive God's love as given in our hearts and then purpose to return His love by submitting to God by setting our human will to love Him with all the heart, soul, and body; and likewise, give the love of God we receive to others. See Acts 3:6.

LIFE: Our love relationship with Jesus should give our hearts wings to love and give selflessly, as 1 Corinthians 13:4-8 admonishes us to do. Write out these love verses, meditate on them first as your Fathers love to you and next as your love to the Father and others. Ask the Holy Spirit to help you in the weak areas. Then speak them over yourself and any relationship you have, especially the difficult ones. Ask the Holy Spirit to work the love of God to fill your heart, so God's love can flow generously to all those you meet. See John 17:23; Colossians 1:20-22.

TWO SIDES OF LOVE

*"He loveth righteousness and judgment: the earth is full
of the goodness of the Lord."* —Psalm 33:5

TRUTH: We are children of a God who is Love. According to Psalm 33:5, God's love is both righteousness and judgment. Just as a parent love by cuddling and firm discipline, so God in His goodness loves by blessing and giving discipline or correction and judgment. We are eternally grateful to God that when we believe in Jesus, He has already dealt our eternal judgment and damnation for sin on Jesus on the Cross. God has no more judgment unto death for the believer living by faith, only His training and discipline by His Word, His Spirit, and His ordained circumstances or tests. See 1 Peter 1; 4:12-13; Hebrews 12:5. When Adam was cast out of the garden, it was God showing goodness for the entire human race. He prevented them both from eating of the tree of life and living forever with sinful hearts because then redemption for humanity would not be a possibility.

God allowed His servant Job to endure harsh trials, which later proved His love for God, and corrected his theology on his lack of faith concerning his sons. See Job 1:4-5. He, however, was proven to be, as God said of him, perfect and upright, and in the end, after he endured, he was doubly blessed by God. In the Old Testament, Lot and his wife were instructed to leave Sodom and Gomorrah, but his wife was judged for disobedience. In the New Testament, Peter sinned in denying Jesus but repented, and instead of judgment, received forgiveness and restoration. God allows us to reap the consequences of our disobedience depending on our relationship and dependence on Jesus. See Galatians 6:7 and Judges 13-16 (the life of Samson).

LIFE: God has unfailing love for all His children. In love, He sometimes does His correction in difficult times to lead us into repentance, faith, and a closer relationship with Him. See 1 Peter 1:7-9. He has, however, reserved judgment unto eternal death only for sinners. See Revelation 21:7-8.

TWO SIDES OF LOVE — DAY 2

"He loveth righteousness and judgment..." —Psalm 33:5

TRUTH: Saul was on his way to persecute Christians, and God struck him down blind in the eyes, to stop and redirect his zeal. Later with his name changed to Paul, he was allowed a thorn in his flesh for the sanctification or the purification of his heart in preparation to teach the body of Christ God's gospel of grace to move him from being a legalist and murderer to becoming an Apostle. Paul received God's love in forgiveness and mercy in God's grace, with chastisement in correction seeking to re-direct him in a new path of God's grace. See Acts 9.

In our relationship, we should never doubt God's goodness when He seems far away or doubts His love in times of discipline when correction seems painful. God's love, whether positive and intimate or disciplinary and difficult, will always work for our good. See Romans 8:28; Ecclesiastes 3:11, 14; Hebrews 12:5-7.

So, never misread God and judge Him harshly because you wrongly hold on to the judgment side of the Cross, focusing on sin and punishment and God's anger. Instead, become alive unto God's love and pursue the mercy side, in His righteousness and power in love to guide, deliver, and give peace and His glory. Remember the story of Job, though a challenging experience for his family, it ended in more incredible blessings for him. *"For the eyes of the Lord run to and fro throughout the whole earth, to shew himself strong in the behalf of them whose heart is perfect towards him"* (2 Chronicle 16:9).

LIFE: Speak to your heart always, "God loves me—in times of blessings, in times waiting, and in times of discipline." Say, "I will continually trust Him because His every Word, thought, and action towards me is for my good." In times of trial, ask for His wisdom and strength to guide and help you endure, fully expecting His goodness and blessings to shine forth in the end. God's love for me is pure, true, absolutely good and infinite. I can always fully trust His love for me. Meditate on Jeremiah 29:11.

ESTABLISHED IN LOVE, NOT FEAR

"In righteousness shalt thou be established: thou shall be far from oppression; for thou shalt not fear: and from terror; for it shall not come near thee." —Isaiah 54:14

TRUTH: When we love, we are established in righteousness. As seen in Romans 13:8-10, we obey all Ten Commandments when we love. God has given us a new commandment of love to live by. See John 13:34-35. His archenemy, Satan, has his counter to God's love: fear. There is no middle ground in between; either we are in God, love, and gain peace, or we side with Satan in fear and gain torment. See 1 John 4:17-19.

The world has endeavored to fill in a middle ground with words such as tolerance, inclusiveness, being inoffensive, and politically correct—no such thing. God has called us to love. We are to love the person, speak the truth in love, and not tolerate sin by agreeing with it just to be socially acceptable.

It must be established in our hearts that God loves, cares, and blesses us over and above so that we can always do good and be a blessing. That is why we will not be afraid despite any oppression, and evil Satan puts in our way. We trust God that though Satan's attack may hurt and cause us pain, he cannot harm us with eternal death because we have eternal life. *"And they loved not their lives unto the death"* (Revelation 12:11b). Remember the life of Stephen in Acts 7.

LIFE: You should know that Jesus loves you infinitely and with everlasting love and has commanded you to love with the love you have received from Him. In all situations, ask the Holy Spirit to help you know how to show forth God's love even at the point of death. See Jeremiah 31:3; John 3:16; Ephesians 2:4-5; 1 Timothy 1:14-15; John 13:34-35; Matthew 22:36-40; 1 John 2; 1 John 4:18-19; Matthew 10:29-31; Romans 8:35-37; Romans 12: 14- 21;1 Corinthians 13:3-8; 2 Timothy 1:7.

GRACE IN GIVING

"In righteousness thou shalt be established." —Isaiah 54:14

TRUTH: Katharine Hepburn says, "Love has nothing to do with what you are expecting to get only with what you are expecting to give, which is everything." There must be a willingness, joy, and peace in our giving while fostering and protecting the other without being afraid of losing from what we have. See Hebrews 12:2. This is how we know we are expressing love; it is in our giving freely, not at others' requests but as the Lord leads from the heart. There will be freedom from sensing abuse and guilt from others. Love gives, willingly and cheerfully. See John 3:16. Even if our giving requires some nudging and convincing from our Heavenly Father, we still give in His grace and love.

But the willingness and cheerfulness must come from God's heart to our hearts. Others may request us, but let God direct your desire to give. It is not the decision of others to tell us what or how to give. It is between you and God alone by His Word and as led by the Holy Spirit, who settles your heart or spirit with peace in believing and joy in giving. See Colossians 3:15-17.

If there is no peace, willingness, and cheerfulness, we are under no obligation to give as it is then not acceptable to the Father. If there is demand, manipulation, condemnation, or any kind of pressure to express our love in giving, it is not love and not of the Father but of necessity or compulsion. See 2 Corinthians 9:7-8. Grace gives with a peaceful, cheerful, and willing heart. It may mean spending time in the Father's presence to arrive at a place of willingness and peace in the heart. But do it!

LIFE: Be like Mary, who sat at Jesus' feet and focused on Jesus. Focus your love on Jesus and His love for you. His Words will bring faith and peace to believe His promises. You can depend on His perfect love and care in your heart to be infinitely blessed in all areas of your life, including His grace to give willingly and cheerfully of yourself and your resources. Read Acts 5.

ANANIAS AND SAPPHIRA

"Ananias, why hath Satan filled thine heart to lie to the Holy
Ghost, and to keep back part of the land?" —Acts 5:3

TRUTH: Revival flames were burning; the Holy Spirit worked mightily with signs and wonders. People were being blessed, and none was lacking in the church. People were selling lands and giving to the Apostles to meet the growing congregation's needs. Ananias and his wife, wanting to seem more generous than they were in their hearts, sold their land and pretended they gave the whole sum to the church when they intentionally held back a portion. They sinned when they lied and tried to deceive by misrepresenting their gift.

Neither Peter nor the Holy Spirit was fooled; the Holy Spirit called Ananias out, and he fell dead. Within three hours, his wife came, and she was asked to confirm if the total sum was given as her husband claimed. She joined the lie and fell dead too. Lying, white lies, misrepresenting the truth, pretending when some say they misspoke are all quite acceptable these days. But it is not to be so among God's people. Our motives must be pure, not driven by a need for popularity, power, or respect. God wants us to speak the truth from a pure heart. Amid a great move of God, when truth and holiness are required in the presence of the Father, these two people lied to God about the truth in their giving. God had to stop it then and there. See James 3:14-18. God was establishing His kingdom, and it cannot be built on lies, which could destroy the church's integrity and trust in the Gospel.

LIFE: The kingdom is within us and requires a foundation of truth, as only truth can build a heart connection with God and a relationship with the Holy Spirit. Ask for the Lord's help to always speak the truth in love. Because only truth can set you free. Proverbs 12:22; Ephesians 4:15, 22-25; Colossians 3:9; 2 Timothy 2:15; John 8:32,36.

NO FEAR IN LOVE

"There is no fear in love; but perfect casteth; out fear because fear hath torment. He that feareth is not made perfect in love." —1 John 4:18

TRUTH: God is love, and therefore love begins with God. Perfect love is only possible from God. In the natural, when we are sure someone loves us, we feel secure and confident in the relationship or marriage. Fear in a believer's heart for any reason means they are unsure of how much God loves and cares for them. They are uncertain of what Jesus has done on the Cross to make them blessed and free. See Matthew 6:31-33. Sometimes we have difficulty believing the depth of His love given in His only Son and that He fully forgave us of all sins restoring us into a relationship with Him despite our imperfections.

He provided (Genesis 2:15-16). He blessed us abundantly (2 Peter 1:3-4). His love is great and forever (Jeremiah 31:3; Hebrews 13:5). He forgave us of all sins and removed its consequences (Hebrews 8:12). He is entirely infatuated and in love with us (Matthew 10:29-31). He will care for us continually (Ezekiel 34:28; Psalm 23). He will come back for us because He loves us and never abandon us (John 14:2,18). Knowing God's perfect love for each of us will cast off any fear towards God or of the devil. See Ephesians 3:17-19; Psalm 34:17; Psalm 91; 1 John 4:4. God's love casts out fear that may arise in our hearts when we face trouble (2 Timothy 1:7; Psalm 112:7; Proverbs 3:5-8). We can be sure our Father's love will always keep our feet from falling because of our Father's passionate love for us in Christ Jesus. To show our love, we will be led to study His Word, prayer, and fellowship with God through the Holy Spirit, which will grow our faith to stand. See Romans 10:17. Loving God builds faith in Jesus, releasing power to drive Satan and fear away. See Isaiah 54:14; 2 Timothy 1:7.

LIFE: Take God's love personally. Meditate on the Scriptures about God's love for you. Believe them. Receive His love by faith and settle in your heart that you are loved. Confess His love over yourself every day to assure your heart, especially when facing trials. Trust His grace, depend on His unchanging love and power to provide and deliver, rejecting all feelings of fear. Meditate on Isaiah 41:10; Jeremiah 31:3; 1 Corinthians 13:1-8.

FEAR NOT

"What time I am afraid, I will trust in thee...In God I will praise his word, in God I have put my trust: I will not fear." —Psalm 56:3-4

TRUTH: God is love, and He is good, while Satan is evil and brings fear. There is only one way to access these two powers in the unseen realm, believing by faith. In what or whom do you believe or trust? Fear is negative faith and trust. Adam in the garden was made in God's image and had absolute faith and confidence in his relationship with God. He flourished and prospered until he sinned, showing he had more faith in Satan's word than God's. Again, later lacking confidence, he became afraid and hid when God called him.

Because of redemption, Jesus' death, and His shed Blood on the Cross, He purchased us back from Satan and evil. When we believe Jesus, we have faith, and we know God always has our back. He will love, care for, protect, provide, and sustain us by His mighty power. Therefore, we can have faith and trust in Him and His Word and never fear. Faith is positive trust.

We will not fear when we have complete abandonment, and God's love swallows up our whole being. *"Perfect love casteth out all fear"* (1 John 4:18). God through Jesus Christ His Son and faith in Him as Lord over everything that concerns us is the source of a life free from fear. When we are sick and get a positive diagnosis from the doctor, we can turn to God and be assured that our faith in His love will drive out fear with the accompanying spirit of infirmity to manifest healing. By His stripes, we are healed. When afraid in strained relationships, we can trust God to reconcile. See Psalm 23; Isaiah 43:1-5; Colossians 1:20.

LIFE: Read the Word of God and always see His goodness, grace, and love, even in times of His correction. Believe that if we ask anything according to His will, He hears and answers. Our God who said this to us will never abandon or neglect us, so receive His love, have faith, and fear not. Meditate on Deuteronomy 31: 7-8; Mark 11:22-24.

NO FEAR, BUT POWER

*"For God hath not given us the spirit of fear, but of **power**, and of love, and a sound mind."* —2 Timothy 1:7

TRUTH: When born into this natural world, our human spirit is dead to God's love and life because of the sin we inherited from Adam, which immediately exposed us to the influence of Satan, evil, and fear.

The reverse occurs when we are born again; the Spirit of God full of love and resurrection power now dwells inside our hearts. This new life of power is now our actual reality, our true self in having an inheritance as a partaker of God's nature, with power in His anointing abiding in our new heart. Now what we do with our inheritance of God's power within us is up to us. We can either invest what we have been given to gain greater rewards, bury or squander it. See Matthew 25:14-30; Luke 19:11-27. We should invest in our actual reality in God and first acknowledge and receive His love. Become passionate about God in His Word. Become passionate to pray and fellowship until faith comes. Continual faith in God releases His power in the Holy Spirit to grow until He drives all fear from our souls. The power of God within as the anointing will increase to destroy your burdens. See Isaiah 10:27; Romans 15:13; 1 John 2:27.

"For the kingdom of God is not word, but in power" (1 Corinthians 4:20).

"Now unto him, that is able to do exceeding abundantly above all that we ask or think, according to the power that worketh in us" (Ephesians 3:20).

"And what is the exceeding greatness of his power to us-ward who believe, according to the working of his mighty power..." (Ephesians 1: 19-20).

LIFE: Hear, read, meditate, and speak the Word in fellowship and in a love relationship with God your Father, through Jesus His Son by His Spirit. As you do, you will by your spirit gain the God-centered force of faith, power, and authority to speak the Word, submit to God, resist Satan and fear, and watch him flee. See Mark 11:23-24; 1 John 4:18; Luke 10:18-19; Romans 8:11; James 4:7-8.

NO FEAR, BUT POWER — DAY 2

*"For God hath not given us the spirit of fear, but of **power**..."* —2 Timothy 1:7

TRUTH: God has not given us a spirit of fear but power and love in the Holy Spirit. We have seen the power of the Holy Spirit at work in creation; we saw His power split the Red Sea wide open. The power of God by the Holy Spirit that conceived Jesus in Mary's womb, a miracle that is still the stumbling block that has kept many present-day Jews from believing in Jesus. They are still resisting God's omnipotent power in Jesus' birth. We saw the power of God everywhere throughout Jesus' ministry when He was here on earth. He taught in power and authority, cast out devils, healed the sick, made the lame to walk and the blind to see. God of all power and might in the Holy Spirit lives in you and me, and nothing is impossible to Him. Because we are in Him, nothing is impossible to us through Jesus. See Luke 1:37; Matthew 17:20.

With God's power working in and through us, we can overcome all things through the power of the Blood of the Lamb and by the word of our testimony that He that is in us is greater than every force of Satan. See Revelation 12:11; 1 John 4:4. How do we grow in God's power? It's as we read, meditate, focus, and believe on Jesus, abide in His Word and His Spirit in the power of the gospel. At the Cross we have (power over sin and death) In His burial we have (control over the world), in His resurrection we have (power in receiving righteousness in God's love), and with the ascension we were seated with Christ and possess (power over Satan and evil). Our faith in God's grace activates His power. We must trust in and depend on God's grace in the power of Jesus in His Blood, in His Word, in His name, and in the Holy Spirit. Independence brings fear. We are never to trust in our thinking, reasonings, or self-effort to fix the things in our lives. Always trust God's power in and for us.

LIFE: I claim my victory and stand resolute and unmovable in His power by believing His Word and resisting the devil until my deliverance comes. Love and faith in Jesus activate His power, and I am not afraid of evil tidings as my heart is fixed, trusting in the Lord. See Ephesians 1:19-23; Psalms 16:8, 112:7.

NO FEAR, ONLY LOVE

*"For God hath not given us the spirit of fear; but of power, and of **love,** and of a sound mind." —*2 Timothy 1:7

TRUTH: Fear in our hearts comes from living from sight, and not faith, as we seek to control self, people, and situations to our advantage. We must trust to let go and let God. Fear in our hearts shows we have not yet received the fullness of how much God loves us, wants to, and will care for us even in life's greatest difficulties. See 1 John 4:18; Philippians 1:6. He deposited Himself in us by the Holy Spirit, represented by the fruit of the Spirit, who is love. God then commanded us to live by His love and His life in us. See Romans 5:5; Galatians 5:22; John 13:34; 15:12-13; Matthew 22:37-40. There is no need to interpret God's Word given in 1 John 4: 13-21. We are to live by the Spirit by both the love for God and love for man. This is God's righteousness, His way to live given to us in Romans 13:8-10. Love fulfills the Ten Commandments.

Satan will do everything to stop God's love from maturing in our hearts because faith works by love. If he stops us from loving, he stops our faith. See Hebrews 11:6; Galatians 5:6. But Satan's power is defeated. See Luke 10:19. When we love God with our whole heart, mind, and soul, we become passionate about Him in His Word, prayer, and fellowship. We also seek to let the heart's attitudes and motives honor God. We are complete in Him and will learn to trust Him. With love, faith, and trust, fear cannot reside in us. See 1 John 4:18; Isaiah 54:14. It was the love of God, sending Jesus to the Cross who established us in His righteousness and His love which builds faith. Faith then releases power to spoil principalities and disarms Satan's power over us to set us free to choose to yield to God's Spirit. See Colossians 1:13-14; 2:14-15.

LIFE: *"That Christ may dwell in your hearts, by faith; that ye, being rooted and grounded in love. May be able to comprehend with all saints what is the breadth, and length, and depth, and height; and to know the love of Christ, which passeth knowledge, that ye might be filled with all the fullness of God"* (Ephesians 3:17-19).

NO FEAR, ONLY LOVE — DAY 2

"Fear thou not: for I am with thee: be not dismayed, for I am thy God: I will strengthen thee: yea I will help thee: yea I will uphold thee with the right hand of my righteousness." —Isaiah 41:10

TRUTH: It was God in Jesus, full of love and the joy of procuring our salvation, who went to the Cross and defeated Satan. And it is the Holy Spirit's power in God's love through Jesus which by faith cause our spirit to rise above Satan to cancel and reject the spirit of fear. We can be sure of His love because He promised us, He is with us, He is our God, He will strengthen and uphold us.

"Who shall separate us from the love of Christ? ... neither death, nor life, nor angels, nor principalities, nor powers...shall be able to separate us from the love of God, which is in Christ Jesus our Lord" (Romans 8:35-39).

When we know deep in our hearts how much God loves us, we also know that He will never leave us and that He will care for us. Through the power of His love, we can stand and declare Jesus is Lord over every area of our lives, and therefore, we will not fear because we know He's greater than all evil and will work all things for our good. Romans 8:28. When we believe He loves us and His Word being true cannot fail, we have nothing to doubt or fear. Because we know He's Truth, we know we can trust Him and never fear. As we stand in faith, we can cooperate with the leading of His Holy Spirit and watch Him bring our deliverance to pass.

If we love other people, as seen in Romans 13:8-10, we will not want to think evil thoughts about harming them; instead, we bless and curse not, thereby giving Satan no access to our soul to bring fear. Loving God with all the heart, mind, and soul, trusting Him, and loving others by esteeming them and forgiving them eliminates independence, selfishness, and fear. See Romans 12:14-21.

LIFE: God's love firmly held in our hearts gives assurance, confidence, faith, peace, and blessing. Knowing God's love is always good and will never fail increases faith and causes us to trust Him completely. He will be with us and for us to always be our good shepherd, always giving His goodness and mercy. See Psalm 23; Philippians 1:6.

A SOUND MIND

*"For God hath not given us the spirit of fear, but of...a **sound mind**."* —2 Timothy 1:7

TRUTH: God has not given us the spirit of fear because we have God's love in the Holy Spirit. The word *sound mind* is translated from the Greek *Sophronismou* to mean self-discipline or self-control, the last fruit of the Spirit mentioned in Galatians 5:22. Self-control causes us to discipline our soul (mind, will, and emotions) and our bodies to conform and be transformed into the image of Christ and in His likeness. Self-control builds Christlikeness and gives us peace. See Isaiah 11:2, 5; Isaiah 32:17-18. We know all believers are born and sealed by the Spirit and are led by the Spirit. A spirit of fear is developed as we look at things in the natural, considering only the negative possibilities that our eyes see. See 2 Corinthians 4:18.

To have a sound mind, we need self-control over the natural eyes and what we allow to enter our souls. We often see failure, apathy, darkness, timidity, hopelessness, cowardice, an unknown future, or a seemingly impossible situation when facing trouble. We may allow our minds to camp at questioning what the doctor said, being fearful about our job, our children's future, terrorism, the coronavirus...and then more fear comes. But when we discipline our minds to focus on God's love, we will trust God and not fear. Because God is in charge, we can have a sound mind of peace with the capacity to think, meditate, understand clearly and find rest. See Isaiah 26:3.

LIFE: When fear comes, lift your heart to Jesus and say, Father, I trust You in Jesus, as my Lord, I trust Your love for me. I trust Your faithfulness and Your care for me completely. Father, I abide in you and rest in Your grace, and I have nothing to fear. Spirit of fear, I reject you because Jesus' love in the anointing now raises a standard to cast out all fear and gives me peace and a sound mind. Jesus, I abide in Your love, and I reject the spirit fear, Your grace is Lord over sin, Your light drives out all darkness, and Your righteousness over all oppression and gives me a sound mind. Thank You, Lord, for Your grace. Amen. See John 8:12; Isaiah 54:14.

A SOUND MIND — DAY 2

"Wherefore gird up the loins of your mind, be sober, and hope to the end for the grace that is to be brought unto you at the revelation of Jesus Christ."—1 Peter 1:13

TRUTH: We are to establish our minds on God's Word for us to have a sound mind. We must set our affection on things above and not focus on things that are seen. See Colossians 3:2-3; 2 Corinthians 4:18.

All believers are to allow the Holy Spirit to help us to discipline our minds and exercise self-control. Galatians 5:22.

- We are to spend time with God, filling our hearts with His Word, His Spirit, and with prayer. See Psalm 119: 11-12.
- Recognize and resist Satan's suggestions of fear, casting down his negative imaginations. Jesus loves us; we trust Him and will not fear. 2 Timothy 1:7.
- Focus on Christ Jesus alone, recognizing His grace is sufficient. Cast every care to Him. See Matthew 6:28-34. Worship and praise Him, for He is gracious.
- See ourselves "In Christ" as a victor and conqueror, unmovable in our faith. See Romans 8:36; Philippians 4:13; Colossians 1:22; 2:7.
- Be intentional about guarding our minds against lies, as well as replacing all negative thoughts with the opposite Word of truth found in God's Word. See 2 Corinthians 10:4-5; Philippians 4:8.
- Remain and rest in God, read, speak, sing, express joyfulness to draw strength from God our Father. See Nehemiah 8:10; Philippians 3:3.
- Exercise self-control with the spiritual gifts in church for us as a body to keep a sound mind. See 1 Corinthians 14, Verse 32.
- Rejoicing keeps our focus on God that He is the "Greater One" in us, and we know that no weapon formed against us can prosper. See Philippians 4:4; Isaiah 54:17.

LIFE: Fill your mind with things eternal while trusting God's power and love to work for you, and the result will be a sound mind. God will give you a mind at rest filled with faith, trust, joyfulness, boldness, success, and peace.

TRUE RELATIONSHIP

"I am the good shepherd and know my sheep
and am known of mine." —John 10:14

TRUTH: To have any meaningful relationship, one must know the other person well. *"And this is life eternal, that they might know thee the only true God, and Jesus Christ, whom thou hast sent"* (John 17:3).

Jesus had an authentic relationship with God His Father. *"If ye had known me, ye should have known my Father also..."* (John 14:7).

We have heard of God; we have read of God and may have even experienced Him in one way or another, but we may know God only when He is our truest reality. When by His Holy Spirit, He is the only person who is most real to us, and He is the One who is the truth for us in every situation we face.

We know He is the only One who is entirely kind and trustworthy. We know we can abandon ourselves and depend on God, knowing we are not perfect as even with our imperfection, we need not fall into condemnation. See John 3:16-17; Romans 12:1-2. As our Shepherd in a genuine relationship, Jesus tells us He will lead, correct, protect, uphold, and catch us if we are wrong or if we fall. We can trust Him completely because we know He is faithful, even when we do not know the how, where, when, and why.

"Know therefore that the Lord thy God he is God, the faithful God, which keepeth covenant and mercy with them that love him...to a thousand generations" (Deuteronomy 7:9). Is our God an expert in maintaining the best relationships or what? Even to a thousand generations.

LIFE: You will get to know God better in His character, His love, His ways, and know His heart desires as you draw close to Him in a relationship by faith. As you fellowship with Him by His Spirit and experience Him, He will lead you by every Word proceeding out of His mouth through Jesus and His Holy Spirit in a true relationship to make His life in you victorious. Meditate on Psalm 23:1-2.

TRUE RELATIONSHIP — DAY 2

"I am the good shepherd, and know my sheep..." —John 10:14a

TRUTH: Believers, we are one spirit with the Father, in a union relationship, living by the very life of God as His Holy Spirit leads us. This is our secret place in God. See 1 Corinthians 2:16; 6:17; John 17:22-23; John 8:14; Psalm 91:1.

God, Himself by His Holy Spirit, is the very life of God living inside us with the ability to know us and for us to know Him. As we fellowship and connect with Him not only as our Heavenly Father but also as our friend, we will develop genuine relationships. See John 15:13-15; James 2:23.

God does not want us to live in a static way only by His Word, as doctrine and principles, coming to Him only for information to try to achieve results on our own. Instead, He desires a dynamic relationship of interaction as we draw near to connect, hear, respond to, have experiences with Him and depend on Him to lead and direct us in the relationship by His Holy Spirit.

In John 21, although there were approximately seven disciples fishing and they all saw a man standing on the shore, verse 4 says the disciples knew not that it was Jesus. But after He spoke, they obeyed Him, still not knowing who it was until John, the disciple whom Jesus loved, recognized Him and said, "It is the Lord."

LIFE: My sheep know my voice. Seek to develop a sincere relationship with God your Father, making Him your highest priority in an environment of honor, commitment, and worshipful fellowship. Knowing Jesus in a relationship brings success just as it brought for the disciples with the multitude of fish. Join in following your all-powerful, all-wise, and great Shepherd, Jesus.

Meditate on Psalm 23: 3-4.

RELATIONSHIP WITH THE SHEPHERD

"The Lord is my Shepherd; I shall not want." —Psalm 23:1

TRUTH: This Psalm was given as the pattern and the way of life in the relationship God desired in the Old Testament and today, for us as the church. David, as we know, had a close relationship with God, who called him a man after His own heart. We can learn from him. David openly and unashamedly admitted the Lord was his Shepherd, and he was willing to submit himself to God's leadership. David realized that he was in a relationship with a God who was greater than himself and who was to be honored and worshipped. We know God can and will do work on our behalf because we saw Jesus fed the five thousand, helped His disciples catch a boatload of fish, deliver a man from demonic oppression, and raise His friend Lazarus from the grave. The greatness of David's God and his dependence on Him assured David's heart he would never lack because His Shepherd will find him provision in green pastures.

We can trust God to take care and provide. See Psalm 34:8-10. David failed to depend on God and relied on his instincts led to his biggest sin of adultery and murder. See 2 Samuel 11-12. Like a good Shepherd, Jesus in a relationship led the way, and by going to the Cross, He secured the very best way to satisfy all our needs, refresh, and restore. We prosper as we follow His lead and take the opportunities, He gives us. God leads us in paths of righteousness, along the right paths as He removes the obstacles and makes our way right and straight, or He gives us the faith, wisdom, and strength we need to climb over them or be sustained as we pass through the valley. See Isaiah 45:2-3; Psalm 23:4. He does this not only to be a good Shepherd but also for His own name's sake, to protect the integrity of His reputation as a good Father to us.

LIFE: Give yourself over in a relationship with God through Jesus and trust Him as being genuine and sure. He is the source of all our wisdom and strength. Jesus is your only actual reality; let His life lead you to prosper and be in good health. Meditate on Psalm 23:4-5.

RELATIONSHIP WITH THE SHEPHERD — DAY 2

"The Lord is my Shepherd." —Psalm 23:1a

TRUTH: Though trouble comes against us, we can have the security and assurance that our Father is always with us and that He is for us. See John 14:17. He goes before and thinks ahead in defending, protecting, providing, and comforting us. He is so lavish, and He prepares a table of blessings for us by Jesus, His grace.

God, through Jesus, adopted us as His children and anointed our heads with oil. Although we are His sheep, He has raised us to be priests and kings, belonging to King Jesus. He is our Shepherd and our King. See Ephesians 1:3; Revelation 17:14.

God has made us kings and partakers of His divine nature, and all His promised blessings can be ours until our cups run over. His grace in Jesus, who provided goodness and mercy, will follow us and keep us sustained all the days of our lives by His power in the Holy Spirit. Therefore, we have nothing to fear. He is our good Shepherd, and we can trust Him.

God's Spirit in us will lead us daily and guide us along the best path to our best destination in this life until Jesus comes back to take us into eternity. God, through Jesus and His Holy Spirit in relationship with us, will be in and with us, leading and guiding us into all of God's goodness all the days of our lives.

LIFE: We have a great God of abundant goodness and mercy, and as sheep, we are in desperate need of Him. Scripture says we can do nothing without Him. See John 15:5. Get in a relationship. See John 3:16 or get in a closer relationship. See Psalm 23; Galatians 2:20 and follow our Great and Good Shepherd, Jesus who knows His sheep. See John 10:14. It is He who promised to supply all your needs according to His riches in glory. See Philippians 1:19; 4:19. Believe Him!

RELATIONSHIP BY GRACE

"For by grace are ye saved through faith; and that not of yourselves: it is the gift of God. —Ephesians 2:8-9

TRUTH: Relationships are the essential thing in life. It is why we came into the world, to have a relationship with God our Heavenly Father and next with family and others. Having good relationships is the best reason for our existence in the world and the only thing we can take with us into eternity. God has commanded us to love. See John 13:34. "And *the world passeth away, and the lust thereof: but he that doeth the will of God abideth forever"* (1 John 2:17). We can have a relationship with God through observing nature in His creation and by what Jesus did on the Cross for us. See Romans 1:20; John 3:16. We have the power of His grace as we humble ourselves to believe and receive Him into our hearts—grace through faith and not by anything we have done.

Grace in salvation is receiving Jesus and the magnificent and mighty work God accomplished on the Cross to provide power in our hearts to receive Him and every spiritual blessing we need. A believer is one who, having seen the enormity of God's grace in Jesus, loves, honors, fears, and believes and bows to worship Him. See Proverbs 9:10. Present-day people who have never seen a display of God's power and His glory or have never been exposed to a demonstration of the manifestation of His presence by the Mighty Holy Spirit may find it difficult to understand how to fear the Lord and still have an intimate relationship with the Father as Christ had with the Church. See Ephesians 5:19-33.

LIFE: Grace is appropriated by faith in our submission to God's love and His Word. As you submit your human will into an abiding love relationship from the heart, you will have shown your highest love for the Father. Jesus laid down His life, so receive His sacrifice, His love, His promises, His commandment, and His truths with a committed heart. By faith, depend on Him to be led by His Holy Spirit, into a relationship by grace, and into all His goodness and mercy.

RELATIONSHIP BY GRACE — DAY 2

*"For by grace are ye saved through faith; and that
not of yourselves..."* —Ephesians 2:8

TRUTH: At present, the lack of experiencing God's tangible presence in the church may be one reason why there are many casual Christians. Relationship with God may seem platonic instead of intimate because we do not fear God enough to be driven to our knees to worship Him. See Isaiah 6:4-5; Acts 9. Our relationship with God by grace must begin with our humility because we have seen His immense sacrifice in His grace on the Cross and how worthy He is of our worship and praise. As we become thankful for His goodness and mercy, we joy in the God of our salvation and draw strength to keep being passionate and growing in dependence on the Lord.

"Wherefore God also hath highly exalted him, and given him a name above every other name. That at the name of Jesus every knee should bow, of things in heaven, and things in earth, and things under the earth..." (Philippians 2:9-11). Just as a bride has given herself over exclusively to her spouse, so are we to be given over to God in an exclusive relationship of love, in dependence, and allegiance to Jesus led by the power of the Holy Spirit.

LIFE: We are His purchased possession, and we belong to God. He has a claim on our lives in exchange for the price of our salvation, the death of His Son. But are you completely yielded to Him? Is He more than just your Savior, but also Lord, Baptizer of the Holy Spirit, and King? Let us all ask Him to lead us into a place of the exaltation of God and dependence on Jesus by His Spirit, above all else.

Prayer: Heavenly Father, I confess I have been somewhat casual with our relationship. I desire to make You the priority in my life. Thank You for leading me to a deeper place in my heart for You. Pray the Ephesians 1:16-20 prayer every day. As you spend time in the Word, prayer, and worship, be expectant and watch for His answer and His leading by the grace of His Holy Spirit.

OUR WHOLE LIFE IS JESUS

"And whatever ye do, do it heartily, as to the Lord,
and not unto men." —Colossians 3:23

TRUTH: Our life is made up of a series of decisions and choices which give us character, purpose, and ultimately, our destiny. All our desires, plans, attitudes, character traits, motives, and choices should point to Jesus for Him to bless us and help us grow in relationship to glorify God.

We are to glorify God with our worship, giving Him a priority in all things. We are to glorify God with our time; we are to give Him more time in our thoughts and prayers than anything else. See 1 Thessalonians 5:17. As we raise our families, we are to give them to Him, trusting His abundant grace and His righteousness to do good by each member and love them with the love of God. See Romans 5:17.

The lifestyle we choose, with friends, entertainment, food, and drink to satisfy our appetites, and our spiritual walk, are not to be of our efforts or works but of His grace, as we ask Him and trust Him to lead us into what will please the Father. The Holy Spirit will help us glorify our Father God by being watchful to be ready for His second coming through Jesus Christ, our King, and our eternal hope.

Our whole life and attention are to be God-centered regardless of our vocation in life. Because God paid such a huge price for us, and we belong to Him, we should always be mindful to walk by faith, abiding in His grace and His love so we can be pleasing to Him. See Hebrews 11:6. Do others see Jesus in the life you live on the job, in your family, during times of recreation?

Life: The Holy Spirit is in us and with us always. He is just a breath of prayer away for us to call on Him and ask Him to help us to please the Father in everything we say and do. And He will help us and cause Christ to be our life, a life which testifies of the image of Jesus in us. See Hebrews 4:16; John 15:26.

GLORY IN RELATIONSHIP

"And the glory which thou gavest me I have given them; that
they may be one, even as we are one." —John 17:22

TRUTH: Jesus received God's glory when the Holy Spirit descended on Him at the river Jordon. The Father spoke from heaven and said, *"This is my beloved Son, in whom I am well pleased"* (Matthew 3:17). Jesus, the Son of man, was made a little lower than the angels; as the Living Word, He was made flesh and dwelt among men, the glory begotten of the Father. See Psalm 8:5; John 1:4.

God's glory was displayed at the Cross in His grace, His goodness and mercy offered in forgiveness and the gift of righteousness, His love. *"Jesus said, Now is the Son of man glorified, and God is glorified in him. If God be glorified in him, God shall also glorify him in himself, and shall straightway glorify him* (John 13: 31-32).

God gave believers His Glory in the Spirit of Jesus when we believe in Him. The Spirit of God entered our hearts and made us one with Jesus. *"The Spirit itself beareth witness with our spirit, that we are children of God: And if children, then heirs; heirs of God, and joint-heirs with Christ: if so be that we suffer with him, that we may be also glorified together* (Romans 8: 16-17).

God's glory in the power of the Holy Spirit has joined man to God in a holy union, *"For God, who commanded the light to shine out of the darkness, hath shined in our hearts, to give the light of the knowledge of the glory of God in the face of Jesus Christ* (2 Corinthians 4:6).

LIFE: We are created for God's glory, *"Even every one that is called by my name: for I have created him for my glory"* (Isaiah 43:7). Through the power of God's Spirit in ours, if we will continue to be participants in His glory, we will see the same glorious works Jesus did. *"For the earth shall be filled with the knowledge of the glory of the Lord, as the waters cover the sea"* (Habakkuk 2:14).

GLORY IN RELATIONSHIP — DAY 2

"And the glory which thou gavest me I have given them." —John 17:22

TRUTH: The Holy Spirit is the One who will demonstrate God's glory in and through us. But we have nothing to fear because He will help to prepare us to grow in God's glory. He will draw us into greater love relationships and holiness and allow us to obey the Father. See Philippians 2:13. God's purpose of union relationship is that together He will endeavor to keep us in the unity of the Spirit in the bond of peace. See Ephesians 4:3. We are to trust God's love in us to manifest in His glory. Jesus walked in a perfect love relationship with the Father, His Word, and power. He also demonstrated God's glory to a dying world in need of His salvation.

"It came to pass, as the trumpeters and singers were one, to make one sound to be heard in praising and thanking the Lord..." (2 Chronicles 5:13). Exaltation of the Word, holiness, unity of relationships, praise, and worship bring God's glory on the scene. We need to bring this back into our hearts and into our churches, so God can manifest in, and through His body again.

"He that hath my commandments, and keepeth them, he it is that loveth me: and he that loveth me shall be loved of my Father, and I will love him, and will manifest myself to him" (John 14:21). God's glory will manifest in and through us, not when we are sin-free but when we maintain the union connection of our hearts with His heart by the power of the Greater One, the Holy Spirit in us, to flow and bring His power and glory to a needy world. Christ in you is indeed the hope of your Glory. See Colossians 1:27.

LIFE: Meditate on these Scriptures on God's Glory and let Him fill your heart: Exodus 40:34-38; 2 Chronicles 5:11-14; Psalm 72:17-19; Isaiah 60:1; John 1:14; 11:40; John 15:5-7; 1 Corinthians 1:23; 1 Corinthians 6:17; Ephesians 1:12; Colossians 3:1-3; Hebrews 3:1-6; 1 Peter 1:18-23; 1 John 4:15; Revelation 21:11.

ONENESS IN RELATIONSHIP

"That they all may be one: as thou Father, art in me and I in thee." —John 17:21

TRUTH: The presence of the Holy Spirit in us creates a union, a restored relationship with God our Father, and oneness in spirit. The heart of the Father for us is to have a connection to Him in a love relationship in unity and intimacy which brings peace. *"... That they also may be one in us..."* (John 17:21). Believers must receive by faith their union with the Father by agreeing with His Word that we are one spirit with Him and complete in Him. See 1 Corinthians 6:17. *"And what is the exceeding greatness of his power to usward who believe, according to the working of his mighty power.... when he raised him from the dead, and set him at his own right hand in heavenly places"* (Ephesians 1:19-20).

From this secret place of union, love relationship, and completeness, we are seated in heavenly places taking our place of victory, which Christ imputed to us as new creation believers. See Colossians 2:15; Ephesians 1:3. We can claim our identity "in Christ" and be secure to relate to our Father in oneness, to see Him as Lord dominating all evil under our feet. And as Lord, He qualified us to be in His presence to receive His love and care.

No one can snatch us or His blessings from His hands. There is no need to try to earn His love or closeness and no need to fear, as His victory qualified us to stand in authority and power against Satan. As we resist him, reject fear, and enforce his defeat, he will get tired of our resistance and leave to find an easier target. See James 4:7; Luke 4:13.

LIFE: In a union relationship, I am one spirit with the Father as His love is shed abroad in my heart. I set my affections on Him because I am hidden in Him. Lord, I delight in and choose to do Your will. In union with Your Holy Spirit, I trust Your power to lead me into truth, intimacy, into my destiny. I am established in righteousness, Your love, and I rest in and trust You. Because of my oneness, I am perfected in Your love, and I reject all fear. You are light, and I am a child of light abiding and resting in You my secret place, and no evil shall befall me. See 1 John 4:18; John 8:12; Psalm 91:1.

ONENESS IN RELATIONSHIP — DAY 2

*"...That they all may be one: as thou Father, art in
me, and I in thee."* —John 17:21

TRUTH: Stand in whom we have been made, a new spirit in union relationship. Know the Holy Spirit empowers us to come boldly and confidently into our Father's presence at any time. See 1 Corinthians 1:4-9; Hebrews 4:16. *"And this is the confidence that we have in him, that, if we ask anything according to his will, he heareth us: And if we know that he hears us, whatsoever we ask, we know that we have the petitions that we desired of him"* (1 John 5:14-15). Let the truth of our union relationship keep us connected to our Father in oneness and closeness, whereby we both look forward to meeting together in times of fellowship. Our union relationship will keep us out of religion, works, and its futility with struggle and striving on our Christian journey. It will also keep the devil and his effects of religion from leading us into sin—consciousness unworthiness, and condemnation.

Union relationship will align us in righteousness and bring security, rest, and peace in our relationship with our Father. Our union with God will cause us to abide in Him and bring His love and power to appropriate blessings and enforce Satan's defeat. God's love and power and Satan's defeat will give us rest and peace in our hearts and unity with others. We'll have a union relationship with God our Father in Jesus Christ our secret place of rest and provision, and the world will know we are His disciples sent to spread love and expand the kingdom. See John 13:35.

LIFE: God made you one with Christ when Jesus became your righteousness. You are to take your seat with Christ in heavenly places, knowing that fear and darkness must flee in the presence and light of Jesus. If you're sick say to Satan, *"Jesus is my righteousness. He bore the stripes for me to make me well and whole, therefore I am healed." As Jesus is healed and whole, so am I. Spirit of infirmity, go! in Jesus' name. I am healed and free.* Do the same for any other need you may have, for example, oppression of the mind. See Isaiah 53:7; 54:14; 1 John 4:17.

AUGUST 5

HUMILITY BEFORE GOD

"He hath shewed thee, O man, what is good and what doth the Lord doth require of thee... and love mercy and to walk humbly?" —Micah 6:8

TRUTH: Humility before God believes God is greater than us, greater than circumstances, greater than the devil, and we exist for His glory. *"All things were created by him, and for him. And he is before all things, and by him all things consist"* (Colossians 1:16-17). We bow in humility because:

- He made us in His image to be in relationship with Him. See Psalm 139:14-16; John 17:21-22.
- He is the Creator of the universe, the Omnipotent One. See Nehemiah 9:6.
- He is Omniscient and Omnipresent. See 1 John 3:20; Jeremiah 23:24.
- He is God's Son who died for our salvation. See John 3:16; Philippians 2:7-10.
- He altogether is good and gracious. See Isaiah 30:18.
- He is worthy of glory and worship. See Psalm 29:1-2.
- He is coming back for His children. See John 14:3.

As believers, we are humbled when we see God in His greatness and graciousness, and, therefore, we choose to live by faith to please Him. See Hebrews 10:38-39; 11:6. We keep His commandments and do His will by loving and exalting Jesus in our hearts. Exaltation of self is dishonoring to God, so avoid it. See Luke 14:11; 1 John 5:2-3. God has prescribed the way to walk for success, and it is with humbleness of heart in dependence on His love, wisdom, power, and guidance. We humble ourselves and receive His forgiveness to maintain the relationship when we sin. See Colossians 2:2-3; Micah 6:8; 1 John 1:9.

LIFE: Jesus' path and life were lowly, in His birth, His brutal crucifixion, and burial, all in humility before God His Father. We must abandon pride, and in humility, we must first see our wretchedness, sinfulness, and need for a Savior, Lord, and Baptizer of the Holy Spirit. Only then can we receive in humility by grace all that Jesus did for us on the Cross and end self-reliance and its consequence of pride.

HUMILITY WITH MAN

"Fulfil ye my joy, that ye be likeminded, having the same love, being of one accord, of one mind. Let nothing be done through strife, or vainglory; but in lowliness of mind let each esteem other better than themselves." —Philippians 2:2-3

TRUTH: The church age in which we are currently living commands us to love God and love people. See Matthew 22:37-38; John 13:34-35. Only with humility can we obey God to love even our enemies and esteem others in love. See Matthew 5:43-48. We exercise humility as we have the mind of Christ to love as Christ loves and to forgive as He forgives. See 1 John 3:10; 4:10-11. We are to humble ourselves and ask the Holy Spirit to develop in us the character of Christ and to help us to love others. See 1 John 3:14-15; Colossians 3:12-17.

We are to endeavor to live with the life of God in us, to build unity. See John 17:21. It takes humility to forgive others. See Matthew 18:21-35. We love in humility when we refrain from flattering others and at the same time reject self-praise for us to maintain a righteous heart before God. See Proverbs 28:23; Proverbs 27:2. We also love with humility as we regard the lowly and show no favoritism. See Romans 2:11; 12:16; 1 Timothy 5:21; James 2:8-10. Also, as we submit ourselves one to another, we show Christ's humility. See Ephesians 5:21. Let us learn humility from Jesus and find rest for our souls in Him. See John 13:1-17.

LIFE: As Jesus is, so are we in this world to show God's love to all. He overcame, and so can we. In humility, receive love from God your Father and open the door wide to forgiveness and love for others. His love in you will eliminate fear, and the world will see God's boldness in you. Humble yourself and yoke yourself to your Father's love. Receive all His spiritual blessings, be blessed, and share them with others to fulfill His commandment to love, always showing by your humility that you're truly His disciple. See Matthew 11:29-30; John 13:34-35.

TEMPORAL THINGS ARE SEEN

"While we look not at the things which are seen...for the things which are seen are temporal." —2 Corinthians 4:18

TRUTH: God has commanded His children to live by faith. Faith is the substance of things not seen. It believes that God will provide whatever He promised and that He will do it even though we cannot see it with our natural eyes. If we are looking at our life's situation and all we can agree with are those things we can see, feel, touch, think and understand, we are seeing only the temporal. We see, feel, and handle only the temporary issues, conditions, and possibilities of our life.

One's natural life consists of happiness, joy, and success. However, these are punctuated with trials, trouble, lack, loss, sickness, and death. When these difficulties present the opportunity, we fear because we live with a temporal earthly mindset. This mindset lacks the fullness of love and trust towards the Father. Our enemy, the devil, fights to keep us at this temporal level, to keep us out of faith.

However, our love for Jesus and His Word creates faith and trust in our hearts and drives out fear. See Romans 10:17; Galatians 5:6; 1 John 4:18. The temporal realm sees us more concerned with our situation, self-effort, appearance, status, and the opinion of others over the Word of God. When we look to please God by what we do and our efforts rather than trusting His Grace in Jesus, the result is us being bound by earthly constraints and temporal limitations. Living in the temporal occurs when our attitudes of selfishness, self-will, reasonings of the mind, leave us constantly trying to figure out life on our own and confines us to fleshly living and earthly or temporal possibilities.

LIFE: Seek not to live by your thinking, emotions, feelings, or being controlled by the body's appetites with evil desires, immodest clothes, gluttony, drink, and pleasure. These show you live in the flesh and are controlled by temporal things. Meditate on Colossians 3:1-4.

TEMPORAL THINGS ARE SEEN — DAY 2

"For the things which are seen are temporal." —2 Corinthians 4:18

TRUTH: The result of temporal living is a carnal mindset. Living in the flesh gives Satan access to our soul (mind, will, emotions), resulting in negative behaviors. *"For to be carnally minded is death, but to be spiritually minded is life and peace. For if ye live after the flesh, ye shall die: but if ye through the Spirit do mortify the deeds of the body, ye shall live"* (Romans 8: 6, 13).

When Satan captures the mind with temporal thoughts and actions, he traps us in the flesh and keeps us from walking in the Spirit. The fleshly mindset will distract and draw us away from the Word and our relationship with our Heavenly Father and loving people. This hinders our faith as faith works by love, love for God, and people. See Galatians 5:6. *"This I say then. Walk in the Spirit, and ye shall not fulfill the lust of the flesh"* (Galatians 5:16).

"Being then made free from sin, ye became the servants of righteousness" (Romans 6: 18).

LIFE: Look to Jesus as the solution for your every need. He is the Author and Finisher of your faith. Do not seek to depend on yourself to do what needs to be done to satisfy your needs or fix your problems. Instead, have faith by looking to things eternal, the heavenly things, and depend on God. Pray, read, and meditate on His Word, spend time in fellowship to hear from Him, and apply His leading, wisdom, guidance, and correction to your life to open your eyes to see the unseen. *"To open their eyes, and to turn them from darkness to light, and from the power of Satan unto God, that they may receive forgiveness of sins, and inheritance among them which are sanctified by faith that is in me"* (Acts 26:18).

This book of the law shall not depart out of thy mouth: but thou shalt meditate therein day and night, that thou mayest observe, to do according to all that is written therein: for then thou shalt make thy way prosperous, and then thou shalt have good success" (Joshua 1:8).

"For as many as are led by the Spirit of God, they are the sons of God (Romans 8:14).

THE ETERNAL IS UNSEEN

"While we look not at the things which are seen...but at the things which are not seen... but the things which are not seen are eternal." —2 Corinthians 4:18

TRUTH: Eternal life by faith results from receiving the God of love, the God of all eternity, living within, leading, guiding, teaching, and empowering us by His grace in the Spirit of Jesus to love Him and to love others from now and into our eternal home in heaven.

God is eternal, spiritual, and supernatural. He created the earth supernaturally, rose from the grave supernaturally, recreated man as born again beings supernaturally, and commanded believers to walk in both the eternal and supernatural realms by walking in faith. Faith requires that we look away from ourselves or anything natural and look to Jesus, the Eternal One. Faith requires we look to the worth, ability, and power of one greater than self, and that is the Greater One, our God.

Eternal things are not seen. This list is not exhaustive, but here are some eternal things we know: God, love, hope, the Word, faith, righteousness, grace, Jesus, the Holy Spirit, the spiritual realm, heaven, hell, angels, and Satan. For anyone to believe God, it must be by faith as the Bible starts with *"In the beginning God."* We have no explanation of His prior existence, but we must believe Him and receive Him by faith. Likewise, we receive eternal things by faith.

LIFE: As believers, we must look to God first as our priority by accepting His truth given on Himself and on creation to see and receive Him. See Romans 1:19-21. And having believed, we continue by faith to trust His grace in His righteousness and all Jesus accomplished on the Cross. We must acknowledge God's love given on the Cross and believe by faith in God's grace and all things eternal, shown to us in the gospel and as taught in Acts 2:22-41.

THE ETERNAL IS UNSEEN — DAY 2

"...But the things which are not seen are eternal." —2 Corinthians 4:18

TRUTH: Faith in God's grace is looking unto the eternal, the things which are not seen. So, we walk by faith and not by sight. See 2 Corinthians 5:7. We walk even as He (Christ) walked. See 1 John 2:6. We walk in the Spirit as we walk in the truth of God's Word. See Galatians 5:16. We set our affections on things above. See Colossians 3:2. We call those things which be not as though they were. See Romans 4:17. We see godliness with contentment is great gain. See 1 Timothy 6. We put on the whole armor, love and submit to God and resist the devil. See John 13:34; 1 Peter 1:13-15; James 4:7.

When we remember that we are citizens of heaven and are only sojourners here on earth, we will look to the eternal and loosely hold on to the temporal or material things on earth. Instead, we hold onto Jesus as Lord and Master of all God's blessings and all situations. We seek to lay up treasures in heaven where rust does not corrupt nor where thieves can steal. See Matthew 6:19. And in all life's trials, we put all our troubles back in our Heavenly Father's hand, trusting Him to work all things for our good. See 1 Peter 5:7; Romans 8:28. By faith, we focus on the eternal as God continues to deliver us from Satan's darkness and into Christ's light.

"God is light, and in him is no darkness at all... But if we walk in the light, as he is in the light, we have fellowship one with another, and the blood of Jesus Christ his Son cleanseth us from all sin" (1 John 1:5, 7).

More than conquerors and overcomers, we are victorious as we focus on eternal things by faith and rest in Christ Jesus' victory, causing us to overcome all things. See 1 Corinthians 15:57; Romans 8:37; Revelation 12:11.

LIFE: Start looking at your life and your life's situations through the eyes of God's love, faith, and eternity. It will put your present challenges and pain in the correct perspective and help you endure and succeed as you look forward to your present victory and later see Jesus face to face. Revelation 21:3, 22:4.

"I will lift up mine eyes unto the hills, from whence cometh my help. My help cometh from the Lord, which made heaven and earth. He will not suffer thy foot to be moved: he that keepeth thee will not slumber" (Psalm 121:1-3).

GIVE THE LORD YOUR CHOICES

"Commit thy way unto the Lord; trust in Him;
and he shall bring it to pass." —Psalm 37:5

TRUTH: A self-directed and independent lifestyle has caused many, including believers, to unconsciously try to find their way in life, living by trial and error or by the desires and choices of their limited minds.

Only God knows all things. He is our Father and willing to guide us into what is best for us. So, He tells us to commit our thinking, choices, and decisions to Him. We do that by comparing our thoughts to God's, His Word or as we hear Him speak to us by His Spirit. We will discern Him by "a knowing" in His voice speaking to our hearts. See 1 John 2:20.

Since God's Word shows us that God is love and truth, when we choose God's way, we will walk in love and truth, making good choices, fulfilling His commandment to love God and others. See Romans 13:8-10. At all times, we need to make choices to do as the Word of God says, even if it is difficult. It may seem impossible to do for ourselves when we see God directing us to forgive those who have badly hurt us. He says to commit it to Him. Give Him the situation, cast it as care upon Him, and ask Him to help us forgive. See 1 Peter 5:7; Matthew 18:34-35. When we are tormented with ungodly thoughts from the enemy, we are to cast them down and immediately choose to side with God. Tell Satan what God's Word says and that you agree with it. Then speak God's Word, confirming who you are in Christ, what you have in Christ, and the choice you've made for Christ. As you resist Satan, he will realize he cannot overcome you and flee. See Ephesians 1:3, 19-21; 2 Corinthians 10:4-5, 5:17; Philippians 4:8; 1 Peter 2:9; Psalm 37:23-24.

LIFE: *"Teach me thy way, O Lord; I will walk in thy truth; unite my heart to fear thy name"* (Psalm 86:11).

GIVE THE LORD YOUR CHOICES — DAY 2

"Commit thy way unto the Lord; trust also in Him;
and he shall bring it to pass." —Psalm 37:5

TRUTH: First, we commit our desires and choices to God's Word and His way, and then we must trust Him to do it. Rest in our union relationship by meditating on the Word, in prayer, fasting, and fellowship, and let Jesus bring it to pass. We leave it in His hands by our praise, worship, and thanksgiving, and His goodness, faithfulness, and trustworthiness will cause our needs to be met. Worshipping God keeps our focus on Him, not on ourselves, our feelings, the situation, Satan, or the outcome, only on Jesus. Let our union in Christ lift us to be seated with Him on the right hand of the Father, remaining steadfast, knowing we have His victory. Speak the Word of God with His power and authority, knowing in our hearts it is already done, and Satan must bow to your choice of Jesus our Lord and His resurrection power. See Philippians 2:9-11.

Watch out for the enemy Satan, who will be working to get you to un-commit and to depend on yourself or others. He will appeal to our human desires of comfort, panic or confusion, or the path of least resistance. He will try to get us to avoid our responsibility and discipline to the Word, make compromises, excuses, or blame ourselves or others. But none of his tactics will work because we have cast down our anchor of truth in the solid Rock Christ Jesus and His Word and have made Him our choice as Lord of all. See John 1:17; 2 Peter 3:8-9.

LIFE: Commit your choices to Jesus, see His Spirit, character, nature, and love for you in His Word, and yield to Him. Turn from your selfish and fleshly ways, thoughts, and actions, which are enmity against God, and trust Him to lead you into all truth, life, and peace. See Romans 8:6-7; John 16:13. Have patience as you trust God and wait as your choice in Christ Jesus brings forth your peace and blessings and fills you with His life. See Hebrews 10:35-38.

KNOWING GOD

"That I may know him..." —Philippians 3:10

TRUTH: As Christians, we are called out from the world to be children and followers of God in relationship with Jesus. God's goal is that we get to know Him and imitate Him to bring the Kingdom of heaven here on earth in His salvation to the lost, for healing, deliverance, and restoring power to the weak and oppressed. See Luke 4:18. Our first goal should be the same as the Father's of old, to know Jesus and His love that others may know Him as Father through us. Some enter the Christian life with many goals, which may be:

- To try to live the Christian life and be a better person.
- To obey the rules to be pleasing and acceptable to God.
- To obey and please God, even if by methods or formulas.
- To work for Jesus so they can hear Him say, "well done."
- To climb the spiritual ladder and become known.
- Do the works of Jesus to prove the heights of our spirituality.
- To go to heaven and avoid hell.
- To have a personal growing relationship with Jesus by His Spirit; to know Him, be guided by Him, and become like Him.

LIFE: The latter point is God's primary goal for you. And He'll say the same as He said to Solomon. *"Because thou... hadst not asked for thyself long life; neither hadst asked riches for thyself... behold I have done according to thy words* (1 Kings 3:11-12).

"And be not conformed to this world: but be ye transformed by the renewing of your mind, that ye may prove what is that good, and acceptable, and perfect will of God" (Romans 12:2).

Though we will never know God in entirety on this side on earth, as Christians, we can through faith see the love of God through Jesus His Son and desire to draw close to Him in a personal, growing relationship; we can know His heart in His Word, love Him and become like Him. With our union relationship growing, some works by our efforts as some mentioned above are then acceptable to Him, but not before. Always relationship first. See Ephesians 3:16-19; James 2:17-26.

KNOWING GOD — DAY 2

"That I may know him..." —Philippians 3:10

TRUTH: Jesus is to be our highest priority. Even Satan knows where Jesus' position is to be, in the highest place. As in the wilderness temptation, Satan took Him to the pinnacle and told Him to cast Himself down from the pinnacle. See Luke 4:9. We place Jesus at the highest place when we honor His Word in our thoughts, words, and actions, which gives us authority. God is love in our spirit, and when we live in and demonstrate love for God and others, living by faith from the spirit and in the eternal, we will know God because He'll manifest Himself. See John 13:34-35; Romans 13:8-10; 2 Corinthians 4:18; John 14:21.

The devil wants us to be preoccupied with him by living in the temporal, carrying cares, worry, disobedience, envy, bitterness, fear, and hatred, all of which open the doors for him to prevent us from loving and therefore from knowing God our Father in a growing faith relationship.

Our highest good and best will be found in Christ when God is the head of our lives. We know Him best when we experience Him in a dynamic relationship of faith unto obedience, trusting Him to lead us by demonstrating His character of love for us to follow.

We know Him when we know His Words and live by them; We know Him by knowing His heart and His ways; We know Him by living by the power of His Spirit daily and moment by moment, trusting His Word and His Spirit to lead us. We also know Him by experience as we draw close to Him in times of fellowship. We get to know Him better in times of trials as we must endure and watch Him work to stretch us and grow our character from selfishness and self-righteousness to be more like Him, a God of righteousness and love. When we know God and His goodness, we will love Him with all our hearts.

LIFE: Meditate on Psalm 9:10-11; Ephesians 3:14-21.

KNOWING GOD BY HIS RESURRECTION POWER

"That I may know him, and the power of his resurrection." —Philippians 3:10

TRUTH: We know God by His resurrection power when we become born again by that glorious, omniscient power of God which defied every power of darkness and raised Jesus from the dead for our salvation. We can know Christ fully only if we experience Him in the spiritual realm by what His resurrection accomplished for us. See Romans 8:11.

- The resurrection is central to our Christian faith and the main reason to believe in God. See 1 Corinthians 15:14-20.
- By the power of Jesus, death can be raised to life. Jesus raised Lazarus. See John 11:42-43; John 10:17-18.
- Because of the resurrection, the spiritually dead, the sinner, can be given spiritual life. See Ephesians 2:4-8; Acts 26:18; Colossians 1:13.
- Believing the resurrection power of God can change lives. The weak, discouraged, and even the one who denied Jesus became a bold and fearless leader willing to die for Him. For example, Peter in Acts 1.
- The same Holy Spirit who defeated the whole hosts of hell and raised Jesus from the dead lives in us to make us overcomers of sin, death, sickness, demons, and the Law. See Romans 8; Luke 10:17-19.

"And God wrought special miracles by the hands of Paul: So that from his body were brought unto the sick handkerchiefs or aprons and the diseases departed from them, and the evil spirits went out of them" (Acts 19:11-12).

LIFE: Jesus' resurrection power gives us salvation with a changed heart and a new spirit full of Jesus' righteousness. His resurrection by the power of the Holy Spirit will continue by sanctification to bring change in us to live as new creation beings. We will also walk in power, authority, and victory over Satan, sin, and all things evil. Regularly pray the Ephesians 3:14-21 and 1 Corinthians 13:4-8 prayers.

AUGUST 16

GOD IN YOU BY HIS RESURRECTION POWER

"The Spirit of truth...but ye know him, for he...shall be in you." —John 14:16-17

TRUTH: God is connected to us in a relationship by Jesus and the Holy Spirit. After Jesus ascended, He promised the Holy Spirit, about whom the Word in Ephesians 1:13-14 says, *"In whom ye also trusted, after that ye heard the word of truth, the gospel of your salvation: in whom also after that ye believed, ye were sealed with that Holy Spirit of promise. Which is the earnest* (down payment) *of our inheritance."*

"For ye are the temple of the living God; as God hath said, I will dwell in them, and walk in them; and I will be their God, and they shall be my people" (2 Corinthians 6:16).

GOD IS IN YOU: In the oneness of Spirit, we are to receive all our sins as forgiven by the Blood of Jesus. This will witness to our hearts that we are children of God and eliminate Satan trying to make us sin-conscious, insecure, or feeling unworthy. All the nature of God is in us, His righteousness in His love and acceptance, His peace, His wisdom, and His strength; His power in the fruit of the Spirit has made us complete and secure in God, knowing His presence and help is only a prayer away. Read Ephesians 1-3 and learn who we have been made "in Christ."

"What? know ye not that your body is the temple of the Holy Ghost which is in you, which ye have of God, and ye are not your own?" (1 Corinthians 6:19).

LIFE: The Holy Spirit is in you and me, and we belong to Jesus. You have been established in Him. Do you believe it as a truth that cannot be shaken from your heart? Do you believe God the Holy Spirit in you, full of resurrection power, greater than every evil thought from the devil, greater than sickness, lack, and oppression? God is in you; let Him rule from your spirit by His Holy Spirit in Jesus' power to influence your soul to be an overcomer. See 1 John 4:4; Romans 8:37.

GOD IS FOR YOU

"And I will pray the Father, and he shall give you another Comforter." —John 14:16

TRUTH: God is for you because He gave you His greatest gift, His Son, who suffered on the Cross to cancel sin's power and its effects and give us all His spiritual blessings. Romans 8:32 tells us how God in His goodness shall with Christ Jesus freely give us all things. God will bless us, take care of us, lead us into all truth, and meet the needs we give to Him in faith. God is for you; believe and be assured of His power and ability to cause you to overcome. Believe nothing can come against you and succeed outside of His will for your life. Father, let Your will be done on earth, as it is in heaven. See Matthew 6:10. Can you release God to do His will in your life as He sees it in heaven? There is no temptation, sin, sickness, or death in heaven. Have faith that God's grace will cause you to overcome trials and multiply heaven's atmosphere here on earth. See 1 John 4:17b.

God is for you when He removed all sin, justified you, and declared you innocent, when He freed you from all guilt and shame so that, when in faith, no one can successfully lay a charge against you. Faith, forgiveness, and innocence render Satan incapable of accusing you and bring you down to feel condemned, low, and depressed in your soul. No accusation or condemnation of the enemy can succeed against you. And no death can ever rob you of life because, in Christ, you have eternal life. See 1 John 5:20.

"There is therefore now no condemnation to them which are in Christ...For the Spirit of life in Christ Jesus hath made me free from the law of sin and death" (Romans 8:1-2).

LIFE: God is for you because no one and nothing can condemn or defeat you. Not Satan with sickness or threats of death, no calamities, no lack, no evil person seeking your downfall. God says if you walk according to His Spirit, by His Word, and in love, your faith in Him will cancel Satan's effort to bring you down. No weapon formed against you will prosper. See Isaiah 54:17. And when trouble comes, He says to call, and He will answer. See Psalm 91:15. God is for you.

GOD IS FOR YOU — DAY 2

"And I will pray the Father, and he shall give another Comforter." —John 14:16

TRUTH: We also know God is for us because He says nothing can separate us from His love—neither tribulation, distress, persecutions, famine, nakedness, peril, or sword. No weapon formed against us can prosper, and nothing can separate us from His love. WHY? Because the Holy Spirit is God and the God of love, He has deposited love in our hearts. See Romans 5:5; Galatians 5:22. No one can make us feel less than we are in Christ because our Great God is living in us, and no one can take God from our hearts. He is in us to give us strength, and He is for us to provide divine assurance and His help. He has got us imprinted on the palm of His hand. See Isaiah 49:16.

"If God be for us, who can be against us?" (Romans 8:31).

God is our source, and we are recipients of all His blessings. He says further that we can do nothing without Him, But OH! We can do all things through Christ which strengtheneth us. See John 15:5; Philippians 4:13.

And if we are tempted to or have sinned, He is still for us; we can run to His throne for grace to help us receive the gift of repentance in His mercy and never fall into condemnation. See Hebrews 4:16; 1 John 1:9; Romans 8:1-2. God is for us; He strengthened us in the inner man to stand strong in Him and to know that, by His Spirit, we can overcome all and be victorious, that we can say, *"But thanks be to God, which giveth us the victory through our Lord Jesus Christ"* (1 Corinthians 15:57).

LIFE: *"My sheep hear my voice, and I know them, and they follow me: And I give unto them eternal life; and they shall never perish, neither shall any man pluck them out of my Father's hand"* I and my Father are one (John 10: 27-30).

"When I cry unto thee, then shall mine enemies turn back: this I know; for God is for me" (Psalm 56:9). God is for you always!

GOD WITH YOU

"Even the Spirit of truth...for he dwelleth with you." —John 14:17

TRUTH: God is with you. God can keep this promise because of the person of the Holy Spirit. Are you feeling lonely? Do you feel abandoned? Do you have needs that, despite your prayers, seem to go unanswered? Does it seem God is never there when you think you need Him the most? Turn back the pages of history and remember the people of Israel traveling from Egypt to the promised land. He led them by day in a pillar of cloud and by night in a pillar of fire. Can we recount the ways God was with them? They were innumerable! See Exodus.

God is with you. He is Emmanuel, meaning *God with us,* in Jesus Christ His Son. Jesus gave all of us a promise that where two or three are gathered in His name, He is there in our midst. We have the continual presence of God the Holy Spirit with us and in us, and as we trust Him, we cannot fail. 1 Corinthians 13:8.

God, the Holy Spirit, is God with us in a very intimate and personal way. He is with us everywhere we go, and we can call on Him every time. Whatever our need, even in our darkest time and greatest need, we can call on God our Heavenly Father and be confident even if we don't sense His presence, by faith we believe that He hears and answers to provide, heal, deliver, comfort, teach and correct us. Be always expectant for His response to us.

"For they shall fight against thee; but they shall not prevail against thee; for I am with thee, saith the Lord, to deliver thee" (Jeremiah 1:19).

LIFE: Confession: God is in me, and He is greater than all. God is for me; nothing and no one can succeed against me. God is with me, and I will never fail because He is love, and love will never fail. *"I will love thee, O Lord, my strength. The Lord is my rock, and my fortress, and my deliverer, my God, my strength, in whom I will trust; my buckler, and the horn of my salvation, and my high tower"* (Psalm 18:1-2). Meditate: on Jeremiah 31:3; Hebrews 13:5.

THE GREATER ONE

"Greater is he that is in you, than he that is in the world." —1 John 4:4

TRUTH: The Greater One in us is God the Holy Spirit. He is God's perfect love deposited in our hearts. See Galatians 5:22; 1 John 4:18. He is the Anointing. See 1 John 2:27. Satan is the one who is in the world, and he is the lessor one. 1 John 2:27 says, *"But the anointing which ye have received of him abideth in you."*

John 14:16-17 says, *"And I will pray the Father, and he shall give you another Comforter, that he may abide with you forever... but ye know him, for he dwelleth with you, and shall be in you."*

The Holy Spirit came in at the born again experience. All the might and power of the God of heaven came to live within. See John 1:12; 3:3-5. He abides in us and is with us. He is to be acknowledged, recognized, honored, and called upon in all situations. Because He is greater than all. We are of God because we have received the truth about Jesus and are the children of God. As Children of God, having the power of the Holy Spirit, the Anointing in us, we have dominion and have overcome the world, Satan, and his demons operating through; sin/flesh; death/sickness; Law/self-effort. We have a Helper in the Holy Spirit, the Greater One as our God. If we keep our eyes mostly on our lives and our faith, we will be sidetracked by Satan to neglect the Holy Spirit and the Anointing and become weak, as we are pushed into works to become self-sufficiency orientated. See 1 John 2:15-17.

LIFE: Whenever we are challenged, with trouble or facing trials we are to be still and call upon God's Spirit the Anointed One and His anointing, the Greater One abiding in us to raise a standard against the enemy of our soul, and defeat Satan's attack against us. And He will show us how to stand and having done all to stand, because the Greater One in us overcomes all. See 1 John 4:4. Draw near to God in the power of His Spirit and the Greater One who will help us to submit to God and to resist until the enemy flees. See James 4:7-8.

THE GREATER ONE — DAY 2

"Greater is he that is in you, than he that is in the world." —1 John 4:4b

TRUTH: Satan is no match for the believer filled with the Holy Spirit and who believes the anointing within is greater. It is God's perfect love within the anointing who will move on our behalf to take care of business, to deliver, and cause us to have nothing to fear. *"Perfect love casteth out fear"* (1 John 4:18b). It is God's power within us, the Holy Spirit, who will face those challenges, that trial, that oppression, those seemingly impossible situations and cause us to overcome. God told Moses to stretch forth his hand and divide the Red Sea, but God's power did the work. See Exodus 14:15-16.

Stand firm and unmovable and believe that the Holy Spirit in us is greater than Satan's plans. He is greater than sickness, He is greater than any lack we are facing, and He is greater than death. He will also protect us from any untimely death. See Psalm 118:17. If fear has gripped your heart, if it seems fear will not leave you alone despite your commanding it to go, stop the self-effort, the striving, and fighting; sit down on the inside as you surrender your human will to the Lord. Be still, rest, and call upon the GREATER ONE inside to give you revelation knowledge on how to stand and cause you to overcome. He will show you the way out. All things are possible to him that believeth. See Ephesians 1:16-23; Mark 9:23.

LIFE: My Jesus is Lord. I keep my eyes on Him and His blessed Holy Spirit. The Anointing in me is greater than any force of darkness coming against me. Your love is greater than fear, and Your truth is greater than lies; Your righteousness in me is greater than condemnation. Jesus is light, and His light expels all darkness. Your grace is greater than sin. Jesus loves me, and I trust His love and care for me, which is greater than fear. Meditate on these Scriptures to increase belief in the Greater One who will overcome all: See 1 John 4:4; Isaiah 54:17; 2 Timothy 1:7; John 10:27-30; John 12:31-32; John 17:21-23; Romans 8:10-11,31,37; 2 Corinthians 6:17; 1 John 4:13-18; 5:4-5; Revelation 12:11.

TASTE AND SEE THAT THE LORD IS GOOD

"For thou, Lord, art good, and ready to forgive; and plenteous in mercy unto all them that call upon thee." —Psalm 86:5

TRUTH: God is absolutely and completely good. This is one truth we must never doubt, regardless of what our experience or situation tells us. Everything God is, has done, or will do is for the ultimate good of His children because He is good. The slaughter of animals was God's mercy in the Old Testament, to cover sin until the complete sacrifice for sin could be made through Jesus' death and resurrection.

Under the Law of Moses, where people died for disobedience, it was a good God preserving holiness in the hearts of men and women so that in the fullness of time, Jesus, His grace, could come forth of a virgin to bring eternal salvation. We must always and in all situations trust His goodness to come out of every problem we face. How we view, God will determine our thoughts, words, faith, behavior, and hence our relationship with Him and our success.

If we are an outer court believer remaining distanced and going to God only for advice, blessings, or when in trouble, He will remain small in our eyes. But we know His goodness is forever turned towards us, and we can, through worship, enter the inner courts in a more intimate relationship to hear from His heart. Then we will see Him as He is, a big God. In our eyes and in our hearts, we must see God as BIG! always good and always a God of tender mercies.

LIFE: Your God is perfect, faithful, and trustworthy. When prayers seem unanswered, you must trust the situation to Him and stay in prayer, expecting to hear from Him simply because we know He is good, and we can trust that He will work it out in His way for our good in the long run. See Nahum 1:7; Romans 8:26-28.

MADE TO PARTAKE

"...confirmation of the gospel, ye are all partakers of my grace." —Philippians 1:7

TRUTH: As the Lord was leading me into His grace to live by faith, He gave me this dream. I was in a shopping plaza, and I was hungry. I stopped by a supermarket and peered through the glass; there, I could see the shelves laden with all kinds of food. My mouth watered. But somehow, the scene changed, and I was on the beach (I lived close to one). As far as my eyes could see were tables filled with every imaginable food fit for a king. I awoke. I deduced from the dream that I was thinking small, desiring packaged food on shelves when there was more. A banquet of more good things than I ever anticipated, imagined, or knew of was already provided by my Heavenly Father. On my side of the equation, something (represented by the glass) was keeping me from partaking in God's abundance. What limitation could the glass represent in a believer's life?

- There is a lack of knowledge of God's grace in His provisions in Christ Jesus.
- Not knowing who we have been made in Christ as qualified partakers.
- Self-effort and pride in trying and striving to find the bread for oneself, instead of sitting at the table already prepared.
- Not knowing we are qualified to sit at the table because of small thinking.
- Not discerning the Body and the Blood of Jesus Christ?
- Not knowing what God's Word says about obtaining His provision by faith.
- Lack of faith to sit at the table and partake of what was already provided.
- Hindrances to partaking because of condemnation from the enemy.
- Inability to sit at the table because of fear of the presence of the enemy.
- Prayerlessness which leaves us clueless, powerless, and defenseless.

LIFE: If you are not like a tree planted by the rivers bringing forth fruit (see Psalm 1:3), Satan is using some hindrance against you. Examine the points above against your life and situation and ask the Holy Spirit to expose lead you out of any of Satan's similar bondage and limitations and into becoming a willing partaker.

OFFENSE

"The discretion of a man deferreth his anger; and it is his glory to pass over a transgression." —Proverbs 19:11

TRUTH: Offense and walking out of love, either with God or man, is one of Satan's tactics to keep us paralyzed or preoccupied with him. See Luke 7:23. Satan entices us into offense so very quickly, as sometimes we may hear a statement and quickly jump to an illogical or wrong conclusion; at other times, we retaliate because we say we are no one's doormat. Sometimes, we're insulted or neglected or hear about another's problem and join them in taking offense. God wants us to resist offense and look past the offense to His love, forgiveness, and grace.

We have examples in Scripture of Jesus Himself saying while He was on the Cross, *"Father, forgive them: for they know not what they do"* (Luke 23: 34). We see Stephen being stoned, yet he did not get offended and curse his attackers; instead, he asked the Father to forgive them. So, guess what?

God wants us to do the same. When others hurt us, we are responsible for remaining at peace and resisting anger or retaliation. The harboring of offense will harden our hearts toward others with unforgiveness, bitterness, grudges, and hatred; it opens the door to the enemy. See 2 Corinthians 2:10-11; Ephesians 4:26-27. Satan will then attack by causing that offense to:

- Build fear, worry, robbing us of our blessings. See Luke 7:23.
- Break relationships. See Matthew 18:15-17.
- Rob us of our peace. See Psalm 119:165.
- Build anger, bitterness, and pride. See Proverbs 13:10; 18:19.
- Quench the Holy Spirit. See 1 Thessalonians 5:15-19.
- Bring fear and build strongholds. See Psalm 112:7 and rob us of our victory. See 1 John 5:4

LIFE: When offense comes, immediately look to Jesus and ask His help to overlook, forgive, and bless and curse not. This will free you and will not clutter your heart with hindrances and worry, robbing you of close fellowship with Jesus and being able to live in peace both with God and with man. Give all offenses to God and be free to enjoy your relationships.

OVERCOME OFFENSE

*"Great peace have they which love thy law: and
nothing shall offend them."* —Psalm 119:165

TRUTH: To overcome offense, first acknowledge Christ. The anointing is in us, and He is greater than the pressure of the offense and the fear coming against us. Therefore, we will forgive and seek not to retaliate. We forgive because the love of Christ deposited in our hearts covers a multitude of sins. See 1 Peter 4:8. We will keep our peace, as anger gives Satan and others control over us. Let our words minister grace unto the hearers. See Ephesians 4:29. Seek to remain calm and remain the same; do not change the good actions we are used to doing towards the person, and the offense will end. *"If the spirit of the ruler rise up against thee, leave not thy place; for yielding pacifieth great offenses"* (Ecclesiastes 10:4).

"A soft answer turneth away wrath: but grievous words stir up anger" (Proverbs 15:1).

All people are made in the image of God, even those with ugly behavior and in whom the image of God is barely visible. Ask God to let His love for them flow through us so that they can see a new light in His love. Forgiveness quells offense; move quickly to forgive and release others who have wronged us. Ask for the help of the Holy Spirit to be pleasing to God.

"Let all bitterness, and wrath, and anger, and clamor, and evil speaking, be put away from you, with all malice: And be kind one to another, tenderhearted, forgiving one another, even as God for Christ's sake hath forgiven you" (Ephesians 4:31-32).

LIFE: Never harbor offense in your heart. Right at the offense, even under your breath, ask the Holy Spirit to take the offense from you and help to keep the offense from seeping into your heart. Ask the Holy Spirit to keep you from retaliating. Forgive and release the person or situation to God. God says vengeance belongs to Him. See Hebrews 10:30; Romans 12:9-21. Meditate on 1 Corinthians 13:4-8 and let God's love fill your heart.

AUGUST 26

OVERCOME OFFENSE — DAY 2

*"Great peace have they which love thy law: and
nothing shall offend them."* —Psalm 119:165

TRUTH: When bad things happen, we are not to withdraw into ourselves with self-pity, replay, and relive the bad experience over and over in our heads. Instead, we walk by faith in the fruit of the Spirit of love, exercising self-control while pursuing peace and holiness so that we will become peacemakers. See Galatians 5:22-23; Romans 12:14; Matthew 5:9.

"Follow peace with all men, and holiness, without which no man shall see the Lord" (Hebrews 12:14).

Only God can see the entire situation and who contributed what to the problem; we are to, without judgment, cast it as a care to the Lord. He will apply His righteousness and His abundant grace to make things right and cause peace to reign in the hearts of all concerned, either by forgiveness, repentance, self-control, or setting boundaries. See 1 Peter 5:7; Romans 5:17; Galatians 5:22; Colossians 3:12-15. If we know someone is offended at us, even if they are the cause, Scripture says if we go to the altar, we are to leave our gift at the altar and seek reconciliation with them. See Matthew 5:24-26. Seek to reconcile differences quickly. If the stronger person in faith seeks reconciliation first, it will end the offense in a reasonable time. If the offended refuses to receive your request for forgiveness, let it go in the hands of the Lord. Another solution to preventing offense is to speak less and listen more.

"Wherefore my beloved brethren, let every man be swift to hear, slow to speak, slow to wrath" (James 1:19).

LIFE: Meditate and obey the Scriptures in Matthew 18:15-17, so that blessing will follow us. Let us take charge of our hearts, resist offense, and choose to walk in love, kindness, tenderheartedness, and forgiveness, even as God in Christ Jesus forgave us. See Ephesians 4:31-32.

PURPOSE OF TRIALS

"My brethren count it all joy when ye fall into divers temptations: Knowing this, that the trying of your faith worketh patience." —James 1:2-3

TRUTH AND LIFE: Temptations, trials, and trouble come to every person living in this fallen world. A Christian's faith does not exclude them from experiencing trials. What is the purpose of these trials? Trials test us to show us the level of our relationship with God and, consequently, our faith and endurance. See Romans 5:3-4. Do we have a close relationship resting and trusting God as we believe and receive His blessings and deliverance by faith? Or do we have a distant relationship experiencing doubt and fear and then complain and remain lacking?

Trials purify us as they expose and destroy any false hope and security we put in ourselves or our idols of money, possessions, pleasure, status, or other people. See James 1: 2-5. When they fail, as they always will, we must turn to God for His help. As with Job's trials, God used tests to work faith and endurance and give glory to Himself as the One in charge of Job's life. God proved to the enemy His child Job maintained faith in Him, and His pleasure was to greatly bless Him more in the end when by faith he overcame. God displayed His power and His grace in Job's life. Trials also drive us to the Father to seek His help. He is always gracious to respond to our call and to lead us back to Himself to produce the fruit of righteousness.

Trials work eternal benefits in us.

Blessed are ye, when men shall revile you, and persecute you, and shall say all manner of evil against you falsely, for my sake. Rejoice, and be exceeding glad: for great is your reward in heaven: for so persecuted they the prophets which were before you" (Matthew 5:11-12).

"That the trial of your faith, being much more precious than of gold that perisheth, though it be tried with fire, might be found unto praise and honour and glory at the appearing of Jesus Christ" (1 Peter 1: 7).

PURPOSE OF TRIALS — DAY 2

"Knowing this, that the trial of your faith worketh patience." —James 1:3

TRUTH: When trials come, we usually become preoccupied with ourselves, wanting it to stop. But God knows that there are areas of our lives that need to be purified or corrected at times. And He will use these difficult times when we are turned to Him in prayer to reorient us to Himself and His righteousness. In Psalm 73, we see the writer preoccupied with the wicked prospering while he, as the righteous, was suffering. But when he took His eyes off himself and others, he saw God for who He is, His source and defender. Trials in our lives allow God to show up as Father for His children and as the healer, provider, protector, sanctifier, and deliverer to meet our needs and display His power on our behalf against the enemy. See Luke 8:22-25; Psalm 34:18.

We can count trials all joy because they work in us an eternal reward of helping us walk in greater faith, patience, and in the Spirit. Trials will cause us to pray more and draw us into a more intimate relationship with the Father. Often the result is that we learn righteousness, faith, patience, endurance, and trust. See Isaiah 26:9; Hebrews 12:11; James 1:2-6. In the end, we are shifted from focusing on ourselves, our situation, or the devil and begin to focus on God, His purpose, and His goals for our life even in and through the trial.

LIFE: Because Christ is our life when trials come, let our posture be to embrace the trial and take it to God. Do not waste much time fighting the devil or being anxious, wanting the trouble to end or instantaneously go away without knowing God's plan or purpose in the matter. Instead, we are to ask our Heavenly Father to give us His mind on the situation, His wisdom, His direction, His strength, and His way forward and out of the trial. Keep your eyes on Jesus through the Scriptures He places on your heart. Keep standing on His Word concerning your situation. Listen and follow the leading of God's Spirit, and you will overcome and endure a shorter trial and a lasting benefit of growing in your faith as you overcome. See 1 Peter 1:2, 7-9.

RESPONSE TO TRIALS

"My brethren, count it all joy when ye fall into divers temptations." —James 1:2

TRUTH: God does not bring temptations, trouble, or trials on people for any reason, including to teach them a lesson. But the Word says, whatever is not of faith is sin. Satan latches on to any kind of sin we may be entertaining, for example, unforgiveness or self-righteousness. If a person is not in faith, they are in sin, and any sin would have opened the door to the devil to bring trouble, seeking to rob, kill and destroy. See John 10:10; 1 Peter 5:8. But since there was a lack of faith in that area, God's desire may be to use the trouble we are facing to help us grow in relationship and therefore in our faith and learn to forgive or yield to Him in faith-righteousness more quickly. See Matthew 18:34-35.

When trouble or torment comes, God may not always and immediately pull us out of the trouble, as He may desire for us to endure, grow in faith, and overcome and learn to trust Him. See James 1:2-8; 1 Peter 1:6-7; Revelation 12:11. Jesus defeated Satan in the wilderness, at the Cross, and from the grave; likewise, we must enforce his defeat to maintain our victory over him in our daily lives.

"For whatsoever is born of God overcometh the world: and this is the victory that overcometh the world, even our faith" (1 John 5:4).

LIFE: What are our responses when troubles or trials come? Is it to fear and begin to worry? You may become paralyzed by asking, why me, God? Others may blame God or other people. You may blame the devil and begin spiritual warfare, binding and loosing the devil without faith and knowledge of the source of your exposure to the devil. If the devil has a legal right to cause you trouble because of sin, you gave him access; and no amount of warfare can expel him. You must close the opened door by repentance, and by obeying God's Word and the leading by the Holy Spirit in that area. Live in faith and love; follow and trust God's Word. God's Word as truth will set you free, as even your trials can work for your good. Meditate Romans 8: 26-28.

RESPONSE TO TRIALS — DAY 2

"...When ye fall into divers' temptations." —James 1:2

TRUTH: In a time of trial, we may seek to become self-sufficient and plan our escape route or fix the problems we face by ourselves. At the very worst, we may give up on ourselves or our faith in God.

However, our first response in any trial should be to look to God in faith. Because our salvation is grace through faith, always look to God's grace in Jesus and all He accomplished at the Cross and find joy in the truth that God has already done everything about our situation and has given us faith and promises concerning it for us to hold on to Him. See 2 Corinthians 1:20-22; 1 Corinthians 10:13.

Keep looking to God as we embrace the trial by faith, prayer, and even fasting, asking God to give us wisdom, direction, strength, angelic help, or comfort, whatever we may need in the trial.

"For thou hast delivered my soul from death: wilt, not thou deliver my feet from falling, that I may walk before God in the light...?" (Psalm 56:13).

On a personal basis, If God shows you, whether by His Word or His Spirit or in a dream, the weakness or flaw to be corrected, thank Him for His revelation knowledge, give the weakness over to Him and ask for His help to fix. See 1 Peter 5:7; Hebrews 4:16. Ask God to sanctify you by His truth, point you in the right direction, and help you to guard your mind, thoughts, words, and actions from the enemy's attack. Ask Him to help you align with His will. Expect to hear from Him as to His path for you out of the trial.

LIFE: Keep in close union with your Heavenly Father, hear from Him, yield to Him, and obey. He will lead you out stronger in faith because you overcame your weakness and Satan's attacks. God is pleased with you as you look to Him in faith, trusting Him. He will keep your feet from falling again a second time. Meditate on Psalm 143:8-12.

PATIENCE IN TRIALS

"But let patience have her perfect work, that ye may
be perfect and entire, wanting nothing." —James 1:4

TRUTH: In this highly electronic age in which we live with Alexa and Siri to instantly respond to our commands, we may have become negligent in seeking God. The Android phones are constantly being upgraded to new models to respond with even speedier and more personal responses. It is difficult to still our souls or to be quiet and patient. It is becoming increasingly difficult to persevere and wait. See Psalms 116:7; 131:1-3.

What is often extremely hard for us is that, while waiting, we must bear the pain of our trial, whether hardship, sickness, lack, or grief from the death of a loved one, when what we want is a quick deliverance. We want to be delivered from our pain and anguish immediately or at least quickly.

God in His wisdom does not always pull us out immediately but instead gives us His wisdom in the Word and His strength and comfort in the Holy Spirit to go through the trial. When we do, we always are stronger because of it. God's thoughts and ways are not ours, as He often looks at the big picture of our lives and then decides where He desires us to be patient in a trial, to experience spiritual, financial, or some other type of growth. See Isaiah 55:8; John 15:7-8; Ephesians 5:8-11.

LIFE: God expects us as His children to grow up and mature. Most of the time that happens only in trying times, when we must endure hardships while exercising faith and patience to overcome. In the process of enduring and overcoming, we grow up in faith spiritually with the ability to build character, increase faith and trust in our Father more as not only Savior but also as our Lord, Master, Baptizer, and soon coming King. Meditate on 2 Timothy 4:18.

TRIALS AND PATIENCE

"But let patience have her perfect work..." —James 1:4

TRUTH: When trials come, we are to run to God and hand it to Him. We can ask Him to show us the source, if our trial was a direct attack from Satan to hinder us, or from our sin, or if it was being used for His divine purpose of sanctification. See 1 Peter 1:5-9; Jonah 1. For any answer the Holy Spirit gives, we are to stand in faith and turn to the Word to read, meditate on, and speak God's Word concerning His heart while expecting His intervention.

We then become a doer of the Word as God gives us clarity and, if it was sin, we repent. If the trial is from Satan or God Himself, do not respond by fighting, rebuking, binding, and loosing to seek an immediate escape or reprieve. See Matthew 18:18. Ask the Father for His eternal perspective on how we respond, for Him to show us His way and path to overcome. See Matthew 18:19-20; Psalm 32:8. Listen to God, agree with His Holy Spirit, and follow what you hear. Patience with faith will result in God coming to us with deliverance, spiritual maturity, blessings, and peace. From these lessons on trials, the next time the devil attacks, you should have learned to stand first by submitting to God in prayer and then locate the source and then resist the devil more quickly, efficiently, and successfully.

LIFE: Always Keep your eyes on your Heavenly Father in a trial. Run to Him, give Him your troubles, pray, worship, and praise Him for whom you want Him to be. If you need healing, worship Him as your Healer. Listen when He speaks to your heart, and yield to Him; you will be 100% successful because He is love and truth. He loves you, and you need not fear Him, but know His love will never fail you. Instead, He will always lead you through the valley and out beside still waters. See Psalm 23.

"And not only so, but we glory in tribulations also: knowing that tribulations worketh patience; and patience, experience, and experience, hope" (Romans 5:3-4).

JOY IN TRIALS

"My brethren, count it all joy when ye fall into diver's temptation." —James 1:2

TRUTH: We can count trials as joy because we have salvation in our God. We joy not at the trial but in God during the trial, knowing He is faithful with us. As we demonstrate faith in Him, we believe His Word that He will never leave us. We know that faith in the Blood of Jesus will bring a reward in blessings from heaven. We can have joy because trials, though challenging, get eternal benefits as they increase and perfect our love and our faith.

We can joy in trials because, though painful, God promised trials would not cause our downfall because He will never leave us nor forsake us. See Jude 24-25; 1 Corinthians 10:13; Hebrews 13:5.

We can also joy because God has given us what we need to overcome, faith in His grace, His Word, His Spirit, His anointing, and fellowship and answers in prayer. We can rejoice because our situation is temporary, as our God will deliver. After all, He loves us. See Matthew 5:11-12; Acts 16:22-31.

"If ye keep my commandments, ye shall abide in my love; even as I have kept my Father's commandments, and abide in his love. These things have I spoken unto you, that my joy might remain in you, and that your joy might be full. This is my commandment, that ye love one another, as I have loved you" (John 15: 10-12).

LIFE: Believers can count it all joy because we know our God is faithful. And as you embrace trials while depending on God, His Holy Spirit will utilize the joy in your heart to sustain you with strength as He works out your salvation, and until Christ is formed in your heart for the Holy Spirit to raise a standard against the enemy to change your situation. God is the hope of your glory and your salvation, so joy in Him even during your trials. Rejoice, and again I say rejoice. See 2 Corinthians 12:9-11; Colossians 1:27; Philippians 4:4.

BENEFITS OF TRIALS

"That ye may be perfect and entire, wanting nothing." —James 1:4

TRUTH: Trials have many benefits, as they allow God to intervene in our situation and be our God, Savior, Healer, Deliverer, Comforter, and Provider. We can joy in Him for His great salvation. Trials show us where our hope and faith lie, whether in ourselves, other people, or the world system. These tests help us recognize the problem and reorient our priorities and direction from self-directed efforts to dependence on God.

Trials help us to develop faith and patience. When the answer is delayed, we must remain in faith and wait patiently on God with full knowledge that He is faithful and will come through for us.

Trials expose where we lack faith or have character flaws that need correction. God does not bring problems as trials to us, but He uses them to sanctify our hearts. In the process, we can have joy and be excited in our relationship because of God's direct involvement in our life to change us and grow the fruit of the Spirit in us. Our response is to follow God as He trains and refines our character to remove weaknesses, flaws, and open doors the enemy could use to hurt us. God closes the doors by making us stronger through the trial. God watches over us and protects us from Satan. He does this as He increases love, faith, righteousness, prayer, and authority in us, which in the end will defeat Satan. See Isaiah 26:9.

Trials will cause us to run to God our Father for help, and as we interact with Him by His Spirit, we increase our relationship. We rejoice as we grow in our relationship with Him, faith, and patience until we are delivered. When we exercise our human will to rejoice, it increases intimacy and trust. Overall, we grow in more profound dependence on God as our Father, source, provider, and deliverer.

LIFE: The Word tells you to rejoice in God's grace for all His blessings because God remains with you through your trials and will always sustain and deliver. Face difficulties with joy because of who God is and because with Him, you always win, as He will never leave you and will work all things for your good.

TRIAL BY FIRE

"All that he hath is in thy power; only upon himself put not forth thine hand." —Job 1:12

TRUTH: God has a stake in our lives, and it is not all about what He does for us to prosper, but also what He does in us for His character and glory to be seen and demonstrated in us. Job, His servant, was one example who went through the fire. Others were Jacob wrestling with God; Joseph was banished to Egypt, David was driven into the wilderness, Saul, who later became Paul had a thorn in his flesh, and Peter, who denied Jesus three times, was frustrated. These all suffered pain but, in the end, through the sanctification process, gained God's grace in His power. We are called to fellowship in His suffering for us to mature into His image and Christlikeness. See Philippians 3; 2 Corinthians 11:24-31.

God did not cause trouble in the lives of those Old Testament saints, but He used their trials to remove weakness, bad habits, or questionable character traits in them. Paul was practicing religion and self-righteousness, and Peter was impetuous and rash. God will likewise do the same for us. Sometimes we may not even know we have something that needs changing, like pride or self-righteousness. But God knows all things and will bring the necessary change we need even by fiery trials.

"I have redeemed thee; I have called thee by name; Thou art mine. When thou passeth through the waters, I will be with thee; and through the rivers, they shall not overflow thee..." (Isaiah 43:1-3).

LIFE: Fire of adversity can be exceedingly difficult to understand and endure, and we all need God's help, strength, wisdom, and direction to go through. Trial by fire comes to grow God's character in us, both for spiritual maturity and for us to minister at a more profound and higher level in our calling. The fire will burn until all God's enemies and the dross (like a lack of understanding of His love and compassion, pride, self-righteousness, greed, fear, and others) fall from our lives to make Christ Lord of each life.

IN THE FIRE

"That the trial of your faith, being much more precious than of gold that perisheth, though it be tried with fire, might be found...honor and glory." —1 Peter 1:7

TRUTH: Trials, hardships, and trouble are all part of our normal life, and God uses them to train us to become transformed Christians. See Deuteronomy 8:5; Proverbs 13:23; 19:18; 23:13-24; 1 Samuel 3:13-14; 2 Samuel 7:14-15; Hebrews 12; John 16:33.

Every person would prefer to go through life without dealing with trouble or its consequences, but God sometimes permits difficult situations where we cannot help ourselves and must run to Him. He wants to get our attention and build love, faith, patience, His compassion, authority, or whatever need He sees in us. Unfortunately, the difficulty is the only way to build Christlikeness as we are often so preoccupied with ourselves or other interests. God cannot get our full attention until we are forced to run to Him. The COVID 19 pandemic is an example of people being in the fire by losing a job or loved ones.

Our first natural response to trial and pain is for it to leave, to end now! We become desperate and begin our efforts by doing all we know to do by faith. When nothing works, we run to the One overseeing our trial and ask for help, wisdom, direction, and patience through prayer. In the problem, stay in communion with Jesus and let Him show you what is coming against you and adjust or make the necessary changes day by day. Above all REJOICE, and again I say REJOICE as God will strengthen you and see you through to victory.

When God is in control, others will see our faith and trust in Jesus. They will see the fourth man, like the Son of God, in the fire with us, and we will come out of our trial showing it had no power over us. We will be rejoicing in the greatness of our God and His faithfulness to deliver.

LIFE: *"And exhorting them to continue in faith, and that we must through much tribulation enter into the kingdom of God"* (Acts 14:22).

IN THE FIRE — DAY 2

*"...Though it be tried with fire, might be found unto praise and honor
and glory at the appearing of Jesus Christ."* —1 Peter 1:7

TRUTH: When we face trouble, we should run to God first and ask for His wisdom before doing what we think we know to do. See 2 Chronicles 16:12. Do not fall back into a Law mentality of self-effort. Always depend on the Holy Spirit to help us grow up more quickly. This will save us time and shorten the time in the fire when we hear from God, listen, ask Him questions for clarifications and wisdom, and then do as He leads. See Luke 1:34-35. We are to ask God for His grace, power, and ability to keep us through our ordeal. See 2 Corinthians 12:9; Philippians 4:4. God wants us to depend on Him first and foremost and consistently.

Fire will draw us into a closer relationship with the Father as we will have had to draw nearer to pray and hear what He has to say about our situation. We must receive His grace and obey to be led out of our trial. In difficulties, yielding to God leads to growth in character, faith, trust, patience, and blessings. The more quickly we yield, the more God gets to do His work in us, and the shorter our time will be in the fire. See Isaiah 48:10-11; Jeremiah 18:1-6; Psalms 66:8-20; 118:18; 119:67; Malachi 3:3-4; Galatians 4:19; Hebrews 2:10-11; 5:8-9; 1 Peter 4:1-2, 12-13.

LIFE: The results of coming out of the fire will be God-dependence instead of self-reliance, patience instead of haste, God's glory instead of self-glory, greater fear of God's love instead of carnality. It is doubt changed to faith, Law to God's grace, weakness to strength, dependence on natural knowledge to God's revelation knowledge, pride to humility, torment to peace, darkness to light, prayerless to prayerful, and from lack of trust to trusting God. Though you have passed through the fire, you were not burnt and have become a better Christian because of it. Therefore, rejoice and let the treasure of God in you, which has been polished, now shine!

FELLOWSHIP IN HIS SUFFERINGS

"That I may know him, and the...fellowship of his sufferings being made conformable unto his death." —Philippians 3:10

TRUTH: God sent His love, Jesus, to earth and the Cross to suffer in our place. After much suffering, God resurrected Jesus and glorified Him. God revealed Himself to us in Jesus. Adam was formed with love in his heart in a relationship and fellowship with the Father. However, pride in self-centeredness caused him to sin and consequently all humanity after him. See Psalm 51:5; Romans 5:12. Jesus came to reverse this and for man to be conformed, restored, and transformed through God's Word and His Spirit, back to His nature of love and being God-centered.

Just as Jesus suffered in His flesh, God will allow us to suffer in our flesh to put the old man under and bring an end to the old life, habits, and desires to cause us to grow, mature, and be conformed into Christ's image, likeness, and character.

Many believers over the years have done one of two things: first, they have neglected to apply the power of the Word and the Spirit to effect change in their lives, or they have tried to change by means other than God's way of the Word and His Spirit. One such means is religion and self-effort, trying in our strength and works of self-effort to know God, sense His love, and be accepted or fight the devil in spiritual warfare but not in faith. Religion negates the power and benefits of our salvation, keeps us weak, and perpetuates the work of the evil one.

LIFE: To end man's independence and efforts to please God in his strength with self-righteousness and religion, God in His wisdom often steps in and allow trials by fire in our lives to strongly encourage us to turn from self to God, from fear to love, from our will to God's will that we may know and worship Him. He did this with Saul, who later became Paul. Give up religion in self-effort for an intimate relationship with your Father. Jesus in a relationship will show up in our trials and, with patience, teach, lead, and deliver us, which then brings joy, peace, love, and rest to our souls.

FELLOWSHIP IN HIS SUFFERINGS — DAY 2

"Know him...and the fellowship of his sufferings." —Philippians 3:10

TRUTH: We do not suffer in God's will with anything from which we have been redeemed, such as sin, sickness, or any curse. If suffering comes to us with any of these, it is not from God; but He is sovereign and can use them for our spiritual benefit, just as Jesus suffered in the flesh to bring us His righteousness. Trials by fire bring suffering to our flesh in our soul (mind, will, and emotions) and work righteousness as we die to self and the flesh and are transformed into Christlikeness as the Holy Spirit dominates us. We partake in His sufferings as we enter the process of sanctification by which we endure trials and pain in the flesh for us to align our hearts with the heart of God more closely.

Also, as we deny ourselves in the flesh and take up the Cross, we are more inclined to obey the Word, forgive, and love our enemies. See Matthew 16:24-26. Persecution for the gospel's sake is also fellowshipping in His sufferings. And when we endure suffering in trials, we learn how to comfort others. See 2 Corinthians 1:4-5.

Jesus suffered when He confronted the world and was accused and spat upon. He was grieved at their hardened hearts and when people doubted in unbelief. Hebrews 5:8 tells us Jesus learned obedience through what He suffered. This, I believe, means Jesus, through the things He suffered, learned to surrender and be obedient to His Father so He could be our High Priest.

"But rejoice, inasmuch as ye are partakers of Christ's sufferings; that, when his glory shall be revealed, ye may be glad also with exceeding joy" (1 Peter 4:13).

LIFE: We can share Jesus' suffering and pain as we die to self in the flesh and become alive unto His love. We can also do that as we see the need of others and receive the burden of another given by the Holy Spirit and respond to help. See Galatians 3:13-14; Matthew 11:19; Galatians 6:2; Romans 8:17-26; 2 Corinthians 1:4-9; 1 Peter 1: 2:21-23; 4:12-19.

GODLY FRUIT

"It was planted in a good soil by great waters, that it
might bring forth branches, and that it might bear fruit." —Ezekiel 17:8

TRUTH: A born again believer has God's Spirit in his heart or human spirit, full of everything God possesses—love, faith, righteousness, peace, goodness, authority, power, and infinitely more. John 15 tells us God is the Vine, and we are the branches to bear fruit such as the fruit of repentance (Matthew 3:7-8.), abiding in Christ (John 15; Matthew 13:3-23), the Spirit within for character building (Galatians 5:22; Ephesians 5:9-22), giving in grace (Philippians 4:15-19), righteousness (Hebrew 12:11), holiness (Romans 6:17-22), evangelism, seeking the precious fruit of souls in the earth (James 5:6-8; Romans 1:13).

A Christian's goal is to live by faith in a relationship with Jesus, seeking to bear fruit and grow in Christlike character. God deposited His Spirit within us, not to be hidden, but to grow as we nurture and water the fruit of love within with the Word of God to increase faith and to bear more excellent fruit.

And he *"shall be like a tree planted by the rivers of water, that bringeth forth his fruit in his season; his leaf also shall not wither; and whatsoever he doeth shall prosper"* (Psalm 1:3).

God will be enlarged in our hearts to subdue everything fleshly or demonic in our soul and body and for His Spirit to shine in and through us to bear fruit for the world to see Jesus showing forth His glory in and through us.

LIFE: We are called by God not just to keep His image inside but to grow in and become like unto the image of Jesus. Father, help us give ourselves over to You in relationship with Jesus, depending on the Holy Spirit to guide and direct our spiritual growth into bearing good fruit. See Matthew 5:14-16; John 15; Galatians 5:22-23; Titus 3:14.

FRUIT OF LOVE

"But the fruit of the Spirit is love, joy, peace, long-suffering, gentleness, goodness, faith, meekness, temperance: against such there is no law. — Galatians 5:22-23

TRUTH: God is love, and the fruit of His Spirit is love. Love as the fruit has components mentioned, from joy to self-control. Think of the fruit of the Spirit as an orange. God's love as the whole orange, Jesus' love as the segments, and the Holy Spirit's love as the seeds planted on the inside. Jesus deposited His Spirit of love by His grace in our hearts the moment we are born again to establish His character within us. See Galatians 5:22. We must all seek to grow in this love relationship and the likeness of Jesus. As we water and nurture the seeds (mentioned from joy to self-control) the fruit and segments representing Godliness and Christlikeness will grow. We should study the Word and ask the Holy Spirit to teach us about the fruit of the Spirit and how to abide in Him, to draw nearer, and to fellowship with Him. He will help us hear from Him and build faith enough to obey God and walk in the Spirit. *"Take my yoke upon you, and learn of me; for I am meek and lowly in heart: and ye shall find rest unto your souls. For my yoke is easy, and my burden is light"* (Matthew 11:29-30).

God is love, and I believe the yoke here is God's love in a relationship with Jesus. See John 13:34-35. We know because Satan also has his yoke. See Isaiah 10:27. Yoked with God's love, we plant and nurture the seeds of love within for them to grow in the fruit of God's love. Seek to learn of Him by His Spirit, abide and fellowship with Him so that His love in us will grow and mature until we know we are complete in Him and can display His love and life to others. See Colossians 2:9-10; 1 John 4:6-11. As we walk in the love of God, our faith will grow because faith works by love, and faith will release God's power. See Galatians 5:6; Romans 15:13.

LIFE: Draw nearer to Jesus and yoke yourself in a closer relationship and fellowship to learn of Him. And let His life of love first flow to you and then from you to show your beautiful Savior and Lord to the world. See 1 John 3:16; John 13:34-35.

FRUIT OF JOY

"But let all those that put their trust in thee rejoice... let them
also that love thy name be joyful in thee." —Psalm 5:11

TRUTH: *"Who for the joy that was set before him endured the cross"* (Hebrews 12:2). It was a joy for Jesus to purchase our salvation and redeem us from the hand of Satan. No, it was not joyful in the way He suffered or in the things He endured, but He rejoiced in the partnership with His Father and for the result of setting us free. Jesus went to the Cross with joy and gave us His joy in our hearts. See Galatians 5:22. Joy is one of the elements, the seed of love that springs forth with jubilation at the goodness of God. God gave us salvation that made us no longer slaves to sin, Satan, death, and the Law but freed us unto God to love Him.

There should be great rejoicing in our hearts for so great a redemption, a constant source of joy for every believer because it was not just a nominal price that God paid for us; it was the life of His only Son. When we consider how far God stooped to recover us from our sin, shame, weakness, and rebellion, we can rejoice in His graciousness and choose to trust His Lordship. When we joy in the Lord and all Jesus has done for us, resting in His strength, it makes us strong to endure until a change from our hopelessness comes. *"The joy of the Lord is your strength."* (Nehemiah 8:10).

LIFE: Joy comes only from your spirit where Jesus dwells. Let joy arise as Jesus has set your heart free from the bondage of Satan and sin and unto Himself. Jesus Christ is in charge, and as you feed your spirit-man the Word, you will see God at work in the situations of your life, and this should cause eternal joy to spring forth. Let thankfulness and gratitude to Jesus fill you with joy as you trust Him for the blessings even before they come as well as afterward, *"Rejoice in the Lord always and again I say rejoice."* Sing songs of joy to Him and let His joy within give you strength to cross your Red Sea or to endure and overcome all trials. See Philippians 4:4.

FRUIT OF PEACE

"Peace I leave with you, my peace I give..." —John 14:27

TRUTH: The gospel of Jesus is a message of peace, for He is the prince of peace. Peace can be looked at in two ways: having peace *with* God and having the peace *of* God.

Peace with God comes when we receive Jesus as our righteousness; that is, His love at salvation in forgiveness ended our separation. See Romans 5:8-10. His righteousness by faith made us alive unto God one spirit with Him resting in union relationship. See Colossians 1:20. We have peace because it is the Blood of Jesus which justified us, declared us innocent, righteous, and reconciled to God, as guiltless, blameless, and innocent, accepted, worthy, and sufficient in the sight and presence of God. God's peace was deposited in us when we were born again. See Galatians 5:22. Jesus brought us peace when He ended the harsh and wrathful Law and gave us grace in His righteousness or love. See Isaiah 9:6; Luke 2:14; Romans 5:8, 17; 2 Corinthians 5:19-21.

Having peace with God is having faith in His love to produce righteousness which makes things right in your life, bringing peace. See Isaiah 32:17-18. We were justified and restored in love and right standing before the Father in peace. See Romans 5:1; 2 Corinthians 5:21. God's grace ended the Law mentality of trying, striving, struggling, and feeling unworthy. Peace is love at rest in our hearts by having an intimate love relationship with our Father. Knowing we belong to Him, that we're His charges and that He is faithfully working, leading, and guiding our life to have peace within, we can come boldly to His throne of grace to find help and mercy without unworthiness and condemnation. See Hebrews 4:16; Ephesians 1:6; Romans 8:1.

LIFE: Jesus's love in righteousness gives us peace with God. When our righteousness or standing before God is of faith and not in our goodness, we will have peace in our relationship with our Heavenly Father. His love, acceptance, assurance gives confidence, boldness, and assurance of His care for us, bringing us peace before God. See Isaiah 26:3; 32:17-18; Philippians 4:7; Hebrews 4:9-10; 13:5.

FRUIT OF PEACE — DAY 2

"Thou wilt keep him in perfect peace, whose mind is stayed on thee: because he trusteth..." —Isaiah 26:3

TRUTH: God is a God of peace. See Isaiah 9:6; Romans 16:20; 2 Corinthians 13:11. The first step to having the peace of God is to be born again and to walk in the Spirit of faith and love. This is walking in righteousness, always looking to Jesus, who brings peace. See Isaiah 32:17. Trouble and trials will come to everyone, but if we choose faith in God's love, faith will arise for us to trust Him and gain God's peace. Cast the situation over to God for His answer, speak the Word of God concerning your need, as you praise, worship, and thank Him until peace comes. *"For to be carnally minded is death; but to be spiritually minded is life and peace"* (Romans 8:6).

However, if we choose to handle life situations in our strength, the results can be devastating, leading to complaining, worry, strife, fear, failure, and a lack of peace. We have peace as we walk in love, faith, and authority first by declaring our love for the Father and trusting His love and care. He will never fail us.

And as we rest in the truth that Jesus is our righteousness, that He is our peace, our healer, our deliverer. As we stand in faith, He will come to work out our life situations, and peace comes. We can then pass His love and peace to others by taking no offense as our speech is always in God's grace, a soft answer that turns away wrath and shares about His goodness. Satan's strategy is to keep our soul scattered on many things, often worrying, and to rob our peace. But we are to draw near to Jesus and keep our focus on Him, cast our cares, trust in Him, and His peace comes. Let the Word dwell richly within to keep our minds at peace. See Colossians 3:15-16.

LIFE: We are to guard our hearts and minds and let the peace of God rule as we trust Him to work our concerns for our good in all things. See Hebrews 12:2; Psalm 55:16-18, 22.

CONFESSIONS ON PEACE

"The Lord will give strength unto His people; the Lord will bless his people with peace." —Psalm 29:11

TRUTH AND LIFE: The peace of God, which passes all understanding, keeps our hearts and minds in Christ Jesus. See Philippians 4:7. I am justified by the Blood of Jesus, made innocent, worthy, and acceptable, reconciled to my Father in union relationship, and I reject the lie of Satan that I am justified by my obedience and good performance to please God. Jesus' obedience did it all, and now I yield to Him. See Romans 5:16-21. The chastisement of my peace was upon Jesus; He bore my punishment and gave me His peace. I receive it by faith. See Isaiah 53:5. I am justified by faith and have peace with God through our Lord Jesus Christ; therefore, I am just, and I live by faith. See Romans 5:1; 1:17. Jesus loves me, and I am reconciled into His love, one Spirit in Christ Jesus. See 1 Corinthians 6:17

Therefore, no accusing voice of Satan bringing doubt that God does not love me can stand, as the law of the Spirit of life has freed me from the law of sin and death. See Romans 8:1-2, 10. I do not look at myself and my sin; I look to Jesus. See Hebrews 12:2; 1 John 1:7, 9. God will grant me wisdom when I ask, without faultfinding in me. Father, in this situation, I thank You for Your wisdom and Your peace in Jesus' name. See James 1:5-7.

God's peace can never be removed from me, and it will rule my heart. See Isaiah 54:10; Colossians 3:15. God is never the author of confusion but peace; He is peace in my heart. See 1 Corinthians 14:33; John 14:27. I will rest in the Lord, and I shall be still. He always gives me peace as I cast my care on Him. See Psalm 46:10; 1 Peter 5:7. I keep my mind and thoughts on Jesus. I will meditate on and speak His Word of peace, and He blesses me and keeps me in His perfect peace as I trust in Him. Father, thank You for showing me the path of Christ's life into Your peace. Amen. See Psalm 16:11.

FRUIT OF PATIENCE

*"For ye have need of patience, that, after...ye might
receive the promise."* —Hebrews 10:36

TRUTH: Patience is about forbearing in faith, being the same in a problem without anger or retaliation. It is love's victory in trials, as it endures until the time of manifestation and rejoicing in the natural comes. Patience is a virtue that is difficult for most of us to acquire and impossible without God's help. What is it that makes us impatient? Is it waiting on others? The intellectually slow? Is it driving in traffic? Listening to others speak? Waiting for a character change in a child or a loved one? Waiting for our desired blessing from the Lord? Whatever it is, God sometimes uses extended trials and times of waiting to build our faith to be patient. Although we would like to hurry things along, try to force the issue, or even fix things ourselves, God will let us try and fail; then, we must turn to Him to fix things. Looking to and trusting Jesus and patiently waiting on Him will bring His promise, His perfect blessing, and deliverance in His timing.

We can be patient with ourselves and others because God has been patient with us. See Ephesians 2:4-5; Romans 2:4. Patience also includes perseverance and bears up under weariness, strain, and persecution. The book of James admonishes us to be patient in trials and count it all joy because we can look to God and trust Him to work things out for us. When exercised, we have joy in our spirit, which gives us the strength to endure and wait on God's timing for our deliverance. The trying of our faith works patience, which perfects our faith. See James 1:2-4.

LIFE: *"Followers of them who through faith and patience inherit the promises"* (Hebrews 6:12).

*"Patience graciously, compassionately and with understanding judges
the fault of others without unjust criticism"* —Billy Graham.

FRUIT OF GENTLENESS

"Thou hast also given me the shield of thy salvation...and thy gentleness hath made me great." —Psalm 18:35

TRUTH: In a relationship, gentleness is the softness of our response in love. Gentleness is also referred to as kindness and tenderness. Our God is gentle, kind, and tender. He never disciplines us as much as we deserve; instead, He has tender feelings towards us. See Psalms 103:10-14. He is kind to the unthankful and the evil. See Luke 6:35. *"He shall feed his flock like a shepherd: he shall carry them in His bosom, and shall gently lead those that are with young"* (Isaiah 40:11). The opposite of gentleness could be hardness, harshness, inflicting punishment, revenge, severity, none of which applies to our Lord Jesus. He is always good even when His discipline seems severe. See Psalm 107:1; Jonah 1-4.

God admonishes us to be Christlike and gentle: *"But the wisdom that is from above is first pure, then peaceable, gentle, and easy to be intreated, full of mercy and good fruits..."* (James 3:17).

We are to love and be gentle with others: *"Forbearing one another, and forgiving one another, if any man have a quarrel against any: even as Christ forgave you, so also do ye. And above all these things put on charity"* (Colossians 3:13-14).

Kind words warm the heart, and kind deeds lighten another's load, which builds more profound love in the relationship. As believers in the body of Christ, let us be gentle as a dove, the form of the Holy Spirit who landed on Jesus at His baptism and led Him in gentleness and power into His earthly ministry.

LIFE: To whom much is given, much is required. God has been kind to us, so pay it forward; let us share our seat with the elderly, provide Bibles to those in need in persecuted nations, bless those who curse us, and do good to those who despitefully use us. Let us give brotherly kindness and love to all so that the world may see the life of Jesus in and through us. See 2 Peter 1:5-8.

FRUIT OF GOODNESS

"For how great is his goodness, and how great is his beauty!" —Zechariah 9:17

TRUTH: Goodness is the character of love displayed when people are good to each other in an honest and healthy relationship. However, God is everlastingly and absolutely good, just as everything He made in creation was good. See Genesis 1. The Israelites exodus and journey from Egypt show the goodness of God, as He led them by cloud in the day and fire by night, He fed them manna, pulled water out of a rock to satisfy their thirst, kept their shoes like new, and delivered them from their enemies.

The goodness of God is the foundation of our faith, as the more, we believe He is good, the more we will love Him and trust His actions towards us to be good. Our faith is to be grounded in God's love. See Colossians 2:6-7. We see Jesus walking the earth in the gospels, displaying God's goodness as He healed the sick, raised the dead, and caused the lame to walk, the deaf to hear, the blind to see, and the demon-possessed to be free from bondage. In our new relationship with Jesus Christ by faith, if we were poor, we should be poor no more without love and trust. As with love and trust in Jesus, God will bless us to be a blessing. See Genesis 12:2. If we are in bondage, His goodness gives us the authority to be free. As a good Father, He loves and forgives us that we too may love and forgive others.

LIFE: God is a good God, and we have a good Father who blesses His children with good things. Heavenly Father, You are good to me, and I receive Your goodness and all Your blessings, that I shall prosper and not want in Jesus' name, Amen. See 3 John 2; Psalm 23; Psalm 107:8; Luke 11:9-13; 2 Peter 1:3-4.

GOD'S GOODNESS IN REPENTANCE

*"Not knowing that the goodness of God leadeth
thee to repentance?"* —Romans 2:4

TRUTH: God in Jesus' shed Blood and His death on the Cross forgave all our sins, gave us His love in His righteousness, and loosed us from the slavery of Satan, sin, death, and the Law. See Ephesians 2:8-9; Colossians 1:13-14; 2:13; Mark 3:28.

What did God's goodness in redemption do for us? He sent His only Son to die in our place for sin that we can repent and not die for sin. See 1 John 1:9. By His Blood, He justified us, declared us innocent, pure in heart, and reconciled unto the Father in a love relationship. See John 3:16-17; Romans 5:5. He gave us the gift of righteousness for love, fellowship, and intimacy. See Romans 5:17. Jesus destroyed Satan's power at the Cross when He made us dead to sin, which will never be held against us because of repentance. See Romans 4:8; Psalm 32:1-2. Jesus gave us His life, power, and authority in the Word to defeat Satan, death, and sickness. See Luke 10:18-19; Philippians 2:9-11. Jesus canceled the Law as it stimulated self-effort and failure and caused Satan to accuse us of sin, sin-consciousness which brings condemnation. See Hebrews 7:18-19; Colossians 2:14-15; Romans 8:1-2.

LIFE: Jesus gave us the New Covenant of grace to love Him from our hearts by faith instead of the Law and rules to obey with fear of punishment. In His goodness, God's grace in Jesus ended self-effort and trying, for us to live by faith in the power of the Holy Spirt. God's goodness lifted us from striving to obey and from obligation, to depending on and delighting in and trusting Christ Jesus. Hebrews 8:8-13; Psalm 37:4-6; Philippians 2:13. God is a good Father in salvation, with forgiveness. The gift of the Holy Spirit will help to keep us free as we live in forgiveness, repentance, holiness and walking in the Spirit. Meditate on God's goodness to Paul in 1 Timothy 1:11-17.

FRUIT OF FAITHFULNESS

"God is faithful, by whom ye were called unto the fellowship of his Son Jesus Christ our Lord." —1 Corinthians 1:9

TRUTH: Faithfulness in a relationship speaks of being consistent, reliable, loyal, steadfast, diligent, and trustworthy. *"I will sing of the mercies of the Lord forever: with my mouth will I make known thy faithfulness to all generations"* (Psalm 89:1). This Scripture tells us God was there for our forefathers Abraham and his people when they needed Him. When Abraham needed a son as his heir, God provided. He was there for Moses, who needed to cross the Red Sea. He was there for Daniel in the lions' den and the three Hebrew boys in the fiery furnace. And because He's faithful to all generations, He will be devoted to us. Psalm 89:24 says, *"But my faithfulness and my mercy shall be with him: and in my name shall his horn be exalted."* When we know how much God loves us, we can trust and never doubt His Word to us. As we trust His faithfulness, He will bless and lift us out of any harmful or impossible situation.

Because we are made in God's image, we are to walk in faithfulness. Faithfulness is of the Spirit, as the Father's love full of faith is deposited in our hearts. Romans 12:3; Galatians 5:22. When believed, received, and acted on consistently, God's love will create faithfulness in our character too. We are to be faithful to our word given in a promise, faithful with the ministering of God's Word. See Acts 20:27. We are to be faithful in our relationships. See 1 Timothy 3:2. We are to be faithful with our gifting, talents, and time. We must be faithful to God to the very end. See Luke 18:8; Hebrews 6:11.

LIFE: Let the faithfulness of God in you give contentment and assurance. Depend on God and live by His faith. See Mark 11:22-24. Show forth His faithfulness in all you say and do. Christ's faithfulness will manifest in you as His disciples, having integrity because Christ is your life. See Psalm 25:21; Galatians 2:20.

FRUIT OF MEEKNESS

"Put on therefore, as the elect of God, holy and beloved, bowels of mercies, kindness, humbleness of mind, meekness, longsuffering." —Colossians 3:12

TRUTH: In a relationship, meekness is love expressing humility, mercy, gentleness, and submission to one another. Meekness patiently endures offense, trusting God for His righteousness. It is, therefore, love showing the quality of strength in one's restraint, being free from pride and arrogance. People sometimes consider a meek person weak, but a vulnerable person retaliates to provocation while the meek uses wisdom and chooses not to. We see an example of Moses in Numbers 12:1-13. See also Matthew 23:11-12; Isaiah 57:15.

Meekness is vital as it enables us to develop self-restraint, as we saw with Moses. It also helps us be less selfish, self-focused, self-assertive, and more willing to esteem others. See Philippians 2:3. Meekness allows us to honor God as we correct others with the gentleness of heart when they are wrong. See Galatians 6:1.

Meekness causes us to be humble and teachable, like Nicodemus in John 3:1-2. And the church in James 1:21-22. At all times, let the Word of God be our priority and final authority, not church elders, church traditions, or denomination standards. We all need to be corrected and sharpened, and we should receive the Word with meekness and grow in God. See Acts 18:24-28. Meekness helps us to develop and walk in wisdom as we grow spiritually in the things of God. We will continue to walk with peace and joy in our hearts as we refrain from absorbing offense and as we continually depend on God's strength within to be our strength and defense. Meditate on Ephesians 4:14-16; James 3:13.

LIFE: Meekness shows the strength of character. Let the joy of the Lord, which brings strength, give you the needed control to walk in humility, gentleness, and meekness. See Ephesians 4:1-3.

DEVELOPING MEEKNESS

"Seek righteousness, seek meekness: it may be ye shall be hid in the day of the Lord's anger." —Zephaniah 2:3

TRUTH: God deposited meekness within us and, as we depend on Him and nurture the seed, He will develop the fruit to work His plans and purposes for us to grow more like Jesus each day. See Galatians 5:22. God desires that, with the help of the Holy Spirit, we cultivate the fruit of meekness before we can rule well in the kingdom on the earth. *"But the meek shall inherit the earth: and shall delight themselves in the abundance of peace"* (Psalm 37:11).

LIFE: In Psalm 35:11-13, David was accused and lied on, but in meekness, he turned to God and humbled his soul with prayer, fasting, praise, and thanksgiving. Satan has used food to deceive God's people many times: Eve in Genesis 3:6; the Israelites in Exodus 16:3; Esau in Hebrews 12:6; Samson in Judges 13:4; 14:8-9. Satan knows food is one source of temptation and condemnation in keeping us preoccupied and away from God. He even tried to use it against Jesus in Matthew 4:3. We must sometimes practice self-denial and subject our appetite for food to God. Fasting from food will clear and free our hearts and minds to be quieter to listen in meekness to hear from God our Father.

Secondly, we can cultivate meekness during difficult times. In times of trials, we should always ask our Father God for His wisdom and purpose in the trial. He will always work them for our good. See Romans 8:28. Moses learned humility and meekness in the desert, and the children of Israel learned it in the wilderness. See Exodus 2:11-25; Deuteronomy 8:2-5. Yielding to God and trusting Him in difficult situations will often humble us unto meekness. Meekness helps us to be humble enough to learn from God and be able to comfort others. See 2 Corinthians 1:4; Hebrews 5:8-9. A spiritual posture of gentleness, humility, and obedience are qualities of meekness. Let us be swift to hear, slow to speak, slow to wrath. See James 1:19.

"The meek will he guide in judgment: and the meek will he teach his way" (Psalm 25:9).

FRUIT OF SELF-CONTROL

"But the fruit of the Spirit is... temperance (self-control)." —Galatians 5:22

TRUTH: Self-control in a relationship is love under restraint. It is temperance or mastery over something and speaks of discipline, self-restraint, self-denial, and moderation. Paul says in 1 Corinthians 9:25, *"And every man that striveth for the mastery is temperate in all things."* We are expected to conduct ourselves appropriately at the right time. God deposited this fruit of the Spirit in us, but we must depend on God by His grace and power for the Holy Spirit to help us to grow up in them, for them to be seen in our natural lives. See Romans 8:29; 12:1; 2 Peter 3:18. Scripture has given us some areas where self-control is greatly needed. Self-control is needed: in our appetites (Colossians 3:5), with our tongue (James 3:5-11), in our thoughts (Proverbs 4:23), in our actions (Galatians 5:19-20), and in our emotions (Proverbs 16:5-7), when operating in the gifts of the Spirit (1 Corinthians 14:26-33.

The fruit of self-control will help us mature as we develop Christian disciplines in Bible study, prayer, fellowship, relationship, and ministering in the gifts. See 2 Timothy 2:15. It will aid us in crucifying the flesh. See Galatians 5:24-25. It will help us develop godliness. See 1 Timothy 4:7-8. Self-control helps us to persevere. See Galatians 6:9. It helps us to deal with our responses to adverse situations. See Romans 12:20-21. It helps us to remain steadfast in trials. See James 1:12. Self-control will allow us not to become castaways but to be purposeful in achieving goals in life. See 1 Corinthians 9:27. It will aid us in not being overcome by the flesh. See Mark 7:20-23. Self-control will prevent failure, as the Israelites did in the wilderness. See Exodus 20:4-6.

LIFE: Prayer: Heavenly Father, please help me exercise self-control in my life in my thoughts, words, attitude, body, motives, and actions. Grant me Your grace, strength, and mercy every time I need it. I choose to put on Jesus as my full armor and the mind of Christ as my helmet of salvation as I trust You to develop this precious fruit in my life. Amen. Read the story of Joseph in Genesis 42-45 and see his extraordinary self-control.

DEVELOPING SELF-CONTROL

"Therefore it is of faith, that it might be by grace: to the end the promise might be sure to all the seed." —Romans 4:16

TRUTH: Self-control, like all the fruit of the Spirit, can be developed only by asking for God's help and depending on His grace, love, and power to increase them in us. Our trying, goodness, or performance does not achieve it. See Romans 5:1-2; 11:6; Ephesians 1:7-9. Trusting God's grace and the Holy Spirit with our desires and habits will prevent them from enslaving us, for example, food and gluttony. By God's grace, as we spend time in the Word, prayer, and fellowship with the Holy Spirit, His power working in us will strengthen the inner man. Our spirit will be fed and developed to dominate the soul and body and lead us to self-control and victory in our Christian life.

Meditate on Scriptures in the areas where God's help is needed; faith will increase to be a doer of the Word. Pray and listen, then do as the Holy Spirit says, and your spirit-man will grow and begin to direct and dominate your soul to give you victory.

Use Scriptures to develop self-control over body and soul in our thoughts, words, appetites, motives, and actions as we walk in the Spirit of truth and not in the flesh. In the natural and in our daily lives, we must train ourselves by practicing self-discipline in some of these ways: to keep our word; complete given tasks well; clean up after ourselves; listen more and speak less; be slow to anger; avoid excuses and obey God; keep the Word of God in the forefront of our minds and use it to make consistently good choices; forgive often; walk in love; be punctual; take no offense; exercise self-control over food, selection of friends, money, reckless speech, and driving and to daily guard our minds.

LIFE: You and I are to live as God purposed, to have an abundant life. Practice saying NO! to anything that would hinder God's grace, relationship, and witness in and through you as you practice developing self-control.

BENEFITS OF SELF-CONTROL

"He that hath no rule over his own spirit is like a city that is broken down, and without walls." —Proverbs 25:28

TRUTH: The main benefit of the fruit of self-control is to be controlled by the Holy Spirit unto godliness and not the flesh unto lawlessness, *"All things are lawful unto me, but all things are not expedient: all things are lawful for me, but I will not be brought under the power of any"* (1 Corinthians 6:12). Although there is no law against some things, Paul says that he abstains from them because he does not want to be controlled by anything harmful. Self-control, therefore, protects us from being overcome. See 1 Corinthians 10:5-13. Self-control closes the door to sin and from Satan's accusations against us and gives us long life. See Psalm 91:16. It also provides a balanced and orderly lifestyle free from stress. See Psalm 9:9-11. Self-control works righteousness in our hearts to:

- Develop the fruit of the Spirit and conform us into the image of Christ (Ecclesiastes 7:8-9).
- Give us protection as we discipline our thoughts and mind to have the mind of Christ (1 Peter 5:8-9).
- Give us the credibility and integrity as Christ's ambassadors (John 13:35).
- Bring self-discipline in our daily lives both naturally and spiritually (2 Thessalonians 3:6-13).
- Help us to die to self and the old man (Romans 6:5-11).
- Create better relationships (1 Thessalonians 5:8-14; Romans 12:16-21).
- Make us more successful in finances (1 Timothy 6:17-19).
- Help us to overcome temptations (1 Corinthians 10:13).

LIFE: Prayer: Father, in the name of Jesus, I come to You for grace, and I depend on Your Holy Spirit to help me to be more self-controlled. By Your grace, deliver me from my weaknesses. Give me strength when needed and help me to practice and obey Your Word and be consistent in following Your leading to be more like Jesus, Amen. See Proverbs 16:32; Ephesians 4:20-32.

BE SPIRITUALLY MINDED

"That the righteousness of the law might be fulfilled in us, who walk not after the flesh but after the Spirit..." —Romans 8:4-6

TRUTH: The righteous requirement of Moses' Law for sin was death. See Romans 6:23. We are born in sin and shapen in iniquity and deserve death. But God! He fulfilled the requirement of death on our behalf by the death of His own Son, Jesus. Hallelujah! Sin was paid for. As such, we are indebted to Jesus and should no longer be self-directed but walk and live by the Word and the Spirit. Satan uses the flesh to fight against the Holy Spirit, seeking to captivate us to live carnally and for him. See Romans 7:22-23; 8:6-10.

LIFE: Be spiritually-minded. See Romans 8:5-6. Paul tells us to have a mindset focusing on Jesus and His Spirit within, to set our affection on things above and not on things on the earth. See Colossians 3:1-2. Having done nothing to gain our salvation, we are to recognize our helplessness and hopelessness to save ourselves or to navigate all of life's challenges successfully. See John 15:5. We worship God, but not with such earthly things as money, power, status, and pleasures. See Colossians 3:2.

Secondly, the Word is Spirit and life, so we are to fill our minds with the Word of God and live by faith. See John 6:63;1 Corinthians 2:10-12; Mark 11:22-24. We must present our bodies as a living sacrifice as we lay aside the old life and take up our new life in Christ. Read, meditate, speak, believe, and do the Word of God, both written and spoken by the Holy Spirit. See James 1:22.

Thirdly, be led by the Holy Spirit, depend on Him, and ask for His help in all things. See Romans 8:14.

Fourth, obey, our New Covenant law to love. Let everything be done with the motive of love. See 1 Corinthians 13:4-8.

Lastly, because you have submitted to God, resist the devil when he comes; worship, praise, and adore God as you enjoy His presence daily. Rest and receive the peace which only He, the Spirit, can bring. If we do these things, we will be on our way to being spiritually-minded.

WALK IN THE SPIRIT

"This I say then, Walk in the Spirit, and ye shall not fulfil the lusts of the flesh." —Galatians 5:16

TRUTH: Scripture tells us to live according to the new life of love deposited in our hearts and by the power of the Holy Spirit. By doing this, we will be kept from yielding to the sinful desires of our soul and body. Many believers have gotten this backward and try to stop sinning to be good. When we feed our spirit with the Word of God to build faith and truth, we are beginning to walk in the Spirit. The fruit of the Spirit within will arise to demonstrate Christ in our lives, and sin-producing thoughts and desires will fall away.

LIFE: Be born again by grace through faith as a new creation; acknowledge that you are forgiven of all sins, dead to sin, and alive unto God. See John 3:16; Ephesians 2:8-9; 2 Corinthians 5:17; 1 John 1:7; Romans 6:11. By faith, you are to receive your gift of righteousness, God's love for you, deep in your heart. Believe His character of greatness and goodness is always for you. See Romans 5:17. Renew your mind about all that the shed Blood of Jesus accomplished for you and acknowledge God as the source and strength of everything in your life. Live your life walking in God's grace, Word, faith, love, and authority. See Colossians 2:6; Hebrews 11:6; 1 John 4:9-15.

We are to walk in the truth of the Word of God and with the leading of the Holy Spirit and align our life accordingly. *"The words that I speak unto you, they are spirit, and they are life"* (John 6: 63). Keep your eyes on Jesus and the eternal. Trust His goodness and mercy, for your sufficiency, is from Him, not ourselves or others, as these are temporal and will fail you. See Matthew 14:22-28; 2 Corinthians 4:18. Develop the fulness of the fruit of the Spirit and be fruitful in every good work. Walk in the Spirit of truth until Jesus' second coming to take us home to be with Him, enjoying life forever. Meditate on Colossians 1:9-23.

PRAISE AS A WEAPON

"And when they began to sing and to praise, the Lord set ambushments." —2 Chronicles 20:22

TRUTH: Jehoshaphat, the king of Judah, feared the Lord and was faithful to seek Him. He was in great distress when armies of great multitudes came against him to battle. He knew he was no match for his enemy's troops, so in verse three, he set himself to seek the Lord for help. Always an excellent first response to anyone in trouble, pray and seek God. In his seeking in verses 6-14, Jehoshaphat first began to magnify God. He worshipped God and told Him:

1. He was the God of heaven and ruler over the kingdom of His enemies.
2. He was the most powerful and mighty.
3. That none can stand before Him and succeed.
4. He was their deliverer from the time of their forefather Abraham.
5. He is faithful to hear and answer them when they cry unto Him.
6. He praised Him for His promise in giving them the land.

After all of this, Jehoshaphat gives God his problem and asks Him to judge his enemies because his army is outmatched. This is a good pattern of warfare, in prayer and praise. God will build a habitation among us and defend us when we worship Him. *"Let the high praises of God be in your mouth, and a two-edged sword in their hand"* (Psalm 149:6).

LIFE: God responded, *"Be not afraid, nor be dismayed by reason of this great multitude; for the battle is not yours, but God's"* (2 Chronicles 20:15b). There are times when God requires us to be still and know that He is God. At these times, the battle is the Lord's to fight and bring deliverance by Himself. Our role is to cooperate as well as worship and praise. See Exodus 14; 2 Kings 3. At other times, God will engage us to fight as we fight the fight of faith. See 1 Samuel 30:8. Therefore, relationship and fellowship with the Lord are of utmost importance, as in any battle, we must always inquire of the Lord regarding the strategy. As we listen, hear, and obey to do as He says, we will always have the victory as we praise!

PRAISE AS A WEAPON — DAY 2

*"I will call on the Lord, who is worthy to be praised: so, shall
I be saved from mine enemies." —2 Samuel 22:4*

TRUTH: Jehoshaphat praised, magnified, worshipped, and prayed to God and asked in faith for his need to be met. God heard him and showed up big! He dispatched angelic hosts of heaven who ambushed their enemies and confused them so that they turned against each other, then fought among themselves until they were destroyed.

"I will love thee, O Lord, my strength. The Lord is my rock, and my fortress, and my deliverer: my God, my strength, in whom I will trust: my buckler, and the horn of my salvation, and my high tower. I will call upon the Lord, who is worthy to be praised: so, shall I be saved from mine enemies" (Psalm 18:1-3).

Our worship in faith strengthens God's resolve to move on our behalf to help us and deliver.

"The righteous cry, and the Lord heareth, and delivereth them out of all their troubles" (Psalm 34:17).

"Many are the afflictions of the righteous: but the Lord delivereth him out of them all" (Psalm 34:19).

"He shall call upon me, and I will answer him: I will be with him in trouble; I will deliver him, and honor him" (Psalm 91:15).

"The Lord is my strength and my shield; my heart trusted in him, and I am helped: therefore, my heart greatly rejoiceth; and my song will I praise him" (Psalm 28:7).

LIFE: We find much value in these examples of using praise as a weapon. Seek God and when He says to be still, put on your praise and let God battle for you to bring your deliverance. Praise the Lord always. *"Before they call, I will answer; while they are yet speaking I will hear"* (Isaiah 65:24).

ACCESS INTO BLESSINGS

*"I am the door: by me if any man enter in, he shall be saved,
and shall go in and out and find pasture." —John 10:9*

TRUTH: We access God, and He saves all who ask, including all whosoever's that come to Him. See John 3:16. He then blesses all with whatsoever they will ever need to prosper them as children of God. *"Blessed be the God and Father of our Lord Jesus Christ, who hath blessed us with all spiritual blessings in heavenly places in Christ"* (Ephesians 1:3).

We have an inheritance in Christ; are you accessing yours in:

- God's grace and the gift of righteousness (Ephesians 2:8-9; Romans 5:17).
- All spiritual blessings, like healing, (Ephesians 1:3; 2 Peter 2:24).
- Believing all your sins are forgiven, and you have no sin-consciousness in your life (1 John 1:7; Hebrews 10:2).
- A purged conscience (Hebrews 9:14; 10:22).
- In the loving relationship with God that you received with the gift of righteousness (Romans 5:17; 1 John 1:4-5).
- God's peace (Romans 5:1; Ephesians 2:12-22).
- His boldness increases confidence (Ephesians 3:12).
- The fruit of the Spirit (Galatians 5:22).
- The baptism of the Holy Spirit as your Helper (Acts 1:8; John 14:16-17).
- Freedom from and authority over Satan (Luke 10:19).
- Eternal life in His Son Jesus and preparing for your life in your eternal home in heaven (John 3:17; John 17:3.).

LIFE: We have an inheritance, and by grace, through faith, we have access into God's rest in Christ Jesus. Stop trying to do it on your own and learn of Him and depend on Jesus just as He depended on God His Father. See Matthew 11:29-30; John 5:30; 8:28-32; Luke 22:40-46; John 6:40; John 15.

PROVISION

"And God blessed them, and God said unto them, be fruitful, and multiply." —Genesis 1:28

TRUTH: Every believer can be an heir of this promise: *"Beloved, I wish above all things that thou mayest prosper and be in good health, even as thy soul prospereth"* (3 John 2). As we read and meditate on God's Word regarding provision and prosperity, the power of God's Word in our spirit will increase. Our spirit, dominated by God's Word, will direct our soul (mind, will, emotions) not only to think God's thoughts but also to be led by the Holy Spirit into making wise decisions to prosper in every area of our life.

God provides for His children and sets them up to prosper and multiply as we believe His Word to us. He will bless us abundantly so that we will abound in all things and always in every good work. His divine power has given us everything we need for a godly life through our knowledge of Him, who called us by His glory and goodness. Consider the ravens. They do not sow or reap; they have no storeroom or barn, yet God feeds them. How much more valuable are we than birds. We begin to prosper when we first seek the kingdom of God and His righteousness. The love of God will lead us into all the blessings and provisions we need to prosper. Do not be anxious about anything, and do not follow our chosen path, but in every situation, by prayer and petition, with thanksgiving, present our requests to God and trust Him to provide. See 2 Corinthians 9:8; 2 Peter 1:3; Luke 12:24; Matthew 6:33; Philippians 1:6, 19; 4:6-7, 19.

LIFE: Christ is your life for provision and prosperity. Will you turn wholeheartedly to Him in faith, pray, listen, and follow His Word to lead you into His best path of provision for you? *"For the Lord God is a sun and a shield: the Lord will give grace and glory: no good thing will he withhold from them that walk uprightly. O Lord of hosts, blessed is the man that trusteth in thee"* (Psalm 84:11-12).

ACCESSING HIS MIND

"But we speak the wisdom of God in a mystery, even the hidden wisdom, which God ordained before the world unto our glory." —1 Corinthians 2:7

TRUTH: 1 Corinthians 2:1-16 tells us that the mind of Christ, encompassing His truths, standards, morals, and values, is the opposite of man's (Vv. 4-6). His wisdom is revealed in mysteries to believers (Vv. 7), that all believers were given the mind of Christ in the Spirit of God that we might know supernatural things (Vv. 10-12). We are told the natural man, or the unsaved person, does not have the mind of Christ (Vv. 14). The mind of Christ gives believers supernatural discernment and wisdom in spiritual matters, which can be imparted to the natural mind through prayer.

All believers, therefore, can be led by the Holy Spirit. See Romans 8:14. We access the mind of Christ by faith, as we believe and receive His truth in the Word as we read, meditate, pray, and listen for His answer.

Praying in the Holy Ghost is the ideal way to access the mind of God and to build up and edify ourselves. See Jude 20. And as we listen and obey the Holy Spirit, God gives us the wisdom and understanding of His mind, and we grow up and mature spiritually and naturally. See 1 Corinthians 14:1-5; 2:16. We are to believe in our hearts that we have the mind of Christ and thank God for the unction of the Holy Spirit within to lead us to pray (Romans 8:26), we pray the perfect will of God with the interpretation (1 Corinthians 14:13) and be conformed to His perfect will (Romans 12:1-2) and heal the sick (James 5:15).

LIFE: The Holy Spirit will speak the hidden wisdom of God from our spirit to our minds, emotions, and will, making our soul fruitful by giving us inside information of what is in the Father's heart, to show us things to come, and to bless and prosper us. See John 14:26; 16:13; Acts 13:2; 3 John 2.

WRITE IT DOWN

*"Write the vision, and make it plain upon tables, that he
may run that readeth it."* —Habakkuk 2:2

TRUTH: The Christian journey is not a hundred-yard dash; instead, it is more like a marathon. And it is simply about taking Jesus in our hearts to love, learn of Him, depend on Him, and trust Him. In this union relationship with the Father, we have communion as He talks to us and as we listen and respond. But what do we do after we have heard a Word from God our Father?

Sometimes we just keep going as if we did not hear, or we trust what is heard to memory and soon forget. We then allow the enemy to steal the Word from our hearts with trouble, trials, strife, and busyness. He distracts and robs the Word from our hearts and hence robs us of God's wisdom, direction, and blessings. In the story of the sower and the seed, God told us how Satan would seek to rob us of the Word and or us to be mindful. See Mark 4:14-20.

God told Habakkuk to write down the vision. God intended for us to read, re-read, memorize, meditate, speak, and obey the vision He has given in His Word and by His Spirit so that we can draw our reference from His wisdom, His goals, and His process to reach victory.

The vision written down also protects us from the evil one. As when he comes to rob, kill, destroy and sidetrack us, we can look back at God's Word written down and use it as a weapon of warfare against the devil to remain steadfast because we know what our God said and that He is faithful to His Word. He will keep His promise never to leave nor forsake us, and He will help us, deliver us and cause us to win if we remain steadfast and believe what he says.

LIFE: God speaks to bring you, His life. Therefore, you are to be intentional not to forget but to hear, write it down, speak in faith, and watch as you prove His Word to you is accurate. You can trust Him to lead you to overcome and give you a new path to victory and newness in every area of your daily life.

GOD IS OUR SUPPLY

"But my God shall supply all your needs according to his riches in glory by Christ Jesus." —Philippians 4:19

TRUTH: The Bible tells us our Heavenly Father knows what we need even before asking Him. See Matthew 6:8. *"Every moving thing that liveth shall be meat for you; even as the green herb have I given you all things"* (Genesis 9:3). See Psalm 84:11. The Philippians church, despite their poverty, were givers and supporters to Paul and his efforts to spread the Gospel, and God blesses all givers. See Philippians 4:16.

Paul knew that God was the source of his supply, as seen in the Word in James 1:17. If our need is in the Word of God, then the power to supply that need is available if we believe God by putting faith in that Word. For our provision, each of us must find Scriptures on God's provision for our need, look to the Cross, stand firm and believe the thorns which pierced Jesus' head and shed His Blood in His hands broke the curse of toil and lack, to give us God's wisdom for prosperity.

God can supernaturally provide or lead you to your supply. See Genesis 3:17-19; Deuteronomy 11:14; 8:3-4; Proverbs 3:9-10; Psalm 36:8; 2 Corinthians 9:8-11; Philippians 1:19.

If your need is not explicitly mentioned in the Bible (like, for example, whom to marry), pray in the Holy Spirt, speak His Word about mates or marriage and ask for His leading. He will answer and be your supply. See Luke 11;11-13; Isaiah 34:16, 62:5 ;1 Corinthians 14:1-14; 7:2; 1 John 5:14-15; Jeremiah 1:12.

LIFE: Jesus by His Spirit is the supplier of your every need. Look to Him, ask Him, rest in faith, believe, receive, and rejoice as you can expect Him to come through for you. *"For I know that this shall turn to my salvation through prayer, and the supply of the Spirit of Jesus Christ"* (Philippians 1:19).

OUR ABBA FATHER

"For ye have not received the spirit of bondage again to fear; but ye have received the Spirit of adoption, whereby we cry, Abba, Father." —Romans 8:15

TRUTH: *Abba* is an Aramaic word for "father" used as a term of devotion and endearment. Therefore, some have placed this term in our modern-day language of calling God *Papa* or *Daddy*. *Abba* is a believer's way of expressing a close relationship with God our Father where we see Him as He sees us, as the "beloved." After we are born again, the Holy Spirit comes inside to live and bears witness to our spirit that we are the children of God who can have a close relationship with a loving Father, our Abba Father.

LIFE: He is Abba, our Beloved Father.

Although He is God, He humbled Himself and came in the flesh for your salvation. For such grace, you are to be joyful and endear Him to your heart in gratitude for His great love in making you His beloved child. He is your Beloved because He loved you first in His Son Christ Jesus, and He draws you into an intimate relationship with Himself when you believe. See 1 Corinthians 13:2-8; 1 John 4:19. Because God is your Abba Father, you can be secure in knowing He is love, and His love will never fail you.

Your God is all-knowing and full of wisdom. See Psalm 139:1-13; Proverbs 9:10. You can have assurance that your Abba always knows what is best for you. He knows what will benefit, hinder and what will harm you. Your Abba, the source of all wisdom who gave you His wisdom in His Word and by the leading of the Holy Spirit, will keep you always succeeding in life. See Psalm 119:14-16; Romans 8: 14. He even went as far as to tell you how to get His wisdom by simply asking Him. See James 1:5. And then as you draw near to experience His affection, as you listen for His answer and receive His blessings given to you by faith and wrap yourself in His love, you will always succeed so you too can say in love Abba Father!

OUR ABBA FATHER — DAY 2

*"But ye have received the Spirit of adoption, whereby
we cry, Abba, Father."* —Romans 8:15

TRUTH: God is our Abba Father because He is loving, merciful, and kind. We did not get the penalty of death we deserve for our sin; instead, we received a full pardon which completely removed our sin and forgave us. See Romans 3:10-18, 21-26; Titus 3:5-7; 1 John 1:8-9. As His disciples, our Abba Father has also given us the ability to be merciful and kind. See John 8:4-15. Our Abba Father showed compassion for us when He sent His Son Jesus for our salvation, drawing us into His loving arms. First, God saved humanity at the Cross, and by His faith, He deposited Himself within our spirit to save us and meet all our other human needs. This shows us that we, too, by the Spirit of God in us, can be compassionate as we bear with the suffering of others. See Matthew 18:23-35; Mark 1:41-42.

Who is a God like our God, Abba Father, as we endearingly worship Him. Our Abba Father is the only One who is absolutely good, the One who is always giving and will never extinguish Himself. The Lord is good to all. *"How God anointed Jesus of Nazareth with the Holy Ghost and with power: who went about doing good and healing all that were oppressed of the devil; for God was with him"* (Acts 10:38). God's Spirit living in us makes us righteous, able to be good, do good, and do what is right in God's sight. God's holiness in us will cause us to experience freedom from Satan and from sin. See 2 Corinthians 3:17; 5:21.

LIFE: Our Abba is gracious. He gives us good even when we do not deserve it. He gave us the gift of His Son with forgiveness of sins, His righteousness, eternal life, and relationship as with a friend, whereby we can cry Abba Father, our personal Father and love. See Ephesians 1:7; 2:7-9; Galatians 4:4-7; 1 John 5:13. Love Him and worship Him as your ABBA!

GOD HEARS

"The righteous cry and the Lord heareth, and delivereth out of all their troubles." —Psalm 34:17

TRUTH: Troubles abound and seem to surround us, some of which are of our own making. Others have wronged us, and we sometimes lash out at them or accuse them until we get into worry, strife, and fear. But God wants us to remember we are children of God, new creation beings made wise, accepted, holy, and free. See 1 Corinthians 1:30. We are righteous and restored in a right love relationship with a God who sees and responds to our faith when we cry out for the needs in our lives. We are to always maintain our relationship and communication in prayer because He is a God of love who hears.

When we call on the Father, we must listen to hear and never behave as if God is deaf. *"And this is the confidence that we have in him, that, if we ask anything according to his will, he heareth us: And if we know that he hear us, whatsoever we ask, we know that we have the petitions that we desired of him"* (1 John 5:14-15). Have faith that God not only hears but responds. If our answer seems late, we are to trust His knowledge and love about our situation that His best for us is in the waiting. Will you trust your Father God's heart and wait patiently for your supply?

"But my God shall supply all your need according to his riches in glory by Christ Jesus" (Philippians 4:19).

LIFE: Christ will always respond to your every call, every time. Do not give in to the enemy's pressures to get it now! Don't give in to fear. In the tough times, you are to remain in faith, prayer, and thanksgiving, which will bring peace to your heart and strength from the rock of your salvation. He is your provider who will get your supply to you. Your Lord will answer and deliver, for as Christ of your life, He hears.

OCTOBER 7

SAFE AND SECURE

"He that dwelleth in the secret place of the Most High shall abide under the shadow of the Almighty." —Psalm 91 :1

TRUTH AND LIFE: As believers, John 17:21-23 is our secret place. When we sit enthroned in the oneness of El Shaddai, we are hidden in the strength of our God, the Most High, our secret place.

1. He is the hope that holds us in His stronghold. He is our great confidence. See Psalm 42:11; 1 John 5:14. He rescues us from every hidden trap and protects us from any deadly curse. See Galatians 3:13.
2. His massive arms are wrapped around us, protecting us. We can run under His majestic covering of love and hide. His arms of faithfulness are a shield, keeping us from harm. See Colossians 3:3-4.
3. His love enfolds us. We are not afraid of any attack of demonic forces at night nor fear the spirits of darkness coming against us. Psalm 112:7.
4. We are never to be afraid! Whether by night or by day. No demonic danger will harm us, nor will the powers of evil launched against us prosper, as the Blood of Jesus covers us. See Isaiah 54:17.
5. Even in a time of disaster, when thousands are being attacked, we will trust in Him, for God is our fortress. See Psalm 18:2.
6. We will be a spectator as the wicked perish in judgment, for they will be paid back for all the evil they have done! Psalm 7:9.
7. When we live our lives within the shadow of God Most High, our secret hiding place, we will always be shielded from harm. How could evil prevail against us or disease infect us unto death, when we have eternal life? John 17:3.
8. God sends angels with special orders to protect and guide us wherever we go, defending us from all harm. Acts 12: 7-9.
9. If we walk into a trap, the angels will keep us from falling into it.
10. We will even walk unharmed among the fiercest powers of darkness, trampling every one of them beneath our feet! We are safe! Daniel 6:16-17.
11. No unlucky number 13 here for us! With long life will He satisfy us.

SAFE AND SECURE — DAY 2

"He that dwelleth in the secret place of the Most High..." —Psalm 91

TRUTH: Psalm 91 is God's Word of divine protection to us all. Considering the recent COVID 19 pandemic where many died, and many hearts became afraid, God gave us His Word to strengthen our hearts.

Here is what the Lord has spoken to us in Psalm 91:14-16 (TPT):

"Because you have delighted in me as my lover, I will greatly protect you. I will set you in a high place, safe and secure before my face. I will answer your cry for help every time you pray, and you will find and feel my presence even in your time of pressure and trouble. I will be your glorious hero and give you a feast. You will be satisfied with a full life and with all that I do for you. For you will enjoy the fullness of my salvation!"

Did you really hear your Father's heart!

Read Psalm 91 repeatedly from the King James Version of the Bible and meditate on Scriptures on protection until faith for divine protection comes into your heart. Become assured that your Father's love will protect you like a hen covers her chicks, and you feel safe and secure. Resist every fear, for Christ Jesus, is our life. See Matthew 23:37. Remember, He who dwells in the secret place of the Most High shall abide under the shadow of the Almighty. God is our protector, our refuge, our fortress. We will not be afraid of evil.

LIFE: Read and speak protection Scriptures over yourself and your family daily and be not afraid: Psalms 20; 31; and 107; Psalms 5:12; 17:4; 32:7; 18:1-2; 34:7; 97:10; 119:116-117; 121:8; 46:1, 10, 11; Zechariah 2:5; Proverbs 1:33; 3:25-26; Isaiah 32:1; 41:10; Mark 16:18; Romans 8:2, 37; 2 Thessalonians 3:3; Revelation 12:11.

ANGELS

"Bless the Lord, ye his angels, that excel in strength, that do his commandments, hearkening unto the voice of his word." —Psalm 103:20

TRUTH: Angels are the hosts of heaven. They are God's powerful beings, greater in might and power, stronger than us humans because they are the ones who encamp round about us to protect us. See Matthew 28:2; Psalm 37:4.

God has assigned an angel to every child. See Matthew 18:10. They are also God's ministering spirits sent to do His bidding to bring messages to His people. God also uses angels as a mighty army to battle on our behalf against Satan and his evil forces. See Daniel 10:13.

Angels are not to be worshipped. See Colossians 2:18. Neither are people to pray to them. See 1 Timothy 2:5. We are to talk to Father God in the name of Jesus Christ, His Son in prayer, asking Him to fulfill His promises of angelic help.

Angels are the ones carrying out God's will in heaven, and they are present here as we pray to carry out God's will for the gospel and our lives here on earth. They minister for our protection, provision, instruction, and deliverance. See Hebrews 1:14.

To bring us messages from heaven: *"There stood an angel of God...saying, fear not Paul: thou must be brought before Caesar."* See Acts 27:23-24.

LIFE: For protection: *"For He shall give his angels charge over thee, to keep thee in all thy ways. They shall bear thee up in all their hands, lest thou dash thy foot against a stone"* (Psalm 91:11-12).

"The Angel of the Lord encamped round about them that fear him, and delivereth them" (Psalm 34:7).

Ask for and expect angelic help from heaven in your time of need.

ANGELS — DAY 2

"...Angels, that excel in strength, that do his commands." —Psalm 103:20

TRUTH: Angels hearken unto God to fight for us, to secure our release, as was the case with Daniel when they shut the lions' mouths. See Daniel 6:22. An angel brought the world's most powerful message from heaven to Mary, the mother of Jesus, announcing the birth of our Savior. See Luke 1:28.

Angels carry out God's judgments against our enemies and those who dishonor Him. See 2 Chronicles 32:21; Acts 12:23.

Angels are ministering spirits on our behalf. *"Are they not all ministering spirits, sent forth to minister for them who shall be heirs of salvation?"* (Hebrews 1:14). When needed, when we speak God's Word in authority and faith, God can and will release angels to minister on our behalf. In our prayers, we ask God to dispatch angels to do our bidding for protection, for finances, to battle against our natural or spiritual enemies. Psalm 103:20 says angels hearken to our voice when we speak God's Word.

Angels will be with Jesus when He returns to earth. See 2 Thessalonians 1:7; Revelations 18:1-2, 21.

Angels worship God in the beauty of His holiness. The Lord's prayer says, *"Thy will be done, as in heaven, so in earth"* (Luke 11:2).

Angels worship God in heaven, and we too must begin to worship God and start practicing by doing what the angels do—worshipping and praising God. We are embracing His presence now as we prepare for our future time and destiny of worshipping in heaven.

LIFE: Let us not ignore the presence of God's angelic hosts. We live in tumultuous times, so ask for angelic help any time you are in need; believe and expect God to move as He desires to help on your behalf, even with His angels.

HEALING BY FAITH

"And great multitudes followed him, and he healed them all." —Matthew 12:15

TRUTH: Sickness and disease are part of the curse of the Law from which Christ has redeemed us. See Galatians 3:13-14.

If we believe in God for healing or are standing in faith for someone else's healing, God is able. He is willing to heal, and, as Christ the Healer, He is *"Jesus Christ the same yesterday, today, and foreve*r" (Hebrews 13:8).

There are many stories in the Bible of Jesus healing people: He healed all those who came to Him, some in faith and even others who were not fully sure. The woman with the issue of blood and the man who was let down through the roof by his friends came in faith. Those who knew they wanted to be healed but were not fully in faith still came and were also healed. See Mark 1:40-41; 2:1-13. Many near and far were healed; Simon Peter's mother-in-law was healed. See Mark 1:29-31. And the centurion's servant was healed. See Luke 7.

Faith to be healed is the same faith and belief we used to receive salvation or be saved. Believe in God's Word of grace and receive. See John 3:16; Romans 10:9-10; 1 Peter 2:24. By simple faith, hear the Word that God heals and believe Jesus accomplished your healing on the Cross. Use your imagination, your eyes of faith, and see that Jesus on the Cross bled and took that sickness from you. Believe that He carried it away and, in exchange, gave you healing. Receive, in faith, and rejoice in advance that you got your blessing, and you are healed.

LIFE. All of salvation's blessings, including healing, are to be received by grace through faith. In relationship, believe all Jesus did on the Cross for you, speak His Word on healing, then rejoice, receive and again rejoice. See Ephesians 2:8-9; Colossians 2:6; Isaiah 53:4-5.

HEALING BY FAITH — DAY 2

"...And he healed them all." —Matthew 12:15

TRUTH: Healing is God's grace to make us well and prosperous.

1. Hear the Word concerning healing. See 1 Peter 2:24; Isaiah 53:4-5.
2. Read and meditate on what God's grace did through Jesus on the Cross and build our faith. See Romans 10:17; Psalms 103:1-4; 107:19-20.
3. Believe all that Jesus did to grant us healing. This anchors our faith in God's grace to build more faith trusting His relationship. See Matthew 8:17; Galatians 3:13.
4. Meditate on Healing scriptures until faith arises in your heart to believe.
5. After we believe, pray, and ask God for our healing. See Mark 11:22-24.
6. Just as we are done praying, receive healing as if it is already given. If someone asks how you are, there is no need to deny your condition. You can state your diagnosis but always end with your faith in God. Tell them what the doctor said and end with, "But I believe God that by His stripes I am healed. He has delivered me. I am healed."
7. Listen for any instructions from the Holy Spirit and obey. See Luke 1:35.
8. We are to stand firm in our belief that we are healed. Let the Word of God be the final authority, not our feelings, not the symptoms, not the doctor's report, and not Satan's lies. Speak life. See Proverbs 18:21.
9. In response to your conviction, do something you couldn't or found difficult to do. It may be to get up out of bed or to dance, rejoicing that you are healed.
10. Continue to praise, worship, thank, and rejoice in God through Jesus Christ His Son until your healing manifests.
11. Give your testimony; tell others to help build their faith to receive.

LIFE: Healing Scriptures for meditation: Exodus 20:12; 23:25; Deuteronomy 7:15; Psalms 30:2; 91:16; 103:1-3; 107:2, 19-20; Psalm 118:17; Proverbs 3:26; 4:20-23; 9:11; Isaiah 53:4-5; 58:8; Ezekiel 16:6; Jeremiah 17:14; 30:17; 32:27; Nahum 1:9; Matthew 8:17; 15:13; Mark 10:27; Romans 8:23; Galatians 3:13; James 1:12; 1 Peter 2:24; Revelation 12:11.

HEALING CONFESSIONS

*"Heal me, O Lord, and I shall be healed: save me, and I shall
be saved: for thou art my praise."* —Jeremiah 17:14

TRUTH AND LIFE: Father, I believe Jesus' Blood was shed on the Cross for my healing, and His grace is sufficient for my recovery.

1. I approach Your throne of grace with confidence in Your faithfulness to receive mercy in Your healing power to deliver me from (name the situation). See Jeremiah 17:14.

2. Thank You that Your face is ever turned to give me healing and peace. I believe You are the God of all grace, who called me to Your eternal glory in Christ. Restore me, and as I meditate on Your Word, increase my faith to make me strong, firm, steadfast, and healed. See 2 Corinthians 12:9; Hebrews 4:16; Numbers 6:26; 1 Peter 5:10.

3. Father, Your Word said, *"I call heaven and earth to record this day, ... I have set before you life and death, blessing and cursing: therefore, choose life...."* Father, I trust Your grace and choose life and blessing, that I may love the Lord my God and obey His voice and cling to Him, for He is my life and the length of my days. See Deuteronomy 30:19-20.

4. *"Who his own self bare our sins...that we, being dead to sins, should live unto righteousness: by whose stripes ye were healed"* (1 Peter 2:24).

5. Father, I believe every Word Jesus spoke concerning healing is true, and I accept it as truth. Jesus took my griefs/sicknesses and carried my sorrows/diseases away from me to be healed. He was wounded for my transgressions and bruised for my iniquities, the chastisement of my peace was upon Him, and by His stripes, I am healed, and I rejoice. See Isaiah 53:4-5.

6. Thank you, Father. You are God of all flesh, and there is nothing too hard for You? I call myself healed in Jesus' name. See Jeremiah 32: 27

7. You Lord will make an utter end to this affliction, and it shall not rise a second time. See Nahum 1: 9. Amen.

HEALING CONFESSIONS — DAY 2

*"Healing every sickness and every sickness and
every disease among the people."* —Matthew 9:35

TRUTH AND LIFE:

1. I bless the Lord; I bless His Holy name. I will not forget Your benefits in forgiving all my sins and healing all my diseases, redeeming my life from destruction, and crowning me with your lovingkindness and tender mercies. Psalm 103:1-5.
2. No harm comes near me, and no plague comes nigh my dwelling, for You, Lord, shall give Your angels charge over me to keep me in all my ways. See Psalm 91.
3. I shall not die but live and declare the Lord's works. See Psalm 118:17.
4. No weapon of death, sickness, disease, or pain formed against me shall prosper because You, Lord, have sent Your Word, healed me, and delivered me from all destructions. See Psalm 107:20.
5. Any bleeding in or from my body, I command you to cease now! By the stripes of Jesus, I am healed. See Ezekiel 16:6.
6. I apply the Blood of Jesus upon every area of my body, and I command every spirit of infirmity to leave me now in Jesus' name. I speak to every cell, every muscle, and every organ to come in alignment with the Word of God and function normally and accurately and be healed in Jesus' name.
7. The Word tells me God only gives good and perfect gifts. I speak to any abnormalities in my body to go now and command you to become normal in Jesus' name. Romans 4:17.
8. I am the redeemed of the Lord, and the Blood of Jesus has redeemed me from the hand of the enemy. I accept only healing and wholeness in my body in the name of Jesus, amen. See Galatians 3:13.
9. REJOICE! This is the day the Lord has made. I choose to rejoice in my healing and be glad in it. I rejoice, and again I say that I rejoice that I am healed. I will always bless the Lord and praise Him continually. I am healed.

PRAISE

"Whoso offereth praise glorifieth me: and to him that ordereth his conversation (lifestyle) aright will I shew the salvation of God." —Psalm 50:23

TRUTH: Everyone likes to be praised, especially after doing what we think to be a good job. We also want to give praise to encourage and motivate others. We are inherently born to praise and to receive praise always with the intent to give God the glory. We tend to praise what we love and value highly, and we often find it easier to praise our loved ones, family members, or even our favorite sports figure. But praise is an outflow of the love deposited in our spirit man, firstly for us to acknowledge God the One most worthy to be praised.

It was God who made us, not just to exist on our own, but to be in a love relationship with Him. He wants to be seen for who He really is. He is our good Father, our good Shepherd and King, the Supplier of our needs, our Way Maker, our ever-present Helper in times of trouble, our Rock, our Refuge, our Strong Tower, the Faithful One, our Sufficiency, our Deliverer, our Healer, our Baptizer, our Wisdom, and our Victory. He is our all in all, and He desires our praise.

Once we are born again, we can joy in all God has done for us in Jesus and praise Him. We have a lot to rejoice and praise God about. A heart in union relationship with our Heavenly Father, seated in the heavenlies, one Spirit victorious over Satan under our feet will overflow in praise for His love in His grace, provision, goodness, and mercy. When we believe God's grace, we are saved. See Ephesians 2:8. For His salvation, God desires us to praise Him, not for His benefit but ours. We are also to continually praise God for His love and care in our daily lives. Praise opens our hearts to hear God and to respond to Him. Praise gives us an entrance into our Father's presence to receive His blessings. See Psalm 100:4.

LIFE: Praise honors God and softens our hearts to relate to God our Father and each other in His kingdom and to give and receive love. Meditate on 1 Chronicles 29:10-13 and praise the Lord!

PRAISE — DAY 2

"Whoso offereth praise glorifieth me..." —Psalm 50:23a

TRUTH: If we are unforgiving, angry, resentful prideful, and judgmental, praise will lead us to Jesus, who will nudge us to receive the Spirit's help into repentance and transformation. Praise is our language of gratitude in response to God's love. When we praise Him, we are yoking ourselves in a relationship with God the Father through Jesus His Son.

God desires our fellowship and praise as we honor and draws near Him. In response, He will draw near to us. Let our praises come from our hearts as led by the Holy Spirit because God inhabits the praises of His people. As we praise, God abides with us and delivers us in our relationship with Him.

Praise will dethrone Satan. "Your adversary the devil, *as a roaring lion, walketh about, seeking whom he may devour*" (1 Peter 5:8). If we know who we are in Christ Jesus, that roaring lion cannot defeat us. A joyful heart raised in praise to God builds faith and trust, which closes the door to the enemy.

"Praise ye the Lord. Praise God in his sanctuary: praise him in the firmament of his power" (Psalm 150: 1).

"By him therefore let us offer the sacrifice of praise to God continually, that is, the fruit of our lips giving thanks to his name" (Hebrews 13:15).

"But ye are a chosen generation, a royal priesthood, an holy nation, a peculiar people; that ye should shew forth the praises of him who hath called you out of darkness into his marvelous light" (1 Peter 2:9).

LIFE: I love You, Lord my God, and I will praise You with all my heart and all my strength, for You are my King. You are worthy of my praise because You are exalted above all to keep me by Your love, grace, and power.

"Worthy is the Lamb that was slain to receive power, and riches, and wisdom, and strength, and honour, and glory, and blessing" (Revelation 5:12).

GOD IS FAITHFUL

"Faithful is he that calleth you, who also will do it." —1 Thessalonians 5:24

TRUTH: To be faithful is to be loyal, conscientious, consistent, and genuine. God is truth and, if He says something or gives a promise, you can take it to the bank and cash it because, by Him, all things consist. See Colossians 1:17. His only request of us is to live by faith and patience, believing that His promises to us will save and bless us. *"God is faithful, by whom ye are called unto the fellowship of his Son Jesus Christ our Lord"* (1 Corinthians 1:9). We must be assured that God is faithful; otherwise, we will waver in tests or trials.

It is God who made creation, and everything functions perfectly and consistently. The sun shines by day, rises in the east, and sets in the west. The moon shines by night, and each season flows uninterrupted and without fail, winter, spring, summer, and fall. If we can depend on God's faithfulness in creation, we can daily rely on Him by His Word. When temptations come our way to derail us, we can trust God. See 1 Corinthians 10:13.

"But the Lord is faithful, who shall establish you, and keep you from evil" (2 Thessalonians 3:3).

LIFE: Where a believer has failure or unanswered prayers, ask the Father for His wisdom. With the delay, He could be keeping you from danger or building faith and patience, or it could be a weakness needing time to be corrected, or God could be waiting on another person to obey for Him to fulfill His promise to you. See Hebrews 6:12; 2 Corinthians 4:13. Pray about everything and trust God to deliver. Sarah judged God faithful who had promised. See Hebrews 11:11. Like Job, we can trust God to keep and restore everything the devil has stolen. See Job 42. See these Scriptures on God's faithfulness for meditation: Deuteronomy 7:9; Numbers 23:19; Lamentations 3:22-26; 2 Peter 3:9; Joel 2:25-26. God's faithfulness is seen by us because of Jesus Christ our life. He is faithful believe Him in His Word to you.

OUR FAITHFULNESS

"Moreover, it is required in stewards, that a man
be found faithful." —1 Corinthians 4:2

TRUTH: Christianity is a joyful relationship of believers reconciled to their Father God because of Jesus. As His children, God commands that the just shall live by faith. We are to live by faith and be faithful. *If therefore ye have not been faithful in the unrighteous mammon, who will commit to your trust the true riches?"* (Luke 16: 11).

"His Lord said unto him, Well done, thou good and faithful servant: thou hast been faithful over a few things, I will make thee ruler over many things enter thou into the joy of the Lord" (Matthew 25:21).

One part of our faithfulness before God is to abide in Him. See John 15:7. Another which makes us good witnesses of His faithfulness is for us to love. See 1 John 4: 8,11. We are to keep our word to others, even to our own hurt. See Deuteronomy 23:21-23; Numbers 30:2-4; Ecclesiastes 5:4, 33-36; Mark 6:23; James 5:12; 1 John 2:5-6. God is true to His Word and, as He trains us unto Christlikeness by His faith and His power, we are to be the same as He is. See 1 John 4:17. If we do not keep faith with someone by failing to keep our word, it is a sin. See Numbers 32:20-23; Romans 14:23.

LIFE: Just as we are to be faithful in aligning our thoughts, words, and actions to God's Word, so must we ask Him to help us by His grace to be the same in faith, to be faithful before man here on earth.

Prayer: Heavenly Father, please help me walk faithfully before You and before man. Let Your grace in Your goodness and mercy keeps following me and cause me to walk in faithfulness and Your love. Give me Your wisdom and strength to stand as You live in and through me in the small and big things. Let Your faithfulness in me cause me to abide in You that my joy may be full.

HONESTY

"But have renounced the hidden things of dishonesty, not walking in craftiness." —2 Corinthians 4:2

TRUTH: Honesty is a facet of moral character showing positive virtues such as integrity, truthfulness, straightforwardness, transparency, trustworthiness, fairness, loyalty, and sincerity, along with the absence of lying, cheating, and stealing, among others. Honesty is highly valued in every area of life—on the job, in marriage, and any relationship. We are made in the image of God, who is truth, and as a believer, He has stamped His character onto our hearts. God is truthful, and He desires truth from us, His children. See Psalm 51:6. The commands which God gives are not to restrict or to confine us because He is High and Mighty; but they are for our highest good, to maintain in clear conscience, and for our protection, *"For we trust we have a good conscience, in all things willing to live honestly"* (Hebrews 13:18). Failure to live truthfully relegates us to living dishonestly with lying, deception, shame, and guilt, which harms us and our relationships.

"Lying lips are abomination to the Lord: but they that deal truly are His delight" (Proverbs 12:22).

God has given us a new commandment to love, and therefore any form of dishonesty, shadiness, manipulation, or craftiness that we tolerate is unacceptable to Him. It is intolerable because it is the opposite of His character and Commands to love. We can understand why God dealt severely in His punishment for dishonesty in Joshua 7 and Acts 5. In addition to these two chapters, meditate on these Scriptures and let them build faith to desire the image of God growing on the inside with honesty.

LIFE: *"Who shall ascend into the hill of the Lord? He that hath clean hands, and a pure heart; who hath not lifted up his soul unto vanity, nor sworn deceitfully"* (Psalm 24; 3-4). Meditate on Romans 13:8-10; Proverbs 6:16-19; 19:1; Isaiah 33:15; Luke 3:12-14; Ephesians 4:25.

PROSPERITY

"Let them shout for joy, and be glad, that favor my righteous cause...Let the Lord be magnified, which hath pleasure in the prosperity of his servant." —Psalm 35:27

TRUTH: Delight in the Law of the Lord... *"But his delight is in the law of the Lord... and he shall be like a tree planted by the rivers of water, that bringeth forth his fruit in his season; his leaf also shall not wither; and whatsoever he doeth shall prosper"* (Psalm 1: 2-3). We are to declare God's love and care over ourselves and our families; say: "I am blessed in the city, I am blessed in the field, I am blessed in my career or job, I am blessed with innovative and Godly ideas to increase my income. I am blessed coming in, and I am blessed going out. I am blessed and protected against the enemy's attacks because they shall flee from me seven ways. My savings and potential savings are blessed, and everything I set my hand to is blessed. I am established in God's righteousness, and I will not fear because He will help me walk in His ways and protect my every step."

God will not cover His blessings under a bushel but will cause the people around to see His blessings on our lives because we are His children. He shall bless us with plenteous blessings in every area of life—our children, work, finances, and friends. We will be the head and not the tail, above and not beneath, because we will joy in the God of our salvation. We will rejoice in our bountiful God. We will trust His Holy Spirit to lead us and help us obey the Father as our priority and serve Him in all the ways and for all the days of our lives.

LIFE: I meditate, speak, and do God's Word concerning my prosperity. I believe and receive God's promise that He shall make my way prosperous and give me success. I abide in Christ, fellowship with Him, I rest in, trust and obey Him. As I act on the ideas presented me in His promises, I will always prosper by the Holy Spirit's power, wisdom, and direction. See Joshua 1:8; Philippians 4:19; 3 John 2; Psalm 84:11.

CONFESSIONS ON PROSPERITY

"...Which hath pleasure in the prosperity of his servant." —Psalm 35:27

TRUTH: Abide, rest in, trust in Christ, and confess His Word: My God shall supply all my needs according to His riches in glory by Christ Jesus. See Philippians 4:19; Psalm 1; Deuteronomy 28:1-14.

- Jesus came to bless me and offer me abundant life; by faith, I receive it as I prosper in my soul. See John 10:10; 3 John 2.
- Because I put the Lord before me and seek Him, I shall not want any good thing. See Psalm 34:10.
- Wealth and riches shall be in my house, and His righteousness endureth for ever. I prosper in all things in His love. See Psalm 112:3.
- Because I know the Lord loves me, and I love Him in return, I will inherit His substance; and be filled with His treasures. See Proverbs 8:21.
- I do not cover sin. I repent, and God's continued mercy causes me to prosper. See Proverbs 28:13.
- The Lord leads me, teaches me to profit, and gives me ideas to prosper. See Isaiah 48:17.
- God's Word in my mouth shall go forth like a sword, and it shall not return void, but shall prosper in the area that I am praying. See Isaiah 55:11.
- Items lost or stolen from me shall be recovered in full. See 1 Samuel 30:19.
- I am righteous, a good man/woman, and my prayer availeth much. I am blessed abundantly to leave an inheritance to my children and grandchildren. See James 5:16; Proverbs 13:22.

LIFE: I am blessed above and beyond in every area of my life. It may not yet manifest, but I believe the thorns that broke Jesus' head and the nails that pierced His hands broke the curse of poverty from my life. As I pray in the Spirit, God will give me direction on my path to prosperity, and as I stand in faith and speak His Words of provision over my life and act in faith on His Words to me, things will change, and my blessings will abundantly manifest.

OBEDIENCE AND LEADING

"But if ye be led of the Spirit, ye are not under the law. Now the works of the flesh are manifest... adultery, uncleanness, ...variance emulations, wrath, strife, seditions, heresies." —Galatians 5:18-20

TRUTH: As believers, God loves us and has given us commands to keep, not as the 'thou shalt nots' of the Old Testament as rigid rules demanding obedience or punishment, but a command of giving love to Him with sincerity through a willing and glad heart led by the Holy Spirit. God has called us to surrender to Him because of His great love and to follow His Holy Spirit into obedience because He is entirely for our good. Some Christians are afraid to think about obedience as they know it seems almost impossible to get everything right in their hearts. This view comes from looking at obedience from an Old Testament viewpoint of the Law as something to obey and be blessed or to disobey and suffer the consequences of God's wrath in punishment. See Deuteronomy 28.

This Law mentality approach to obedience opens the door to Satan to cause feelings of a lack of assurance and acceptance with God and for Satan to accuse us of disobedience and deserving of punishment. This is a lie from the evil one, as what he's really saying is that you are not justified, not made innocent by the Blood of Jesus, but by your perfect behavior, obedience or actions. Reject Satan and his lies and his accusation of disobedience that brings false guilt and condemnation. Do not let him tell you that you deserve to suffer. He will be seeking to push you into some action to be obedient, which cannot make you free. Only obedience to the truth that you are justified by the Blood of Jesus alone can make you free.

LIFE: A believer is led into obedience by the Holy Spirit and the Word as we abide in Jesus, never by being pushed or coerced into obedience by doing some action to end Satan's torment and condemnation. Yield to God and be led into repentance by the Word and the Holy Spirit only! Declare you are justified by the Blood of Jesus alone. Read, meditate on Philippians 2:13 and follow the leading of the Holy Spirit into obeying God.

OBEDIENCE, OUR FOUNDATION

"If ye love me, keep my commandments. If a man love me, he will keep my words: and my father will love him, and will come unto him, and make our abode with him." —John 14:15, 23

TRUTH: Just as the Old Testament saints had to obey God, we as church saints who now live under the New Covenant of grace are also required to obey God to prosper. The Law of the New Covenant of grace is love. See John 13:34; Romans 13:8-10. We do not have to be afraid that the weaknesses and faults we see in ourselves will prevent us from obeying God or disqualify us from our Father's presence. On the contrary, God's covenant of love in Jesus is so much better as even with sin; we can still run to our Father and ask for His help, mercy in forgiveness for cleansing, and freedom. See Hebrews 4:16; 13:21.

Just as God's love made sin and punishment for sin a non-issue unto condemnation, likewise, love makes disobedience with immediate sentence a non-issue as our dependence on God by faith in Jesus will cause His Spirit to speak and guide us into truth, repentance, and obedience. See John 15:26; Romans 2:4; Philippians 2:13. Instead of getting stuck worrying about whether we're disobedient, we are to spend the time drawing closer to our Father in a relationship, abiding in His Word, praying, worshipping, and praising God for His love, wisdom, guidance, and the leading of His Spirit in our lives. With our faith turned to Jesus, He will help us obey Him. Our faith in love relationship and meditating on His Words will give wisdom, guidance, assurance, and peace in our hearts. God did it for Peter after he denied Jesus. He'll do it for us. Our dependence on Jesus' love will flow forth with joy and the willingness to bring guidance and rest to our souls. See Hebrews 4:2-3; John 16:13.

LIFE: God will teach and work obedience in your heart by the Holy Spirit, who is our Helper. See John 14:26; 16:13; Philippians 2:13; Hebrews 8:10-11; 13:20-21. Rest and let Him help you to love Him sincerely with obedience.

OBEDIENCE TO GOD'S WORD

*"And Mary said, Behold the handmaid of the Lord; be it
unto me according to thy word."* —Luke 1:38

TRUTH: Our obedience is essential because, as believers, our salvation grace through faith, and our obedience are to be from a joyful heart of gratitude and thanksgiving for God's love and grace. However, we are not justified or made right with God by our strict obedience. Believers are by faith to keep an open and a free heart towards the Father to be convicted and led by the Holy Spirit into obedience. We should not hold on to sin while waiting until the enemy brings agitation and torment before we realize we need to repent. Obey the Word. Our obedience to God's grace and yielding to the conviction of the Holy Spirit will keep us from torment, sin-consciousness, guilt, accusation, and condemnation.

Mary was rewarded for her obedience, blessed, and revered to be the mother of our Savior. She also received God's protection, peace, comfort, salvation, and baptism of the Holy Spirit. Our abiding and yielding to God unto obedience proves our union relationship and love for the Father, enough to desire to be a part of His end-time harvest of souls. We obey God as we love Him and allow His love and power of the Holy Spirit in us to love others. He that loveth not knoweth not God; for God is love. For this is the love of God, that we keep His commandments: and His commandment to love is not grievous. See 1 John 4:8, 11; 5:3. We should love others enough to be concerned about their souls. See Mark 16:15-18. Before obeying, Mary was not in unbelief with her question but showed her love, faith, and trust in God, by asking for clarification. It pleases God when we walk in faith, not according to our own way. See Luke 1:34; 1 John 2:3-8; 2 Corinthians 5:7.

LIFE: Our obedience living by faith leads to Christlikeness and the presence and power of the Holy Spirit in us. Just as He moved upon Elizabeth to prophesy and Mary in worship, God will lead me to obey Him, of which I am thankful. See Luke 1:41-56; Psalm 119:1-10; Hebrews 13:21.

HOLY SPIRIT LED

"But if ye be led of the Spirit, ye are not under the law." —Galatians 5:18

TRUTH: Why do we fear in the first place? The Scripture says perfect love casts out fear. See 1 John 4:18. Therefore, if we fear, we are not fully established in how much God loves us and all He has offered to help us, by his character, in His Word, His Holy Spirit, and by His angels. We will not fear when we believe the Greater One on the inside is greater than Satan's effort on the outside to condemn or harm. We obey because of God's great love to us, and we respond in obedience to His everlasting love, which never fails. We are living under the New Covenant of God's grace. This means we are not on our own to stress about obeying God. Isaiah 53:5 says, *"the chastisement* (correction) *of my peace* (well-being of a sound mind) *was upon Him; and with His stripes I am healed."* We are led into obedience by the Holy Spirit if we'll allow Him. See Romans 8:14; Philippians 2:13.

Our correction in walking this Christian path, or our obedience and the peace that comes from it, was upon Jesus. We are His, and our sound mind comes from His love and the power of the Holy Spirit in us, helping us to obey and be at peace. See 2 Timothy 1:7. We have no business trying to obey God by engaging in legalistic self-efforts or putting out a fleece, See Judges 6:36-40, or listening to or allowing Satan to drive us, by our fear of disobedience, into guilt and condemnation. Reject any leading from Satan, period. Tell the devil, "No! I will not be led by fear through your accusation of disobedience and condemnation. My leading and correction come only from Jesus by His Spirit of peace. The Holy Spirit will teach me and lead me into all truth by His peace." See Romans 5:1; Hebrews 13:21; 1 John 2:20.

LIFE: *"And let the peace of God rule in your hearts, to the which also ye are called into one body; and be ye thankful"* (Colossians 3:15).

BLESSINGS AND OBEDIENCE

"And Mary said, Behold the handmaid of the Lord; be it unto me according to thy word." —Luke 1:38

TRUTH: God accomplishes His will on the earth through His children obeying Him. God wanted to bring revival to earth by sending His Son Jesus to preach the gospel. He had to find a virgin to bear the Godchild. God sent an angel to Mary, who told her she had found favor with the Lord and would conceive a Son in her womb, to be named Jesus.

Mary did not hesitate to believe but was perplexed how could it be, since she was a virgin. She possibly was not acquainted with the Holy Ghost, so the angel explained. She never wavered with unbelief but agreed to do as God had asked through the angel.

It is never wrong to ask the Lord questions for clarification or understanding. See Luke 1:34. But it is wrong to ask in unbelief or make statements of unbelief. See Luke 1:11-20.

As a child of God, Mary had her heart turned to her Father; she heard Him, abided in, and yielded to Him. The Holy Ghost confirmed the Word of God given to Mary through Elizabeth. See Luke 1:43-45. Mary then rejoiced in the Lord and said, *"My soul doth magnify the Lord."*

LIFE: God desires to bring another revival to earth before Jesus' second coming, and He is preparing hearts to be obedient, as Mary was to Him. As believers, we are called to a life of obedience to fulfill His plans and purposes in these last days. Therefore, we must trust, yield and obey. We are never to be fearful about our obedience, just yield and He will lead you into all truth.

"What doth the Lord thy God require of thee, but to fear the Lord thy God, to walk in all his ways, and to love him, and to serve the Lord thy God with all thy heart and with all thy soul. To keep the commandments of the Lord, and his statutes, which I command thee this day for thy good" (Deuteronomy 10:12-13).

TEACH OUR CHILDREN

"Train up a child in the way he should go: and when he is old, he will not depart from it." —Proverbs 22:6

TRUTH: *"Though he were a Son, yet learned he obedience by the things which he suffered"* (Hebrews 5:8). If Jesus was perfectly obedient to the Father and yet suffered, we too can expect to go through trials as we seek to obey God. As we walk by faith, we will not get everything correct all the time; but as we remain in faith, looking to Jesus, His Spirit will help us and lead us in the right path, into obedience and His power as we minister to and for the Lord.

Jesus helped Peter the Apostle through many trials and failures as he learned not to depend on himself but God's power. As Peter learned obedience, He became fruitful and used God on the day of Pentecost to lead many souls to salvation. See Peter's journey to obedience and power. Mark 14:27-30; Matthew 26:34-35, 69-75; Matthew 14:22-36; Acts 2.

Just as God is our Father and He leads and trains us to obey Him, we too are to do the same for our children.

"Train up a child in the way he should go: and when he is old, he will not depart from it" (Proverbs 22:6).

LIFE: The emphasis is on training. If we raise our children with a Law mentality of obeying or else, they are punished, we control them, which will later lead to disobedience and rebellion when they are young adults. We train our children when we depend on God's grace to show us how to help each child grow. This is because each child is different, and God alone knows how best to help each one obey their parents and ultimately obey Him. As we depend on God's wisdom and being led by the power of the Holy Spirit, we are to abide in God and ask the Holy Spirit to teach us how to train our young ones to love and obey their parents and by His grace to love the Lord.

TEACH OUR CHILDREN — DAY 2

"Train up a child in the way he should go..." —Proverbs 22:6

TRUTH: Control is appropriate and necessary when children are small and at times to correct or pull a child from harm, but even then, we can trust God to help us to remain connected to our children with love. We must teach them in the simplest of ways how much God accepted us even in our sin, then He washed and made us clean by the Blood of Jesus. By extension, we are teaching them the same acceptance God gave us; we must assure them that we will never separate from them or leave when they sin... See Hebrews 13:5. Always love and grace over Law and control.

"Suffer little children, and forbid them not, to come unto me for of such is the kingdom of heaven" (Matthew 19:14). We are to teach our children to love. Tell them God loves them and that we love them too. Let them believe our love is love from God our Father as we show it to them by our behavior, exhibiting God's grace in His goodness and His mercy; this is what will help them learn to believe in God's love.

Children need love, boundaries, discipline, and correction in love to grow into well-balanced adults. See Proverbs 22:6, 15. *"And that from a child thou hast known the holy scriptures, which are able to make thee wise unto salvation through faith which is in Christ Jesus"* (2 Timothy 3:15). As parents, we can seek to better understand our children in their thoughts, feelings, and choices as we seek to help them obey God's boundaries and limits given in His Word.

"And thou shalt teach them diligently unto thy children, and shalt talk of them when thou sitteth in thine house, and when walkest by the way, and when thou liest down, and when thou risest up" (Deuteronomy 6:7).

LIFE: *"Lo, children are an heritage of the Lord: and the fruit of the womb is his reward"* (Psalm 127: 3). As parents, we must assume the responsibility to be parent leaders and train them well to believe God and trust Him as we teach them to believe us. The Lord will help us, and we can depend on Him for guidance as well as the teaching they will receive in Sunday school.

CHILDREN, OBEY YOUR PARENTS

"Children, obey your parents in the Lord: for this is right." —Ephesians 6:1

TRUTH: All children must be taught to obey, and as they are being taught the Word, they will be helped to choose to follow.

"My son, hear the instruction of thy father, and forsake not the law of thy mother" (Proverbs 1:8).

*"With*hold *not correction from the child; if thou beatest him with a rod, he shall not die. Thou shalt beat him with the rod, and shalt deliver his soul from hell* (Proverbs 23:13-14).

LIFE: We are to train our children to understand that:

1. Maintaining a tender heart turned to Jesus and their parents in obedience will ensure their place in heaven. See Matthew 18:3.
2. When children honor their mother and father, they will live a long life. See Ephesians 6:2-3.
3. When children obey, they will show their love for Jesus and their parents and others. See John 14:23.
4. Obedience is not a choice; it is a given. We are to teach them that Jesus obeyed to bring us salvation, even when it cost Him His life. Likewise, it will cost them their pride to humble themselves and listen and obey their parents' instructions. Jesus had joy in obeying God, and children become more like Jesus as they obey their parents. We can help them to see that obeying the Word will bring them joy in the end as they are becoming fruitful and succeeding in their life.
5. Obedience builds faith. If our instructions to them are based on the Word and God's grace, we are ultimately helping them to obey the Word; and faith pleases God. See Colossians 3:20.
6. Obeying their parents is learning to love God and practicing following Him.

CHILDREN, OBEY YOUR PARENTS — DAY 2

"Children obey your parents in the Lord..." —Ephesians 6:1

LIFE CONTINUED: As parents, we obey God as His disciples; as we show that example to our children, they too will find it easier to follow God as they follow us. When they become adults and are away from us, we will not have to worry if they are doing right or making good choices because we've trained them to listen and obey their Father God in the Word. As we pray, we know they now have a Father and leader in Jesus in our absence to help them obey Him and take good care of them. See Philippians 2:13; Proverbs 22:6.

1. As we lead by example in obedience to God's Word, we can expect them to be consistent in their obedience, just as we are consistent with our instructions and actions. Over time, by experiencing God's grace, they will learn to trust our judgment and later God's. Consistency will build good habits of yielding as they repeatedly practice obedience.

2. We help our children to obey by following the boundaries set by God's love. As parents of teens, if they fail to see that our desire for their obedience is for their good, we can let them see the effects of disobedience. For example, we could take them to an emergency room and let see the devastating effects of driving and texting accidents. Along with the Word, they can be encouraged to obey. See Ephesians 6:1-3.

3. Obedience is a God-ordained structure with God at the Head of the church. See Ephesians 1:22; Romans 13:1; Matthew 15:4. Children were meant to depend on parents and parents on God. We are to continually use God's grace to point our children to Jesus. He will hold them and lead them into all truth with our help guiding them. See Proverbs 6:20-23; John 5:19; 2 Timothy 3:16; John 15:26.

"And all thy children shall be taught of the Lord; and great shall be the peace of thy children" (Isaiah 54:13).

CONFESSIONS FOR CHILDREN

"And that from a child thou hast known the holy scriptures, which are able to make thee wise unto salvation." —2 Timothy 3:15

TRUTH AND LIFE: As early as a child begins to process information, we are to start the discipline of building faith to help them to honor God as they honor their parents and build healthy esteem for God, others, and self. We can help them by making scriptural confessions.

- I am beautiful/handsome because my Heavenly Father fearfully and wonderfully made me. See Psalm 139:14.
- God chooses me and I am loved. See Ephesians 1:11-12.
- He is my perfect Father. See Matthew 5:43.
- Jesus made me wise, acceptable, holy, and free. See 1 Corinthians 1:30.
- God has given me wisdom, knowledge, and skill in all things concerning my life and school. See Daniel 1:4, 17; My memory is blessed. See Proverbs 10:7.
- The Holy Spirit will teach me and bring all things to my remembrance. See John 14:26.
- I can do all things through Christ … See Philippians 4:13.
- I obey my parents, and I have a long life. See Ephesians 6:1-3.
- I choose to delight in the Lord, and He will bless me. See Psalm 37:4.
- I will seek the Lord with all my heart. See Deuteronomy 4:29.
- The Lord is my Shepherd, and I shall not want of His love, provision, or protection. See Psalm 23:1.
- God's angels have charge over me to keep me safe. See Psalm 91:11.
- I am more than a conqueror through Christ. See Romans 8:7.
- Jesus loves me. See John 3:16. His love is in my heart. See Romans 5:5.
- God lavishes His love on me. See 1 John 3:1.
- God sings love songs to me and rejoices over me. See Zephaniah 3:17.
- When I am sick, I know by His stripes I am healed. See Isaiah 53:4-5.
- His favor, like a shield, surrounds me. See Psalm 5:12.
- Nothing can separate me from God's love for me. See Romans 8:38-39.

SATAN IS DEFEATED

"For this purpose, the Son of God was manifested,
that he might destroy the works of the devil." —1 John 3:8

TRUTH: The Scriptures tell us that Satan is a real entity.

- He is a thief who has come to steal, kill, and destroy. He is as a roaring lion walking about seeking whom he may devour. See John 10:10; 1 Peter 5:8.
- Jesus defeated Satan at the Cross. See John 16:11; Romans 5:12-21.
- Jesus vanquished death from Satan. His victory accomplished healing from all sicknesses unto death. See Isaiah 53:4-5; 1 Peter 2:24.
- Jesus took away Satan's control over our soul when He ended the Law in self-effort, strengthening sin, accusations, and sin-consciousness. And in its place gave us faith in God's grace with dependence on the Holy Spirit to lead us. Flesh gives the devil power while the Spirit defeats him. See Romans 8:2; Ephesians 2:8; Colossians 2:14-15.
- Jesus' shed Blood released God's power and authority over every force of Satan to make us overcomers. See Luke 10:19; Revelation 12:11.
- Jesus' resurrection lifted us by faith from spiritual death to eternal life. We are no longer guilty. See John 3:16-17; Colossians 1:13-14.
- We are also raised and seated in heavenly places in Christ, and Satan is placed under Jesus' feet and consequently ours. See Ephesians 1:3, 19-21.
- We have the Word and the Holy Spirit's power to abide in truth and enforce the devil's defeat. See John 15:7; Philippians 2:9-10.

LIFE: As a believer, you must believe in your heart that Satan is defeated and that whatever he brings against you cannot succeed. You must feast at the table of faith Jesus set for you, filled with God's promised blessings even while you are enduring Satan's pain or pressure. See Psalm 23:5-6. In your heart, believe he is defeated. Abide in Christ, speak the Word, pray, taking your stand knowing he is defeated. Listen to what God says and do it. Satan may hurt you but never harm you unto destruction. See Job 5:19-22; Psalm 91:10; 1 John 5:18.

SATAN IS DEFEATED — DAY 2

"...That he might destroy the works of the devil." —1 John 3:8

TRUTH: As believers needing healing or deliverance, we may have been taking medicine as well as standing on God's promises by faith without knowing what caused our dilemma. This approach will not help us get to the real root of our problem. The same applies to the spiritual. Satan has been using his various tactics to harass our body and soul, as he brings torment, temptations, dark thoughts, depression and entices us into works, legalism, sinful pleasures in our bodies, and idolatry in our desires. Meanwhile, we just keep trying harder, struggling to grow up as a Christian using our faith to fight him off. We are seeking to overcome, but it seems we are fighting a losing battle.

Although we know legally Satan is defeated, he may still seem to be extraordinarily strong against us. Why is this so? We must be aware and know his tactics against us. We must know which tactic he is using to apply the right Word as a remedy. Remember only the right Word as truth to your specific need can set you free. See John 8:32. For example, His attack by condemnation must be remedied by the Word of Jesus' righteousness in us. We will know the truth as we abide in Christ and depend on Him by the Holy Spirit to lead us into revelation knowledge.

Despite the severity of his attacks, we must daily enforce his defeat as we resist him with the truth until he flees. Jesus says He has made a table in the presence of our enemies. See Psalm 23:5. We must possess our blessings amid the enemy's attack. We must, by faith, stand and believe that Jesus overcame and defeated him and made us overcomers even while we may be suffering.

LIFE: Satan employs many weapons and tactics such as fear, worry, doubt, lies, guilt, accusations, condemnation, shame, distractions (modern technology), strife, jealousies, sickness, confusion. Submit to God in His Word seated in Christ in authority or repentance. Draw near in your union relationship, believe you have the victory remain in Christ to hear from your Father, and do as His Spirit leads you. His truth will succeed every time.

ENFORCE SATAN'S DEFEAT

"Whatsoever ye shall bind on earth shall be bound in heaven: and whatsoever ye shall loose on earth shall be loosed in heaven." —Matthew 18:18

TRUTH: When we are weak, we must know what is coming against us and how Satan hurts us. We must pray for wisdom about what and how the attack is being carried out against us. First, seek God's wisdom if the attack is from the evil one alone or with permission from God. See Matthew 18:34-35. If we feel fearful, determine what specific situation he uses to bring that fear. It could be fear of the coronavirus or some other sickness, fear of our children messing up, fear of financial insecurity, fear of marriage failure, fear of being unprepared for retirement?

Satan cannot attack and succeed without us first succumbing to fear. The Scripture says perfect love casts out all fear. Therefore, when we believe God loves us deeply, that He will care for us, and has provided for our deliverance and success through the Cross, we will trust Him and not yield to fear. Using relevant Scriptures, give the situation to God in prayer and pray in the Holy Spirit for greater wisdom. See Matthew 6:33, 34; Philippians 4:6-7; 1 Peter 5:7.

LIFE: When you hear what God has to say about your way of escape from the attack, worship and praise Him for His goodness, grace, and faithfulness, then do as He says. See James 1:22. It may be to forgive, cast down imaginations, guard your mind, warfare against the enemy speaking Scriptures, stand in faith abiding in your union relationship, or go to the doctor or the deliverance minister. Obey Him as you stand and believe God, speak, act on His Word, and rejoice for the victory. Jehoshaphat placed singers in front and started to praise God for His victory. Guard your mind from the enemy taunting failure. He's a liar. Worship and trust Jesus' love to protect and care for you. His love will drive fear far from you to quench and reverse Satan's attack. For He is your life.

ENFORCE SATAN'S DEFEAT — DAY 2

"I have pursued mine enemies, and destroyed them; and turned not again until I consumed them" —2 Samuel 22:38

TRUTH:

- We are to meditate on God's Word and believe in our hearts that Satan is defeated, despite how we sense him attacking us. Joshua 1:8.
- Speak the Word to enforce his defeat. If the attack is within your soul/mind and you do not know the cause, go to God and pray in the Holy Spirit for revelation truth about the attack and how to overcome it. It may be to guard the mind or cast down imaginations, get out of self-righteousness. Truth exposes Satan's lies to defeat him.
- We all must speak the Word and worship as we seek to come to a place of the oneness of our spirit with Jesus as Lord and His Word, that we know Christ in us has already defeated Satan, and at our command, he must bow. As an example, for fear in sickness, say, "Jesus is my Lord my righteousness, my justifier. I am established in righteousness; Jesus loves me. He has by His stripes healed my body. Therefore, by His Blood, I am healed; oppression is far from me, and I will not fear. Spirit of fear, I reject you; spirit of infirmity, leave now in Jesus' name." Speak the Word. See Isaiah 53:4-5; 54:14,17; 2 Timothy 1:7; 1 John 4:4.
- Follow God's leading by speaking the Word; listen to the Holy Spirit follow Him step by step, and stand unmovable until you are free. Psalm 112:7.
- During the process, worship and praise God for His grace, goodness, truth, and power to give you victory. *"No weapon that is formed against thee shall prosper...."* See Isaiah 54:17; Philippians 2:9-10.

LIFE: Prayer: Heavenly Father, I thank You for Your love and grace. In You, Lord is life, and Your life is the light in me. I plead the Blood of Jesus against every force of darkness and agree that greater is God's anointing that is in me than Satan, who is in the world. God's power in His anointing deposited in me by His love is greater than sickness and fear. God's perfect love in my heart cast out all fear and make me healed, delivered, and free, in Jesus' name, amen.

IN THE PRESENCE OF THE ENEMY

"Thou preparest a table before me in the presence of mine enemies." —Psalm 23:5

TRUTH: The first inhabitants of the garden of Eden lived in infinite love, abundance, and the goodness and faithfulness of God's presence. When Adam sinned, and rebellion severed his spiritual relationship, he lost his righteous position as a son when he gave his dominion, authority, and blessings over to Satan. In return, he received shame, sin-consciousness, and toil of labor for him to eat. He lost the table of infinite goodness and blessings God gave him. To retrieve His children from Satan's grasp, God sent Jesus to redeem humanity back to Himself and restore His goodness, blessings, fruitfulness, and intimate relationship. The Cross defeated Satan, sickness, death, the Law, and its power of sin in the life of anyone who believes in Jesus. See Isaiah 54:17; Romans 5:12-21.

God through Jesus has a new spiritual table spread, with Jesus seated at the head and laden with even better blessings than Adam's. God's table, however, is prepared and spread in the presence of our enemy Satan. Here on earth, we must, by faith in God's grace, stand in authority and power against Satan even as we partake of our blessings at the table. To do that, we must stand in faith and the victory, Christ imputed or gave to us and acknowledge we are righteous, loved, seated in Christ already victorious and not afraid. In the presence of the enemy, we declare to him that we know he is defeated. And we call those things which be not as though they are. See Romans 4:17. Believe we are healed even when we feel sick in the presence of the enemy. Call ourselves provided for amid empty pockets. Stay in faith, enforcing the enemy's defeat by abiding and rejoicing until our blessing manifests. Don't wait until the enemy leaves to rejoice.

LIFE: Remain steadfast, abide and speak God's Word, believe, resist, rejoice, and partake in the presence of the enemy. We have the power to do so and prosper. See Deuteronomy 30:19-20; John 10:9-10; Psalms 23; 78:19.

GRACE AND SATAN

"Who hath delivered us from the power of darkness, and hath translated us into the kingdom of his dear Son." —Colossians 1:13

TRUTH: Very often, the oneness we have with God may feel like the opposite as the chatter and temptations of the enemy seem to crowd out our sense of oneness and peace with Christ Jesus. At times, we may get overwhelmed with the clutter and noise in our soul and dark feelings, which originate from Satan. Because we are united unto the Father, we must simultaneously believe through God's grace in Jesus that we are fully separated from the kingdom of darkness. See Ephesians 1:19-23. Paul prayed that our eyes might be opened to the riches of our inheritance, to know the grace, power, and dominion we have over Satan and all his darkness.

But why do we so often think and feel that he is not under our feet? Most likely, we are inadvertently believing some lie of the devil. Here are some suggestions of lies he could be telling us:

- If I sin, I am instantly qualified to receive his torment.
- When I have sinned, I have failed God and myself and am unworthy.
- I must feel guilty, ashamed, and condemned until I make it right.
- If I sense turmoil in my mind, I must hurry and do something for the turmoil to stop, as I will only have peace when I am right with God in my heart because all stirrings of discomfort are of the devil.
- I cannot defeat Satan; he is too strong for me. It is not true that no evil shall befall me, and greater is he that is in me than he that is in the world.
- Your righteousness or position before God is determined by your goodness, and not the Blood of Jesus.

If we believe these lies, we will in the spirit realm be attached at the hip to the devil because we have discounted everything the Blood Jesus has done for us.

LIFE: Stand in your oneness with Jesus' in His victory which defeated Satan by God's grace. Oneness, abiding, and remaining in Jesus gives us the same power and authority as Jesus to command the devil who must flee. As Jesus is so we in this world. See 1 Corinthians 6:17; 15:57-58; Romans 8:11; Ephesians 1:18-22; Colossians 2:6.

SEPARATED FROM SATAN

"Who hath delivered us from the power of darkness." —Colossians 1:13

TRUTH: *"And having spoiled principalities and powers, he made a shew of them openly, triumphing over them in it"* (Colossians 2:15). First, Satan had power over us because he became god in the earth, and when we were born in this world, he was our master. See Psalm 51:5. We have changed allegiance when we are born -again; God is now our Savior, Lord, and Master.

Secondly, Satan had power over us by using an annulled Law of Moses, against us...a Law which says, obey or suffer the consequences. See Deuteronomy 28; Romans 3; 10:4; Ephesians 2:13-16. Jesus ended the Law and separated us unto God by the power of the Holy Spirit within to guide and help, us to obey. See Hebrews 13:20-21.

Third, Satan had power over us with sin. But Jesus became sin, forgave all our sins, and made us free with His righteousness. See 2 Corinthians 5:21.

And fourth, Satan had power with sickness, physical death, and destruction. Jesus by His shed Blood gave us healing and has delivered us from all of Satan's power when He arose from the dead and gave us His eternal life in His promises, His righteousness, and the power in His Blood, His stripes for healing. See 1 Peter 2:24. His Word as truth, His armor as our protection, His Spirit as our Helper within us to stand in His victory, His name, and His authority are weapons to enforce Satan's defeat and will cause us to overcome. See Psalm 103:1-5.

LIFE: We have been separated from Satan and his works of darkness with sin, sickness, poverty, death, and the Law with self-effort. *"For the law of the Spirit of life in Christ Jesus hath made me free from the law of sin and death"* (Romans 8:2). The separation God made between us and Satan through the power of His Spirit, are the truth of His Word, the Blood and His name as Lord, when enforced gives us complete authority over the enemy and total overcoming victory. So, resist him with truth and power and declare your victory. Truly the anointing in you is greater than Satan. See 1 John 4:4

SEPARATED FROM SATAN — DAY 2

"And hath translated us into the kingdom of his dear Son." —Colossians 1:13

TRUTH: The Blood of Jesus shed on the Cross separated us from Satan and all the powers of darkness. See Titus 3:3-7; Hebrews 2:14-15. As believers we are to use the keys to the Kingdom and our oneness in our relationship by faith in God's grace: Our salvation, forgiveness, righteousness, the name of Jesus as Lord; the Blood of Jesus; the Word, putting on the whole armor and praying in the Holy Spirit, guarding our minds and casting cares and imaginations will cause us to stand and keep ourselves separated from Satan.

Satan often tries to keep us attached to himself by using sin, lies, half-truths, accusations, and the flesh to lead us onto his path, as he did with Eve. Reject him. Satan also often tries to lead us with agitation and torment, trying to force us into impatience, strife, and rash decisions. But when we surrender to God, it is His Spirit who must lead us, not us listening and yielding to Satan's voice to end his torment. We are united unto God by our union relationship with His Holy Spirit. The Word is Spirit and life; believe, speak, and overcome.

LIFE: *"Howbeit when he, the Spirit of truth, is come, he will guide you into all truth"* (John 16:13).

"For it is God which worketh in you both to will and to do of his good pleasure" (Philippians 2:13).

"Who shall separate us from the love of Christ? shall tribulation, or distress, or persecution, or famine, or nakedness, or peril, or sword?" (Romans 8:35). The answer for everyone should be no!

"My son, despise not thou the chastening of the Lord, nor faint when thou art rebuked of Him" (Hebrews 12:5). Chastening and rebuke were by the exhortation, not the chastisement of Satan and his terror. See Hebrews 12:5-8

"Looking unto Jesus the author and finisher of our faith..." (Hebrews 12:2).

Nowhere was Satan mentioned here, he is defeated. Jesus is our conqueror.

NOVEMBER 9

HUMAN AUTHORITY

"Let every soul be subject unto the higher powers. For there is no power but of God: the powers that be are ordained of God." —Romans 13:1

TRUTH: Who are the people out in front, leading us...in our nation, our job, community, and church? The Word of God says we are to submit to their leadership. This can be an exceedingly difficult thing to do if, as believers, we are still living by our self-will, our thoughts, and our opinions instead of accepting God's Word. It has become extremely easy for Christians to think we can join the rest of the political world and treat leaders with derision, speak derogatorily about them, and resist their efforts to lead us. We do not want anyone with whom we do not agree to lead us. This is not God's way. God says we are to submit to the authority that He has placed over us, whether we agree with their way or not. See 1 Peter 2:13-18 *"Whosoever, therefore, resisteth the power, resisteth the ordinance of God: and they that resist shall receive to themselves damnation"* (Romans 13:2). When we have evil leaders, we cry out in prayer to God for deliverance, and He will go before us and deliver. Sometimes God will use an evil leader to show us our sins for us to repent, as seen in the books of Kings.

"Submit yourselves to every ordinance of man for the Lord's sake: whether it be to the king...or governors...them that are sent by Him for the punishment of evildoers, and for the praise of them that do well... As free, and not using your liberty for a cloak of maliciousness, but as the servants of God. Honor all men. Love the brotherhood. Fear God. Honor the king" (1 Peter 2:13-17).

LIFE: The castigating, name-calling and derogatory character bashing of the nation's leaders must not be found among Christians. Always speak the truth in love, as if honoring God. Take the stand which God is leading you to take and pray. Never take things into your own hands to create your peace; always be led by the Holy Spirit.

"I exhort therefore, that, first of all, supplications, prayers, intercessions, and giving of thanks, be made for all men; For kings, and for all that are in authority; that we may lead a quiet and peaceable life in all godliness and honesty" (1 Timothy 1:1-2).

HUMAN AUTHORITY — DAY 2

"Obey them that have the rule over you, and submit yourselves:
for they watch for your souls." —Hebrews 13:17

TRUTH: God has placed leaders over His people to watch our national affairs, our economic welfare, or our souls. This means we must first obey God and then the laws of the land and the officials set over us to enforce the law. Children obey their parents, employees, employers, and church members their pastors as they follow Christ. See 1 Corinthians 11:1-2;1 Peter 2:12-21; Ephesians 6:1-2; Hebrews 13:17-18. God is not asking us to be nice only to leaders who are nice to us, but also to them who are mean. See Romans 13:5-7; 1 Samuel 24:1-22; 1 Peter 2:17.

God is our highest and final authority, and although He has called us as believers to respect, honor and obey our natural leaders when their leadership and laws are in direct conflict with the Word of God and the expansion of the kingdom of God, we are to submit to God, our highest authority. We can fast and pray for wisdom and understanding in how best to respond. See Acts 4:18-23; Acts 5:12-29. As we cry out to God, we may not have to do anything because He does the work and delivers, or we may have to defy man and love, not our lives unto the death. See Revelation 12:11. The common response in the world today, even in our churches, is of ignoring and or rebelling against bringing division. This is not God's way. It is carnal and of the devil. See Romans 1:16-17; Romans 8.

LIFE: We are accountable to those God has placed above us but even more so to God. If asked to disobey God or our conscience, we can make the choice to disobey but be willing to suffer the consequences of retaliation or even death, knowing God is in charge. See Acts 8; Revelation 20:4. Pray, obey God, and let Him manage the consequences.

AUTHORITY OVER EVIL

"Behold, I give unto you power to tread upon serpents and scorpions, and over all the power of the enemy: and nothing shall by any means hurt you." —Luke 10:19

TRUTH: It was prophesied as early as Genesis 3:15 that God would deal a blow to Satan, His archenemy. To do this, God sent Jesus to die and forgive our sins and give salvation in His righteousness to restore us into a right love relationship with God the Father. This separated us from Satan back to God. But God did not stop there. He deposited His love, full of the anointing, in us and raised us to be seated in heavenly places with Him at the right hand of God the Father, in a place of power, authority, and victory. God in Jesus placed us far above every work of darkness. See Ephesians 1:16-23. The Holy Spirit in us made us one with God, and we have now been made a partaker of God's divine nature in our spirit. We have His power and authority within us. God delegated His power in Jesus to us and commanded us to put on the armor, Jesus Himself, and resist the enemy of our souls. We have been given the power of God in, with, and upon us by His Spirit. See Psalm 91:13; Mark 16:17-18; Luke 10:18-19; Romans 8:11; 1 John 2:27; 1 John 4:4; Revelation 12:11.

"Above all, t*aking the shield of faith, wherewith ye shall quench all the fiery darts of the wicked*" (Ephesians 6:16).

LIFE: Paul prayed that our eyes would be opened to see that God has given us this power over all evil. See Ephesians 1:18-23; 2:4-7, 3:10-11. We must know that the believer who thinks he is weak is mistaken, as the Word says Satan is under our feet because we are raised "in Christ," and whatsoever we bind on earth shall be bound in heaven, and whatsoever we loose on earth shall be loosed in heaven. See Matthew 18:18-20. Often pray these Ephesians prayers for yourself and others to maintain your authority over all evil.

Take your seat in Christ at the right hand of God the Father rest in Him claim His power, His anointing in His name, Jesus my Lord. As Lord, every evil, every sickness, every lack, every need is under His feet and must bow and leave. I have the victory in Christ Jesus. Meditate Philippians 2:9-11.

AUTHORITY OVER EVIL — DAY 2

"...Hath quickened us together with Christ... And hath raised us up together, and made us to sit together in heavenly places in Christ Jesus." —Ephesians 2:5-6

TRUTH: To begin to walk in our authority, we must know the exalted Christ and our exaltation in Him at the right hand of the Father. And Christ's victory is given to us. See Ephesians 1:16-23, 2:6; Hebrews 2:14-15; 1 Corinthians 15:51-57; Ephesians 6:11-18; Philippians 2:9-11; Revelation 12:11.

Secondly, we must know that we have been given power over Satan and all the hosts of hell. *"Behold, I give unto you power to tread on serpents and scorpions, and over all the power of the enemy: and nothing shall by any means hurt you"* (Luke 10:19).

God said here that the Law which held us captive to self-will and death, and which gave Satan access to us in our soul and the appetites of our bodies was removed by His Son Jesus on the Cross. Jesus, by the Spirit of God, died for us and got the victory according to God's will. He gave us the victory in His resurrection power, which justified us as innocent and free from sin and worthy to go into our Father's presence for Him to meet our every need. Self-will, which leads to sin, and sin-consciousness, which held us captive to Satan, was defeated. God's will for us, living by faith, being led by the Holy Spirit into righteousness and peace, will defeat Satan every time. See Romans 14:23, 5:17; 1 John 5:1-5; 1 John 4:4.

"Blotting out the handwriting of ordinances that was against us, which was contrary to us, and took it out of the way, nailing it to the cross. And having spoiled principalities and powers, he made a shew of them openly, triumphing over them in it" (Colossians 2:14-15).

LIFE: We must develop our spiritual authority by renewing our minds to see the exalted Christ and our place in Him. Search the Scriptures above and others regarding who we are in Christ. Find references on being 'in Him' and 'in Christ' and meditate on them until your heart is lifted and seats you with Christ in the oneness of Spirit in the secret place in heavenly places established in the victory Christ gave us to resist the enemy and watch him flee.

EXERCISING AUTHORITY

*"And whatsoever thou shalt bind on earth shall be
bound in heaven..."* —Matthew 16:19

TRUTH: We receive God's power and authority when we are born again, but this could lie dormant if we do not act upon this knowledge. We are to build our awareness of our authority and exercise it. We have control over Satan, his demons, and every effect of his evil kingdom. We have authority over sickness, lack, oppression, fear, darkness, accusation, depression, all animals, and destruction and all forms of death. *"...Put on the whole armor of God that we may be able to stand against the wiles of the devil..."* (Ephesians 6:11). We must put on the armor and exercise our authority.

We have the keys of the kingdom. See Matthew 16:19. Some of which are: The Word of God as truth. Jesus spoke the Word; it is written. See Luke 4:1-14; We have the name of Jesus as Lord. See John 21:5-7. With the Word, we have rest in the faith of God. See Mark 11:22-24; We have the Blood of Jesus. See Revelation 12:11; The power of casting care ensures our humility and allows us to retain our authority. See 1 Peter 5:7. In Genesis 44 and 45, Joseph is an example; Another key in the kingdom is our gift of righteousness, which keeps us in God's love, assurance, boldness, and out of unworthiness, condemnation, and fear. See Isaiah 53:14; We have power in the key to bind and loose in faith. See Matthew 6:19; We also have the anointing of the Holy Spirit. See Isaiah 10:27; Finally, we have the authority to call upon God for help from angelic hosts. See Hebrews 1:14. I'm sure there's more you could add. So, keep adding and keep the keys turning.

LIFE: Jesus said all power is given unto me in heaven and on earth. See Matthew 28:18. And this power was delegated to all believers. See Luke 10:19. Authority is best exercised in partnership and oneness with Jesus as heirs and joint-heirs seated in Him at the Father's right hand. We must believe our God is the Greater One within and that we are one with Him having the same power and authority as Jesus to enforce Satan's defeat. Be strong in the Lord and in the power of His might, fighting the good fight of faith, abiding in Christ until you see the victory of Christ manifest.

PUT ON ARMOR

"Put on the whole armor of God, that ye may be able to stand against the wiles of the devil." —Ephesians 6:11

TRUTH AND LIFE: God has given us all the blessings of heaven in Christ Jesus to enjoy. However, the spiritual forces of evil in the lower heavenlies above the earth will seek to block our prayers and our freedom in Christ Jesus. Whenever a believer stands in the power of God and takes authority, Satan takes notice and resents it because we are succeeding against him. Never make the mistake of fighting the devil, trying to get him to leave you alone. We are to stand in the power of God and our authority in the Word; resist the devil from our place of victory seated in Christ, and command him to leave. We resist, and he flees; we do not fight him. See James 4:7-8.

Our place of authority is in Christ, seated at the Father's right hand and abiding in Him. Therefore, to maintain our jurisdiction, we must be suited with Christ Himself, fully covered by Him as our armor. Jesus is our armor. Abiding in Christ suits us up with the armor of God and gives us dominion and power over evil. The different armor parts represent other parts of Christ Jesus' character given in redemption for our protection from Satan. We should endeavor to put on Christ by abiding in Him in every area of our life every day.

Truth as the first piece of armor is Jesus Himself, the Living Word. See John 1:17; 14:6; 17:17; Revelation 13:19. Take up God's Word as truth and discern the devil's lies, reject them, and come out of agreement with him. Cast down lies and abide in the truth. Replace them with the Word of God, then abide and reign in His abundant grace and His gift of righteousness. See Romans 5:17; 2 Corinthians 10:4-5; Philippians 4:8. One truth is that Jesus is our Lord of righteousness, God's love in our hearts made us pure, holy, and acceptable to the Father. Every day we must speak that Jesus is our righteousness, who rights all the wrongs we give to Him in faith. Jesus is my righteousness; by His Blood and His power, I am delivered, healed, and made whole, free and filled with His peace.

PUT ON ARMOR — DAY 2

"Put on the whole armor of God... and having on the breastplate of righteousness." —Ephesians 6: 11, 14

TRUTH AND LIFE: The breastplate of righteousness protects God's love in our hearts so that when we fail or sin, the devil does not rob us of our right standing or right love relationship and peace with God our Father. He will try to cause us to forget that it is Jesus who makes us in right standing with the Father and instead try to let us believe that we must be perfect with no sin before God loves and accept us.

He further tries to let us think that our imperfect actions or flawed performance or sin deserves punishment or feelings of unworthiness, a lack of acceptance, and condemnation. These feelings often make us feel that we do not measure up to God; instead, we feel distanced and disconnected. See Romans 5; 2 Corinthians 5:21; 1 Thessalonians 5:8. Righteousness will bring peace, quietness, and assurance to our hearts before God knowing we are loved and accepted. Isaiah 32:17-18; Ephesians 1:6.

Our feet shod with the gospel of peace is another piece of armor. Daily we are to walk in the gospel of Jesus Christ, the Prince of peace, not in our strength, religion, legalism, or works. The gospel of God's grace, abiding, trusting, and yielding to Jesus will keep us protected. See Ephesians 1:13 Our willingness also to share the gospel will keep our hearts turned to Jesus and joyful as we share Jesus, the Prince of Peace, who brings peace to all hearts. See Romans 5:1.

The shield of faith protects us from the fiery darts of the enemy. When we lift the shield of faith in Jesus, we raise the spoken Word and resist Satan. Our oneness in the relationship and the Word we believe as truth, abide in, and speak in authority causes every knee to bow and every tongue to confess that Jesus Christ is Lord. See Colossians 2:9-10. When we hope in God and His Word, faith comes to raise our expectations for more positive outcomes and blessings, which creates peace as we trust in God instead of ourselves.

PUT ON ARMOR — DAY 3

"Put on the whole armor of God... and take the helmet of salvation" —Ephesians 6: 11,17-18

TRUTH AND LIFE: The helmet of salvation is Jesus Himself as our Savior, the Author of our salvation and our hope. Hope always in God. Isaiah says we will be kept in perfect peace when our mind stays on Jesus. The helmet protects our mind as we keep our focus on Jesus instead of ourselves, others, circumstances, and certainly not on Satan. Set our affections on things above, for our life is hidden in Christ Jesus. See Colossians 3:2-3; Isaiah 26:3. Cast down all negative thoughts and cares of the enemy and replace them with the Word of God. See 2 Corinthians 10:4-5; Philippians 4:8, 1:6; 1 Peter 5:7.

The sword of the Spirit is the Word of God. See Ephesians 6:17. We are to use the Word of God offensively as we stand in authority, face the enemy, and speak the Word of truth we believe in our hearts. The Bible says that when we do, no weapon that is formed against us can prosper because the truth makes us free. See Isaiah 54:17; John 8:32,36.

Prayer is the last weapon, and we should be praying all kinds of prayers while exercising faith and patience to hear from God. On hearing, we respond accordingly for Him to give us divine protection from the enemy. Prayer is very often a weak area in the lives of some believers. But we must all seek to talk to the Father more to know if we have a hole in our armor (any one or more pieces of the armor missing), giving the enemy a reason to attack.

When we are fully arrayed in our Jesus armor, we are empowered by His love and free from fear, and no devil in hell can touch us: *"There shall no evil befall thee, neither shall any plague come nigh thy dwelling"* (Psalm 91:10). See Job 5:17-27; 121:7-8; John 14:30; 1 John 1:18; 4:4; Romans 8:37-39.

Suit up with Christ Jesus daily. Dwell in Him, be seated with Him. Your oneness in His presence is your secret place of the Most High God, in whom you shall abide under the shadow of the Almighty. As you trust Him in your armor of defense, He will be your refuge and fortress and will surely deliver you from all destruction.

COMPONENTS OF DELIVERANCE

"And they overcame him by the blood of the Lamb, and by the word of their testimony." —Revelation 12:11.

TRUTH AND LIFE: And they overcame. Who are they? It is us, the believers. To overcome and receive deliverance, we must become established in our hearts with the critical components of self-deliverance. Make the Word personal.

1. Know our God's goodness in what Jesus by His shed Blood accomplished on the Cross and be saved and delivered. See John 14:6, Jeremiah 32:17, 27; John 3:16; Colossians 1:13-14.

2. Receive the gift of righteousness and stand in boldness and confidence that Christ loves you and already overcame imputing His victory to you. See John 16:33; Ephesians 1:12-23; 1 John 5:4.

3. Know that you have been made new creation beings in Christ with a new heart to live by a new and living way by faith in Christ alone. See 2 Corinthians 5:17, 21; Romans 8:14-17; Hebrews 10:20; Galatians 2:20.

4. You must know you overcame Satan by the Blood of Jesus and that He is defeated. See Luke 10:18-19; John 8:36; 16:11; Ephesians 1:22-23; Philippians 2:9-11; 1 John 4:4; Revelation 12:11.

5. Be deeply in love with your Heavenly Father enough to trust and yield to Him. Walk in love with others. See Matthew 22:37; 1 John 4:4-18.

6. Stand in faith, knowing God is the Greater One, trusting Him to work on your behalf and bring deliverance. See Mark 11:22-24; 2 Corinthians 4:13-18; Galatians 5:6; Romans 4:17-21; 10:9-10; Hebrews 10:22-23.

7. Repent, forgive and renounce, submit to God to release any legal ground you may have given Satan. See 1 John 1:9; Matthew 18:34-35.

8. Rejoice in the graciousness and willingness of your God to deliver. See Isaiah 55:11-12; Philippians 4:4.

9. Stand in authority and command Satan to leave, taking his curses with him. Matthew 18:18; Philippians 2:9-11; Galatians 3:13; 1 John 4:4; Revelation 12:11. With full confidence in the name of our God Christ Jesus our Lord we win.

DELIVERANCE FROM ACCUSATION

"For the accuser of our brethren is cast down, which accused them before our God day and night." —Revelation 12:10

TRUTH: Jesus came to give us abundant life. Satan will steal, kill, and destroy, trying to rob us by any means. Externally he will try disasters, catastrophes, sickness, strife, destruction, accidents, and death. Internally he uses his voice to accuse, guilt, castigate, discourage, condemn, diminish, and deceive. In these last days before Jesus' return, as our text tells us, Satan's greatest weapon of accusation has already been unleashed. Nationally in the United States in the year 2020-21 accusations are widespread, calling others racist, white supremacist, fake media, sexist, all aimed at leading to condemnation, fear, low feelings of depression, rebellious and devilish behaviors. See Revelation 20. Satan will raise accusations against you, your spouse, children, and others. He aims to get you to believe his lies, become fearful, and either retaliate and be involved in strife or rebellion against God's command to love or become paralyzed and a passive target for him as a roaring lion devour. Either response gives him access to wreak havoc. See Genesis 37; 39:7-20; Luke 6:40-46.

LIFE: Guard your mind and heart against negative voices and influences. See Proverbs 4:23; 1 Corinthians 10:4-5; Philippians 4:8. Fill yourself up with a daily intake of the Word of God so that you'll get to know the voice of the enemy. See Romans 10:17; John 10:3-4. Receive your gift of righteousness and know how much God loves you and will keep His promise to love and care for you. His love will cast out all fear. See 1 John 4:18; Isaiah 54:14. Hear, meditate, and speak the Word of God on whom God made you in Christ and reject Satan's lies. Stand on Isaiah 53:7 and declare, "Jesus was oppressed and afflicted, yet He opened not His mouth. He remained silent, bearing all accusations for me. And now I stand in Jesus' silence and open my mouth and reject every negative voice speaking against me. I cancel every negative voice in my head because no weapon formed against you can prosper. I know my Shepherd's voice and a stranger's voice I reject. Now rest and let Jesus work on your behalf. Meditate on Isaiah 54:17; Psalms 33: 9-10; 144:7,8.

DELIVERANCE FROM A BAD REPORT

"And there we saw the giants... and we were in our own sight grasshoppers, and so we were in their sight." —Numbers 13:33

TRUTH: In life, there will be good times and bad times. Times of pleasures, blessings, and peace and times of sadness, pain, strife, and trials. The times may seem mostly bad for some people, and they want to give up, but God encourages us to keep our faith turned to Jesus. What do we do when faced with a negative report, or maybe even a fatal diagnosis?

Firstly, affirm God's goodness in our hearts. See Psalms 25:7; 27:13; 31:19; 107:1; Zechariah 9:17; 2 Thessalonians 1:11. Believe His faithfulness is sure. See Psalms 40:10-11; 89:1-3; 119:89-90; Lamentations 3:22-24; 1 Corinthians 1:9; 1 Thessalonians 5:24; Hebrews 10:23-24; 1 John 1:9; Revelation 17:14. Declare we belong to Jesus and are assured of His love, presence, and grace, as we speak His Word concerning our need. Meditate on healing Scriptures invoking the Blood of Jesus to work on your behalf. See 1 Corinthians 15:58; 1 Peter 2:24; Isaiah 53:4-5; Jeremiah 17:14; 30:17.

Each person must enforce Satan's defeat as you speak with authority Scriptures on deliverance. See Luke 10:18-19; Philippians 2:9-10; 1 John 4:4; Revelation 12:11; Philippians 4:4-8. Declare your trust and speak the promise you need; believe and rest. See Joshua 1:9; Isaiah 26:4; Jeremiah 17:7; Psalm 28:7, Proverbs 3:5-6; 2 Timothy 4:18; 1 John 5:14-15. Believe you are delivered even when symptoms still exist. We must partake and be free in the presence of the enemy. Peter's chains fell off, and he was free inside the jail. God first delivers us in the spiritual realm and tells us we are free before it manifests. Therefore, believe Him and receive.

LIFE: Have faith in God's promises from His Word about deliverance. Know that Satan is defeated and has no legal right or power over you. Where he gained the legal right, for example, with unforgiveness, or sin, repent and free yourself from his stronghold. Stand fast, believe, command, and receive. We shall not be afraid of evil tidings; instead, we fix our hearts, trusting in the Lord. See Psalm 112:7.

DELIVERANCE FROM WITHIN

"And his yoke from off thy neck, and the yoke shall be destroyed because of the anointing." —Isaiah 10:27

TRUTH: As believers, the Anointing, the Spirit of Christ, lives within us. See 1 John 2:27. The Anointing is the Holy Spirit is the power of God with the ability to do what only God can do for us. Only He can take away burdens or remove and destroy the yoke of the enemy from our shoulders. Yokes can be any hindrance, sickness, grief, sadness, pain, guilt, depression, demonic oppression, or accusatory voices. The Holy Spirit as God comes in and deposits His fruit of love because God is love. See 1 John 4:8. God's love within our human spirit will increase when fed and nurtured with the Word of God. He will release in our natural lives the power to develop joy, peace, patience, gentleness, goodness, faith, meekness, and self-control to overcome all attacks from within.

The fruit of the Spirit grows and matures, as we speak and become doers of the Word, the Holy Spirit exposes and expel any stronghold of carnality in sinful thoughts, attitudes such as anger, jealousy, wrong thinking, or fears, and immoral actions which may still be lurking in our soul (mind, will, emotions). Satan can only attack us in the soul, body, or life situations. He will seek to bring us bondages, weights, hindrances, strife, and burdens. However, as we guard our minds, take our position of victory in Christ seated at the right hand of the Father, subject our human will and emotions to obey the Word of God, and become doers of the Word, we are strengthening our human spirit within, which will then arise to dominate our soul, body, and life situations with power as the anointing from within to set us free.

LIFE: The anointing within is the Greater One, greater than all evil of the enemy on the outside. As we hear, read, meditate, believe, abide and speak with a command from our spirit, we activate the anointing for self-deliverance to drive the enemy out. "*... And the yoke shall be destroyed because of the anointing* (Isaiah 10: 27). Practice self-deliverance often. For example, if you felt jealousy against a friend, repent and pray for God to continue to bless them, or you bless them in some way, and then command that evil spirit of jealousy to leave, you'll then be free.

SELF-DELIVERANCE

"But if the Spirit of him that raised up Jesus from the dead ...quicken your mortal bodies by his Spirit that dwelleth in you." —Romans 8:11

TRUTH: I honestly believe the body of Christ needs to assume greater responsibility to expunge Satan with the hindrances and bondages he brings to us daily. Self-deliverance is having the revelation knowledge, wisdom, and confidence in Jesus and His Word of truth to confront Satan and command him to leave our mind, body, children, or resources. In the power of the Holy Spirit, when the enemy attacks, we must daily cast the devil and his thoughts, ideas, suggestions, and actions from our souls. And when we sin and know an evil spirit became attached to our soul, we are not only to repent, but we command that evil spirit to leave.

LIFE: For you as a believer to command the devil to leave and have him obey, you must: Always abide in Christ, knowing that your union and oneness in Him makes great power available. See John 15:7.

- Submit to God. Submit to Jesus' love deep in your heart, His written Word, and His Spirit. See Ephesians 3:17; John 13:34; Romans 8:11.
- Stand as the "just," righteous and bold. See 1 Corinthians 1:30.
- Believe the Word that Jesus is your righteousness, and you are established in His righteousness of healing or any other need. For provision, see Philippians 4:19; for His righteousness of protection, see Psalm 91.
- Acknowledge that you have the greater power of God within, and you are one spirit with Him. See 1 John 4:4; 5:4; Ephesians 6:10-18. Believe God's Word is true that His Spirit within you, His love in the anointing, is greater than Satan and anything he brings against you. Walk in love with others, give Satan no place to want to stay. See John 14:30. Repent, forgive, and renounce any agreement with Satan. See 1 John 1:9; Mark 11:25; Romans 12:14, 21; Philippians 2:3; 1 Thessalonians 5:13-15. With the Word as a sword, command Satan and his evil spirits and fear to leave. If you are still not free, seek the help of a God anointed Deliverance Minister.

DEPEND ON GOD

"For we are the circumcision, which worship God in the Spirit, and rejoice in Christ Jesus, and have no confidence in the flesh." —Philippians 3:3

TRUTH: Human beings are inclined to want independence, to go after our thinking, reasoning, and solution. We, however, could only receive salvation from the Cross. This is God's grace, and we did nothing to obtain this salvation, but we believe by faith in Jesus and receive. See 2 Timothy 1:9.

The Galatians received salvation by faith, depending on God's grace, but later made the mistake of relying on themselves, "Are *ye foolish? having begun in the Spirit, are ye now made perfect by the flesh?*" (Galatians 3:3).

The same way we received salvation in our spirit, grace depending on God through faith in Jesus, is the same way by the power of the Holy Spirit we are to walk out our entire Christian life. Maintain a relationship by abiding in your Father as you go to Him first, with everything that concerns you.

Put no confidence in the flesh or yourself, others, worldly pursuits, money, status, power, sinful pleasures, or human intellect. These are all idols, which contaminate our hearts with spiritual adultery. See Exodus 20:3. Idols will lead to weakness, failure, destruction, fear, and death, and with these idols contaminating the heart, one cannot live a life pleasing to God.

LIFE: Go to God your Father with your questions, needs, trouble, joys, failures, and successes. We are to depend on Him to lead us into what is good, right, and profitable and away from evil. Look to Him, according to His Word, in whatever situation you find yourself. Look for His way in the Word and listen for His way in His answers to your prayers. Look for His providence in open doors or opportunities and choose to walk in them. Walk away from the doors He closes. Do not be independent; depend on God and let His Spirit of life be your life. Meditate on Isaiah 41:13; Proverbs 3:5-7; Zechariah 4:6; Galatians 5:6.

BE STILL

*"Be still, and know that I am God: I will be exalted among
the heathen in the earth."* —Psalm 46:10

TRUTH: Being still does not mean relaxing and doing nothing. Being still means to acknowledge we are finite, but that we have an infinite God with the fulness of power living inside us, for us to abide in Him, He will do whatever is needed to cause us to overcome. See Colossians 2:10; John 1:16; Ephesians 3:19. On a personal level, have you been binding and loosing or casting out fear only to have it come back? Have you been fighting with Scriptures, striving to make confessions to build your faith to eliminate fear? You may need to consider if self-righteousness is present because the human will may not yet be fully surrendered, or you may be in works more concerned about what you do! Be still. Stop striving, stop fighting, stop fearing and acknowledge the Greater One in you and abide in Him by trusting and yielding to Him in all things. His love for you makes Him your refuge and your strength. He is your assurance, your security, and He makes all things well. Whatever the situation, God will work it for our good as we look to the Greater One, our mighty God within, for the deliverance of whatever is coming against us...not at what we see in front of us or the fear we feel. Be still and rest.

LIFE: How can you be still?

1. You are not in charge by what you do. Surrender your human will. Look to God the Anointing within for His power to work on your behalf. Speak Scriptures of God's power and greatness in you by faith and believe them.
2. Trust that God's power in the Holy Spirit is greater than any trial, lack, sickness, or fear. Rest in Him.
3. Find Scriptures supporting the attack and hold them up against it; speak and believe, standing unmovable and receive.
4. Stay in an attitude of prayer, praise, and worship, looking unto Jesus as the Author and Finisher of your faith. Listen and do what He speaks to your heart; be still, rejoice and watch for His salvation. See Exodus 14:14; Psalms 46:10-11, 62:5.

TRUST

"O Lord my God, in thee do I put my trust: save me from all them that persecute me, and deliver me." —Psalm 7:1.

TRUTH: Trust is to place confidence, hope, reliance, and dependence in the character or resource of something or someone greater. God in Jesus Christ His Son is the Greater One worthy of our trust. Why can we trust Him?

- He is a Father who loves and cares for His children, just as a shepherd cares for his sheep. See Psalm 23.
- He is a covenant-making and a covenant-keeping God. He chose us as His bride and promised never to leave us nor forsake us. See Revelation 22:17; Hebrews 13:5; Psalm 105:8-15.
- He is faithful and true. He never lies. See Revelation 19:11; Numbers 23:19. His faithfulness is from everlasting to everlasting. See Psalm 93:2.
- He is love, and His steadfast love is unchanging. See Hebrews 13:8; John 3:16.
- Our Father saved us and continues to save and keep us, giving us security and great assurance that, as His children, we can depend on and trust Him. See Psalm 16:5-11; Lamentations 3:23; 1 Corinthians 10:12-13.
- God is our all-sufficiency. See 2 Corinthians 3:5, 9:8; Philippians 1:6; 4:19.
- He is no respecter of persons; He will meet all needs asked for in faith and patience. See Acts 10:34; Hebrews 6:12.
- We can trust God as our healer, provider, deliverer, sanctifier, and protector because He causes us to always triumph in Christ Jesus our Lord. See Ephesians 1:3; 2 Corinthians 2:14.

LIFE: God is fully invested in and committed to you and me. Abide in Him, Trust His character of love and His integrity in His Word, and the power of His Spirit to deliver. Yield to Him as you say, *"I have set the Lord always before me: because he is at my right hand, I shall not be moved"* (Psalm 16:8). *"He shall not be afraid of evil tidings: his heart is fixed, trusting in the Lord.* See Psalm 112:7.

TRUST — DAY 2

"The Lord is my rock, and my fortress, and my deliverer; my God, my strength, in whom I will trust." —Psalm 18:2

TRUTH: We can trust God because His Word says, *"The Lord redeemeth the soul of his servants: and none of them that trust in him shall be desolate"* (Psalm 34:22). We can trust God when our hearts become established in God and His love and know that everything, He says is true because He cannot lie. The more we get to know God, the more we can trust Him because we get to know His character in how much He loves us and cares for us, never to let us fall. The knowledge of our Father's love will anchor our faith to trust and abide in Him in love, which will drive fear far from us. See 1 John 4:18.

We trust God when we absolutely and completely depend on His Word and are not worried by the circumstances, of what others say, or how we feel. See Matthew 8:5-13; Numbers 13. We trust God when we believe His Word and stand by those Words, and, having done all, we stand unmovable in our belief. God will see us through even when the evidence seems otherwise or if we must pass through treacherous situations. See Psalm 125:1; Isaiah 12:2-3; Nahum 1:7; Romans 8:28.

LIFE: How can you show your trust? First, give up depending on yourself for your answers. Go to the Father with all your needs, both large and small, in your job, family, future, relationship difficulties, sickness, and all seemingly impossible situations. Spend time getting to know your Heavenly Father in His Word, in His goodness and mercy, and see how beautiful He is. Talk to Him and hear His answer to you in prayer. Draw close in relationship to hear what He has to say, and in faith do as He says. Trust, abide, rely, depend on Him in praise, worship and thanksgiving; God will bring it to pass for you. Trust no matter what, as then He will make all things beautiful in His time. See Isaiah 46:9-10; Ecclesiastes 3:11; Psalm 5:11-12, 18:2; John 10:28-30; Romans 8:28, 31.

TRUST GOD, NOT SELF

"Trust in the Lord with all thine heart; and lean not unto thine own understanding." —Proverbs 3:5

TRUTH: Some believers know they are saved and that God loves them and commands them in return to love Him and others. See Romans 10:9-10; John 13:34. But trouble comes when we seek to obey God by following our understanding of what He requires. For faithfulness, some choose to follow the norms, disciplines, and formulas such as church attendance, prayer, Bible studies, faith formula, confessions, cautiously walking in love to maintain one's faith, and fasting as the means to connect with or love God. Instead of trusting God, they have leaned to their own understanding of loving and obeying God. As believers, we do this when we make assumptions, try to figure out things ourselves, and solve our problems in our wisdom. We will fail when we put our confidence in idols, such as riches, pleasures, other people, government, our righteousness, and abilities. See Micah 7:5; Jeremiah 9:4; Ezekiel 33:13; 2 Corinthians 1:9.

We love God when we simply live by faith and learn to trust Him. Daily we trust Him by giving Him our needs and thanking Him for meeting them. We make Him our priority to meet our needs, and we give Him total commitment by depending on Him in a relationship as we praise and worship Him. We hear Him in His Word, believe by abiding, and have full expectation that He will turn our situation around. We trust Him when we believe His Word about the situation to be true and hold fast with patience, choosing to rest by faith in God's grace to the end for His best. We are to trust God with all our hearts while remaining steadfast and resolute that our answer is on the way.

LIFE: Keep your eyes and your praise on Jesus, not on yourself, the problem, or on the expected result. Trust by releasing the situation and the answer to God's will, His way and His timing. Abide, yield to Him, and He will bring it to pass. See Mark 11:24; Ephesians 1:11; Philippians 1:6.

TRUST IN RELATIONSHIP

"No good thing does he withhold from those who walk uprightly. O Lord of hosts, blessed is the one who trusts in you." —Psalm 84:11-12.

TRUTH: It takes at least two in a relationship to forge trust. God assumed full responsibility by providing and giving us what we can trust in when He gave us His grace in His Son Jesus and all His work on the Cross to redeem us from Satan, sin, Law, and death. God in Jesus gave us the Blood and the name of Jesus, His Word, and His Spirit to call on Him by faith and trust in Him.

Our part in the relationship is to believe God that what Jesus died on the Cross and said in His Word and by His Spirit is the truth we are to abide and yield. He says that we shall know the truth, and the truth shall make us free. See John 8:32. We must believe the truth even when we do not understand or see the possible outcome. We trust when we look to God and give Him our questions for clarification to help us to stand in greater trust. See Luke 1:34. Mary trusted God upon receiving her call to birth the Son of God into the world and said, *"Be it unto me according to thy word"* (Luke 1: 38). What if every believer said the same thing when we see the promise of God for healing, provision, deliverance, or protection? Our relationship with the Father would be one hundred percent fruitful in our every desire and of every request for His blessings.

LIFE: Grow in your relationship with the Father as Peter, who denied Jesus did. He did not stay distanced in continued fear and denial but drew close to Jesus, abiding in the Living Word. Over time, after enduring many trials, he learned to trust Jesus. And by the power of the Holy Spirit in a relationship, he increased with power in the anointing to minister healing deliverance and grace See Acts 3:6. Rest in the wisdom, power, and grace of God your Father, knowing He is with you, in you, and for you, and we need fear no evil. See Psalm 46:1-2; Romans 4:20-21; 8:31; 39; 1 Peter 5:7; John 8:31-32.

TRUST GOD'S WORD

"All scripture is given by inspiration of God, and is profitable for doctrine, for reproof, for correction, for instruction in righteousness." —2 Timothy 3:16

TRUTH: God's Word was given to instruct us in the righteousness of God's love which by the Blood purchased an inheritance for us in Christ Jesus. All Jesus did on the Cross that was given and promised to us and is written down in the Bible is for our benefit. And the Word says all God's promises are yes and amen unto the glory of God. See 2 Corinthians 1:20. The question today is, do you have a need? If you do, God in Christ Jesus has already provided for that need. And to receive the provision for that need, you must by faith believe with your heart. You must have an encounter with Jesus and the Cross and receive the promise by grace as given. Begin to rejoice that your need is met before seeing it with your natural eyes. You must see and receive with your heart before seeing it with your eyes. God's Word is His will for us, and we can have confidence and trust in Him that when we ask, He will hear, answer, and meet our needs. See Mark 11:24; 1 John 5:14-15.

If there is lack, believers remind God of His Word to us, believe Him, and rejoice in advance that it is received. See Psalms 23; 37:19, 25; Psalm 84:11-12; John 15:7; Philippians 4:19; 3 John 2; 2 Corinthians 9:8. If you are sick and given a bad report from the doctor, pray and hear what God has to say about it and do as He say. Stand on and trust God's Word as we continue to follow the doctor's instructions. See Isaiah 53:4-5; 54:17; Jeremiah 17:14; 30:17; 32:27; Psalm 118:17; Matthew 8:17; 15:13; Galatians 3:13-14; 2 Peter 2:24. If there is strife in your relationships, meditate on Colossians 1:20; Romans 5:17; 1 Peter 4:8; Proverbs 15:1; Romans 12:14, 21. You will always overcome with God's Word.

LIFE: Read about the saints of the Bible who trusted God's Word and were blessed. See Matthew 8:5-13; Luke 5:4-9; Romans 15:13; Hebrews 11.

TRUST AND DOUBT NOT

"Except I shall see in his hands the print of the nails, and put my finger into the print of the nails, and thrust my hand into his side, I will not believe." —John 20:25

TRUTH: The believer is justified by the Blood of Jesus, made innocent of sin, and therefore called the "just." God the Father says four times that the just shall live by faith, which means it is a significant concept. See Habakkuk 2:4; Galatians 3:11; Romans 1:17; Hebrews 10:38. Faith is believing in our heart that we have the promised blessing in our life before it manifests. While we are in the process of believing, Satan will assail us with doubts and fears. If we are sick and believing for healing, symptoms will seem to worsen; yet we must still speak and abide in the Word on healing and stand believing that we have already received. Refuse to give in to fear. We may waver, but we must assure ourselves again and again in our relationship and in the Word to stand in faith.

We are to sit at the table Jesus spread by the stripes on His back to provide healing, and in the face of the enemy telling us we are sick, declare that we trust God and are healed. See Psalm 23:5; 103:2-4; 1 Peter 2:24. Thomas wanted to see before he believed, but God says we live by faith and believe in our hearts before seeing with our eyes. See Joshua 1:3; Hebrews 11:1; 1 John 5:14-15; James 1:5-8. We are in doubt instead of trusting and abiding when:

- We are still wondering if it will happen.
- We are waiting to see the evidence first before we rejoice.
- We are worrying and not at rest.
- We are giving God a time frame before going to plan B.
- We think that God has failed because the wait is long.
- We are murmuring and complaining about not seeing results.
- When we give more ability to the problem harming us than faith in God to deliver.

LIFE: Rest by faith in God's ability and the faithfulness of His Word, and He will bring it to pass. *"Blessed are they that have not seen, and yet have believed."* (John 20:29b).

TRUST GOD, RESIST SATAN

"Resist the devil, and he will flee from you." —James 4:7

TRUTH: The goal of the Christian life is to know the one true God, love and worship Him and let Him guide us into becoming more like Jesus, who gives true success in our natural lives. See John 17:3. Following Jesus pleases God but infuriates the devil who wants us to worship him. Satan tried to get Jesus to worship him and failed. See Luke 4. And he continuously tries at every turn to hinder, harass, and tempt us as believers to sin, fear, doubt, and live in self-righteousness. He uses his voice negatively against us to bring discouragement, pride, failure, accusation, and condemnation. He is the thief who has come to steal, kill, and destroy. See John 10:10. But God says we are to be sober and vigilant because our adversary Satan is walking about as a roaring lion seeking to destroy us. We must submit to God, abide in Him, trust His character and Word, yield to His Spirit, and use our authority to resist the devil. We resist the devil by:

- Submitting to God by believing that His Word is true.
- Trusting, forgiving, renouncing, and repenting.
- Guarding our minds by protecting our ears and eye gate from negative influences, including overstimulation from social media.
- Being conscious of whose voice we are listening to and cast down Satan's.
- Drawing near to our Heavenly Father and knowing His voice so that when Satan comes to us, we can quickly recognize and reject him.

When thoughts, feelings, or instructions come for us to act contrary to God's Word, recognize the source as Satan and reject it by immediately siding with God. Cast down those thoughts and replace them with the Word of God. See 2 Corinthians 10:4-5; Philippians 4:8. Satan will flee. See Luke 4:13-14; James 4:7; Proverbs 4:20-27.

LIFE: *"When he putteth forth his own sheep, he goeth before them, and the sheep follow him, for they know his voice. And a stranger will they not follow but will flee from him: for they know not the voice of strangers"* (John 10:4-5).

REDEEMED AND WILL SAY SO!

"And he saved them from the hand of him that hated them, and redeemed them from the hand of the enemy." —Psalm 106:10

TRUTH: We were slaves to Satan and sin because of Adams's sin. Christ redeemed or repurchased us from Satan, the god of this world. God regained possession of us as His children through Jesus Christ, His Son, and His shed Blood at the Cross. Satan's power was destroyed in the legal sense by our Advocate, Jesus. Jesus then gave us the knowledge of the truth of the gospel in authority and the power of His crucifixion, burial, resurrection, ascension. He gave us power in the Blood and Words of life to remain free by keeping Satan defeated and under our feet.

We know God's love is shed abroad in our hearts, and by His love, we have full assurance that we are loved and that God will never abandon or leave us. Knowing God has bought us back to Himself will free us from sin, a guilty conscience, and fear. Our freedom makes Him a good God of love, forgiveness, mercy, and kindness; this should bring joy and peace to our hearts. The spirit or heart belongs to God because He dwells there. The devil cannot contaminate or possess the spirit of a believer, but he can negatively influence our soul, in the mind, will, and emotions to bring fear and torment. See Ephesians 1:13; Romans 8:6-7; 12:1-2. God has told us to renew our minds so that God in our spirit can arise and dominate our soul and lead us by His love into experiencing the victory Christ has legally won for us. We have been redeemed, and we believe we have freedom in Christ.

LIFE: Understand the truth that the God of love in your heart has fully and completely provided your deliverance and freedom from death by His payment of an extremely high price, the life of His Son. "Know that ye *were not redeemed with corruptible things, as silver and gold...But with the precious blood of Christ, as of a Lamb without blemish and without spot*" (1 Peter 1:18-19). You have redemption in His Blood. You are the redeemed made free. You are SPECIAL, AS THE REDEEMED AND WILL SAY SO!

REDEEMED, AND WILL SAY SO! — DAY 2

"...Redeemed them from the hand of the enemy." —Psalm 106:10

TRUTH: Christ's redemption gave us back our full inheritance. God held nothing back from us, *"According as his divine power hath given unto us all things that pertain unto life and godliness,* (2 Peter 1:3). We must have faith in His love to believe we belong to God and are provided and cared for in our every way. We will be joyful and thankful that we belong and are perfectly loved, having NO FEAR! God's perfect love casts out all fear. See 1 John 4:18. We are the redeemed and must say so to Satan when he comes with pain, sickness, lack, worry, negative thoughts, depression, and fear. Tell the enemy:

- We have been saved and have eternal life. See 1 John 5:11.
- All our sins are forgiven. See Ephesians 1:7; Titus 1:14.
- We are adopted into God's family. See Galatians 4:5-7.
- We have the right relationship as worthy children of God. See John 1:12.
- The Holy Spirit, the Greater One, dwells within us. See John 14:16-18.
- We possess a sound mind redeemed from worry and fear. See Mark 5:36; Philippians 4:6-7; 2 Timothy 1:7; Revelation 12:11.
- We abide in Christ and have peace with God. See Colossians 1:20-22.
- We believe God loves us and redeemed us from the enemy, and by faith, we stand on His Word as truth. See Psalm 91; Isaiah 54:17; 2 Timothy 4:18.
- We believe God's Word and agree with Him completely; we surrender all to Jesus and shall not be moved to worry, as we trust in the Lord.

LIFE: I confess that I am saved, redeemed, and made free. See 1 Corinthians 1:30. The anointing in me is greater than any attack of the enemy. I will not fear but stand and believe Jesus made me new, loves me, and gave me my inheritance in deliverance on the Cross. Satan, I do not fight you; I stand in faith as I abide in the Word and enforce your defeat because I overcame by the Blood of the Lamb, Amen. Meditate on Isaiah 55:11; 2 Thessalonians 3:3.

PROTECTION BY THE BLOOD

"There shall no evil befall thee…For he shall give his angels charge over thee, to keep thee in all thy ways." —Psalm 91:10-11

TRUTH: Divine protection is God's promise to all His children who believe in Jesus. We are reminded of God's protection at the Passover in Exodus 12. The Israelites were to kill a spotless lamb and place the blood on the doorposts. When God's judgment of death came, those not within a house covered by blood died. This event foreshadowed the death of Jesus on the Cross, shedding His Blood which, when applied to our lives and situations, gives divine protection.

"And they overcame him by the blood of the lamb, and by the word of their testimony" (Revelation 12:11). Words of our testimony are *"no weapon that is formed against us can prosper"* (Isaiah 54:17). "Greater is he that is in you, than he that is in the world (1 John 4:4). Speak the Word.

We are to claim our protection using the Blood of Jesus. "Father, in the name of Jesus my Lord, and by His Blood, I cover myself, my home, my resources, all my family, my children and grandchildren not living at home, my vehicles, protection from accidents, and all possessions, and finances exposed to digital media. Romans 8:2 tells me that the law of the Spirit of life in Christ Jesus hath made me free from the law of sin and death. We have been redeemed from the curse of the law because Christ has been made a curse for our deliverance and protection. I receive protection by the Blood in Jesus' name." See Psalms 31:4-5; 41:2.

LIFE: Father, in the name of Jesus, I plead His Blood over myself, my family, my home, my possessions and claim Psalm 91 as my divine protection. I cover everyone and everything with the Blood of Jesus and declare we overcome all evil and are sheltered in our Father's everlasting arms. Amen.

Learn Psalm 91 by heart and be ready to speak it when in a hurry or immediate danger.

PROTECTION BY THE BLOOD — DAY 2

"For he shall give his angels charge over thee." —Psalm 91:11

TRUTH: I fully expect the blessings of Abraham to be mine and that I am divinely protected and kept safe.

I have set the Lord always before me, and I shall not be moved because Philippians 2:9-10 tells me that God has exalted Jesus and His shed Blood over and above every attack of the enemy against me. By the Blood of Jesus, every plan of Satan to cause sickness, accident, death, or destruction is nullified. Satan, I bind you from myself, my family, my church, my resources, and we stand protected by the Blood of Jesus and shall not be moved.

I plead the Blood of Jesus, and with it, I draw a bloodline around everything that concerns myself and my family, my community, my country. We claim divine protection and deliverance as children of the Most High God.

Father, as we go about our daily tasks today, we ask that You go before us and make every crooked way straight. See Isaiah 45:2. Dispatch angels to protect us from harm, danger, accidents, any destruction, and all evil.

Because we have delegated power and authority, I plead the Blood over every mode of transportation we utilize today and upon every other vehicle in proximity, they too will not cause us harm. We will travel safely and get back home safely in Jesus' name.

LIFE: The Blood of Jesus forgives, cleanses my conscience, purges my soul, protects, and delivers because I put my faith in God today and abide in His Word every day. Father, I have spoken Your Word, and I know that You watch over Your Word to perform them, and I am safe. Father, for all Your goodness and faithfulness, I rejoice and say thanks in advance.

"But I trusted in thee, O Lord; I said, Thou art my God. My times are in thy hand: deliver me from the hand of mine enemies, and from them that persecute me" (Psalm 31: 14-15).

THE SPIRIT WITHIN

"But whosoever drinketh of the water that I shall give him shall never thirst; but the water that I shall give him shall be in him a well of water springing up into everlasting life." —John 4:14

TRUTH: The Holy Spirit indwells a believer the moment they are born again by believing in Jesus. This is also known as salvation, regeneration, or conversion. See: John 3:16; 4:14, 20:22-23; Romans 10:9-10.

When one surrenders to God, the Spirit of Jesus enters a person's human spirit and lives there for salvation or redemption in the forgiveness of sins. See John 3:16 and Ephesians 1:7. For transformation and character development of the believer, see Galatians 5:22 and Romans 12:1-2. For deliverance, see Isaiah 10:27; Galatians 5:16. Jesus promised the Holy Spirit would live in us as our Helper. See Ezekiel 36:25-27; John 14:16-17. The Holy Spirit came into our hearts, and we were born again, made new creation beings in Christ as adopted sons. See Hebrews 8:10; Titus 3:5; 2 Corinthians 5:17.

He deposited the love of God in our hearts, which is the fruit of the Spirit to build God's character in us. *"The love of God is shed abroad in our hearts by the Holy Ghost which is given unto us"* (Romans 5:5). *"But the fruit of the Spirit is love, joy, peace, longsuffering, gentleness, goodness, faith, meekness, temperance: against such there is no law"* (Galatians 5:22-23).

The Spirit within is God's equipment of power and anointing in us to assure us we are children of God, guiding us to live for God, and for the anointing to raise a standard against all evil that comes against us from within. See Romans 8:15-17; Luke 10:19; 1 John 2:5-6, 27.

LIFE: God is love, and by depositing love within, He adopted us unto Himself in a love relationship with the Godhead to make us sons and daughters of God, filled with all His fulness and capabilities. See Romans 8:15; Galatians 4:4-6; Colossians 2:9. Believe He is the Spirit of love within and that He is greater than all. See 1 Corinthians 13: 13; 1 John 4:4.

HOLY SPIRIT IN US

"And I will pray the Father, and he shall give you another
Comforter... and shall be in you." —John 14:16-17

TRUTH: God is a Spirit, and He sent Jesus His Son in the flesh that we may get to know Him in character, in His thoughts, His love, His ways, and His purpose. After ascending, Jesus sent His Holy Spirit so He could indwell us at the born again experience. His purpose at salvation is to fill and direct our soul, but at the baptism of the Holy Spirit, He gives us power to live the Christian life and be His witnesses to the lost. See John 4:14, 24; 1:14; 14:16-17; Acts 1:8. Believing in Jesus seals the Holy Spirit within our human spirit in a union relationship unto God. See Ephesians 1:13-14; 4:30; 2 Timothy 2:19. As our text intimates, the Holy Spirit is a person and talks about He and Him. The Holy Spirit who dwells in us, in addition to sealing us unto God, guarantees we belong to God and confirms our Heavenly Father has adopted us as children of God. See Romans 8:15-17; Galatians 4:6. *"Know ye not that your body is the temple of the Holy Ghost which is in you... For ye were bought with a price ...* (1 Corinthians 6:19-20).

The Holy Spirit in us is the anointing of the Greater One. He is full of power and is greater than all the enemy's power. When we grow in our union relationship with the Father, the Holy Spirit takes greater control within to dispel every force of darkness, not only for ourselves but also for those to whom we minister. We have a deposit or a measure of the Holy Spirit in us given by God for our relationship and communication with Him. See Romans 12:3; Galatians 5:22. The Holy Spirit is God, the third person of the Trinity. See 1 Timothy 3:16. He is in you, upon you, and with you for you to keep in union and direct communion with your Heavenly Father. His anointing will destroy every yoke against you.

LIFE: *"The grace of the Lord Jesus Christ, and the love of God, and the communion of the Holy Ghost, be with you all"* (2 Corinthians 13:14).

"And it shall come to pass in that day, that day, that his burden shall be taken away from off thy shoulder, and his yoke from off thy neck, and the yoke shall be destroyed because of the anointing" (Isaiah 10:27).

GOD'S CHARACTER

"But the water that I shall give him shall be in him a well of water springing up into everlasting life." —John 4:14

TRUTH: The food for the human spirit is the Word of God. As we hear, believe, speak, and act on the Word of God, our spirit grows and begins to manifest the fruit of love causing us to walk in joy, peace, patience, gentleness, goodness, faith, meekness, and self-control. See Galatians 5:22.

The Spirit within was given to help us grow and mature into Christlikeness. Christlikeness is developed as the Holy Spirit within convicts us of God's righteousness, putting on Christ and dropping off old and sinful behaviors, self-centeredness, human effort, and weakness. See Ephesians 4:22-24.

We put on the love and integrity of God's character, who empowers us with the power of the Holy Spirit to overcome all evil.

"And every man that hath this hope in him purifieth himself, even as he is pure" (1 John 3:3).

"But if the Spirit of him that raised up Jesus from the dead dwell in you, he that raised up Christ from the dead shall also quicken your mortal bodies by his Spirit that dwelleth in you" (Romans 8:11).

LIFE: Live the Christian life by first acknowledging that the Holy Spirit lives in you, and He will confirm to you that you are a child of God. You are bought for a price and should live as one belonging to God. Be assured of your salvation. As you feed your spirit with the Word of God, abide in Him, and yield to what the Word and the Holy Spirit say, He will lead you into all truth for your sanctification. He will enforce the truth that you are dead to sin and alive unto God in the newness of life, capable of putting off the old man and putting on Christ in all His mercy, goodness, and glory as you grow and mature in the image of Christ. He will help you surrender your human will to the truth that the Holy Spirit in you is greater than all. His greatness will give you authority, dominion, and rest within. Meditate on Numbers 23:19; John 15:1, 2; 17:17; 1 Thessalonians 5:23; 1 Peter 1:2, 22; Hebrews 4; Colossians 1:22; 1 John 2:27; Revelation 5:13.

THE SPIRIT UPON YOU

"But ye shall receive power, after that the Holy Ghost is come upon you." —Acts 1:8

TRUTH: We know the Holy Spirit lives in and indwells a believer. See John 4:14; 14:17; Romans 8:16. Jesus, speaking to His disciples, breathed on them and said, *"Receive ye the Holy Ghost"* (John 20:22). The Holy Spirit came within, and the disciples became born again and were equipped to be led and used by God. But there is also a subsequent work of the Holy Spirit upon a believer. See John 7:38-39; Acts 2:4; 8:17. The Holy Spirit will empower us to live the Christian life with greater assurance, to overcome life's challenges, and give us power to be witnesses for Jesus utilizing the gifts of the Holy Spirit. See 1 Corinthians 12.

The Spirit, however, came upon them when they were commanded to wait in Jerusalem for the Holy Spirit. After the Holy Spirit came, we observed the Holy Spirit's transforming the disciples into bold men and women of God, filled and equipped with power, doing the works of Jesus. See Acts 1-3.

In the same way, the fruit of the Spirit was given within, I believe God also deposited and downloaded all nine gifts of the Spirit into our spirit (word of wisdom, word of knowledge, faith, healing, miracles, prophecy, discerning of spirits, tongues, and interpretation). As we lay aside weights and feed on the Word of God and grow in holiness, the Holy Spirit will arise and pour out His gifts in power through us to minister using the relevant gift as needed at the time.

LIFE: The Spirit upon us, also called the baptism of the Holy Spirit, gives more extraordinary supernatural ability to live the Christian life and to minister. On a personal level, as you fellowship with Him, He empowers you to pray supernaturally in tongues to connect to God to hear and receive truths, revelation knowledge, and quicker and more accurate answers to your prayers. His supernatural abilities will cause you to live victoriously in Christ because Christ is your life full of supernatural power. See 1 Corinthians 14; John 14; 16:13.

DECEMBER 9

THE SPIRIT UPON YOU — DAY 2

"For ye shall receive power, after that the Holy Ghost is come upon you" —Acts 1:8

TRUTH: The direct evidence of being filled with the baptism of the Holy Spirit is speaking in other tongues. See Acts 2:4, 41. There are many benefits of having the Spirit upon us. God says, *"But ye, beloved, building up yourselves on your most holy faith, praying in the Holy Ghost."* See Jude 20-21. Praying in the Holy Spirit charges us up and empowers us spiritually for God to operate more powerfully in and through us with supernatural revelation and power.

The Spirit will give us spiritual refreshing and is necessary to open the door to begin operating in the nine spiritual gifts and to endure and face challenges. See Isaiah 28:11-12; 1 Corinthians 12.

The Holy Spirit will improve our prayer life as He helps us pray and keep our prayers in line with the will of God. See Romans 8:26-28. The Holy Spirit will also help us pray out unknown mysteries and know the things we need to know to succeed, which only God knows. God will give us the answers to our impossible situations and make them possible as He gives the mind of God with solutions to our hearts. See: 1 Corinthians 14:2; Matthew 19:26; Acts 21:9-11. Praying in tongues offers pure and perfect worship unto God as through the Holy Spirit we talk to Him directly and perfectly. See 1 Corinthians 14:2.

LIFE: The Baptism of the Holy Spirit is for all believers. You will be filled with power for witnessing and service in the kingdom of God. See Acts 2:38-39. *"And these signs shall follow them THAT BELIEVE; In my name shall they cast out devils; they shall speak with new tongues...They shall lay hands on the sick; and they shall recover"* (Mark 16:17-18). Each of us must humble ourselves and put aside self-reasoning and church doctrine and accept the Word of God on the Baptism of the Holy Spirit. Believe, pray, and ask God for His gift and by faith receive that you may be the church, holy, equipped with power, without lack or blemish preparing for Christ's return. You have received Jesus as Savior and Lord now receive Him as your Baptizer. See Luke 11:9-13; Ephesians 5:26-27; John 1:33.

344 | PATRICIA MARAGH

THE WORK OF THE HOLY SPIRIT

"But the Comforter, which is the Holy Ghost, whom the Father will send in my name he shall teach you all things, and bring all things to your remembrance, whatsoever I have said unto you." —John 14:26

TRUTH AND LIFE: The Amplified Bible describes the Holy Spirit in our text above as the Counselor, Helper, Intercessor, Advocate, Strengthener, and Standby. As believers, we possess the Holy Spirit dwelling in us, and God has provided the power of the Holy Spirit to come upon us to be all the things we just mentioned. He is present to work in, with, through, and for the children of God.

- The Holy Spirit will lead one into salvation, fellowship, and relationship with the Father. See John 3:16; 17:3; Romans 10:9-10.
- The Holy Spirit helps us to give thanks and become more compassionate. See Philippians 4:6; 1 Peter 3:8-9.
- The Holy Spirit helps us to worship God. See John 4:24; Philippians 3:3.
- The Holy Spirit gives a greater desire for the Word of God. See John 14:26; 16:13; Ephesians 1:17-18.
- The Holy Spirit gives spiritual refreshing. See Isaiah 28:11-12.
- The Holy Spirit builds faith and our ability to hear from God our Father. See Jude 20; 1 Corinthians 14:12-15.
- The Holy Spirit will teach us all things and bring things to our remembrance. He also guides us into truth. See John 14:26; 16:13.
- The Holy Spirit comforts. See John 14:16, 26; Acts 9:31.
- The Holy Spirit gives power and strengthens with might. See Acts 1:8; Ephesians 3:16.
- The Holy Spirit will speak through us. See Mark 13:11.
- The Holy Spirit gives us confirmation. See 1 John 5:6.
- The Holy Spirit gives God's wisdom, understanding, and revelation of mysteries. See 1 Corinthians 2:19, 14:2.
- The Holy Spirit gives testimony of and always points to Jesus. See John 15:26.

WORK OF THE HOLY SPIRIT — DAY 2

"...The Holy Ghost, whom the Father will send...
shall teach you all things..." —John 14:26

TRUTH AND LIFE:

- The Holy Spirit guides us into all truth and shows us things to come. See John 16:13-14.
- The Holy Spirit will help us pray when we do not know how to pray. See Romans 8:26-28; 1 Corinthians 14:14-15.
- The Holy Spirit gives us the power to live the Christian life. See 1 Peter 1:5.
- The Holy Spirit opens eyes and hearts to convict us. See Luke 24:32.
- The Holy Spirit helps our infirmities and weaknesses. See Romans 8:26.
- The Holy Spirit reproves the world of sin, believers of their righteousness, and the truth that Satan has been judged a defeated foe. See John 16:8-11.
- The Holy Spirit helps us yield and obey the Father. See Philippians 2:13.
- The Holy Spirit is the anointing abiding in us to destroy every yoke in us. See Isaiah 10:27; 1 John 2:27.
- The Holy Spirit helps us with sanctification. See John 15:2; 1 Thessalonians 5:23.
- The Holy Spirit helps us focus more on eternal things than on temporal things. See 2 Corinthians 4:18.
- The Holy Spirit leads us continually. See Romans 8:14.
- The Holy Spirit gives us power and authority in the name and the Blood of Jesus over Satan and all evil. See Luke 10:19.

As the Holy Spirit hovered the face of the waters at creation, so let Him hover over your life situations causing you to stand, abide, and overcome. As you acknowledge, recognize, fellowship, and receive the Holy Spirit, you will be guided and helped by Him. In every decision and area of your life that you surrender to Him and abide in Him by His Word, He will bring the power of Jesus to deliver and for you to take His power to minister to the world who needs Him.

SIGNS FOLLOWING

"And these signs shall follow them that believe; In my
name shall they cast out devils." —Mark 16:17

TRUTH: This verse is the Word of God to all believers. In Christ, we know the Holy Spirit, the greater One full of resurrection power, lives in us to cause signs and miracles to follow us. We know the Holy Spirit who lives in us is God Himself, full of power and might. So, why are we limited in working signs as the disciples did? What stood out to me is that they all went through the process of sanctification. They were sanctified by Jesus, the Living Word, and the Holy Spirit, yielding to a change in their character as with Peter the Apostle who cut off the soldier's ear, denied Jesus, tried to stop Jesus from going to the Cross; Saul who, after he changed direction from a murderer and a legalist in doctrine, became the Apostle Paul; and John Mark over whom a dispute ensued between Paul and Barnabas for his lack of usefulness. See Acts 15:36-41. He became useful later, as seen in 2 Timothy 4:11. When born again, we are made holy and unblameable in our spirit, but our soul is not saved and still has remnants of the old man, the old mindsets we had before our salvation, which the Word must purify for us to think and act like Jesus. See John 4:23-24.

LIFE: For us to do the greater works and have signs follow us, we too must:

- Be sanctified in our souls and bodies unto holiness and be renewed in our minds, transformed from the old man to the new man in Christ. See Romans 12:1-2; Ephesians 4:20-25.
- Become dead to sin and self, dead to the opinions of man. See Romans 6; Proverbs 29:25-26.
- Be dead to the world and its ways. See John 17:15-17.
- Be dead to the fear of Satan and his demons. See Luke 10:19; Mark 5:2-6.

When sanctified, the Spirit can arise in us unhindered to make us whole and operate in and through us with signs following. Be prepared!

JESUS IS GREATER

"If God be for us, who can be against us?" —Romans 8:31

TRUTH: God, the Anointing in us, is greater than all. He is greater than Satan and any force which can come against us. Our God is all-powerful, all-knowing, all-present, infinite, and He loves us. He says, *"Call unto me, and I will answer thee, and shew thee great and mighty things, which thou knowest not"* (Jeremiah 33:3). Satan tries his best to assert himself to dominate our soul (mind, will, and emotions) to cause us to think and feel that he has the upper hand in our life outcomes. But he does not; we must believe God for whom He says He is to us, in His character and His Word.

Our Father tells us He is greater than all. When thoughts, feelings, and situations of sickness, anxiety, fear, lack, strife, and oppression assail us, they contradict the truth that God is greater. We overcome and win in Christ as we stand our ground and keep our focus on Jesus and our unity with His Spirit and His Word. Stand in the victory Christ imputed to us; speak and abide in His Word and receive amid the enemy's attack. *"And what is the exceeding greatness of his power to us-ward who believe, according to the working of his mighty power"* (Ephesians 1:19). As we submit to God and stand on God's Word in faith, the Holy Spirit will arise in power within and begin to rid our soul of every contrary belief. Our God is greater than Satan and all his hosts in hell. Our God's grace is greater than sin, and His healing power is greater than sickness. His ability to provide, deliver, and protect is greater than Satan's lack. Our God is greater than all. Believe it! The greatest battle is for God's will to be stronger than our human will. Surrender it to Him. See 2 Chronicles 29:31; Psalm 40:8; Luke 22:42; John 5:30; 6:38; 7:16-19.

LIFE: *"I shall not be afraid of evil tidings; my heart is fixed, trusting in the Lord."* Psalm 112:7 Meditate on 1 John 4:4; Luke 4:18-19; 10:18-19; Philippians 2:9-11; Psalm 107:2; 112:7; John 15:7; Revelation 12:11. Jesus said it, I believe it, and I claim my victory in His name because He's greater than all. Amen.

FREEDOM

"Stand fast therefore in the liberty wherewith Christ has made us free."
—Galatians 5:1

TRUTH: We have so far seen that God in Jesus has freed us from sin, sickness, death, the Law, and now from Satan himself. In the love of God, we are freed from fear, Satan's main weapon to infiltrate our souls. See Colossians 1:13-14, 2:15; 2 Timothy 1:7; 1 John 4:18. Satan cannot have access to harm us unless we yield to fear; therefore, he forces himself on us with negative thoughts, feelings, and situations to try to get us to be afraid. But God's love given in repentance, forgiveness, abiding faith in God's grace, the anointing of the Holy Spirit, our new identity in Christ, exercising spiritual disciplines such as prayer in the power of the Holy Spirit, the Blood of Jesus, and the casting of cares, the surrender of our human will has destroyed his power over us. See 1 John 1:7-9; Matthew 18:34-35; John 15:7; Ephesians 2:8; 2 Corinthians 5:17; James 1:22; 2 Corinthians 3:17; Revelation 12:11; 1 Peter 5:7. As we abide in Christ's love, recognize, resist, reject, and cast out all fear by the name and the Blood of Jesus, we will be free. If he entered by sin or a curse, he must be ejected by repentance or be cast out.

The love of God, which gave us the New Covenant of grace with a new Law of love in John 13:34, has freed us from the Law of Moses and hence from the dominion of selfishness, pride, and Satan. Jesus' love made us righteous, in right standing with the Father, loved, accepted, and in peace. See 2 Corinthians 5:21; Ephesians 1:6; Romans 5:1. Grace, therefore, has freed our hearts and human will unto God in loving dependence and from the bondage of Satan's control with independence, self-effort or self-righteousness, and self-motivation.

LIFE: Submit to God, resist the devil, and he will flee. There is power and freedom in humility, surrender, abiding in Christ, and our authority. See John 15:7. You are freed unto God from Satan. Receive your freedom as you yield to God's Spirit, obey, and abide in His Word and His love. Love expressed gives freedom as love never fails.

FREEDOM — DAY 2

*"Stand fast therefore in the liberty wherewith Christ
hath made us free."* —Galatians 5:1

TRUTH: The Oxford dictionary defines freedom as the power or right to act, speak, or think freely. To some, being free is the unrestricted use of something. The Gospel of the kingdom of God is countercultural to the world's thinking. God gave us His love in a King named Jesus to set us free. Jesus then told His followers that the way to increase is to decrease; to live is to die; to receive is to give; to be strong, one must be weak; to be exalted, one must be humble; and we rule by serving. If we yield to Jesus, His love frees us to love the Father with all the heart, mind, soul, and body. We will receive from Him to love others and free us from Satan's attacks. We can receive and walk in God's freedom as we assume the responsibility to obey His command to love. Love begets holiness and holiness freedom. See John 14:30.

God, in His great love, sent Jesus who died to free us from sin upon repentance and to receive forgiveness. We were freed when given Jesus' righteousness we could approach and relate to God, loving Him with gratitude, confidence, and peace. Scripture tells us God has removed sin far from us and will never hold it against us. See Isaiah 43:25; Psalm 103:12; Romans 4:8; 2 Corinthians 5:19; Hebrews 9:14, 10:2. Blessed are the pure in heart, for they shall see God. See Matthew 5:8. God in His great love in Christ Jesus freed us from spiritual death when He gave us eternal life and by His stripes freed us from sickness and death. Death here can refer to any negative consequence from the curse, poverty, bad relationships, worry or fear. In Christ Jesus, we are free in our spirit, and we can be free from anything that tries to hinder or harm us in our soul and body. We maintain our freedom through God in the love of Christ Jesus as we abide in Him. See Colossians 2:6.

LIFE: Meditate on John 8:32, 36; John 10:10; Romans 8:1-2; Galatians 5:1; 2 Corinthians 3:17.

WALK FREE IN CHRIST

"...Wherewith Christ hath made us free..." —Galatians 5:1

TRUTH: When Satan is attacking with agitation and torment, trying to get us to act in impatience, we must ask the Lord to give us wisdom according to His will to stop us from yielding to any wrong leading. Stay in prayer, fellowship, and listen as we watch for open doors or opportunities towards the direction God wants us to take and follow His lead. We do not have to be absolutely 100% sure of what God says and be entirely certain before we can obey God and close the door to Satan's torment.

We must only be willing to step out in faith on what we understand, and God will do the rest, even redirect us. Genesis 22:8; Philippians 1:6; 2:13. Satan has no place trying to lead God's children by getting us to be so afraid of disobedience and sin that he coerces us to quickly yield to him just to avoid or to end his agitation and torment.

Scripture says the just shall live by faith. See Galatians 3:11. And the sons of God are led by the Spirit of God See Romans 8:14. God is pleased with our faith and willingness to follow and depend on Him to lead us by His Spirit and not our perfect obedience. Take steps of faith in a relationship with God led by the Holy Spirit. Hear, abide, and follow God's guidance, and He will honor us with wisdom, knowledge, and understanding, and guidance always leading us into truth and victory. See Psalms 27:11; 32:8; John 16:13.

LIFE: Prayer: *"Cause me to hear thy lovingkindness in the morning; for in thee do I trust, cause me to know the way wherein I should walk; for I lift up my soul to thee. Deliver me, O Lord, from my enemies: I flee unto thee to hide me. Teach me to do thy will; for thou art my God: thy spirit is good: lead me into the land of uprightness. Quicken me, O Lord for thy name's sake: for thy righteousness' sake bring my soul out of trouble"* (Psalm 143:8-11).

LOVE MAKES US CONQUERORS

"Nay, in all these things we are more than conquerors through him that loved us." —Romans 8:37

TRUTH: Jesus rose from the grave with resurrection power, conquering death, hell, and the grave and gave us His righteousness, the very love of the Father. His love not only conquered for us when He raised us in Himself, but He also equipped us as conquerors, not as victims. We begin to conquer when our hope is always in God. *"Why art thou cast down, O my soul? and why art thou disquieted in me? hope thou in God"* (Psalm 42:5). Our hope and faith in God the Father through Jesus, His grace, the Living Word, brings the power of His Spirit on the scene to build faith and trust. He promised never to leave us or forsake us and fight for us. *"The Lord shall fight for you, and ye shall hold your peace"* (Exodus 14:14).

God's love assures us that we can hope in Him, look to Him in faith, abide in Him, and believe in Him to deliver us. Because it is His love which gave us His life within us, making us one spirit with Him, faith comes so we can stand against any force of darkness and trust we will conqueror. Romans 8:35 says nothing can separate us from the love of God—neither tribulation, distress, persecutions, famine, nakedness, peril, or sword. Nothing that we face will we have to face alone or be afraid. See 1 John 4:18. For believers who love God and have faith, we will always have His love to care for us and to work things out for our good. Jesus conquered for us and will always move on our behalf to make us more than conquerors. At times you may be overwhelmed or distressed, but believe His love, be seated with Christ at the right hand of God, abide in Him standing on His Word, refuse to be moved, and conquer. Jesus conquered and we were adopted to claim the spoils. That makes us more than conquerors.

LIFE: Meditate on Ephesians 1:19-23; Colossians 2:15; Romans 8:28.

OVERCOMERS

"Nay, in all these things we are more than conquerors through him that loved us." —Romans 8:37

TRUTH: Life is made up of challenges, triumphs, and difficulties. Trouble, hardships, tests, and trials abound, and we all try to do our best in each situation; but we must turn to God for His wisdom to do our best and overcome. As we trust God for His help, we can overcome every hardship that comes our way. Our text says that IN ALL things, we can have God's continual presence, help, and wisdom to be conquerors and overcomers from our enemies. See 2 Kings 7.

We are conquerors because Jesus went before us and conquered Satan, sin, death, and the Law and freed us from their tyrannical rule. This God did through Jesus' death and resurrection, providing everything we would need to sustain us and for us to overcome.

But we are more than conquerors because He also gave us His faith (see Galatians 5:22; Romans 12:3) for us to develop and take hold of all He has provided by His grace. We are in Christ; we are not alone; as we abide in Him, having the faith of Jesus, God will fight for us. See Exodus 14:14; 1 John 5:4-5. Satan, our enemy will try to stop us with sickness, poverty, sin, oppression, and affliction, but through Christ and His shed Blood, we overcome. We have the power in the life of Christ in His name as Lord and in His Blood for us to both submit to God and to stand immovable on the authority of His Word, resist the evil one, overcome and walk forward in victory. We are the head and not the tail, and we will prosper and overcome as our soul prospers. See Deuteronomy 28:13; 3 John 2.

LIFE: Stand steadfast and look at Jesus and receive the power from the Cross. Surrender fully to Him draw strength from His resurrection power and believe that He gave us victory for all our needs to be met. And so, faith take it NOW! *"Now thanks be unto God, which always causeth us to triumph in Christ, and maketh manifest the Savour of his knowledge by us"* (2 Corinthians 2:14).

AN OVERCOMING MIND

*"I have written unto you, young men...and the word of God abideth in you, and ye have overcome the wicked one." —*1 John 2:14b

TRUTH: As Christians, if we are not careful, we can fall into a life of self-righteousness based on what we do, making our confessions, or trying hard in our strength to walk in love so as not to hinder our faith. We may try to build ourselves up spiritually by what we do in our faith walk. We may be binding and loosing indiscriminately because we forget to hold on to grace from the Cross and rest in our relationship with the Father by His Spirit in faith. Instead of self-righteous actions, trusting God, staying in His Word, believing, speaking, and abiding in Him will give us an overcoming mind.

We must not get lulled into Christian passivity, practicing Christian disciplines and working hard to be pleasing to God. Bible disciplines are good and necessary, but if we neglect relationship by abiding in Jesus the Living Word first, we could become hindered by operating in our strength and prevented from overcoming, as whatever is not of faith is sin. An overcoming mind requires a relationship with Jesus, faith in His work on the Cross, and His written Word. Our faith is to be birthed in and lives out of our love relationship with the Father. See Romans 10:17; Galatians 5:6. You were saved when you believed in Jesus. That's a relationship. We overcome in surrender and dependence to the gospel of the Cross as we hear, believe, abide in connection, and do God's Word. Christ delivered us from the kingdom of darkness and placed us into the kingdom of God legally, but we must maintain an overcoming mind that we are over in the light, above and not beneath. See John 8:12; Acts 2:17-19. There is great power in surrender to the God of light, as darkness flees. We walk in Christ's victory at the Cross, His resurrection, grace through faith. In His strength, we rejoice and overcome.

LIFE: We have the victory. Speak, overcoming Scriptures sing, rejoice, and laugh at The devil as the overcomer you are. Psalm 107:1-2; Luke 1:37; John 8:12, 32, 36; Romans 8:15, 31, 37; 1 Corinthians 2:16; 2 Corinthians 2:14; 15:57;1 John 4:4-5.

OVERCOME BY THE BLOOD

"And they overcame him by the blood of the lamb." —Revelation 12:11

TRUTH: All believers overcome Satan by the Blood of Jesus when His shed Blood destroyed Satan's power of sin over us and redeemed us unto God. See Psalm 107:2; Romans 8:37; 1 John 5:4-5. We overcome because the Blood of Jesus on the Cross separated us from the powers of Satan and His kingdom of darkness and gave us divine protection. God established us in the Kingdom of His Son filled with His life and light. It was the Blood of Jesus who forgave all our sins, justified us, and made us righteous, restored us into a love relationship, and in right standing with the Father to live in God's fullness.

When we receive our Father's love by faith, abiding in His Word, we are walking in the Spirit of truth. Satan, therefore, cannot accuse us or bring any charge or condemnation to stand against us. He cannot destabilize our relationship with the Father by causing us to feel unloved or neglected and to have feelings of unworthiness and insecurity. These negative feelings can only come if we seek to be loved by our Father or walk in our strength in the flesh. We are to depend only on what Jesus did for us by His shed Blood.

We walk in a relationship by faith in God's grace, trusting Jesus, in His Word of truth, and as we do, we're walking in the Spirit, and the faith given us by the Blood of Jesus overcomes Satan. See Mark 11:22-24. He has nothing on us to defeat us, just as he had nothing on Jesus. See John 1:33. If there is sin in our life, let repentance, renouncing, and forgiveness made available by the Blood cleanses us of all unrighteousness. And if struggling with temptations, run to His throne of grace. The power in His Blood will provide help in your need. See Hebrews 4:16.

LIFE: Resting in God's grace in a love relationship, by faith in Jesus, God's Word, His righteousness by faith, the power of His Spirit, abiding in Christ, repentance, and forgiveness, all provided by the Blood shuts down Satan and will cause you to overcome, gain victory, freedom, and your eternal reward. See Revelation 3:21.

OVERCOME BY THE WORD

"And they overcame him by...the word of their testimony..." —Revelation 12:11

TRUTH: The second way Scripture says we overcome is by the power of the word of our testimony. Testimony builds faith, not only in our hearts but also in the hearts of those who hear and believe that Jesus is real in our lives today. Let the testimony of our salvation, healing, and deliverance help others believe in Jesus and overcome their bondage of sin and death. See John 3:3, 16-18; John 6:37, 14:6; Romans 10:9-10.

We overcome as we build our faith in the Word of God and speak the Word we believe as truth, *"I have written unto you, young men, because ye are strong, and the word of God abideth in you, and ye have overcome the wicked one* (1 John 2:14b). Whenever we face a challenge in our life, always run to God in His Word first and read, hear, believe, speak and abide in the Word while anchoring our hearts in all that was accomplished at the Cross. Jesus overcame the devil by anchoring His faith in God and His written Word. See Matthew 4:1-11. Satan is a liar, and the Word of God as the sword of the Spirit is truth to cut away lies. See Ephesians 6:17. The truth of God's Word believed, abiding in our hearts, and spoken by our mouths cuts against Satan's attacks and defeats him. Thirdly, as the last two lines of Revelation 12:11 say, we overcome by not giving in to the fear of missing out by being afraid to die. Earth is not our home because we have an eternal destiny in heaven. See Luke 14:26; Acts 20:24; John 14:2-3.

LIFE: I have Jesus as my righteousness, I will take the Word of God and point it to Jesus as a reminder of what He said to me. As I stand steadfast speaking what I want to see, despite the circumstance or the feelings I have, I will overcome them. It is God's truth in His Word which I believe and speak which will set me free. See John 8:32, 36. Jesus as my righteousness will work to make all things right for me according to His Word. See Psalm 34:17.

WALK FREE FROM BONDAGE

"Stand fast therefore in the liberty wherewith Christ hath made us free, and be not entangled again with the yoke of bondage." —Galatians 5:1

TRUTH: Christ defeated Satan and gave us power over him. If you sense this is not true in your Christian life, it means you believe a lie somewhere or not abiding in Christ. One big lie the enemy tells us is that we cannot get rid of him for us to be at peace. Do we wonder why we cannot encounter him incidentally when he attacks, instead of him being like a fixture in our life with worry and fear? We must cut the tie and be separated from his darkness. We must expose his lies, speak God's Word as truth, and abide in our union relationship with Jesus as our righteousness. We must surrender our human will inclined to self-righteousness for Jesus' righteousness and believe we have been made free by God's power in the anointing. We must believe that the greater One in us overcame all not by our might or by our power but by God's Spirit, and He will cause us to walk free from all bondage. See Zechariah 4:6; 1 John 4:4.

Acknowledge our oneness with the Father, His greatness in us, and our new identity with our Heavenly Father frees us as the redeemed to sit in victory with Him in the heavenlies. Psalms 71 and 89. Two's a company, and three's a crowd, so command the third wheel, Satan, to leave from God's presence in and with you. Declare you have been established in righteousness, not performance and you shall not fear. Abide "in Christ," speak the Word, and be not moved. See Romans 8:16-17.

LIFE: Tell Satan, "My God, the Anointing in me, is greater than you and all your hosts of hell, greater than sickness, greater than lack, greater than oppression and anything you throw at me. So, I will stand in union with my Father and abide in His Word until you, Satan the lessor, bow to the Greater One in me. Bow to His resurrection power in the name of Jesus Christ my Lord because Christ redeemed me, and I say so. I worship my Lord, my deliverer, and command all bondages to GO!" See: Isaiah 10:27; Philippians 2:9-10; 2 Timothy 1:7.

WALK FREE FROM BONDAGE — DAY 2

"Stand fast therefore in the liberty wherewith Christ
hath made us free..." —Galatians 5:1

TRUTH: We have liberty and freedom given us by the Blood of Jesus. At times, Satan will lie to us that the Holy Spirit is whipping us back into shape and righteousness. It is a lie; it is Satan himself. We are children of God, and no stranger should be correcting us. The Holy Spirit is the one who convicts us of righteousness, never of sin. See John 10:3-5. The world, in John 16:8, is referring to the sinner. He convicts the sinner of sin. Jesus spoke about us, the believer, in verse 10. Remember Jesus cast our sin as far as the east is from the west. It is also the Blood of Jesus which keeps us free, not our actions or performance. See John 8:32, 36; 2 Corinthians 3:16-17; Romans 8:2; 1 Peter 1:5.

Take authority over the enemy's attack lying to you that you missed it or sinned, and therefore Satan has a right to attack you. This is a lie because Jesus purchased you for a price, you belong to Him, and your sin is between you and God alone. Jesus is your righteousness. As we quickly submit, in repentance, forgiveness, and walking in love, He makes things right in our lives without suffering, torment, or condemnation. See 1 John 4:18; Romans 8:1-2. As believers, we stand in faith, seeing Jesus alone as the One who is right, and believe in His righteousness to help us do right in life. Faith in repentance, forgiveness, abiding in Christ, and trusting God's love will cause us to walk free from Satan and his bondages, including condemnation.

LIFE: We are to maintain our personal relationship always, talking to our Heavenly Father about everything. We hear, abide, yield, and obey. See: 1 Thessalonians 5:17; Psalm 23. It is not about us being or behaving perfect by not sinning, but that Jesus' righteousness in us causing us by His Spirit to do right, even leading us to repent. Repentance, renouncing of sin, and embracing the fullness of God's love in His Spirit's power makes us free from Satan's bondages.

SHOUT THE WALLS DOWN

"Joshua, said unto the people, Shout; for the Lord hath given you the city." —Joshua 6:16

TRUTH: As believers, at times, we may not be overcoming with the victory Christ provided when He overcame for us. Christ walked effortlessly in the things of God, working with and doing the works of God, while we seem to have such a hard time. Like Jesus, we also have the enemies of our soul, Satan, sin, death, Law mentality, and the world; but we are not dealing effectively with the enemies of our souls. God told Joshua He had given the city into his hands, but he had to obey God and march and shout to overcome his enemies.

Joshua circled the city of Jericho once per day, but on the last day, they were told to circle the city not once but seven times before they shouted, and the walls came down. As we trust God for the manifestation of our victory, we must be prepared to increase our persistency, intensity, and volume in speaking while trusting God to act—just as Joshua obeyed and circled seven times before he SHOUTED. He did not just confess Scriptures, pray, and praise God...no! He was told to shout, and the walls came down.

The bigger our problem and the longer its duration, the more consistent we must be in the Word of God, and the bigger our shout needs to be, in prayer and praise, to put the situation under our feet. In Hebrews 11:30, Joshua believed and did just as God said, and he got the victory. Get over thinking about what others may say, rejoice, go forward in the Word, face the enemy, circle him with the Word in God's strength and power, and shout unto God your deliverer!

LIFE: As many obstacles come against you, abide in Him, see God as bigger, hear from Him how to proceed, trust His Words, do as He says and lift your voice and shout all the way along the victory path told unto you by His Word or His Spirit because the truth of God's Word is greater than Satan. Let your praise and worship defeat the enemy of your soul with a SHOUT! Hallelujah!

GOD MEETS MAN

"Therefore also that holy thing which shall be born of thee
shall be called the Son of God." —Luke 1:35b

TRUTH: The virgin birth is still one of the mysteries of the gospel that many people, especially other religions, do not understand or want to accept. This keeps them from Jesus. The sin of humanity in the garden of Eden severed close fellowship with God because He is holy and could not be one in spirit with sinful man. With sin in man's heart, God could not find a sinless human being to pay the penalty of death for sin. He had to sacrifice His only sinless Son to pay the price for sin. See Romans 6:23. When Mary accepted the invitation to bear the Christ-child, His birth and sinless life meant God could once again create a path to have a union relationship with humankind. If after His resurrection they believe in Jesus His Son for salvation.

Jesus, the divine Son of God, took on flesh and became a new species of the divine, the Son of man, able to make us sons of God. See John 1:14; Matthew 8:11; John 1:12. Jesus, the Godman, bridged the gap of separation between God and man and became our mediator, reconciling man to God. See Hebrews 8:6. He was touched with our flaws and frailties so He can relate to us as our Savior, forgiving our sins, and as Lord, watching over our wellbeing. See Hebrews 4:15; 9:12.

God had to become a man to save us. *"Who, being in the form of God, thought it not robbery to be equal with God: but made himself of no reputation, and took upon him the form of a servant, and was made in the likeness of men..."* (Philippians 2:6-7).

LIFE: Jesus facilitated God's involvement to both indwell and flow through us by His Spirit. See John 4:14; 7:38. Because of Jesus the Godman, we can forever be identified with God the Father as sons and daughters, one in spirit and headed for one destiny in heaven. See John 14:2-3. We have good reason to celebrate His birth as the Prince of our Peace and share His love this joyous Christmas season.

KING WORTHY OF WORSHIP

"Where is he that is born King of the Jews? for we have seen his star in the east, and are come to worship him." —Matthew 2:2

TRUTH: Kings of old had complete power, authority, and control of their kingdom and people. This concept is lost to our modern way of thinking as we crave and demand democracy, autonomy, independence, and freedom. But we were created by God and for God. See Colossians 1:16-17.

As children of God, He is our King, and He rules our lives. To gain access to, enter, and prosper in the Kingdom of God, we must surrender to Jesus as Savior, Lord, and King.

"Now unto the King eternal, immortal, invisible, the only wise God, be honor and glory for ever and ever. Amen" (1 Timothy 1:17).

Jesus is Lord and king when His Word rules our hearts first and foremost. And we allow honor and worship to flow from a heart of humility, which acknowledges Jesus by His Spirit as the greater One worthy of worship. We worship our Father God as we acknowledge and receive His sacrifice, His full package from the Cross to the ascension in the gifts of salvation, Jesus' righteousness in the fruit of the Spirit, and His Gifts of the Holy Spirit.

Our worship should flow from a heart of faith that knows God's love and care for us and that He will never fail us. He is faithful and true. The Word says, in the mouth of two or three witnesses shall every Word be established that He's worthy to be worshipped. See 2 Corinthians 13:1; John 4:23; Revelation 5:12-13.

LIFE: *"Thou art worthy, O Lord, to receive glory and honor and power: for thou hast created all things, for thy pleasure they are and were created. And every creature... heard I saying, Blessing, and honor, and glory, and power, be unto him that sitteth upon the throne, and unto the Lamb forever and ever"* (Revelation 4:11, 5:13).

KING WORTHY OF WORSHIP — DAY 2

"...And are come to worship Him." —Matthew 2:2b

TRUTH AND LIFE: God is worthy to be worshipped.

- He is the owner of heaven and earth with blessings to give. See Psalms 24:1; 89:11; 115:14; Acts 7:49-50.
- He is our King to whom we belong. See 1 Corinthians 3:16, 17; 6:19-20; Titus 2:14.
- He is Master over all His creation. See Romans 11:36; Colossians 1:16-17; 1 Corinthians 13:22-23.
- He is a God of integrity. His Word is truth, always whole and complete, and it must be believed. See John 8:40; 14:23-24; 17:17.
- He loves to bless His people who honor Him. See Psalms 34:10; 37:3-4; 1 Peter 3:12.
- He assumes full responsibility for our care. See Deuteronomy 7:13-15; Psalms 23; 48:14.
- He is all-powerful and competent to protect us. See Psalms 91; 34:17; Jeremiah 32:17.
- He meets all needs; we are to have no fear of lack. See Psalms 35:27; 37:25.
- He is our sufficiency. See 2 Corinthians 3:5; Philippians 1:19; John 15:5.
- He is our Strength. See Psalms 18:2; 49:1-2; 29:11.
- He will keep our feet from falling. See Psalm 56:13; Romans 14:4; Jude 24.
- God is our King, not to be ignored in good times and rushed to when things are bad or wondering where He is when needed. Psalm 73:26.

Lord, You are my strength, worthy of all praise and worship for all Your marvelous works in my life. Father, You are in complete control of Your kingdom, to which I belong. You are my King, and I bow to worship You. See Philippians 2:10.

Lord, Your kingdom is at hand. I worship You and await Your glory in the earth, showing forth signs, wonders, and miracles declaring Your greatness!

WE HAVE THE VICTORY

"But thanks be to God, which giveth us the victory through our Lord Jesus Christ." —1 Corinthians 15:57

TRUTH: Jesus is our redeemer. His resurrection made us victorious over Satan, sin, death, and the Law when He arose from the grave. He removed the old and made us new in our hearts by His Holy Spirit's indwelling presence and gave us a New Covenant and gave us victory. We were born in sin and shapen in iniquity. Our sinful hearts would have condemned us to continue sinning and destiny in hell. But Jesus by His Blood made us new, and His Spirit in us made us free! We have victory over sin. Jesus, our Savior, became sin and freed us from sin and all its power and consequences such as guilt, condemnation, and death. See Romans 6; 1 John 5:4-5. His resurrection justified, forgave, and made us innocent, righteous, holy, and reconciled into the Father's heart of love. We are the righteousness of God in Christ, and we reign in life in His Kingdom with resurrection power by faith, seated with Christ above. God's gift of righteousness gave us victory over condemnation from the enemy. See Romans 8:1-2

With the Holy Spirit within our spirit, God can now begin to lead us in His ways to the Father. We must believe this by faith that Jesus is our justifier, and legally from the Cross, we are dead to Satan's accusations that we are justified in our performance by the Law. Tell him you are justified only by the Blood of Jesus. He did it all for us and gave us the victory of eternal life. See John 17:3; 1 Corinthians 15:54-57. Jesus' crucifixion and burial gave us victory over the old man of the flesh, Satan, and the world. See Romans 6. His exaltation raised us seated in Christ at the Father's right hand in dominion over Satan.

Christ by His Spirit in His anointing leads us in our daily life to give us His life, for us to reign in life in overflowing victory.

LIFE: Let the life of God in your spirit give you eternal life now, and all God's blessings until eternity. Meditate on Colossians 1: 12-14.

WE HAVE THE VICTORY — DAY 2

"Which giveth us the victory through our Lord Jesus Christ." —1 Corinthians 15:57b

TRUTH: God by His Holy Spirit and the Word who helps us maintain the victory as we obey and take His help to drop off the old sinful habits and take on the right ones. God's sanctification or purification by His Spirit declutters the soul so that God in relationship with us can arise from within our human spirit and help us to hear, obey, abide, and follow Him. The more we are freed unto God through Jesus, we will have continuous victory. See 1 John 5:4-5; 2 Corinthians 2:14.

We have victory over the Law. The Law refers to the Ten Commandments. The Law was given for humanity to show their love for God and man by obeying it perfectly. God knew man could not keep the Law perfectly, but that man would come to Him in seeing their weakness and futility. Instead, man doubled down and tried harder to keep the Law while continuing to ignore God's love and leadership by His Holy Spirit.

The Law kept the human will of a man tied to self and sin, operating in self-righteousness, doing things their way and in their timing. When God sent Jesus, He blotted out the handwriting of ordinances (the Law) that was against us, which was contrary to us, and took it out of the way, nailing it to the Cross. See Colossians 2:14-15. On the Cross, Jesus fulfilled the Law that man could not keep. See John 7:19. When Jesus ascended, He promised the Holy Spirit who will lead us to Jesus, and into truth and freedom. John 8: 32,36.

LIFE: We are free from the Law which tied us to self-will. See 2 Peter 2:10. We are free unto God the Father, as we are led by the Word and the Holy Spirit into God's will, keeping us victorious in Christ Jesus. See Exodus 20; John 7:19; 14:17, 26; John 16:13; 1 Corinthians 15:21-22; John 14:16-26; 16:13; Acts 1.

EXALTED IN CHRIST

"Wherefore God also hath highly exalted him and given him a name which is above every name..." —Philippians 2:9-10

TRUTH: We are raised with Christ as one spirit. See 1 Corinthians 6:17. It is God Himself who called us and raised us in a union relationship to share the life of His Son in victory as we, by faith depend on Jesus to meet our every need. See 1 Peter 1:1-3. We are seated in victory with Christ. From this secret place, of union, one heart with Christ Jesus we abide and rest. We believe and speak His Word in faith and refuse to be moved as we stand victorious.

LIFE: I am a child of God, exalted in Christ, secure in His love and care, and led by His Holy Spirit in righteousness and peace. See Isaiah 54:14.

- I am one spirit with God in Christ Jesus and as He is free from (name problem) so am I. His Word lifts me up. See 1 John 4:17.
- My Lord Jesus Christ is exalted above every name that is named, and I am exalted with Him. Satan is under my feet. See Philippians 2:9-10.
- I overcome the evil one and rejoice because my God is greater than all. I magnify and exalt Jesus above (name situation). See Luke 10:19.
- The anointing in me is greater than (fill in the blank). The Blood of Jesus silences and rejects the voice of the accuser in Jesus' name. See 1 John 2:27.
- I exalt Jesus in my thought life and cast on Him all my cares (name them). I reject the spirit of worry and fear and command you to leave now as I abide in Christ Jesus, resting in Him and trusting Him to care for me, I am freed from fear. See 1 Peter 5:7; 2 Timothy 1:7.
- The exalted Christ my elder brother loves me, and no one can pluck me from His hand, and no weapon formed against me can prosper. See Isaiah 54:17. I abide in His Word as true and will not be moved. See Psalm 108:1.
- I am delivered from the kingdom of darkness and from fear and made partaker of Christ's righteousness and peace. See Colossians 1:12-13; 1 Timothy 1:7.
- I choose the voice of the Holy Spirit and reject agitation in the enemy's voice because God's love in me rejects all fear. Christ is exalted above all, and in Him, I have the victory.

IT IS WELL

*"And brought him to his mother... and then died...Is it well
with the child?...It is well."* —2 Kings 4:20, 26

TRUTH: The prophet Elisha visited Shunem, where a woman housed and fed him. In return, Elisha asked her what he could do to bless her. Elisha's servant Gehazi answered that she did not have a son. Elisha called her and prophesied the blessing of a son to her. Later, the son died. On her way to see Elisha to report her grief and ask for deliverance, she was asked if all is well. Read the entire story in verses 10-37. In the greatest trial of her life, she replied, "It is well." What made her say it was well?

We can say it might have been because she had faith in Elisha's love and care for her. Maybe, she knew he possessed the power to reverse her situation even if her faith was not strong. (Notice she did not take the staff herself to lay on the child). Yet she remained steadfast in her belief for her son's life. She believed Elisha's God and called those things which be not as though they were. See Romans 4:17. As believers, we must believe and speak as this Shunammite woman because our life is hidden in Christ, hidden in the depth of His love where we abide, and where Christ is our all in all. Our assurance that He is working things for our good, is to be so strong that when we face our greatest trials, in the depths of the darkness in our soul, when we cannot see but we can still look to God our Father of light and say, Jesus, You're my light of life and "all is well" because we know He loves us and will work out all things for our good. See Jeremiah 32:41-41; Romans 8:28; John 1:4. Take God at His Word, believe Him, abide in Him, trust in Him, yield to the leading of His spirit, to do as He says, and all will be well.

LIFE: I have set the Lord before me; I rest in His love and light. I shall not be moved, so situations of darkness around me must flee. As I abide in Christ and my thoughts and words become aligned with what God says, the only plausible belief I have in every situation is "It is well." Jesus is Lord of everything (name the situation and speak the relevant Scriptures) therefore I am afraid of nothing. As I stand in faith and abide in His truth, Jesus goes to work on my behalf, He becomes my life, and all is well. Meditate on Psalm 16:8-11.

REFERENCES

Excuses – January 2, 24; May 10; August 12; September 23

Faith – March 21-28; April 5, 30-31; June 7-10

Faithful/ness – January 13; September 19; October 17-18; November 19

Fear – July 14, 17-24; November 3-4, 18-19

Fear of the Lord – January 15-21; April 20; June 20

Fire – April 28; September 4-6, 8

Freedom – January 26; February 21; December 14-16, 22-23

Food as temptation- May 7; August 23; September 21

Forget – May 1, 3-4; November 15; December 19

Forgive/n/ness – January 23-25, 26-28; February 16; March 15; April 8-9

Fruit of Spirit – September 9-24

God – January 4, 29-30; February 1-3; August 16-19; September 9; October 3, 5-6; December 25

God's Word – February 4-5; April 5; May 10; June 1-6; October 31

Gentleness – April 2; September 16, 20; December 7

Giving – July 15-16

Goodness – August 22; September 17-18

Glory – August 1-2

Grace – January 7-8; February 24-25; May 18, 21-21, 23; June 29-30; July 2-9, 15, 29; November 6

Greater One – August 20-21

Growing Up Spiritually – June 17-18

Healing – October 11-14

Heart – January 10-11; February 27-28; June 14, 18

Holy Spirit – April 29-30; August 20-21; September 25-26; October 25; December 1, 5-12

Honesty – June 20; October 19

Honor – January 11, 15, 19; February 25; June 28; August 14

Humility – May 5-6; June 20, 26-27; August 5-6; September 20

Peace – March 16; September 12-14; November 15

Poor in Spirit – February 18-19

Power – April 4-10, 19; May 18-19; June 2, 4; July 19-21, 23-24; August 15; November 7-8, 11-13; December 8-9

Praise/Worship – May 12-13; September 27-28; October 15-16

Prayer – January 1, 6, 11, 22, 29-30; May 9; July 8, 30; August 15, 22; September 22, 24; November 4, 22; December 16

Pride – April 15, June 26-27

Prosperity – October 20-21

Protection – October 7-8, December 3-4,

Provision – September 30, October 4

Punishment – January 28; March 10; September 14, 16; October 22, 23

Redeemed/Redemption – March 14; September 8; December 1-2, 22

Refuge – October 8, 15; November 16, 23

Relationship – January 22; March 21-23; July 11, 25-30; August 1-4; November 28

Repentance – January 5, 23-24; September 9, 18; December 23, 29

Report – June 19; October 12; November 19; December 31

Righteousness – January 14, 22, 28; March 15-20; April 1-3; May 21-31

Salvation – January 8, 23-24; February 8, 24-26; March 3, 4; April 4; May 18-19; June 9-10, 22-23; November 16, 22

Sanctification – February 26; March 13; April 28; May 20; September 1, 8

Satan – November 1-8, 10, 30

Security – February 6-7; March 1, 3; July 28; November 23-24

Self-control – April 11; July 23; September 22-24

Self-reliance/Effort/Self-will – April 21-22

Sin – January 5-6; May 18-20; July 1-2, 10; November 7-8

Spiritual Vacation – June 13

Spiritual Warfare – August 29; September 5-8, 27-28

Suffering – January 25; February 11; May 6, 17; August 28; September 7-8

Temporal – March 6; August 7-8, 14; September 26; December 11

Trials – August 27-31; September 1-8

Trust – April 5; November 22-23, 24-30

Truth and Life – January 1-3; February 21

Union – January 22; February 1, 17; April 5; August 2-4, 12; December 12

Victory – December 24, 28-31

Vision – October 2

Wisdom – March 11, April 25-27

Word/s – February 4-5; April 23-24; June 1-6; November 29; December 21

Worship – May 12-13; December 26-27

Workmanship – April 13-14

ALSO, BY PATRICIA MARAGH

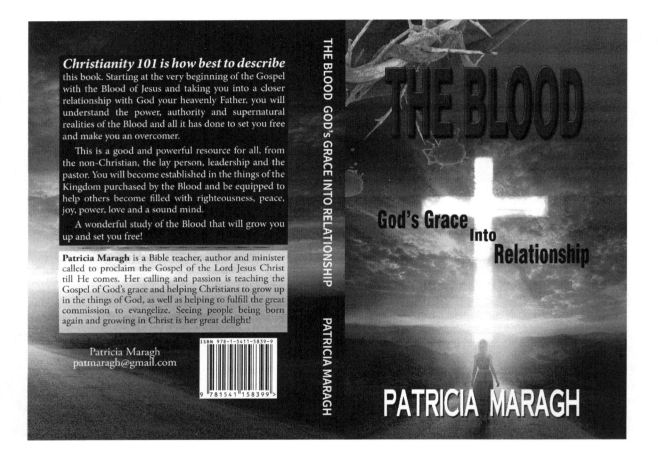

Christianity 101 is how best to describe this book. Starting at the very beginning of the Gospel with the Blood of Jesus and taking you into a closer relationship with God your heavenly Father, you will understand the power, authority and supernatural realities of the Blood and all it has done to set you free and make you an overcomer.

This is a good and powerful resource for all, from the non-Christian, the lay person, leadership and the pastor. You will become established in the things of the Kingdom purchased by the Blood and be equipped to help others become filled with righteousness, peace, joy, power, love and a sound mind.

A wonderful study of the Blood that will grow you up and set you free!

Patricia Maragh is a Bible teacher, author and minister called to proclaim the Gospel of the Lord Jesus Christ till He comes. Her calling and passion is teaching the Gospel of God's grace and helping Christians to grow up in the things of God, as well as helping to fulfill the great commission to evangelize. Seeing people being born again and growing in Christ is her great delight!

Patricia Maragh
patmaragh@gmail.com

ISBN 978-1-5411-5839-9

9 781541 158399

THE BLOOD GOD's GRACE INTO RELATIONSHIP

PATRICIA MARAGH

THE BLOOD

God's Grace Into Relationship

PATRICIA MARAGH

The world has become a dark place where Satan has gotten more prolific in his activities of lying to, accusing, harassing and condemning people—especially Christians. His goal is to separate us from God's love, relationship, power, purpose and eternal life, because he knows his time is short.

The call is NOW for everyone to know your inheritance in Christ and reclaim what the adversary has stolen. *"Awake, awake put on thy strength"* (Isaiah 52:1). It is time to experience abundant life in relationship and true freedom in Christ to fulfill God's purpose and mission for your life, to grow up spiritually and to be prepared to mentor others.

Patricia Maragh is an author and teacher in the ministry of the Gospel. She is a graduate of Rhema Bible Training College Pastoral Ministry. She released her first book, The Blood: God's Grace into Relationship in 2017. She lives in Tulsa, Oklahoma with her husband of thirty-five years.

Freedom from Guilt, Accusation, and Condemnation

Patricia Maragh

This book is available for purchase at http:// www. Amazon. com
And from:
Contact information: patmaragh@gmail.com
GospelDeliveranceMinistries.org

Printed in the United States
by Baker & Taylor Publisher Services